Richard Cunningham Shimeall

Unseen World

The Heavenly Blessedness

Richard Cunningham Shimeall

Unseen World
The Heavenly Blessedness

ISBN/EAN: 9783337389123

Printed in Europe, USA, Canada, Australia, Japan

Cover: Foto ©Lupo / pixelio.de

More available books at **www.hansebooks.com**

THE UNSEEN WORLD.

THE HEAVENLY BLESSEDNESS:

OR,

WHERE AND WHAT IS HEAVEN?

INCLUDING AN INQUIRY INTO

THE STATE AND PLACE OF THE DEPARTED

Between Death and the Resurrection:

AND A CONSEQUENT LOGICAL REFUTATION OF

MODERN SWEDENBORGIANISM, UNITARIANISM, UNIVERSALISM, SPIRITUALISM, AND THE ANNIHILATION OF THE WICKED AFTER DEATH.

INTERSPERSED WITH COPIOUS POETICAL EXTRACTS.

"The world to come, whereof we speak."—(ST. PAUL. Heb. ii. 5.)
"Arise and depart: for this is not your rest."—(MICAH ii. 10.)

BY THE REV. R. C. SHIMEALL,
A Member of the Presbytery of New York.

NEW YORK:
CHARLES SCRIBNER & CO., 654 BROADWAY.
A. D. F. RANDOLPH, 770 BROADWAY; CARTER & BROS., 530 BROADWAY;
SHELDON & CO., 500 BROADWAY.
1870.

Entered according to Act of Congress, in the year 1870,

By R. C. Shimeall,

In the Clerk's Office of the District Court of the United States, for the Southern District of the State of New York.

John J. Reed, Printer and Stereotyper, 43 Centre St., N. Y.

Contents.

	Pages
TITLE AND SUMMARY OF SUBJECTS,	i–xiv
POETICAL EXTRACTS,	xv–xxi
PREFACE	1–11

THE UNSEEN WORLD.

BASIS OF THE EXPOSITION, 1 Peter i. 3-9 13–14
THE UNSEEN WORLD, OR THE HEAVENLY BLESSEDNESS, etc.... 15
INTRODUCTION. Prevalent Views of Heaven—Man's aspirations after, innate—Qu.: Is Heaven a Place? 15–20

PART FIRST.—WHERE IS HEAVEN?

CHAPTER I.

"An Inheritance in Heaven."

SECTION I.—THE PAGAN IDEAS OF HEAVEN.
 Elysian Fields, Hesperian Gardens, Islands of the Blest, etc.—Socrates—Plato—Plutarch—Aristotle—Zeno—Various Heathen Nations—Transmigration of Souls—Plato—Origen—Furnishes a Clue to the Romish Dogma of Purgatory—Their Ideas of, Imperfect—Cicero, Seneca and Plutarch, dreaded Annihilation—Leland on —For the most part denied a Resurrection—Exceptions —Remote Origin of their Ideas of, etc.—A Divine Revelation necessary—The Bible 21–29

SECTION II.—THE JEWISH IDEAS OF THE "INHERITANCE IN HEAVEN."

Priority of, to those of the Pagan—Dean Prideaux on—Their Ideas of, limited—"Died in faith of" that "Better Country," etc.................................. 30–34

SECTION III.—THE CHRISTIAN'S IDEAS OF THE "INHERITANCE IN HEAVEN."

More perfect Views of—Distinction between the "Inheritance" and "Heaven"—"The World to come"—Harbaugh, Dr. Thomas Chalmers, and Dr. Dick on.... 34–39

CHAPTER II.

OF THE HEAVENLY INHERITANCE AS DEFERRED.

"An Inheritance - - - - - Reserved in Heaven."...... 40–42

SECTION I.—CONCERNING THE PLACE AND STATE OR CONDITION OF THE DEPARTED, BETWEEN DEATH AND THE RESURRECTION.

Introduction.—Quotation from Ps. viii. 5, in Heb. ii. 7, 8, "Man a little while lower than the Angels," etc.—Remarks on, by Professor ——— 43–47

The theory, that the *Soul only*, is the Man—Ignores a literal Resurrection—Prof. Hitchcock on—Fallacy of—Re-united with the raised body 48–50

Another Theory, that the Soul of Man was created Mortal—and hence, the alleged Annihilation of the Wicked at Death—Proof of the Fallacy of 50–58

SECTION II.—OF THE SCRIPTURAL DOCTRINE OF THE PLACE AND STATE OF THE SOUL, INTERMEDIATE BETWEEN DEATH AND THE RESURRECTION.

Contents.

1. The Scriptural View—Introductory Remarks—Intermediate Place and State of departed Spirits—Involves Locality—Bp. Horne on—Harbaugh on—Quotes from Trench 58–62

Heaven *Local*—Risen Saints have *Bodies*—Harbaugh on—Gnostic Heresy—Swedenbourg—Prof. Geo. Bush—Proof of a Literal Resurrection—Hence, Man a Complex Being, constituted of Body and Soul 62–64

Qu.: Whither goes the Soul at death?—Dr. Harbaugh on—His Theory examined and refuted—Three remarks on the passage Rev. vi. 9–11, the "Souls under the Altar," etc. 64–75

DEPARTED SPIRITS IN AN INTERMEDIATE PLACE AND STATE, DURING THE INTERVAL BETWEEN DEATH AND THE RESURRECTION, ADAPTED TO THE CHARACTERS OF BOTH THE RIGHTEOUS AND THE WICKED.

Objections to—I. *It is a purely Heathen Fable*—Ans. True, the Greeks and Latins had their Orcus or Hades—But, their knowledge of, proved to be derived from the Hebrews—The same of other Pagan Nations—Egyptians, Chinese, India, etc.—Illustrations of—1. The Hebrews—2. The Septuagint Translators—3. The Pagan Writers—4. The New Testament Writers 75–85

Objection II. *The Hebrew word* SHEOL *and the Greek word* HADES, *mean the* GRAVE—Fallacy of—The Hebrew for Grave is KEBER, etc. 86–90

Objection III. *That it is nearly identical with the Romish Purgatory*—Reply—Explanation of 1 Pet. iii. 19: Christ's alleged Preaching to the Spirits in Prison—Dr. Harbaugh's Theory—Ans. to 91–97

SECTION III.—OF THE WORDS SHEOL, TOPHET, HINNOM—HADES, PARADISE, TARTARUS, AND GEHENNA, ETC.

Dr. Harbaugh on the words *Sheol* and *Hades*—Reply—1. Meaning of the word *Sheol*, in three particulars—Drs. Doddridge, Campbell, Adam Clarke, on the *original* import of these words 97–101

Passages in illustration, *First*, from the OLD TESTAMENT on the word Sheol 101–104

Alleged Ignorance of the Jews of the Doctrine of *Future Endless Punishment*, etc.—Refutation of—Three inferences 104–112

Second, From the NEW TESTAMENT. Preliminary remarks—I. Of the word HADES—Passages examined—Four inferences—Qu.: Whither went the Soul of Christ at the instant of death, if it did not go direct to Heaven? Ans., as based on Ps. x. 16 and Acts ii. 27, 31—Examination of the import of the words *Hades* and *Paradise*, etc., in that connection.................................112–117

II. Of the word "Paradise," Luke xxiii. 43—Also of the phrases "*Abraham's bosom*," "*the Third Heaven*," etc.—Not the same with the "*Highest Heaven*".......117–124 other passages 124–127

III. Of the word GEHENNA—References to all the passages where it occurs...............................127–130

AN HISTORICAL VIEW, AS EMBRACING THE VOICE OF THE CHURCH, ANCIENT AND MODERN, IN RELATION TO THE DOCTRINE OF THE INTERMEDIATE PLACE AND STATE OF THE DEPARTED.

I. The writers of Primitive Antiquity..................131–138

II. Of Evangelical Divines since the time of the Reformation..138–170

Recapitulation..170–173

CHAPTER III.

"An Inheritance in Heaven."

QUESTION—*In what Heaven is the Deferred Inheritance of the Saints Located?* 174

Dr. Harbaugh on—His Theory examined—Fallacy of, shown in four particulars—I. The Lower or Sublunary Heaven, Air, or Atmosphere—II. The Starry Heavens, or Steller Universe—III. "The Third Heaven"—IV. The Heaven of Heavens, etc. 174-180

1. GOD, a SPIRIT—Not subject to a *Local Habitation*— 2. The DIVINE PERSON INCARNATE—His relations to "the Principalities, Powers, etc., in the Heavenly Places"— Christ's Pre-existent State—As "the Word made flesh" on earth—His return to the "Highest Heavens," etc. .. 180-193

The main Question in these Discussions—It respects the Location of that Inheritance of the Saints which is declared to be "Reserved in Heaven for them"— Question: Is it in the "Highest" or Empyreal Heavens? —Dr. Harbaugh on—Fallacy of—Christ again to return from the "Highest Heaven"—His purpose twofold, etc. 193-198

The Millennial State not the final "Inheritance of the Saints 198-202

CHAPTER IV.

"An Inheritance - - - in Heaven."

THE HEAVEN IN WHICH IS LOCATED THE FINAL INHERITANCE OF THE SAINTS.

Recapitulation.—Question: In what portion of the Infinite Expanse of "the Heaven of Heavens" are we to look for it? Ans. It will be constituted of the Post-Millennial "New Heaven and Earth" of St. Peter (2 Pet. iii. 13) and of St. John (Rev. xxi. 1, 5)—Argument derived from the declared Perpetuity of the present Earth and Heavens—Isa. lxv. 17, and lxvi. 22, compared with 2 Pet. iii. 13, and Rev. xxi. 1, 5 204–228

PART SECOND.—WHAT IS HEAVEN?

CHAPTER V.

"An Inheritance incorruptible, and undefiled, and that fadeth not away."

SECTION I.—THE ADAPTATION OF THE INHERITANCE OF THE SAINTS TO THE NATURE OF THE RESURRECTED BODY.

Introductory Remarks—Man's actual Personality after as before Death—Must, as such, have a Local Habitation..229–232

SECTION II.—ON THE PHYSICAL NATURE OF THE FUTURE "INHERITANCE OF THE SAINTS," AS CONTRADISTINGUISHED FROM THE "HEAVEN" IN WHICH IT IS SAID TO BE.

Source of Misconceptions on this subject—Substitution of the Allegorical for the Literal Laws of Scriptural Hermeneutics, introduced into the Church by Origen—Luther, Mosheim, and Milner on, (See Note, pages 136, 137)..232, 233

The Question: WHAT IS HEAVEN?
The formulas, "Kingdom of Heaven," "of Christ," "of God," "of the Son of Man," etc.—Special passages considered—Three Arguments confirmatory of—

Five Illustrations of—Confirmed by the *intensity* of human attachments to the things of earth—Only need to be Sanctified by Grace, and all will be well........233-250

SECTION III.—THE SYMPATHETIC RELATIONS EXISTING BETWEEN THE INVISIBLE AND THE VISIBLE WORLD.

I. Of the DIVINE Sympathy between Heaven and Earth—In Eden—Interrupted—Restored—Cherubims and a Flaming Sword at the Gate of Paradise, Gen. iv. 24—(See Note)..251-255

I. Of the Sympathetic Relations which exist between GOD, the *Earth*, and *Man*.

1. God is present in *Nature's* Work—2. Also in *Providence*—But more especially, 3, in the Person of the LORD JESUS CHRIST—And by the HOLY SPIRIT........255-262

II. *Angelic Sympathy between Heaven and Earth*—Now interrupted, save by their *Unseen* Ministrations......262-269

III. *Human Sympathy between the Departed and the Living*—The basis of—The Communion of Saints in the Invisible and the Visible Church............................269-279

SECTION IV.—Aspirations of the Saints after the Heavenly Blessedness..279-281

SECTION V.—The Heavenly Blessedness in Anticipation, 282-285

SECTION VI.—The Dying Saint at the Close of Life......285-287

CHAPTER VI.

"Receiving the end of your Faith, even the Salvation of your Souls."

The Saint's Final Admittance to the Heavenly Blessedness.

SECTION I.—How the Saints are admitted to their final state of Heavenly Blessedness....................... 288

"By the Resurrection of Jesus Christ from the dead"—Christ's Resurrection a Necessity—His Resurrection the Security and Pledge of ours.....................288–293

SECTION II.—BY WHOM THE SAINTS WILL BE FINALLY ADMITTED TO THEIR ESTATE OF HEAVENLY BLESSEDNESS.
By the Lord Jesus Christ............................293–300
Order of the Resurrection..........................301, 302

CHAPTER VII.

"To an inheritance - - - ready to be revealed at the last time, at the appearing of Jesus Christ."

SECTION I.—WHEN WILL THE SAINTS BE ADMITTED TO THEIR ESTATE OF HEAVENLY BLESSEDNESS?
Recapitulation—*Ans.* "At the Appearing of Christ"....303–308

CHAPTER VIII.

"An Inheritance Incorruptible."

A GLIMPSE OF THE BEATIFIC VISION: OR, THE HEAVENLY INHERITANCE IN ITS RELATION TO THE FINAL BLISS OF THE SAINTS.

SECTION I.—THE UNCHANGEABLE NATURE OF THE SAINT'S INHERITANCE, ETC.
I. *Its Incorruptible Nature*—Argued from the Purification of the Earth and the Heavens by Fire—Adapted to, 1, the Materiality of the Risen Body—Also, 2, to its Spirituality—3. The Power of the Risen Glorified Body—4. The Incorruptibility of—Its Future Glory—Two Inferences 309–322

CHAPTER IX.

"An Inheritance Undefiled."

The Spirituality of the Saints in that State.

Consider—I. The Influence of the preceding Circumstances upon the Glorification of the SENSES. They will be "fashioned like unto Christ's glorious body"—1. The Eye—2. The Ear—3. The Smell—4 and 5. Taste and Touch 323-329

II. Upon the perfection of the MENTAL POWERS 329-333

III. Also upon the MORAL POWERS 333-336

CHAPTER X.

"An inheritance incorruptible, undefiled, and that fadeth not away, reserved in Heaven for you."

SECTION I.—THE SOCIETY OF HEAVEN.

"Ye are come unto Mount Zion," etc. (Heb. xii. 22-25.)

I. The first in order is, THE GOD TRIUNE—
II. "The innumerable Company of Angels"—
III. "The General Assembly and Church of the First-born which are written in Heaven"
IV. "The Spirits of just men made perfect"—
V. Infants in Heaven—The Salvability of Infants—Proof of—Consolation to the Bereaved—Number of—Glorification of—The Saints one Family in Heaven...........339-353

SECTION II.—THE WORSHIP, EMPLOYMENTS, AND ENJOYMENTS OF THE SOCIETY OF HEAVEN.

"All Dominions shall serve and obey Him," etc., etc.—An Inquiry into this Subject lawful and proper—A

Blessing assured—The Employments and Enjoyments of Heaven will consist, I. Of Acts of Pure Benevolence—II. Of ceaseless Praises 353–360

Seven Apocalyptic Anthems 360–365

SECTION III.—Various Orders and Degrees of Blessedness in the Society of Heaven.

"There is one glory of the Sun, and another glory of the Moon," etc.—Diversities of Orders and Degrees of Rank in the Society of Heaven 365–375

SECTION IV.—The Scriptural Doctrine of the Saints' Mutual Recognition in the State of Heavenly Blessedness.

"For now we see through a glass darkly: but then face to face," etc. (1 Cor. xiii. 12.)

Importance of this Subject—All feel an equal Interest in it:

I. *Objections to this Doctrine.* It is urged: *First.* That, if true, the Scriptures would more clearly reveal it—Reply—*Second.* That the Condition of the Glorified will so far transcend that on earth, as to supersede all Earthly Relations—Reply—*Third.* That Saintly Recognition in Heaven, etc., would interfere with our Supreme Love to Christ, and hence, cannot be true—Reply—*Fourth.* That such Recognition would produce Partiality among the Saints in Heaven, etc.—Reply—*Fifth.* That Second Marriages militate against the Doctrine—Reply—*Sixth.* That the Change in the Resurrected Body will be so great, as to render Mutual Recognition impossible—Reply—*Seventh.* That if Heavenly Recognition be true, we should miss some whom we loved on Earth, which would greatly mar our Happiness—Reply—Conclusion. 375–391

II. *Direct Scriptural Proof of this Doctrine.*
   1. Of the Traditionary Legends among the Pagans—Homer, Virgil, etc. 391–393
   2. It characterizes the Belief, Hope, and Desire of All Men 394
   3. Inquiry into the Aspect in which this Doctrine is to be viewed in the light of Reason or Natural Religion—Man's Immortality may be known by—But the Resurrection, never—Dr. Harbaugh on the Intermediate State, etc.—Reply—Dr. Harbaugh's Admission of "Difficulties in the way of Recognition, which will not exist after the Resurrection"—These Difficulties insuperable, separate from that Event—His Admission that Departed Spirits may Recognize each other—But that Recognition in its Consummated Form, depends upon a Re-union of Soul and Body at the Resurrection 394–397
   4. The Teachings of Holy Scripture on this Subject—*First.* Of the Old Testament—Patriarchs and Prophets 397–402
   Second. Of the New Testament. 1st. What our blessed Lord taught—2d. What the Apostles taught 402–415
   Conclusion, in Five Particulars....................415–419

CHAPTER XI.

Preparation for the Heavenly Blessedness.

SECTION I.—On the Scriptural Motives to Faith, Repentance, and a Holy Life.

I. The Popular View. *First.* The alleged coming of the Son of Man to us at Death—Fallacy of—Applied to,

1st, Faith in Christ as it respects (1) the Unregenerate—The passage, "Be ye also ready," etc., examined—(2) As applied to the Regenerate—2. Repentance towards God—Result—3. Holiness of Heart and of Life—Illustrated in Ten Particulars—All demonstrate that the great Scriptural Motives to Faith, Repentance, Holiness, and all the Christian Graces, is, not Death, but the Second pre-Millennial Personal Coming of Christ..419–432

II. It is further alleged, that Meditation on the Glories of Heaven, etc., furnish the Second Class of Motives to prepare and preserve the Mind in a proper frame of fitness for the Future State—Answer: These, though proper and useful, yet are not the Principal Source of those Motives—But, Faith and Hope in the Coming One, the Lord Jesus Christ—The old Patriarchs, Prophets, Apostles, Martyrs, etc., "all died in Faith" of those "Promises" of that Heavenly Blessedness which they "beheld afar off"...................................432–435

CONCLUSION.

What now, Reader, think you of that "Inheritance Incorruptible, etc., still Reserved In Heaven" for the Saints when glorified?............................435, 446

POETRY,

ADAPTED TO THE VARIOUS THEMES DISCUSSED IN THE CHAPTERS AND SECTIONS THROUGHOUT THIS VOLUME.

PART I.

		Page
AN INVOCATION (Preface)		10
SKEPTICISM	Herbert	15
TRUTH	Anonymous	16
THE CHRISTIAN'S HEAVEN	Philip Doddridge	16
LIFE NOT A BREATH	Montgomery	17
THERE IS A LAND, ETC. (A Stanza)		19
"THE BETTER COUNTRY"		19
A DIFFERENCE	Cowper	21
THE PAGAN'S HEAVEN	N. C. Brooks	22
THE SLAVE'S DIRGE	Anonymous	23
THE INDIAN SONG	Pope	24
A COUPLET		26
THE BIBLE	The Synagogue	28
THE JEW'S HEAVEN	Anonymous	30
IN GLORY	Anonymous	31
A COUPLET	Young	31
THE PILGRIM'S SONG	Hymns from the Land of Luther	33
THE FUTURE HOME	Felicia Hemans	34
MISCELLANEOUS		34
GLORIES OF HEAVEN	Pollok	39
THE GOOD MAN'S TRANSIT	Blair, and others	40

	Page
No, no, it is not Dying	41
On Man .... Anonymous	50
Death and the Resurrection .... E. H. B.	55
A Satyre .... Anonymous	58
Earth the Copy of Heaven	61
The Beauties of Nature .... Anonymous	61
Death not the End of Life	70
"The Disembodied Souls of Men," etc	71
A Stanza .... Dryden	76
A Couplet .... Virgil	84
Do. (Tartarus and Elysium)	85
Two Couplets 15,	151
Faith in Things Unseen .... Anonymous	174
Where is God? .... English Pulpit	182
"The Heavenly Principalities"	187
The Heavenly "Powers"	188
The Incarnation .... Anonymous	188
The Presence of the Lord .... "	189
False Philosophy—(An Appeal) .... R. H. Dana	190
On the Millennium .... Joshua Marsden ...	196
The Study of Heaven .... R. H. Dana	203
The Better Land .... Felicia Hemans	203
The Heavenly Blessedness .... Anonymous	212
Home in View .... Newton	227

PART II.

Heaven .... Anonymous	229
Two Couplets—(A Hymn) .... "	229
"O Mother dear, Jerusalem"	245
"O Paradise, O Paradise!"	248
A Couplet	251

		Page
THE PRESENCE OF GOD WITH MAN	Anonymous	255
A STANZA	"	256
HEAVEN AND EARTH RECONCILED	"	258
A COUPLET—(A Stanza)	Watts	260
ANGELIC MINISTRATIONS	Anonymous	262
LAMENT OVER ANGELIC ABSENCE	"	265
HUMAN SYMPATHY PERPETUATED	"	269
CHRIST AND THE SAINTS ONE	Watts	273
A COUPLET—(A Hymn)	C. Wesley	273
SYMPATHY OF THE DEAD WITH THE LIVING	John L. Chester	276
A LONGING FOR HEAVEN	Williams	279
"I WOULD NOT LIVE ALWAY"	Muhlenberg	279
THE HOPE OF HEAVEN	Coleridge	281
DEATH, IN VIEW OF HEAVEN	Wilson	282
HEAVEN ANTICIPATED	Watts	284
"GENTLY, LORD, O GENTLY LEAD US"	Thos. Hastings, 1832	284
THE SAINT'S FINAL EXIT	Blair	285
HEAVEN BEGUN		286
"THE WORLD RECEDES"		287
PARTING ADIEU	Anonymous	287
ON CHRIST'S RESURRECTION	James Edmonson	288
"CHRIST THE LORD IS RISEN INDEED"		291
(Eastern Hymn of the Bohemian Church, 1531.)		
MARY AT THE SEPULCHRE		292
CHRIST, THE SAINT'S HOPE OF HEAVEN	Keble	293
ANOTHER		294
LIFT UP YOUR HEADS, ETC.		297
"THOU, WHOSE NEVER FAILING ARM"	H. F. Lyte, 1834	301
PSALM LXXII	Montgomery	304
GLORY TO GOD AND THE LAMB	Pollok	307
JERUSALEM, THE GOLDEN	Bernard, 1170	309
THE IMMUTABILITY OF THE HEAVENLY STATE	Longfellow	312

Poetical Extracts.

		Page
A Couplet	An Italian Poet	313
A Stanza	Watts	313
The Saints Happy in Death	Mrs. Barbauld	314
The Spiritualized Body	Watts	316
A Couplet	"	318
A Stanza	"	319
The Risen Glorified Body	Anonymous	322
"Arise and Depart, for this is not your Rest."	Anonymous	323
Lines, on the Sense of Smell	"	327
A Hymn	Watts	328
"Watchman, tell us of the Night"	Sir John Bowring, 1776	328
A Couplet	Watts	333
Love of Christ, and Love to Christ	Anonymous	334
The Saint's Final State	"	336
"One Fold under one Shepherd"	"	337
Casa Waddy	"	345
Infants in Heaven	"	346
Miscellaneous	"	347
On Infantile Resurrection	"	348
The Early Lost and Saved	"	350
Longing after Heaven	"	352
We have no Home but Heaven		353
(From Hymns for the Church on Earth.)		
The Flock of Christ	Charles Wesley	356
"Jesus Christ, the same yesterday, to-day, and for ever"	E. Whitfield	358

A SERIES OF APOCALYPTIC ANTHEMS SUNG BY THE REDEEMED IN HEAVEN, CELEBRATING THE PRAISES OF THE TRIUNE JEHOVAH.

ANTHEM I.—(Rev. xv. 3, 4.)

Page
A SABBATICAL HYMN OF TRIUMPH, DECLARING THAT GOD ONLY IS HOLY, AND OUGHT ALONE TO BE WORSHIPED............ 360

ANTHEM II.—(Rev. iv. 11.)

AN ANTHEM, CELEBRATING THE GLORY OF GOD AS THE CREATOR, 361

ANTHEM III.—(Rev. vii. 10, 12, 13.)

A SONG OF THE REDEEMED, CELEBRATING THE GLORY OF GOD AS THE REDEEMER... 361

ANTHEM IV.—(Rev. vii. 10, 12.),

A SONG OF THE REDEEMED, ASCRIBING SALVATION UNTO GOD AND TO THE LAMB 362

ANTHEM V.—(Rev. xi. 17.)

A SONG OF THE REDEEMED, CELEBRATING THE GLORY OF GOD IN THE ESTABLISHMENT OF HIS KINGDOM.................... 363

ANTHEM VI.—(Rev. xii. 10–12.)

A SONG OF TRIUMPH.. 364

ANTHEM VII.—(Rev. xix. verses 1, 2 and 3.)

THE LAST GRAND CHORUS OF THE HEAVENLY HOSTS........... 364

DIFFERENT ORDERS AND DEGREES IN HEAVEN...Bp. Mant...... 365
THE FUTURE PEACE AND GLORY OF THE CHURCH..Cowper..... 374
HEAVENLY RECOGNITION ....Anonymous........ 375
A MOTHER'S LAMENT..................Montgomery....... 377
THE SKEPTIC'S SORROW................Shakspeare........ 378
LINES—The Change from Death to Life..Anonymous........ 383
PERSONAL IDENTITY PRESERVED IN HEAVEN...Bp. Mant........ 384
THE WILL OF THE SAINTS IN HEAVEN IN ACCORD WITH THE
    WILL OF GOD......................Bp. Mant.......... 389
REUNION OF SAINTS IN HEAVEN.........Charles Wesley..... 390
LINES FROM VIRGIL'S ÆNEID 392
OTHERS 392
WEEP NOT FOR THE DEAD ....Anonymous........ 393
OUR ONENESS IN CHRIST...............   "   394
JEWISH HOPE OF HEAVENLY RECOGNITION   "   398
A STANZA.............................Watts 400
A POETIC CHALLENGE ....Anonymous........ 402
A BRIGHTER HEAVEN....................   "   403
GENERAL HEAVENLY RECOGNITION.......Pollok............ 405
CONSUMMATION OF THE PASTOR'S HOPE...Anonymous........ 408
LOVE, THE LAW OF HEAVEN.............   "   412
LOVE ETERNAL........................Robert Southey... 412
ANOTHER ....Anonymous........ 413
THE ETERNAL REUNION IN THE BETTER LAND..Leggett.... 414
THE LAST JUDGMENT..................................... 419
FAITH IN CHRIST......................Watts 424
FAITH'S TRIUMPH OVER DEATH...........   "   426

Poetical Extracts.

	Page
Repentance at the Cross .... Watts	428
Holiness of Heaven .... "	431
The Saint's Perpetual Theme in Glory .. Anonymous	434
A Couplet .... Pollok	435
The Better World	437
Two Stanzas .... Watts	439
"Lo, He Comes," etc.	439
General Ingathering of the Saints—"Egypt and Tyre" ..	441
Mother's Lament over her Dying Boy .. Anonymous	441
"Rejoice, rejoice, believer," etc.	443
Farewell of the Soul to the Body	445

Preface.

"Many have taken in hand to set forth in order a declaration ' of what constitutes the *future* Heaven of Blessedness to the saints, when vision and fruition take the place of faith and hope.

The questions: Where is Heaven? What is Heaven? Is it a *place*, or a *state*, or *both of these conjoined?* often press themselves upon the minds of the pious and devout way-worn sojourner to that "better country, even an Heavenly,"[1] where "the wicked cease from troubling, and the weary are at rest."[2]

Of the ineffable and ecstatic glories of that "world to come" of which St. Paul speaks,[3] we now "know only in part."[4] "Eye hath not seen, nor ear heard, neither hath it entered the heart, the things that God hath prepared for them that love Him."[5] Nevertheless, it is far from being a vain speculation to institute an inquiry into the things *revealed* of that "incorruptible, undefiled, and unfading inheritance" as yet circumscribed to the domain of *faith*. The "*heirs*,"[6] who hold

[1] Heb. xi. 16. [2] Job iii. 17. [3] Heb. ii. 5. [4] i Cor. xiii. 12.
[5] Ib. ii. 9. [6] Rom. viii. 17.

a legitimate title-deed to an estate remote from the place of their birth, and the full possession, which depends upon the *will* of the testator, may form tolerably just conceptions of its real proportions and value, by an examination of *so much* of the details as is contained in the *open* document.

And yet, strange as it may seem, these very "heirs" of the promised Heavenly "Inheritance," form the most divergent views of the import of the things stipulated in the divinely revealed compact in regard to the *locality* of Heaven—the *nature* of the Heavenly Blessedness as connected with the state or condition of its inhabitants—the signification of the term, "an inheritance *reserved in* Heaven"—the *mode* or manner of final admission to it—the *time* of entrance into its full possession—the great matter of what constitutes a proper *meteness* for it—what are the *true Gospel motives* for said meteness, etc.

Our reluctance in making this statement, is counterbalanced by the fact of the generally confused, and not unseldom inconsistent, contradictory, and in some instances presumptuous notions which have obtained on this subject.

This results, we deferentially submit, from the failure to recognize the TRUE STAND-POINT of observation from which the details of the title-deed, as above, is to be viewed. A recent writer has well said, that "the point of observation which commands the popular views of the Heavenly Blessedness, is any one of the many little hills, appreciable as hills by those who live among them. These hills are variously designated, as wealth, respectability, science, poetic imagination, dignity, magnanimity, integrity, generosity, amiability, and the like." [1] And he asks: "Can it be shown that Heaven is visible from these eminences?" It must suffice to observe in reply, that the boastful, self-reliant, and self-righteous *rich young ruler*, being put to the test of his perfect obedience to the law—"Go and sell that thou hast, and give to the poor, and thou shalt have treasure in Heaven; and come, follow me: went away sorrowful, for he had great possessions." Hence the declaration of Jesus: "It is easier for a camel to go through the eye of a needle, than for a rich man to enter into the kingdom of God." This saying of our Lord startled even His own disciples, who, viewing man's *meteness* for Heaven from the little hill-top, "*Wealth*," were exceedingly amazed, and exclaimed, "Who then can be saved?" It behooves those of this day, therefore, who, like the rich

---

[1] Heaven: by James William Kimball, p. 24. Boston, 1857.

young ruler, are "trusting in the *uncertain riches* as a passport to Heaven, to take heed to the reply of Jesus to His erring disciples: "With men this is impossible; but with God all things are possible:"[1] And, with the repentant disciples, descending from this false, insidious, and soul-ruining hill-top, they will do well to take their views of the nature of the Heavenly glory and of their meteness for it, from that point of observation indicated by the words of Peter— "Behold, *we have forsaken all*, and followed Thee."[2] Such, and such only will find that, "in the regeneration, when the son of man shall sit on the throne of His glory, they also shall sit upon twelve thrones, judging the twelve tribes of Israel,"[3] and shall inherit everlasting life. On the other hand, in regard to that little hill-top, "*Generosity*," if found disconnected with that "charity which beareth all things, believeth all things, hopeth all things, and endureth all things" for the sake of Christ and the souls of men, "though we bestow all our goods to feed the poor, and give our bodies to be burned," it will be found to "profit us nothing" in the attainment of a *right* apprehension of or admission to, the future "inheritance of the saints in light."

[1] See Matt. xix. 16–26.   [2] Ib. v. 27.   [3] Ib. v. 28.

Then further. This writer states that he made "a limited experiment by way of putting the question to a number of thoughtful persons, representative men and women, from various positions in life:

What is your most interesting thoughts of Heaven?" The first replied: "O, it's the child's idea of all standing and singing." The next raised his eyes to the ceiling and exclaimed: "Pearly gates, transparent golden streets, the river of life, and ceaseless praise; *all figures of speech.* Paul saw, and could not speak. John was about to write, but was commanded to seal it up." Good old Dr. B. replied: "When I think of character, it is like Christ. When I think of the *astronomy* and *geography* of Heaven, I don't know anything about it. We shall be free from sin, and perpetually serve God." Another made answer: "The presence of Christ, and the sense of the wonderful grace in His coming into our world; that He died for *me;* and above all, the wonder that *I* shall find myself there." Another said: "My most interesting thought of Heaven is that of rest; of freedom from sin, and the fear of sinning." Dr. I— replied: "That I shall *put off a body* that constantly tempts me to sin; that I shall worthily love and perfectly serve my Lord and Saviour, and that my powers shall no longer be restrained by weaknesses, feebleness, and ignorance." One more, and the last answered: "My life has been one of ceaseless and wearying toil, with much weakness; and my first and constant thought is of rest." To the above diversified notions of the nature of the Heavenly Blessedness, we may add: That " Richard Baxter's Heaven depicted in his 'Saint's Everlasting Rest,' is, an eternity of holy repose, free from the sins and troubles of earth." And John Howe's Heaven, delineated in his " Blessedness of the Righteous, 'is a calm, *intellectual* eternity, spent in the vision of God.'"

Very pious ideas and inferences, these, as founded upon that hope which is predicated of the "experiences" of moral fitness for Heaven, and of the nature of its enjoyments, employments, and the like. And, however true and just, as entering into the *elements* of that state, considered in themselves, still, it is a question with us, whether we "*know nothing at all* about the astronomy and geography of Heaven;" and whether or not all the descriptions of Heaven are mere "*figures of speech*." Let it be admitted, for example, that the Heavenly *state* consists of a life of blessedness transcending mere locality; it is nevertheless equally true, that the Heaven " IN ' which that blessedness is enjoyed, *is a place*. It must have an existence of its own, with absolute, and not merely a relative or figurative existence.

On this subject it may be observed, that if Heaven is only a state of ecstatic *spiritual* enjoyment, it will follow, that man's *personality* consists of the soul only; on which hypothesis, the body which it inhabited in life, at death is " put off," that is, it passes into oblivion. This, of course, involves a denial of the literal or *corporeal resurrection* of the body, and of its *re-union* with the soul, after death. But if, on the other hand, Heaven is limited to place, it must remain for ever a tenantless and solitary domain, unfitted for, because unadapted to, the occupancy of a class of *purely* spiritual beings. And, finally, if it should turn out that the two, that is, both *place* and *state* be conjoined, as constituting the future Heavenly Blessedness of the Redeemed, then it will follow, that while the Heavenly place is a material world existing in an organized form, it will possess all the requisites for its adaptation to the *abode* of man in his *organic* and *spiritual* resurrected or glorified nature.

And, unless we greatly err in our conceptions of the teachings of Holy Scripture on this momentous subject, the pious soul, in its aspirations for the "perfect consummation, in *body* and *soul*, of future Blessedness in Christ's eternal kingdom," will find a complete analogy between his *complex* nature, organic and spiritual, and the physical and spiritual *elements* of the Heavenly place and state. In other words, he will discover that there is a perfect harmony between the Heavenly place of his abode, and its relation to the state of blessedness of the saints.

We may, I submit, discover a striking and beautiful illustration of this in "the bride, who is about to go to her *new home*. She feels that she has a *personal* interest in the descriptions which her friends give her of its *site*, of its *appearance*, and of its *furnishings;* for she has upon her soul the sunshine of the gladdening hope, that she is to *spend her future life* beneath its roof."

Still, infinitely more striking, and beautiful, and appropriate, is the celebration of the MARRIAGE NUPTIALS between Christ as the Bridegroom and His redeemed spouse, THE CHURCH, at the time of "the midnight cry" announcing His coming, and of her entrance into "the Palace of the King,"[1] as set forth in the parable of the virgins.[2] But more especially when, at the *re-creation* of "the New Heavens and New Earth wherein shall dwell

---

[1] Ps. xlv. 15.   [2] Matt. xxv. 1-14.

righteousness,"[1] that consolatory assurance given by our blessed Lord, when about to be separated from His disciples, shall be fully verified: "Let not your hearts be troubled. . . *In my Father's house are many mansions:* if it were not so, I would have told you. I go to prepare A PLACE for you. And, if I go, *I will come again,* and receive you unto myself, that where I am, there ye may be also."[2]

That the sentiments indicated in these prefatory remarks, are sustained by what God has revealed to us in His word, concerning the future *place* and *state* of the Heavenly Blessedness of that "multitude which no man can number, gathered from among all peoples, and nations, and kindreds, and tongues;"[3] and that they are in perfect harmony with "the science of astronomy and geography" in their relations to "THE UNSEEN WORLD" or to "the world to come,"[4] it will be our endeavor in these pages to lay open, for the "instruction in righteousness" of the Christian pilgrim, in his advances to that Haven of eternal rest where he would be.

Nor let him be dismayed, if, in regard to all who have "fallen asleep in Jesus"[5] from the

---

[1] ii. Pet. iii. 13. Rev. xxi. 1–5. [2] John xiv. 1–3. [3] Rev. vii. 9; 13 17.
[4] Heb. ii. 5. [5] 1 Cor. xv. 18.

martyred Abel onward, they be found, like the "*souls*" whom St. John "saw"—not sitting with Christ in His throne as described in Rev. xx. 4, denotive of their resurrected state, (verse 5th), but—"*under the altar*,"[1] in the enjoyment of a state of conscious anticipated Blessedness *intermediate* between death and the resurrection.

This additional treatise on that "eternal purpose which God purposed in Christ Jesus our Lord before the world began,"[2] to "make the Captain of our salvation perfect through suffering," to the end that He might finally "*bring many sons unto glory*,"[3] and to "*drive away the wicked in his wickedness*"[4]—"a mystery which the angels desire to look into"—we commit to the blessing of Him who is "able to build us up, and to give us an inheritance among them that are sanctified."[5]

AN INVOCATION.

"O, SPIRIT! that dost prefer
Before all temples th' upright heart and pure,
Instruct us, for THOU knowest.
What in us is dark,
Illume! What is low, raise and support!" *Milton.*

1 Rev. vi. 9–11.   2 Eph. iii. 11.   3 Heb. ii. 10.
4 Prov. xiv. 32.   5 Acts xx. 32; xxvi. 18.

Thou, whose almighty word
Chaos and darkness heard,
    And took their flight;
Hear us we humbly pray,
And where the Gospel day
Sheds not its glorious ray,
    Let there be light!

Thou, who didst come to bring
On Thy redeeming wing
    Healing and sight,
Health to the sick in mind,
Sight to the inly blind,
O, now to all mankind
    Let there be light!

Spirit of truth and love,
Life-giving, holy Dove,
    Speed forth thy flight;
Move on the water's face,
Spreading the beams of grace
And in earth's darkest place,
    Let there be light!

Blessed and Holy Three,
Glorious Trinity,
    Grace, Love, and Might
Boundless as ocean's tide,
Rolling in fullest pride,
Through the world, far and wide,
    Let there be light! Amen.

James Marriott, 1813. (From " *The Sacrifice of Praise*." *Brick Presb. Church Hymns.*)

THE UNSEEN WORLD,
ETC.

1st PETER i. 3-9.

"*Blessed be the God and Father of our Lord Jesus Christ, who according to His abundant mercy hath begotten us again unto a lively hope by the resurrection of Jesus Christ from the dead, to an inheritance incorruptible, and undefiled, and that fadeth not away, reserved in Heaven for you, who are kept by the power of God through faith unto salvation, ready to be revealed in the last time. Wherein ye greatly rejoice, though now for a season, if need be, ye are in heaviness through manifold temptations, that the trial of your faith, being much more precious than gold, though it be tried by fire, might be found unto praise and honor and glory,* AT THE APPEARING OF JESUS CHRIST: *whom, having not seen, ye love: in whom, though now ye see Him not, yet believing, ye rejoice with joy unspeakable and full of glory; receiving the* end of your faith, *even the salvation of your souls.*

THE UNSEEN WORLD;

OR THE

HEAVENLY BLESSEDNESS.

INTRODUCTION.

Prevalent Views of Heaven.

SKEPTICISM.

"Lord, let the angels praise Thy name!
Man is a foolish thing—a foolish thing:
  Folly and sin play all his game;
His house still burns, and yet he doth sing,
    Man is but grass;
    He knows it; fill the glass!
How canst Thou brook his foolishness?
  Why, he'll not lose a cup of drink for THEE.
Bid him but temper his excess;
  Not he: he knows where he can better be,
    As he will swear,
    Than to serve THEE."—*Herbert.*

TRUTH.

"Truth crushed to earth will rise again,
The eternal years of God are hers."

To avoid misery, and aspire after happiness, is innate in man. By nature, he is a *religious* being. This is true of nations the most barbarous, as of the most civilized and enlightened. Be he Egyptian, Hindoo, Mohammedan, Patagonian, Jew, or Christian, it is equally true of all, that

"Man has a soul of vast desires,
Which burns within with restless fires"

that cannot be satisfied with the circumscribed pursuits and attainments of the short span of the life that *now is*. Whether guided traditionally by the dim light of Natural Religion, as the Pagan; or by the superior disclosures of a Divine Revelation, as the Jew and the Christian, man believes that, as God's *gift* to him,

"The soul, *Immortal* as its sire,
Can never die."

And, whatever be his conceptions of a state or condition of future blessedness, that, to him, is HEAVEN.

THE CHRISTIAN'S HEAVEN.

O Zion, tune thy voice
And raise thy hands on high;
Tell all the earth thy joys
And boast salvation nigh:

Cheerful in God, | While rays divine
Arise and shine | Stream all abroad.

Is Heaven a Place?

> He guilds the morning face
>   With beams that cannot fade;
> His all resplendant grace
>   He pours around thy head;
>
> *The nations round* | With lustre new
> Thy form shall view, | Divinely crowned,
>
> In honor to His name
>   *Reflect that sacred light;*
> And loud that grace proclaim,
>   Which makes thy darkness bright:
>
> Pursue His praise | *In worlds above*
> Till Sovereign love, | Thy glory raise.
>
> There on His holy hill
>   *A brighter sun shall rise,*
> And with his radiance fill
>   *Those fairer, purer skies;*
>
> While round Thy throne | In nobler spheres,
> Ten thousand stars, | His influence own.
>
> Philip Doddridge, 1755. (From "*The Sacrifice of Praise.*' Brick Presbyterian Church Hymns).

The Heaven of the *Christian*, as put in contrast with that of the *Pagan*, is the subject of present inquiry. The question is this:—

Is Heaven a Place?

In other words, is it a *state of existence* merely? Has it *locality?* and is it *material?* Will it be what the poet Montgomery has beautifully expressed it—

LIFE NOT A BREATH.

> "Beyond the flight of time,
>   Beyond the range of death,
> There surely is some blessed clime,
>   *Where life is not a breath.*

> Nor life's affections transient fire,
> Whose sparks.fly upwards and expire."

Is this true? It may be observed in reply, that it seems quite in accordance with the suggestions, not only, but with the dictates of Natural Religion. The life-history of man as an intellectual being, is interwoven with a *material* world. It is hence a violation of enlightened reason, to suppose that, at death, the spirit is at once and forever divorced from all ideas of and connection with, that which is visible and tangible to the senses. And so, the soul, in the exercise of its faculties in the future world, would naturally expect to find itself connected with associations and relations analogous to those of the present. Accordingly, while Reason accords with Revelation, in teaching the doctrine of a state of future retributions, *Memory*, aided by the wings of imagination, recalls to mind the deeds of the present life, and of the responsibilities incurred thereby. And, we repeat, these faculties take along with them the *analogy* between the intellectual and the material. None but "the fool," who "says in his heart, There is no God," [1] and who alleges that "death is an eternal sleep," can obliterate from his soul a consciousness of the realities which await him in a *future* state. Disbelieve, laugh at, and reject and scorn an hereafter of blessedness or of woe as he may—be his language that of the God-denying atheist, epicurean, and voluptuary, "Let us eat and drink, for to-morrow we die" [2]—yet, truth eternal receives its vindication in these premises, at the hand both

---

[1] Ps. xiv. 1; liii. 1.   [2] Isa. xxii. 13; 1 Cor. xv. 32.

of enlightened reason and of revelation. These unitedly attest that

> 'THERE IS a land of pure delight,
>   Where saints immortal reign ;
> Infinite day excludes the night,
>   And pleasures banish pain."

"THE BETTER COUNTRY."
(*Heb. xi.* 16).

For thee, O dear, dear country,
  Mine eyes their vigils keep ;
For very love, beholding
  Thy happy name, they weep.
The mention of thy glory
  Is unction to the breast,
And medicine in sickness,
  And love, and life, and rest.

O one, O only Mansion !
  O Paradise of joy !
Where tears are ever banished,
  And smiles have no alloy ;
The LAMB is all Thy splendor,
  The CRUCIFIED Thy praise ;
His laud and benediction,
  Thy ransomed people raise.

Thou hast no shore, fair ocean !
  Thou hast no time, bright day !
Dear fountain of refreshment
  To pilgrims far away !

Upon the rock of ages
  They raise Thy holy tower;
Thine is the victor's laurel,
  And Thine the golden dower.

O sweet and blessed country,
  The home of God's elect!
O sweet and blessed country,
  That eager hearts expect!
JESU, in mercy bring us
  To that dear land of rest;
Who art, with God the Father,
  And Spirit, ever blest.

Bernard, 1150; translated by J. M. Neale. (From "The Sacrifice of Praise." Brick Church Hymns).

Let us then direct our thoughts to the Question—

PART FIRST.

I. WHERE IS HEAVEN?

CHAPTER I.

"An Inheritance in Heaven."

SECTION I.

The Pagan Ideas of Heaven.

A DIFFERENCE.

"In such a world, so thorny, and where none
　Finds happiness unblighted, or, if found,
Without some thistle sorrow at its side;
It seems the part of wisdom, and no sin
Against the law of love, *to measure lots*
　With less distinguished than ourselves; that thus
We may with patience bear our ills,
And *sympathise* with others suffering more."—
　　　　　　　　　　　　　　　　Cowper.

AS we have said: it is innate in man constantly and earnestly to aspire after happiness in a state *future* to the present. "The heathen in his blindness," is a participant of this aspiration. And, however limited and imperfect his conceptions of the immortality of the soul, and of the varying *states* or *conditions* of the hoped-for blessedness,—and which, like the feeble glimmerings of the cold moon shone only by a reflected light—he nevertheless associated in his mind the Idea of a material locality. Both the poets and philosophers of Heathendom, have declared their belief in a *place* and *state* of future blessedness. Hence their Elysian Fields, Hesperian Gardens, and Islands of the Blest, e. g.—

THE PAGAN'S HEAVEN,

"Where vine-clad vale and incense-breathing mound;
And bowers Elysian shed their fragrance round;
Lawns bask in light—in gloom uprise the woods,
And mossy grottoes echo crystal floods
That murmur over sands of gold, and run
Now brown with shades, now glittering in the sun.
Ambrosial trees their buds and fruits unfold
In silver flowers, and variegated gold;
Perennial plants their pulpy treasures spread,
Like rubies gleaming 'mid the leaves o'erhead;
And odorous shrubs shed down their balmy tears
When'er the listening grove the sighing night-wind hears."
N. C. Brook.

Socrates says : "They who live holy and excellent lives, being freed from these earthly places as from prisons, ascend to a pure region above the earth, where they dwell ; and those of them who are sufficiently purged by philosophy, live all their life-time *without bodies*, and ascend to still more beautiful habitations." Plato, a disciple of Socrates, says: "As to bad men, if they be not freed from depravity in this life, that place which is pure from evil, will not receive them when they die." Plutarch, in a citation from Aristotle, endorses the same view, and "represents it as an opinion delivered by the most ancient poets and philosophers, that some kind of honor and dignity shall be conferred upon excellent persons after their departure from this life; and that there is a certain region appointed, in which the souls of such persons reside." Even Zeno, the father of the Stoic sect, placed the abode where the spirits of good men go in subterranean regions, but speaks of them as "pleasant and delightful regions." The same holds true of the ideas prevalent among all tribes and nations of modern times—those of the Society Isles, of the Friendly Islands, the New Zealanders, those of the Pelew Islands, the Kalmuc Tartars, the inhabitants of Northern Tartary, the Birmans, the various tribes of the African Continent, and the Indians of North America. Thus we find the African Slaves who, torn from their home and kindred by monsters in human form, and sold to masters of equally iron hearts in distant lands—though overruled in the purpose of God for their ultimate good—in their song of rapture, as they sit beside the waters of their captivity, sing while they weep,

THE SLAVE'S DIRGE.

" 'Tis but to die, and then to weep no more,
　Then will we wake on distant *Congo's* shore;
　Beneath his plantain's ancient shades renew
　The simple transports that with freedom flew;
　Catch the cold breeze that murky evening blows,
　And catch the palm's rich nectar as it flows;

> The oral tales of elder times rehearse,
> And chant the rude traditionary verse
> With those, the loved companions of his youth,
> When life was luxury, and friendship truth."

And so, also, the ideas of the Indian, driven from his once peaceful habitation, of the felicities which await him after death, as expressed in the following

INDIAN SONG.

> "Even the poor Indian, whose untutored mind
> Sees God in clouds, or hears Him in the wind,
> Whose soul proud science never taught to stray
> Far as the solar walk or milky way—
> Yet simple nature to his soul has given,
> Behind the cloud-capt hill, *a humble Heaven;*
> Some safer world in depths of wood embraced,
> Some happier island in the watery waste,
> Where slaves once more their native land behold,
> No fiends torment, no Christian thirsts for gold—
> And thinks, admitted to you equal sky,
> His faithful dog shall bear him company."—*Pope.*

TRANSMIGRATION.

The doctrine of the *transmigration* of souls, has prevailed amongst almost all the lesser enlightened pagan nations and tribes. It is generally prevalent in the philosophy of India and the East. It was held in one form or other by Pythagoras, Plato, and his disciples. It holds a near affinity to "the doctrine of successive conflagrations and purifications which some of the oriental systems of philosophy taught, which supposes that this *earth* would, by degrees, become a holy habitation, and that *its inhabitants* would become holy with it by the same process." We hence obtain a clue to the origin of the doctrine of Romish *purgatory*, first taught by Plato, and subsequently incorporated into the Christian system by Origen, the famous presbyter and catechist of Alexandria. The theory of transmigrations, in its most ancient and prevalent form, has for its basis the idea of *successive ascensions,*—that is, as the soul is not supposed to reach its final place and state of felicity immediately after death, it passes through successive stages, sometimes entering into another human body, sometimes bodies of animals, and sometimes even of plants and trees; each soul, the virtuous or the vile, inhabiting a body congenial to its character at the time of death. "The Birmans believe in this transmigration of souls, after which, they maintain that the radically bad will be sentenced to lasting punishment, while the good will enjoy eternal happiness on a mountain called *Meru*." "Pythagoras pretended that he had himself passed through a number of bodies, naming the persons in whose bodies his soul had dwelt; and he professed that he had a distinct recollection of his previous existence!" In some systems, it is connected with the doctrine of the pre-existence of souls. Among the Pythagorians and Stoics, many believed that " all souls are *a part* of the Deity, or of the great soul of the world in a pantheistic sense, and that all souls return again to this great source of souls."

But, however this idea of successive transmigrations may have sprung from that deep religious feeling prompted by the aspirations of the pagan after a future state of blessedness, while it is totally devoid of all moral power to restrain from sin and promote holiness, it is equally destitute of affording consolation in a dying hour. Indeed, all the ideas of the pagans regarding a future state of being, were imperfect, unsatisfactory, and false ; and hence involved the mind in the deepest uncertainty in reference to an hereafter. Even Cicero, who wrote well about another life in other respects, said : " If the day of our death brings with it not an extinction of our being, but only a change of our abode, nothing can be more desirable ; but if it absolutely destroys and puts an end to our existence, what can be better than, amidst the labors and troubles of life, to rest in a profound and eternal sleep ?" Ah, that "if." Though he *hoped* to live hereafter, yet he *feared* a total extinction of his being. Seneca too, the most correct moralist among the ancient pagans, speaks of the hopes of a better life as " a kind of pleasing dream, an opinion embraced by great men, very agreeable indeed, but which they promised rather than proved." And Plutarch's comfort in regard to a future life, is equally cold and cheerless. Leland says that, "in his consolation to Apollonius, he observes that Socrates said that death is either like a sleep, or to a journey afar off and of long continuance, or to the entire extinction of soul and body."—Annihilation ! A total extinction of one's being ! Whose soul does not recoil with horror at the thought of

> " This secret dread and inward horror
> Of falling into nothing ! "

We have already quoted Socrates when speaking of the after-life, as saying that the departed live all their life-time *without bodies,*" etc. And, indeed, if we except the Magi of Babylonia, Media, Assyria, and Persia, this formed the staple commodity in the theology of Paganism. These Magi, however, taught that "at the end of the world there shall be a *resurrection* and a day of judgment, after which, the angel of darkness shall take the wicked away to the place of punishment." Then "the angel of light and His disciples shall also go into a world of their own, where they shall receive, in everlasting light, the reward due to their good works."

As to the *origin* of the Pagan ideas of the future blessedness of the departed, Leland says: "Aristotle, cited by Plutarch, speaking of the happiness of men after their departure out of this life, represents it as a most ancient opinion, so old, that no man knows when it began, or who was the author of it, that it hath been handed down to us *by tradition* from eternal ages." And "Lord Bolingbroke, whose interests in the matter would have laid the other way, acknowledges that the doctrine of the immortality of the soul, and a state of future rewards and punishments, began to be taught *before* we have any light into antiquity; and when we begin to have any, we find it established, that it was strongly inculcated from time immemorial, and as early as the most ancient and learned nations appear to us."

It is clear from this, that whatever man may *desire* without a Divine Revelation, he cannot *believe* without it. We gladly, therefore, take our leave of these pagan *idiosincracies* regarding the subject in hand, and turn to the infinitely clearer light reflected in the pages of those Holy "Scriptures given by inspiration of God."

THE BIBLE.

" 'Tis Heaven in perspective ; and the bliss
    Of glory, there,
    If anywhere,
By saints on earth anticipated is ;
    Whilst *faith* in every word,
    A being doth afford."

The Synagogue.

How precious is the Book divine,
    By Inspiration given !
Bright as a lamp, its doctrines shine,
    To guide our souls to Heaven.

It sweetly cheers our drooping hearts,
    In this dark vail of tears ;
Light, life, and joy it still imparts,
    And quells our rising fears.

This lamp through all the tedious night
    Of life shall guide our way,
Till we behold the clearer light
    Of an eternal day.

John Fawcett, 1782. *(From " The Sacrifice of Praise." Brick Presb. Ch. Hymns.)*

HAVING under the preceding section, presented a brief view of the ideas prevalent among the Pagans of antiquity, etc., regarding a future place of blessedness, it is evident from the quotations in the last paragraph, that they could not have sprung from unassisted reason. Their knowledge respecting it, as we have said, was *traditional*. And yet, as "we know that the whole creation groaneth and travaileth together in pain until now," and that "the earnest expectation of the creature waiteth for the manifestation of the sons of God;"[1] it is certainly reasonable to infer that in every *human* breast, there should exist what Cicero calls "a kind of *natural admonition*." And so, "the *Gentiles*, who have not God's law," nevertheless "have the law *written in their hearts*, their consciences either excusing or accusing them"[2] as voluntary and accountable beings, in proportion as their actions are good or bad. Still, a desire after a blessed immortality, and a knowledge and hope of it and faith in it, are very different things. It cannot therefore be strictly true, as is affirmed, that

> "Hope springs eternal in the human breast."

"Faith," only, "is the substance (or confident expectation) of things hoped for, the evidence of things not seen."[3] Hence it is that the natural man discerneth not the things of the spirit of God, for they are foolishness unto him, neither can he know them, because they are *spiritually* discerned. We pass on therefore to—

[1] Rom. viii. 19, 22. [2] Rom. ii. 11-16. [3] Heb. xi. 1.

SECTION II.

The Jewish Ideas of the "Inheritance in Heaven."

THE JEW'S HEAVEN.

> Patriarchs, prophets, priests
> Inspired by mystic dreams, and types,
> And visions of a brighter day, exclaimed—
> *To my fathers gathered I shall be!*
> Thus they "DIED IN FAITH," sure of a passport
> Through death's gloomy vail, to realms
> Of light, and joy, and blessedness :—
> Where Abraham, Isaac, Jacob,
> Throned in Messiah's seat of empire
> O'er all the earth, shall welcome their return.
> Faith said: though "in the dust" I lie,
> "Yet in my flesh shall my Redeemer see!"
> 'Twas thus in hope they wept o'er loved ones,
> Sure of a blest re-union in that "far-off" land,
> At the last loud trumpet's blast.
> *By the Author.*

We shall show, in a subsequent page, the *source* of the traditionary ideas of the Pagan nations of antiquity respecting the future world. Let it now suffice that we advert, by way of illustration, to the learned Dean PRIDEAUX, who, in his "connections of sacred and profane history," has shown conclusively, that Zoroaster, the author of the "*Zend-Avesta*," or Persian Bible, and a cotemporary of the prophet Daniel, stole from that prophet the material for the construction of his entire system of theology.

THE INHERITANCE IN HEAVEN, then, as a matter of divine revelation, comes now to be contemplated in the less brilliant but not less real sun-light of Old Testament *Jewish* faith and hope of a reunion with their pious departed

IN GLORY.

"*There* doth many a loved one dwell
In light and joy ineffable.
Oh, tell me how they shine and sing,
While every harp rings echoing,
And every glad and tearless eye
Beams like the bright sun gloriously.
   Tell me of that victorious palm,
     Each hand *in glory* beareth;
   Tell me of that celestial calm,
     Each face *in glory* weareth."

Thus thought and spake and chaunted the covenanted seed of Abraham, and Isaac, and Jacob, while,

"On heavenly pastimes bent,"

they contemplated the present as but

"The bud of being—the dim dawn,
The twilight of our day, the vestibule."
                                    Young.

Ay, as from the top of Pisgah, they descried the beauties of the Promised Land as it stretched out in the hazy distance before them; so the Heavenly Blessedness—that "*better country*"[1]—revealed to the eye of faith as "afar off," which they beheld from the "hill-top" of the inspired pages. Here

[1] Heb. xi. 16.

was recorded the existence of that first delightful dwelling of man in innocence—the "garden which the Lord God planted eastward in Eden"—(a "country" which signifies *pleasure* or *delight*), and in which was made "to grow every tree that is pleasant to the sight, and good for food ; the tree of life also in the midst of the garden,"[1] and to which came to be appropriated the name of "PARADISE."[2] And, although by sin man forfeited his possession of it, and became a wretched exile "in a desert land and waste howling wilderness ;"[3] yet, the painful and long protracted wanderings and unexampled sufferings of the Jew, with the perpetuated records and traditions of it before him, failed to obliterate from his mind a recollection of it. Nor this only. A foundation was laid, broad and deep, of their *final restoration*, their Lost Paradise, through the promised seed of the woman,[4] the MESSIAH.

The faith and hope, therefore, of every pious Jew, were centered in this "promise" to them of a PARADISE RESTORED. St. Paul, in direct allusion to this, tells us that "these *all died in faith*, not having received the promises, but having seen them afar off, and were persuaded of them, and embraced them, and confessed that they were strangers and pilgrims in the earth. For they that say such things, declare plainly that they seek a country . . . *a better country*, that is, a Heavenly."[5] Yes, their language was that of—

[1] Gen. ii. 8, 9. [2] Luke xiii. 43 ; 2 Cor. xii. 4 ; Rev. ii. 7.
[3] Deut. xxxii. 10. [4] Gen. iii. 14, 15.   [5] Heb. xi. 13, 16.

THE PILGRIM'S SONG.

"A pilgrim and a stranger,
  I journey here below;
Far distant is my country,
  The "*house*" to which I go.
Here I must toil and travel,
  Oft weary and opprest;
But there my God shall lead me
  To everlasting rest.

. . . . . .

Who would share *Abraham's* blessing,
  Must Abraham's path pursue;
A stranger and a pilgrim,
  Like him must journey through.
The foes must be encountered,
  The dangers must be passed;
Only a faithful soldier
  Receives the crown at last.

. . . .

There I shall dwell for ever,
  No more a stranger guest,
With all thy blood-bought children,
  In everlasting rest.
The pilgrim toil forgotten,
  The pilgrim conflict o'er,
All earthly grief behind me,
  Eternal joy before!"

"*Hymns from the Land of Luther.*

In this way the Jew came to associate in his mind the name of *Heaven*, as their future home, which primarily refers, not to the substance of future felicity, but to that which is external and local. In other words, it refers not so much to a state as to a *place*—a visible, tangible, local abode "*in*" Heaven. I only add, that from this Jewish idea of Heaven, was traditionally derived that of the Elysian Fields, Hysperian Gardens, and Islands of the Blest, of the ancient Pagans.

THE FUTURE HOME.

"Call out from the future thy visions bright,
From the world o'er the grave take thy solemn flight,
And O, with the loved, whom no more I see,
Show me my home as it yet may be!
As it yet may be, in some pure sphere,
No cloud, no parting, no sleepless fear;
So my soul may bear on, through the long, long day,
Till I go where the beautiful melts not away."

Felicia Hemans.

SECTION III.

The Christian's Ideas of the "Inheritance in Heaven.

"The more our spirits are enlarged on earth,
The deeper draughts can they receive of Heaven."

FROM the comparative obscurity which vailed the Jewish ideas regarding the "inheritance in Heaven" as a *place*, we now emerge into the noon-tide light of the inspired Oracles, whence, in view of the more perfect developments reflected on this subject, we may say to those to whom the predestined home of the believer is "foolishness," [1]

> "Ye brainless wits ! ye baptized infidels !
> Ye worse for mending ! washed to fouler stains !
> Archangels failed to cast this mighty sum."

Aye :

> "There are more things in Heaven and Earth,
> Than are dreamed of in your philosophy."

In entering upon this branch of our subject, it is important to observe, that the phraseology, "Inheritance," and "Heaven," are often used interchangeably as denoting the same thing. Thus, we read of "an *inheritance* among them that are sanctified" [2]—of the *inheritance* of the saints in light" [3]—of the "eternal *inheritance*" [4]—and of "an *inheritance* incorruptible," [5] etc. On the other hand, we read : "Rejoice, for great is your reward in *Heaven*" [6]—"despise not one of those little ones ; for in *Heaven* their angels do always behold the face of their Father which is in Heaven." [7] "Ye have in *Heaven*, a better and an enduring substance," [8] etc. "Jesus was parted from them, and was taken up into *Heaven*." [9] "The armies that were in *Heaven* followed Him," [10] etc.

And yet, the Scriptures, in speaking of the "inheritance" and "Heaven," represent them as entirely *separate* and *distinct* each from the other. Thus St. Paul : "For we know,

[1] i. Cor. ii. 14. [2] Acts xx. 32. [3] Col. i. 12. [4] Heb. ix. 15.
[5] i. Pet. i. 4. [6] Matt. v. 12. [7] Matt. xviii. 10. [8] Heb. x. 34.
[9] Luke xxiv. 51. [10] Rev. xix. 14.

that if our earthly house of this tabernacle were dissolved, we have *a building of God*, *a house* not made with hands, eternal and IN the heavens."[1] And St. Peter speaks of " an inheritance IN Heaven," etc. And, on this account, St. Paul, alluding to the old patriarchs, who "*now* desire a better country," calls it "a *heavenly;* wherefore God is not ashamed to be called their God, for He hath prepared for them *a city.*" If then, we take the phraseology, "a building of God"—"a house"—"an inheritance"—"a better country"—"a city," etc., and it is the same with "the world—τὴν οἰκουμένην τὴν μέλλουσαν—or habitable earth to come, whereof he speaks,"[2] we get the true scriptural idea of what constitutes the "heavenly blessedness" of the redeemed.

It is clear, therefore, that the Inheritance of the saints in light "as a visible, tangible, and localized *place*, is to be sought for among the numberless" visible and invisible thrones and dominions and principalities and powers IN the heavenly places that "were created by and for Christ."[3] The question, as to *which* of the "heavenly places" the habitable "world to come" is to be assigned, will form a special subject of inquiry in the following pages. We have now to do with that extensively prevalent custom of confounding of things which differ, in these premises, that has led to the substitution of so much of what is vague and conjectural, aye, and fanciful withal, for that which is real, in relation to the Heavenly Blessedness, so common among all classes of Chris-

---

[1] ii. Cor. v. 1. [2] Heb. ii. 5. [3] Compare Eph. iii. 10., with Col. i. 16.

tians of this day. The Rev. Mr. Harbaugh says: It is represented as being such a sublimated—we will not say place, for amid the fashion of the times it is almost heresy to speak of it as a PLACE—it is described as such a sublimated and etherial state, so *purely spiritual*, so abstracted and removed from all the sympathies of the present life, that it must seem to conscientious hearts, almost profane to claim a present fellowship with it! . . . There seems to be an effort to cast an air of strangeness around it, which cuts off all those warm alternations by which it reaches over so lovingly into this life, and makes us feel that *there* is our home—that *there* is "our Father's house," with its familiar, home-like scenes, and not a cold ivory hall of a strange king, which we dread to enter." Dr. Thomas Chalmers speaks to the same effect. "The common imagination that we have of Paradise on the other side of death," he observes, "is that of a lofty *aerial* region, where the inmates float in ether, or are mysteriously suspended upon nothing—where all the warm and sensible accompaniments, which give such strength, and life, and coloring to our present habitation, are attenuated into a sort of *spiritual* element, that is meagre, and imperceptible, and utterly uninviting to the eye of mortals here below—where every vestige of materialism is done away, and nothing left but unearthly scenes that have no power of allurement, and certain unearthly ecstacies, with which it is impossible to sympathize." Dr. Dick says: "The greater part of Christians rest contented with the most vague and incorrect ideas of the felicity of Heaven, and talk and write in so loose and figurative a manner, as can convey *no* rational or definite conception of the sublime contemplations and employments of celestial intelligences. Instead of eliciting, from the metaphorical language of Scripture, the *ideas* intended to be conveyed, they endeavor to expand and ramify the figures employed by the sacred writers still further, heaping metaphor upon metaphor, and epithet upon epithet, and blending a number of discordant ideas, till the image and picture presented to the mind assumes the semblance of a splendid chaotic map, or of a dazzling but undefined meteor. The term " *glory,*" and its kindred epithets, have been reiterated a thousand times in descriptions of the heavenly *state*—the redeemed have been represented as assembled in one vast crowd above the visible concave of the sky, adorned with 'starry crowns,' drinking at 'crystal fountains,' and making ' the vaulted heavens ring' with their loud acclamations. The Redeemer himself has been exhibited as suspended like a statue in the heavens, above the immense crowd, crowned with diadems, and encircled with a refulgent splendor, while the assembly of the heavenly inhabitants were incessantly gazing on this object, like a crowd of spectators gazing on the motions of an air-balloon, or of a splendid meteor. Such representations are repugnant to the ideas intended to be conveyed by the metaphorical language of inspiration, when stript of its drapery. They can convey nothing but a meagre and distorted conception of the employments of the celestial state, and tend only to bewilder the imagination, and to darken counsel by words without knowledge."

"It has hence happened," Dr. Dick continues, " that certain infidel scoffers have been led to conclude, that the *Christian* Heaven is not an object to be desired; and have frequently declared, 'that they could feel no pleasure in being suspended for ever in an etherial region, and perpetually singing psalms and hymns to the eternal'"—an *idea* of Heaven which is too frequently conveyed by the vague and distorted descriptions which have been given of the exercises and entertainments of the future world." [1]

It will be our endeavor to strip the varied and beautiful imagery of Holy Scripture from these and the like "vague and distorted descriptions" of that "better country," and to lay open to the eye of faith and hope a view of the Heavenly Blessedness, in its relation to the future abode of the saints, as depicted in the following lines—

THE GLORIES OF HEAVEN.

Come with us, and behold the higher sight
Than e'er thy heart desired, or hope conceived.
See, yonder is the glorious hill of God
'Bove angels' gaze in brightness rising high.
Come, join our wing, and we will guide the flight,
To mysteries of everlasting bliss,—
The tree, the fount of bliss, the eternal throne,
The presence chamber of "THE KING OF KINGS."

Pollok.

[1] Dick's Future State, pp. 182, 183.

CHAPTER II.

Of the Heavenly Inheritance as Deferred.

"An Inheritance . . . Reserved in Heaven."

WE must here pause the while, to take a view of what the Scriptures teach of the Saint's "Inheritance as *reserved* in Heaven for him."

THE GOOD MAN'S TRANSIT.

In view of the Christian pilgrim's transit from "this present evil world,"[1] it may truly be said, that

> "The last end
> Of the good man is peace. How calm his exit!
> Night dews fall not more gently to the ground,
> Nor weary worn-out winds expire so soft."—*Blair*.

> "As they draw near to their eternal home,
> Leaving the Old, *both worlds* they view."

> "Thou it was
> When the world's din and passion's voice was still,
> Calling the wanderer home!"

> "Thus on he moves to meet his latter end,
> Angels around befriending virtue's friend

[1] Gal. i. 4.

Sinks to the grave with unperceived decay,
While resignation gently slopes the way:
And, all his prospect brightening to the last,
His Heaven commences ere the world be past."

"NO, NO, IT IS NOT DYING."

No, no, it is not dying
   To go unto our God,
This gloomy earth forsaking,
Our journey homeward taking
   Along the starry road.

No, no, it is not dying
   Heaven's citizen to be;
A crown immortal wearing,
And rest unbroken sharing,
   From care and conflict free.

No, no, it is not dying
   To hear this gracious word,
"Receive a Father's blessing,
For evermore possessing
   The favor of the Lord."

No, no, it is not dying
   The Shepherd's voice to know
His sheep he ever leadeth,
His peaceful flock He feedeth,
   Where living pastures grow.

No, no, it is not dying
   To wear a lordly crown;
Among God's people dwelling!
The glorious triumph swelling
   Of Him whose sway we own.

> O no, it is not dying,
>   Thou Saviour of mankind!
> There, streams of love are flowing,
> No hindrance ever knowing;
>   Here, drops alone we find.
>
> Translated by R. P. Dunn, 1852. (From the Sacrifice of Praise. Brick Pres. Church Hymns.)

These lines are no less expressive than consolatory. They naturally open the door to the inquiry: Do the saints pass, *immediately at death*, into the full or consummated and eternal possession of the promised Inheritance? A reply to this, will involve an inquiry into what the Scriptures reveal under

SECTION I.

Concerning the Place and State or Condition of the Departed, between Death and the Resurrection.

INTRODUCTION.

Amid the mazes intricate into which this momentous and much controverted subject is involved, we shall be compelled to tax the reader's indulgence to an extent commensurate with its importance. This will bring us into direct antagonism with those modern un-Scriptural theories, which affirm that the *soul only* is the man or person, on the one hand, and the materialistic or *soul-mortal* theory, on the other. Our plan of argument is simply INDUCTIVE, and hence didactic rather than polemical, showing, by *necessary sequence*, the fallacy of both. The reader will be left to decide for himself, whether or not the Scriptural doctrine of the *place* and *state* of the departed between death and the resurrection, do not furnish a logical refutation of the theories of Swedenborgianism, Unitarianism, Universalism, Spiritualism, and the alleged annihilation of the wicked at or after death.

Let it be observed, then, that we have now to do with man as a COMPLEX BEING in his *disembodied* state and place in THE "UNSEEN WORLD."

If what has been said of the Heavenly Blessedness be true, namely, that it consists of a visible, tangible, local PLACE in some portion of God's universe, then it follows, that the mysterious being, MAN, who is declared to be "fearfully and wonderfully made"[1]—only "*a little while lower* than the angels,"[2]—must be a complex being, constituted of *body* and *soul;* and hence, that his full, perfect, and eternal possession and enjoyment of the "inheritance of the saints in light," must await his *resurrection* from the dead, and the *re-union* of his soul and body, as essential to the preservation intact, of his *entire personality*, and the adaptation, consequently, of his complex nature to that place and state of his future being. On any other ground, the inference is, that only *one-half* the man is the subject of happiness or misery.

"Man a little while lower than the Angels."

A FRIEND of mine, in conversation with me a short time since, expressed some views on this passage in the 8th Psalm, and in the 2d chapter of the Epistle to the Hebrews, in

[1] Psalm cxxx. 14.   [2] Psalm viii. 5; Heb. ii. 7, 9.

which he contended that the marginal note in the authorized version was the true translation of the original Hebrew. Thinking his views deserving of consideration, I requested him to furnish me with a copy of them, and I asked leave to use them, which he has permitted. He says:

"In a sermon by my highly esteemed pastor, this passage, implying the original rank, in the creation, of *man*, was quoted, which led me to investigate the subject.

"The passage in the authorized version, is, '*Thou hast made him a little lower than the angels.*' The marginal note makes it read, '*Thou hast made him for a little time, lower than the angels.*' The difference in this rendering seemed to be of very great importance. In consulting Dr. Clarke, I find he translated the passage '*Thou hast lessened him for a little time from God.*' '*Thou hast made him less than God for a little time.*' This difference in the rendering of the passage, suggested the following reflections:

"In the creation of *man*, as presented in the 1st chapter of Genesis, it is worthy of remark that in the two verses, the 26th and 27th, there is a peculiar emphasis given to the fact that man was created in the *image of God*, for it is emphasized no less than *four* times in these two verses. 'Let us make man in *our image*, after *our likeness*. So God created man in *his own image*, in *the image of God* created he him.' It is on these express declarations, that I have founded my belief that *man*, when created, was the most exalted of all intelligences—superior to all angelic beings: for it is no where declared that any other intelligent beings were created in the image of God. This image, stamping man superior to all other beings, was peculiar to *man*. As this image is not physical but spiritual, man's *soul* was originally endowed with all the communicable attributes of God; that he was in a higher sense than any other created being, 'a Son of God;' that he partook '*of the Divine nature*,' the nature of his Father; that he was emphatically of the blood Royal of Heaven.

"There is, therefore, a difference of great importance in the two renderings. The original status of man at his creation, if he was constituted in any degree inferior to the angels, implies a fixed limit in intellectual and spiritual rank beyond which he cannot naturally pass. In the received version, the angels are assumed to be his natural superiors, notwithstanding they have been declared to have upon them the peculiar stamp of the Godhead. This belongs *only* to man. We can conceive, however, of causes which may temporarily, or even permanently, degrade him from a higher position. We can conceive of a king forfeiting his crown, and driven into exile, so that for a *little while*, he may be lower than any of his subjects, and we can also conceive of his *return* from exile, and his restoration to his former rank. We can understand that sin has cast down man from his original exalted position above the angels, and so become 'lessened for a little time from God.' Man, therefore, in his *fallen* condition, is, indeed, made lower than the angels, but the limiting phrase, 'for a little time,' while it foreshadows a change, also implies an *original superiority*, to which superior condition he is to be restored, after that 'little time' shall have elapsed.

"Redemption through Christ is the revealed means of restoration. The great consummation is the restoration of man, to his original rank *above* the angels; re-union with God in Christ, by which union, man again receives the lost image of God, becomes again a 'partaker of the divine nature;' 'a Son of God;' 'a joint heir with Christ;' 'one with God;' 'one with Christ as he is one with the Father.' In these expressions, we discover clearly the original superiority of man. It is said of Christ as the HEAD of the race, as the representative man, as it was said of man at his creation, that 'he was the express image of God's person;' that '*he was made better than the angels*,' and 'all the angels of God are required to worship Him.'

"The first chapter of the Hebrews seems to be specially devoted to show the inferiority of the angels. All things were put in subjection to man in Christ, and through him. In the second chapter it is also said, 'but unto the angels hath he not put in subjection the world to come.' Yet 'the world to come' must be included in the 'all things;' 'for in that he put all in subjection under him, he left nothing that is not put under him.' Now as 'united to Christ;' 'reigning with him;' sharing with him the inheritance of all things,' as '*coheirs*,' as being one with him, and the Father, man's rank will certainly be above the angels. This, indeed, is in the future. He took on himself, not the nature of angels, but the nature of man, in order to restore that nature to its original condition *above the angels*. Does not this view of the exalted rank of man give an *intensity* to the gravity of man's fall from his original rank, into the condition of temporary inferiority, which is not felt, in the supposition that man fell from a *less* exalted position? A fall from a one story window of a house is not so appalling as a fall from the summit of the tower. Again, this view seems to suggest a reason why Christ the Redeemer should have a peculiar sympathy for *man*, as originally his brother, bearing the image of his Father. It suggests, so to speak, the yearning of family affection, for suffering kindred, which would not be so naturally excited towards beings of an inferior type."

" Much has been said and written on the *dignity of human nature*. But no philosophy concocted from the study of human nature, *outside* of Bible teaching, can conceive of a dignity of human nature like this. Man in the image of God ; man inheriting all things ; man above the angels, but cast down for a little time below these sinless beings ; man with a brother rushing to his rescue ; conquering all adversaries that oppose his final restoration to his natural rank in the Royal family of our common Father. This is a dignity of human nature which cannot generate pride, for it is not of our procuring. It has been purchased for us by the sufferings, and sacrifices, and blood of a brother.

" We cast ourselves down, but he alone redeems us. Helpless, lost, in ourselves utterly unable to regain our forfeited rank, Christ the Redeemer, our elder brother, makes for us a way through humble faith in Him, to be again 'heirs of all things.'"

NOTE.—It may be pertinent to notice that Beza in translating the passage quoted from the 8th Psalm, in the Epistle to the Hebrews, uses the word "*paulisper*," a little while,—and the Tetraglotton of Theile, and Steir, gives in the English note the translation, "*a little while inferior to.*"

The only escape from this inference, is on the hypothesis that the *soul only*, is the man or person; an hypothesis which has originated all those popular misconceptions regarding the Heavenly Blessedness, etc., alleged to be peopled by beings *purely spiritual*, as shown in the quotations from Drs. Harbaugh, Chalmers, and Dick.

But, this theory, in every aspect, totally ignores the Scriptural doctrine of a *literal resurrection* of the same body that dies, and is earnestly advocated by the Rev. Prof. HITCHCOCK, who, in a discourse in the "South Church Lectures" on "the resurrection body," says: "When we sit down to a careful study of the New Testament, we may well be astonished at the crude notions which have in so many quarters been entertained in regard to the resurrection body. The resurrection of the *flesh* is no where affirmed. In cases where the noun is used, the resurrection revealed is the resurrection 'of the dead,' or 'from the dead,' or 'of the righteous,' or sometimes simply 'the resurrection;' *never* is it the resurrection of the flesh; *never*, even in so many words, the resurrection of the *body*. In other cases where the verb is used, the body is spoken of as dying and rising again; but in *no* single passage is there any hint of the resurrection of the flesh. Nay, we are expressly told that 'flesh and blood cannot inherit the kingdom of God,'"[1] etc.

Now, if the learned Professor had not limited our "crude notions" on this subject to the New Testament, we might have quoted those memorable words of the old patriarch,

[1] N. Y. Evang., May 18, 1865.

Job—" I know that my Redeemer liveth, and He shall stand at the latter day upon the earth ; and though after my skin worms destroy this body, YET IN MY FLESH shall I see God : whom I shall see for myself, and mine eyes shall behold, and not another ; *though my reins be consumed* within me." [1] German neologists would convert this sublime passage into allegory, and apply it as denoting Job's restoration to worldly prosperity, etc. But, so far from this, in harmony with the teachings of the New Testament, it is evidently to be taken *literally*, as a prophecy of the *return* of the Redeemer " at the latter day," to raise the *dead bodies* of His sleeping Saints,[2] and re-unite them to their departed souls ; when, each one for himself, and Job with them, " *shall see God* IN THE FLESH," their " vile bodies" being thus " *changed*, and fashioned like unto CHRIST'S GLORIOUS BODY ;"[3] concerning which latter, Jesus himself declared, in proof of *His actual literal* resurrection, " Spirit *hath not* flesh and bones, as ye see ME have."[4] And, as to the Professor's statement, that there is " never even, in so many words, any mention of the resurrection of the *body*," etc., the following passage is a sufficient refutation : " And the *graves* were opened, and *many bodies* of the saints which slept *arose*, and *came out of their graves* after His resurrection, and appeared unto many." [5]

It results, therefore, that Man, being constituted of body *and* soul, " stands as the medium of two worlds. In him,

---

[1] Job xix. 25, 27. [2] Compare Dan. xii. 2, with 1 Thess. iv. 13, 15.
[3] Philipp. iii. 21. [4] Luke xxiv. 39. [5] Matt. xxvii. 52, 53.

Heaven and earth, time and eternity, the finite and the Infinite, meet and exchange their sympathies."

MAN.

" From different natures marvelously mixed,
Connection exquisite of different worlds !
Distinguished link of being's endless chain !
Midway from nothing to the Deity !"

The fair inference from the above is this : that the *consummation* of the Saints' Heavenly Blessedness and of the miseries of the lost, *must await* the resurrection of the " body" or " flesh," and its reunion with the soul.

But, if this be so, then it follows that the *soul*, when separated from the body, whether of the righteous or the wicked, must have a *conscious existence* somewhere, during the *interval* between death and the resurrection. Indeed, we are safe in affirming, that there is no escape from this, unless we admit the modern baptized semi-infidel theory, that the soul of man was *created mortal ;* and hence,—except in the case of the regenerate, who, it is alleged, at the instant of the *new birth* are rendered immortal—that it is subject to *death*. It is on this hypothesis that such writers as Mr Miles Grant, George Storrs, Hudson, Hastings, the Rev. Clinton Colegrove, and others, most of them of the exploded Millerite delusion, affirm the *annihilation* of the souls of the wicked at death, as a caveat against the Scriptural doctrine of future endless punishment.

On this subject of man's *immortality* as a complex being, corporeal and spiritual, we remark that *essential* immortality belongs alone to God. Hence the word *spirit*—in Hebrew רוּחַ, *ruach*, in Greek πνευμα, *pneuma*, and in Latin, *spiritus*,—as denotive of the Divine *essence*, is applied first, to the FATHER : " God is a *Spirit ;*"¹ and of whom Jesus declared, " No man hath seen God at any time." Yes. " He *only* has (inherent) immortality, dwelling in light which no man can approach unto."² And second, to the HOLY SPIRIT, the third person of the adorable Trinity, who, proceeding from the Father and the Son, energized the chaotic elements of the *material* world, bringing order out of confusion ; and in the *moral* world inspires, illumines, regenerates, and sanctifies the redeemed.³ Man's immortality is *derived*. It is God's *gift* to him. This is evident from the following. Of the Lord Jesus Christ, " according to the eternal purpose" of SELF-MANIFESTATION which the " Invisible God" " purposed in Him,"⁴ it is declared that " a *body*," corporeal, was " prepared" for Him,⁵ and " in the fulness of time"⁶ was assumed by Him of the " virgin Mary" by " the power of the Holy Ghost."⁷ So also of the Lord Jesus we read, that " His *soul* was exceeding sorrowful, even unto death."⁸ Hence our blessed Saviour was constituted of a *material* body and a *rational* soul. But HE, as " the second man, the Lord from heaven,"⁹ was the *antitype* of " the first man, who is of the earth, earthy,"¹⁰ and whom St. Paul declares was created as " the FIGURE of Him that was to

---

1 John iv. 24.   2 1 Tim. vi. 16.
3 2 Pet. i. 21 ; 2 Tim. iii. 16 ; Heb. x. 32 ; Titus iii. 5 ; 2 Thess. ii. 13.
4 Eph. iii. 11.   5 Heb. x. 5   6 Gal. iv. 4.   7 Luke i. 35.
8 Matt. xxvi. 38.   9 1 Cor. xv. 47.   10 Ib.

come."[1] There *must*, therefore, be a homogeneity of natures between the two, that is, the corporeal and the spiritual, as indispensable to the proper and essential *personality* of both. And so, the term *pneuma*, as applied to the human soul, which was "*breathed into*" the newly created corporeal form of "the first Adam" by God himself,[2] is used expressly to distinguish it from his *body* ($\sigma o\mu\alpha$, soma.) Indeed, strictly speaking, Man is constituted of THREE PARTS—*body, soul,* and *spirit;* the last, forming the connecting link between the body and the soul, and which, though material, yet being refined and attenuated to its utmost degree, like caloric or heat, is nevertheless invisible and intangible. "*The life is the blood,*"[3] which, at *death*, is subject to decomposition.

But, from the circumstance that the word *soul*, in Hebrew נפש, NEPHESH, is used in Scripture interchangeably with the words spirit and life, and is hence sometimes employed to denote the animal life or the *dead body* of a man; it is maintained by some writers that the soul, in man, is the *same* with that of the animal life or "spirit of, the *brutes which perish.*" If, however, it can be shown that the Hebrew word nephesh, is used in the Old Testament to denote the *rational* soul, when applied to man, and that it is *never* so applied to the lower orders of animals, it will follow that he occupies a scale of being *superior* to them. On this point, we challenge the production of a single passage, where the term nephesh, soul, is applied to the *brutal* creation as denotive of *their* endowment of the rational faculties; while in

[1] Rom. v. 14. [2] Gen. ii. 7. [3] Gen. ix. 4.

Deut. vi. 5, we read of *man*, "Thou shalt love the Lord thy God with all thy heart, and with all thy *soul*."[1] (nephesh.) Here the word soul, is evidently used in the sense of the rational soul or *mind*, properly so called: that principle within us which thinks, and understands, and wills, and exercises the powers and faculties and propensities of our nature. The same holds true of the meaning of the Greek word ψυχὴ, *psuche*, in the New Testament, which corresponds to the Hebrew *nephesh*, in the Old. In the following passages, if there be meaning in words, the term *psuche*—soul—can be understood in no other sense than that of denoting the rational and immortal part of our nature: "Fear not them which kill the body, *but are not able to kill the soul* (ψυχή); but rather fear Him which is able to destroy both *soul* (ψυχή) and *body* in hell,"[2] (not ἅδης *hades*, but γέεννα, *gehenna*, Matt. x. 28): that is, to punish in the torments of "perdition" the spiritual or *immortal* part of man as well as his *corporeal* nature.

Again. In that notable passage quoted by St. Peter, Acts ii. 27, from Ps. x. 16, respecting our blessed Lord: "Thou wilt not *leave my soul* (ψυχή) in hell, neither wilt Thou suffer thy Holy One to see corruption," it is evident that *some part* of the human nature of Christ, called his soul, was to be in hell, but was not to be *left* there; while His *body* was to be in the grave, but was not to see *corruption*. Now, "if soul means merely His *animal* life, this not

---

[1] See also Deut. iv. 29; Ps. xxiv. 4, etc.
[2] See also Matt. xi. 29; xxvi. 28; and John vii. 27.

being a distinct subsistence, there was *no part* of His nature in hell. Soul must therefore refer to some *distinct part* of the human nature of our blessed Lord, which *was not left* in hell. The term soul (ψυχή) cannot mean His body; it cannot mean His animal life, which has *no* distinct subsistence: it must therefore mean His *soul*, properly so called, that is, the *spiritual* and *immortal* part of His human nature," as that which was not to be left in hell.

And finally. With this Scriptural evidence of the *complex personality* of man in view, it will be found in exact harmony with the philosophy of the inspired Paul on this subject, 1 Thess. v. 23, where he says: " I pray God your *whole spirit*, and *soul*, and *body*, be preserved blameless, UNTO THE COMING of our Lord Jesus Christ."

The inevitable sequence from these statements is, that if CHRIST, in body and soul, as a complex Being, is *immortal;* then is MAN, who was created as "*the figure*" of the Incarnate Deity, and from whom He was to descend, *immortal* also. "The children, being partakers of flesh and blood, He also HIMSELF likewise took part of the same"—" not the nature of angels"—*much less* the nature of "the brutes which perish"—"that through death He might destroy him that had the power of death, that is, the Devil; and *deliver* them who, through fear of death, were all their life-time subject to bondage." [1]

So much for the materialistic or alleged *soul*-mortal theory. The words of Martha to our blessed Lord respecting her

---

[1] Heb. ii. 14, 15.

dead brother Lazarus, (John xi. 24,) "I know that he shall rise again in the *resurrection* at the last day," is here in point, and is beautifully expressed in the following lines:

DEATH AND THE RESURRECTION.

Oh, 'tis a thought, most melancholy sad,
A sight which fills the mind with gloom,
A sound, with mournful accents clad—
    We hurry to the tomb!

. . . .

But who is he that calls so loud?
Sure from his grasp there's none can save—
O, I see in his grasp the dead man's shroud,
    His dwelling is the silent grave.

And there he sits with a silent grim,
And revels and feasts most brave;
His meal is brought by his sister sin,
    Down to the silent grave.

And must I there lie down with thee
Since none is found to save?
Come, DEATH, then revel and feast on me,
    When I lie in the silent grave.

From the lonely grave
And the tomb's dark shade,
This body MY SAVIOUR will rise;
Then triumphant I'll sing,
"O Death where's thy sting,"
When His saints I shall meet in the skies?

                                      E. H. B.

In these lines, the poet evidently recognizes a *separation* between the body and soul at death. "After the skin, worms destroy the body"—his "reins are consumed within him." But he rejoices in the faith and hope of a *resurrection* of the body, and its reunion with the soul. It is however clear, that if the soul is the man; or if the body, being raised, is so changed as to destroy its corporeity, man, as a complete being, *loses* his personality. That both these theories are directly at variance with the plainest teachings of Holy Scripture, will appear from the following, demonstrative that man's *personality* in both worlds, consists of the soul *plus* the body.

First. In the *present life*, the Scriptures show that when God speaks *to* or *of* man, they contemplate him in his *complex* nature. Thus, if the term soul only is used when man is spoken of, it is under the form of speech called synechdoche, as in the following passage: "Give me the *souls*, and take the goods to thyself,"[1] where the term "soul" is used to denote the *whole person*, and is equivalent to the "whole spirit and soul and body" spoken of by St. Paul, 1 Thess. v. 23. But,

Second. That this complex personal identity is preserved intact in the *future world*, is evident from the following passage, in reference to the son of the Shumanite widow who died. "And the Lord heard the voice of Elijah; and the *soul* of the child *came into him again*, and he *revived*."[2] Here we ask: Was this the case of a soul *entering into* a

[1] Gen. xiv. 21.   [2] 1 Kings xvii. 22.

soul? or the *return* of a departed soul to and its *reunion* with the body? Take also the case of the daughter of the ruler of the Synagogue in the New Testament: "And He (that is, Christ) put them all out, and took her by the hand, and saith unto her, Talitha Cumi! which is, being interpreted, Damsel, I say unto thee, *arise*. And her *spirit* (or soul) *came into her again*"—that is, returned to her *dead body*—"and she arose straightway,"[1] etc.

We will only add on this subject, that with these statements harmonizes that notable passage which undeniably looks to the future world, as that in which the *final* destiny of man in his complex personality will be *unalterably fixed after* the resurrection, according to his moral character in this life. "Whatsoever a man soweth, that shall he also reap. For he that soweth to the *flesh*," i. e., his carnal desires, "shall of the flesh reap *corruption;*" a term denoting, not annihilation, but the *misery* which awaits him: "but he that soweth to the spirit," i. e., bears the fruits of righteousness, "shall of the spirit reap *life everlasting*," significant of the *happiness* of the redeemed in a future state. But as this is made, in both cases, to depend upon the resurrection of the body, and its reunion with the departed soul, if that body is so transformed into a *purely spiritual* entity, or be so changed as to annihilate or destroy its actual corporeity, it will follow that, by a total loss of its distinctive characteristics as such, only *one-half* of the man will "reap corruption" or "life everlasting" in "the world to come."

[1] Compare Mark v. 35-43, with Luke viii. 40-56.

Evidently, therefore, on the principle of a *resurrection*, the soul, when separated from the body at death, cannot be *instantly* admitted to a state or condition of consummate bliss or woe. And so we find, that while St. Peter speaks of the "Inheritance of the saints" as "*reserved* in Heaven for them;" he, with St. Jude, speaking of "the angels (or messengers) that fell," and of the wicked inhabitants of Sodom and Gomorrah as "examples" of the final doom of the ungodly, says that they "are *reserved* for chains under darkness against (or unto) the day of judgment and perdition of ungodly men."[1] Hence the momentous questions:

Whither does the soul go, when separated from the body at death? *What is its condition* while there? And, Has it a *local habitation*? An answer to these questions introduces us to a direct examination of the next subject of inquiry.

~~~~~~~

SECTION II.

Of the Scriptural Doctrine of the Place and State of the Soul, intermediate between Death and the Resurrection—Its History, etc.

I.—THE SCRIPTURAL VIEW.

A SATIRE.

"O see! an awful world is this
  Where *spirits* are detained. 'Tis half a heaven
  And half a hell! What horrid mixture here!
  I see before me, and along the edge

[1] 2 Pet. iii. 7.

> Of rayless night, on either side, the shades
> Of spirits move ; as yet unjudged, undoomed
> Or unrewarded. Some do seem to hope ;
> Some sit in gloom ; some walk in dark suspense ;
> Some agonize to change their state. Oh ! say,
> Is all this real, or but a monstrous dream." *(Anon).*

INTRODUCTORY REMARKS.

Doubtless, the mind of the author of this poetic effusion was thrilled with a sort of holy horror, at the thought of the departed soul being consigned to a place and state, *intermediate* twixt Heaven and Hell, during the interval between death and the resurrection. And, indeed, this may be regarded as the popular sentiment of the church of this day. A recent writer on this subject observes : " Christians are generally united in the doctrine that there is an *intermediate state*, but not an *intermediate place*," etc. And yet he adds : "it is a doctrine in accordance with the Scriptures, that the *consummation* of happiness to the saints, and of misery to the wicked, will not be experienced till *after* the resurrection." [1]

Now, keeping in view the fact, that we are treating of the soul *after* it has been separated from the body, to the above we reply that, according to this theory, one of two alternatives follow : Either the soul must be *annihilated* at death, or it must exist in some *place*. For, with the existence of all created spirits, is essentially connected the idea of *locality*. On this subject, Bp. HORNE observes : "The soul existing

---

[1] Jewish Chronicle, April, 1849, p. 297.

after death, and separated from the body, though of a nature immaterial, *must be* in some place; for, however metaphysicians may make place as one of the adjuncts of *body*, as if nothing but gross sensible body could be limited to place . . it is hardly to be conceived," he adds, "that any created spirit, of however high an order, can be *without* locality, or without such determination of its existence at any given time to some certain place, that it shall be true to say of it, '*Here it is*, and not *elsewhere*.'" True, "there may be a metaphysical difficulty *how* the soul can exist in an incorporeal state. But does not God, who is a *spirit*, exert an infinite activity as an intelligent Being, independently of material organs? Did not Jesus, the eternal Word, exist in the spirituality of the Godhead *before* His incarnation? And does not the Holy Spirit exert His quickening power without the aid of corporeal instruments?" Even so, *the soul of man* in its separate place of consciousness as an active being after death. Indeed, the writer previously quoted, says: "the righteous, at the time of death, go to *Heaven*, while the wicked are consigned to the infernal pit, the *lower* regions." [1] And so, the Rev. Dr. Harbaugh says: "We consider the true doctrine of God's Word on this subject to be this: the saints do immediately, at death, enter that *place* which is called Heaven, where the body of the Saviour *now* is, where the divine manifestations are most clearly and gloriously made, where angels have their proper home, and where all the heirs of Christ shall finally and for evermore be blessed." [2] And

[1] Jewish Chronicle, April, 1849, p. 298.   [2] Harbour on Heaven, p. 164-65.

yet, we can name no writer, who more ably and satisfactorily demonstrates that Heaven is a *visible, tangible,* and *local* place. "The word Heaven," he says, "refers not, in its primary sense, to the substance of our future felicity, but to that which is *external* and *local* about it. It refers not so much to *state* as to *place*." [1] And again. "There is, furthermore, nothing either in reason, science, or Scripture, to forbid us considering the *material* organizations which beautify the celestial place, as not abruptly dissimilar from those which are familiar to us *in this world*," as says the poet—

EARTH THE COPY OF HEAVEN.

" What if earth
Be but the shadows of Heaven and things therein,
Each to the other like, more than of earth is thought?"

And he quotes Trench, who says : " Many are the sayings of a like kind among Jewish Cabitists. Thus in the book of *Sohar:* 'Whatever is in the earth is also in Heaven ; and nothing is so small in the world, that it does not correspond to a similar thing in Heaven.'" [2] And he adds : "Such is the legitimate *moral* influence of lovely scenery, that he who can be wicked in the midst of it, scarce dares seek repentance ! It is to such that the Poet makes the soul-stirring appeal : " on

THE BEAUTIES OF NATURE.

' O how canst thou renounce the boundless store
Of charms which nature to her votary yields !
The warbling woodland, the resounding shore,
The pomp of groves, and garniture of fields ;

[1] Harbour on Heaven. p. 57.   [2] Ib.—p. 155.

> All that the genial ray of morning gilds,
> And all that echoes to the song of even,
> And all the mountain's sheltering bosom shields,
> And all the dread magnificence of Heaven :
> O, how canst thou renounce, *and be forgiven !* '"—*Anon.*

Speaking of Heaven, this writer further says: "It could not be a suitable abode for the saints, *if* it were not a local, material Heaven. The saints will have *bodies* . . can the *abode* of these bodies be less tangible than the bodies themselves? Certainly not. They cannot be suspended in the air, or float in space eternally ! Though the bodies of the saints will be, in some respects, no doubt, greatly changed,— 'for we shall all be changed, in a moment, in the twinkling of an eye, at the sound of the last trump'—and they will be spirituralized in a way now unknown to us, yet they will be bodies still. 'There is a *spiritural* body.' Job felt confident that he should '*in his flesh* see God.' A human being consists of soul *and* body, the one material, the other immaterial; these two united *make the man,* and they must therefore be united again in the future world, if the man is to retain his nature,"[1] etc.

And, Dr. Harbaugh maintains a *literal resurrection* of the body, after death, in his argument on the revivification of that body in opposition to the Gnostic heresy, "that the resurrection body is in no way a *continuation* or product of this mortal body;"—which heresy has been revived in modern times by SWEDENBOURG, and still more lately by his disciple, the

---

[1] Harbaugh on "Heaven," p. 35.

late Prof. Geo. Bush, in his '*Anastasis*,'—he says: "The history of the whole relation of the present to the future body, is covered by the following points in a process: I. There is a *dissolution* of the present body—its return to its original elements—'That which thou sowest is not quickened, *except it die.*' II. The *evolution* of the future body out of the present. . . 'That which thou sowest, thou sowest not that body that shall be, but bear grain; it may chance of wheat or of some other grain; but God *giveth it a body* as it hath pleased Him,' etc. III. The *continuous identity* of the present and future body through the transformation.* . . God giveth 'to every seed his *own body.*' . . These points are all involved in the apostle's answer to the question: '*How* are the dead raised up? and with what body do they come?' He represents the matter thus: 'That which thou sowest is not *quickened*, except it die: and that which thou sowest, thou sowest not that body that shall be, but bear grain; it may chance of wheat, or of some other grain: but God giveth it a body as it hath pleased him, *and to every seed his own body.*'"[1] On this last point the Doctor says:

"The going down of the body into the grave, is like laying seed into the earth. The seed dies—is resolved into its elemental state. So the (human) body which now is undergoes dissolution. The matter of which it is composed, and which, so long as the spirit (soul) inhabits it, is held under the power of the laws of life, now *loses* its affinities to

[1] i. Cor. xv. 36–38.

those laws, and again becomes entirely subjected to those laws of attraction and gravitation which rule unorganized matter, 'earth to earth, ashes to ashes, dust to dust.' This matter, however, in the case of the *seed*, though it is dissolved, still sustains a *relation* to the new plant and seed of which it is the mother. It nurses the germ of the new plant in its bosom, imparting of itself to it in its growth. It is the condition of its development. Its death is life to the plant. Without its death there is no life to the new plant, for 'that which thou sowest is not quickened *except it die.*' Like this, is the relation subsisting between the *old* (human) body which decays, and the *new* body of which it is the womb. This relation, as that of the old seed to the new, is a *vital* one. It cannot be destroyed. The old body is just as necessary to the new, as the old decayed grain is to the new plant, and to the new seed." [1]

Of course, then, as man is a *complex* being, his "continuous identity" as constituted of body and soul, must await a *re-union* of the "present" with the "future body" at the resurrection. But no one who maintains a *literal* resurrection of the dead, can pretend that that event has already taken place. From the death of Abel down to the last departed saint, a *divorcement* has taken place between the body and the soul. During the *interval*, therefore, between death and the resurrection, the complex personality of man in its original completeness, is broken up. The body lies mouldering in the grave, and the soul has "returned unto God who gave it." [2]

But we again repeat: *Whither has the soul gone?* Dr.

[1] Harbaugh on Heaven, p. 177-187. [2] Eccles. xii. 7.

Harbaugh, who, as we have seen, discourses so learnedly and truly regarding Heaven as a place, and of a literal resurrection of the body, tells us that "the saints do *immediately*, at death, enter that place which is called Heaven, where the body of the Saviour *now* is . . and where all the heirs of Christ shall finally and for evermore be assembled." We must not forget, however, that the learned Doctor repudiates the heresy of the ancient Gnostics and their modern prototypes, viz., " that the resurrection body is in no way a continuation or product of this mortal body." In other words, he *denies* that the body of the saint is raised immediately at death, or that it is so transformed into a *purely spiritual* body, as to lose all corporeity.

It follows, therefore, according to this writer's own theory, that only *one-half* of the saint enters Heaven immediately after death, " to take his place" where "the body of the Saviour now is." For if, as he elsewhere concedes, " the body is not merely a companion to us," but that " it is *a part* of us ;" and that, "to be separated from it must leave, not positive unhappiness," but nevertheless "a sense of want," which must be supplied, for the present, by a "promise," etc.; then we deferentially ask : How is this " *sense of want* " on the part of the saint during its " separation " from the body, to be reconciled with its alleged entrance into Heaven "where the body of the Saviour now is," " immediately at death ?" The "*promise*" above alluded to as given to the saints, is that of St. Paul, Philipp. iii. 21 : "We look for the Saviour, the Lord Jesus Christ : who shall change our vile body, that it may be *fashioned like unto His own glorious body.*" But, as this "sense of want" on the part of the soul while separated from the body, excludes the possibility, during said separation, of its entrance into a state of consummated blessedness in Heaven, it must await Christ's return from Heaven to *raise* His sleeping saints from the dead, that, by a *re-union* of them to and with their souls, they may be made, in their *whole complex nature,* "*like unto Him.*"

We submit, therefore, that it cannot, as this writer affirms, be "the true doctrine of God's Word," that "the saints do immediately at death," enjoy a state of *consummated* blessedness in "that place which is called Heaven." The soul's "sense of want" during its separation from the body, as expressed by Dr. Harbaugh, has its counterpart in the words of the royal Psalmist: "I shall be satisfied, *when I awake* in thy likeness." [1] Not until *then*, will the "vile bodies" of the saints be "changed and fashioned like unto Christ's glorious body." Till *then*, the "promised" Inheritance of the saints is "*reserved* in Heaven for them." Hence their state or condition intermediate between death and the resurrection, is described under the opening of the fifth Apocalyptic seal, where St. John "saw *under the altar* the souls of them that were slain for the Word of God and for the testimony which they held: and they cried with a loud voice, saying, *How long,* O Lord, holy and true, dost Thou not avenge our blood on them that dwell on the earth?"

[1] Ps. xvii. 15.

A "cry" this surely, indicating their "sense of want" of a state of perfect blessedness. "And white robes were given unto every one of them; and it was said unto them, that they should rest yet for a little season, *until* their fellow-servants and brethren who should be killed as they were, should be *fulfilled*." [1]

On this passage, we observe—

1. That we have a description of the *character* of these "souls." This is indicated by the "white robes," or "linen, clean and white," in which they were clad, and were denotive of "the righteousness of the saints," embracing that entire army of the martyrs mentioned by St. Paul, Heb. xi., and onward to the opening of the fifth seal.

2. That their state or condition was one of *conscious blessedness*. There are some writers who allege the *sleep of the soul* during its separation from the body between death and the resurrection. "According to this theory, the soul, *at the moment* of death, sinks into an unconscious lethargy and profound insensibility to all things. In this state it remains, like the body, in the grave, until the final resurrection, at which time, although then awakened to consciousness and life again by the power of God," yet, in the case of the wicked, will be finally annihilated.

This theory, however, is borrowed from the philosophy of the *materialists*, who allege that the soul, being a result of the *physical* organization of the body, is itself material, and hence, that as the body becomes inactive at death, so the

[1] Rev. vi. 9-11.

soul also, when separated from the body, in the relation of cause and effect, *ceases to exist.*

But, to this it may be replied, that so far as the Scriptures are concerned, while they teach that soul and body may *co-exist* together, they also teach that the soul is capable of existence when *separated from* the body. This is predicated of the fact, that in the creation of man, the body remained an *inert* lump of clay, until "God *breathed* into its nostrils the breath of life, and man *became* a living soul,"[1] i. e., was endowed with immortality. It is therefore dishonorable to that Almighty Being who "formed the spirit of man within him;"[2] and degrading to him who was created but "a little while lower than the angels,"[3] thus to place that imperishable jewel, the soul, on a level with the *casket* which by sin had been rendered frail and mortal. Yea, more, it is to *subordinate* the high and noble intellectual and moral endowments and faculties of the soul to that of the material body. It is to make the body the *master* of the soul as its slave!

This, we shall now proceed to show, is as contrary to sound reason and philosophy, as it is repugnant to Holy Scripture. Therein we are taught the *absolute independence* of the soul to the body under certain circumstances. For example: in the instance of St. Paul's ecstatic rapture "into the third heaven," when he knew not whether he "was in the body or out of the body," is a case in point. "If he was *in the body* at the time he was caught up, and heard in Heaven unspeakable words, then it proves that the soul *can*

---

[1] Gen. ii. 7.   [2] Job xxxiii. 4.
[3] See on this, the article inserted in pages 43-47.

act without its being conscious of its connection with the body, and that it is consequently superior to it. If he was *out of the body*, then it proves that the soul *can exist* in a separate state."[1] So also that declaration of our Lord: "Fear not them which kill the body, but *are not able* to kill the soul; but rather fear Him which is able to destroy both body and soul in hell,"[2] (*Gehenna*). An admonition this, of no force or meaning, as a *motive* to patience under suffering, except on the ground that the soul is *independent* of the body in the exercise of its sense of moral obligation and responsibility to God.

Still, the Scriptures do speak of death *as a state of sleep*. Daniel says: "And many of them that *sleep* in the dust of the earth shall awake."[3] Jesus said to Mary and Martha: "Lazarus *sleepeth;* but I go, that I may awake him out of sleep."[4] Matthew says: "Many of the bodies of the saints which *slept*, arose,"[5] etc. And St. Paul says: "Even so them also which *sleep in Jesus* will God bring with him."[6] But, that the term "sleep," in these and other passages, refers to the BODY, and *not* the soul, is evident from our Lord's argument against those sceptical materialists, the *Sadducees*, who denied the resurrection of the dead. This argument consisted of a reference to the fact, that God declares Himself to be "the God of Abraham, Isaac, and Jacob," though their "*bodies*,"—like those of the saints mentioned by Matthew—were then *slumbering* in the grave. The words, therefore, "God is not the God of the dead but of the

---

[1] See 2 Cor. xii. 1-5.   [2] Matt. x. 28.   [3] Dan. xii. 2.
[4] John xi. 11.   [5] Matt. xxviii. 52.   [6] 1 Thess. i. 14.

living,"[1] is proof positive that the Saviour spake of their *souls* as being *then* alive. So also, Christ's declaration to the penitent thief on the cross: "This day shalt thou be with me in Paradise,"[2] contains the highest degree of evidence, that his soul was to retain its *consciousness* after death.

DEATH NOT THE END OF LIFE.

" They err who tell us, that the spirit unclothed,
   And from its mortal tabernacle loosed,
   Has neither lineament of countenance,
   Nor limit of etherial mould, nor form
   Of spiritual substance. THE ETERNAL WORD,
   Before He hung upon the Virgin's breasts,
   Was wont to manifest himself to man,
   In *visible* similitude defined :

.   .   .   .

   The *angels* are but spirits, a flame of fire,
   And subtle as the viewless winds of heaven,
   Yet are they each to the other *visible*,
   And beautiful with those original forms
   That crowned the morn of their nativity.

.   .   .   .

   And so, the spirit inbreathed in *human* flesh,
   By death divested of its mortal robes,
   Retains its individual character,
   Ay, and the very mould of its sojourn
   Within this earthly tabernacle. Face
   Answers to face, and limb to limb ; nor lacks
   The saint immediate investiture
   With saintly apparel. Only then the mind

[1] Matt. xxii. 32.   [2] Luke xxiii. 43.

Which struggles here beneath this fleshly veil,
As the pure fire in a half polished gem—
Ruby or amethyst or diamond—
Imprisoned, *when the veil is rent in twain,*
Beams as with solar radiance forth, and sheds
Its glow o'er every motion, every look :
That which is born of spirit is spirit, and seems
All ear, all eye, all feeling, and all heart ;—
A crystal shrine of life."
Bickersteth. " *Yesterday, To-Day, and Forever.*"

And finally on this subject, the account of the rich man and Lazarus in the future state, furnishes the most irrefragable evidence of the soul's *actual* consciousness after death. The rich man personates

—— " The disembodied souls of men
Who lived and died in sin. Lightly they spent
In godless mirth or prayerless toil unblest
Their brief inestimable day of proof,
Till the last golden sands ran out : and now
Their hour is come, and they are on the road
To that profound abysmal deep, wherein
The rich man lifted up his anguished eyes—
Eyes never to be closed in sleep again :
Nor marvel that one track their footsteps leads
And ours. Remember he of whom I spake,
Himself in torments, though far off, beheld
The holy Lazarus, and call'd aloud—
A bootless prayer—on Abraham for aid.

. . . . . .

All die, for all have sinn'd. Their mother earth
Has but one sepulchre for all. And here

> One Hades, by us called the *under-world*
> Receiving the spirits of the damned and blest:
> One world, but widely sunder'd by a gulf
> Inevitable fixed, impassable,
> Which severs to the left hand and the right
> The prison-house of woe and Paradise."
>
> *Ibid.*

Having thus disposed of this imaginary theory regarding the alleged sleep of the soul after death, we now resume the subject of that *state of conscious blessedness,* of which the souls of departed saints are the participants. It is to be inferred from the import of the term "REST," appropriated to the martyr-souls "under the altar" in the vision of the FIFTH SEAL, Rev. vi. 9–11. It is here almost superfluous to remark, that in whatever that state of blessedness consists, their loud appeal to God to be *avenged* upon their enemies who had shed their blood, proves their *consciousness* of the fact, that their then present state was not *perfect.* They shared in a "sense of want" of something additional to that end. Nor could it be realized by them in its consummated form, "*until* their fellow-servants and brethren who should be killed as they were, should be fulfilled." Meanwhile, they are to "*rest for a little season.*" This term, "rest," therefore, indicates that they were *then* in the enjoyment of a state of peaceful and joyous anticipation, analogous—though under a different form—to the sentiment expressed by St. Paul, when, in his address to his Thessalonian brethren, he said: "And to you who are troubled, *rest with us,* when the Lord Jesus Christ shall be revealed from Heaven in flaming fire with His mighty angels, taking vengeance on them that know not God, and that obey not the gospel of our Lord Jesus Christ" . . . And, "When he shall come to be *glorified* in His saints, and to be *admired* in all them that believe . . . IN THAT DAY."[1] Quere. In what day? The answer is, in the day of the *complete ingathering* of—

"The consecrated host of God's elect,"

"When the Lord himself shall descend from Heaven with a shout, with the voice of the archangel, and with the trump of God: and *the dead in Christ* SHALL RISE FIRST." Nor this only. For, "then we which are *alive and remain* unto the coming of the Lord, shall be caught up together with them in the clouds, to meet the Lord in the air, and so shall we *ever be with the Lord.*"[2]

And so, these martyr-souls, though *now* with Christ, in the enjoyment of a state of "rest," i. e., of conscious blessedness, it is nevertheless to be distinguished from that which *awaits* them, as described in Rev. xx. 4, where St. John in vision "saw THRONES, and they *sat upon them, and judgment was given unto them:* and he saw the souls of them that were beheaded for the witness of Jesus, and for the Word of God, and which had not worshipped the beast, neither his image, neither had received his mark upon their foreheads, or in their hands: and they lived and reigned with Christ *a thousand years.*" Suffice it to add, that in the fifth verse, the Holy Ghost interprets the above thus: "THIS IS THE

[1] 2 Thess. i. 9-12. [2] 1 Thess. iv. 16, 17.

FIRST RESURRECTION," as put in contrast with that of "the *rest of the dead*," (i. e., the wicked dead), "*who lived not again*" (or were not raised) "until the thousand years were *finished*." (verse 5.)

But, what is specially note-worthy, as brought to view in the vision of this fifth seal, is,

3. The *place* or *location*, allotted to those martyr "souls" during the interval of their "rest." St. John says: "I beheld UNDER THE ALTAR, the souls of them that were slain,"[1] etc. Here, the Apocalyptic scenery of this seal, is borrowed from the position of the altar of sacrifice, which was located *before* the Most Holy Place in the Temple. Analogous to this, therefore, must be the *position* of the "altar" under which St. John saw these "souls," in regard to the thing disclosed in the Heavenly vision. Now, taking this statement in its connection with what has been said in the preceding article concerning the "rest" of those "souls under the altar," and it is clear, that the place they occupy, and their state or condition in that place, must be taken together. The one, the *state*, is dependent on and is connected with, the other, the *place*. And, they must have an *adaptation* each to the other. Wherever, therefore, the Scriptures direct us to look for that *place*, it will be in every way *filled* to the occupancy, for the time, of the exalted character of the "souls" assigned to it. Yea, and a place every way *worthy* of that Almighty Being in whose hands and at whose disposal they are.

On this subject then, we observe,—what must be obvious

[1] Rev. vi. 9.

to the plainest mind—that an "*altar*" is not a "*throne.*" Nor is it true in any sense, that our blessed Lord is *now* "under the altar." Nor is He as yet *seated* "in His own throne." For we read that, "when He ascended up on high," it was to "sit down at the right hand of the Majesty in the heavens, far above all principalities and powers, and every thing that is named,"[1] etc., i. e., in the "highest" or empyreal "Heaven,"[2] "*in His Father's throne.*"[3] And, concerning *this Heaven*, He declares, "*No man* has ascended up to Heaven, but He which came down from Heaven."[4] Even of the royal Psalmist David, St. Peter declares that he "*is not* ascended to Heaven."[5] It is clear, therefore, that it is not true, that the "souls under the altar" are, "immediately at death," admitted to a state of *consummate* blessedness in that Heaven "where the *body* of the Saviour now is." Such a representation can never be reconciled with the apocalyptic imagery employed to describe their *present* place and state of "rest." The question then is, *Where are they?* We reply: Not in what is popularly called either Heaven or Hell: but,

IN AN INTERMEDIATE PLACE AND STATE, DURING THE INTERVAL BETWEEN DEATH AND THE RESURRECTION, ADAPTED TO THE CHARACTERS OF BOTH THE RIGHTEOUS AND THE WICKED.

To this view, however, there are several *objections* urged, which deserve a passing notice, before we adduce the Scriptural evidence in support of the above thesis.

[1] Eph. i. 21.   [2] Heb. vii. 26.   [3] Rev. iii. 21.
[4] John iii. 13.   [5] Acts ii. 34.

I. It is objected, that "the doctrine that there is an *intermediate state*, into which the souls of the dead are turned, *separate and distinct from* the Heaven at God's right hand, and the Hell where the devils are held under chains of darkness, is, in our opinion," observes a late writer, "A PURELY HEATHEN FABLE, which finds no countenance in the Word of God."[1] Now, we concede, on this point, that the pagan "Greek and Latin historians, poets and philosphers, e. g., Plato, Virgil, and others, supposed that all the dead were turned into *Orcus* or *Hades*, both the wicked and the good." Thus Plato :—

"From which place two ways lead : the one to the islands of the blest, the other to Tartarus."[2] And Virgil says :—

> " 'Tis here in different paths, the way divides :
> The right, to Pluto's *golden garden* guides,
> The left, to that unhappy region tends,
> Which to the depths of *Tartarus* descends."—*Dryden.*

It is hence alleged, that the Hebrew, Septuagint, and New Testament writers, *borrowed* their ideas regarding the place and state of the departed from "*purely heathen*" sources! Than which, we affirm, nothing can be more at variance with both Holy Scripture and profane historic facts. And, from the fact that this objection forms the *staple commodity* of all classes opposed to the doctrine of the intermediate condition of the departed between death and the resurrection, as maintained in this treatise, if we can sustain the above assertion regarding it, we shall have removed

[1] Jewish Chronicle, April, 1849, p. 297.   [2] In Georgias, p. 524 A.

the *main prop* in support of their various and conflicting theories.

We affirm, then, that the sacred writers, so far from deriving their ideas respecting the doctrine in question from " purely heathen " sources, constituted the *original* fountain whence the remotest pagan nations obtained their notions respecting it. In other words we mean to say—and challenge refutation—that this doctrine was of PURELY HEBREW origin. Of course, if this be so, the Hebrew nation must have existed *prior* to the remotest nations of pagan antiquity. Take the following in proof. Moses declares, Numb. xiii. 22, that " HEBRON was built *seven years before* ZOAN in Egypt," thus furnishing evidence of the fallacy of the ancient Egyptian records in claiming an antiquity *anterior* to that of the Hebrew race. According to Diodorus and other heathen writers, *Menes*, (the same with the *Timaus* of Plato and the *Mestraim* of Herodotus and Erastosthenes,) whom they claim as their first king, is identical with the *Mizraim* of Moses, and a son of Ham, whose posterity settled Egypt. Hence the statement of Plutarch, Philo Biblius, and Porphyry, that the Egyptians, *at the first*, were worshipers of the ONE TRUE GOD. This exactly accords with the Mosaic account of Abraham's reception and entertainment in *Egypt*— which was cotemporaneous with the reign of the Shepherd kings—the same as at *Gerar*, which could not have been had they been idolaters. But, having fallen into idolatry *before* the time of Joseph, it is not strange that their Menes was *deified* and worshiped as a God.

Again—The Egyptian king Shishak, and also Tharaka or Tirhaka, who made war against Sennacherib, king of Assyria—together with Pharaoh Necho, who waged a warfare against both the Assyrians and Jews—and Pheron, or Rameses Tubaete, the successor of Sesostris, and whose dreams were interpreted by Joseph—all occupy their places in our Scriptures. Finally on this subject—

Thebes, or Theba, a name signifying the *ark*, the metropolis of ancient Egypt, is referred to in our Scriptures under the name of "No-Ammon," "Populous No," and was most probably derived from NOAH. The whole valley of the Nile was not large enough to contain it. Its chief temple, that of "*Karnak*," seems to have been built in commemoration of the deluge. But, what is of principal interest to us in regard to this temple is, that among the numerous hieroglyphical inscriptions upon its walls, are to be found inscribed the history of one event connected with the Hebrew race, which is most fully and graphically set forth by the pen of the great Jewish lawgiver. I refer to the bondage of the children of Israel, in Egypt. This is confirmed by a tablet representing them on the tomb of Rekshare, who is known to have been the chief architect of the temples and palaces at Thebes, under Pharaoh Moeris. This tablet depicts the exact physiognomy of the Jews, with their bodies besmeared from the splashes of the clay of which they made their brick, while the hand of the taskmaster is ready to inflict the heavy baton on some worn-out laborer,—illustrating our Scriptural phrase regarding them, "all their service that they made them to serve withal, was with rigor." [1] It also informs us that these Hebrews were "captives brought by his majesty to build the temples of the Great God," doubtless referring to their being marched up from Goshen for this purpose; which corresponds with the narrative of Moses, that they were compelled to build "for Pharaoh treasure-cities, Pithom and Raamses." [2]

Second—In the *Belus* of ancient history, who is supposed to have been the founder of the ANCIENT ASSYRIAN EMPIRE, and of which *Babylon* was the capitol, we find the NIMROD of the Scriptures, the grandson of Ham the son of Noah, "the beginning of whose kingdom," says Moses, "was *Babel* (Gr. *Babylon*), in the land of Shinar." [3] But in addition to the above, to show the absurdity of the extravagance of Diodorus and others—who, in after ages, represent the armies of Semiramus and her buildings at Babylon to be more numerous and magnificent than can be conceived by any who consider the infant state kingdoms were in when she reigned—I have only to mention the fact as recorded by Moses, of the overthrow of Chedorlaomer, king of Elam—Tidal, king of nations—Amraphel, king of Shinar—and Arioch, king of Elassar, by Abraham, for the capture of his nephew Lot, with no other force than his three hundred and eighteen armed servants! [4]

And so, when we come down to a still later period in the annals of heathen writers in this connection, we find a similar coincidence in the facts recorded. Of the three kingdoms into which the ancient Assyrian empire was divided upon the death of Sardanapalus—viz., Nineveh, Babylon, and

---

1 Exod. i. 13, 14.   2 Ib. i. 11.   3 Gen. x. 9, 10.   2 Gen. xiv. 12-16.

the kingdom of the Medes—NINEVEH had for its first king Tiglath-Pileser.[1] His name occurs in our Scriptures in connection with Syria, at first settled by the posterity of Shem, the youngest son of Noah. Of the kings of this country but little is known, till the time of Alexander the Great, except what is related of them in our sacred writings. Of one of them, Hadadezer, we read that he made war, but unsuccessfully, against King David.[2] Another, Benhadad, was three times defeated by Ahab and Ahaziah.[3] Little more is related of the Assyrian kings, till Syria was made a province of the Assyrian empire by Tiglath-Pileser, who defeated and slew Rezin, its king, in battle.[4]

Tiglath-Pileser was followed by Salmaneser, who carried captive into Assyria the ten tribes of Israel:[5] by Sennacherib, who, with his army of 180,000 men, was destroyed for blaspheming the God of Israel:[6] by Esarhaddon, who subdued BABYLON and annexed it to his dominions:[7] by Nebuchadnezzar, who invaded Judea, and carried the Hebrews captive to Babylon:[8] by Belshazzar—the same with the Assyrian Labynit—who was conquered by the Persian monarch Cyaxares II., or "Darius the Mede," of our Scriptures,[9] in conjunction with Cyrus, who subsequently restored the Hebrews to their own land from the Babylonish captivity.[10] But, to return now to the *remoter* ages of antiquity.

Third—Of the INDIAN Bacchus, whom they say was

---

[1] ii. Kings xvi. 7.   [2] ii. Sam. viii. x.   [3] i. Kings xx.   [4] ii. Kings xvi. 9.
[5] ii. Ib. xvii. 3.   [6] ii. Ib. xviii.   [7] ii. Ib. xix. 37.   [8] ii. Ib. xxiv. 1.
[9] i. Comp. Isa. xliv. 28, 45, with 2 Chron. xxxvi. 22; Ezra i. 1-7; v. 13, etc.
[10] ii. Chron. xxxvi. 22, 23.

twice born, and that he was the first who pressed the grape and made wine, etc., we find an exact resemblance in Noah, whose preservation in the ark during the universal flood made him, so to speak, as one *twice born;* and who, Moses says, "began to be a husbandman, and planted a vineyard, and drank of the wine," etc.[1] And so,

Fourth—Of the CHINESE annals, which are next in order, as the most ancient of the nations. They claim *Fohi* as their first emperor. Their traditions regarding him are, that his mother was surrounded with a *rainbow* at the time of his conception; and, that he sacrificed *seven* sorts of creatures to the Supreme Spirit of heaven and earth: both of which facts coincide with the "rainbow," etc., of the NOAHIC COVENANT,[2] and with the clean beasts and fowls which Noah offered by sevens in sacrifice to God, on leaving the ark after the subsiding of the flood.[3] The same will be found to hold equally true,

Fifth—Of the GREEKS, who account that *Chronos*, their first king, was the *second* father of mankind, which circumstance makes him identical with the NOAH of the Old Testament. Finally—

Sixth—A few *miscellaneous* facts will close this evidence. Of the ancient Phœnicians, Herodotus claims for the older Tyre—the principal cities of which were Sidon and Tyre—a great antiquity. Now, of the kings of Sidon we know but little. But we know that *Hiram*, king of Tyre, was cotemporary with DAVID and SOLOMON, two of the mightiest Hebrew monarchs.

[1] Gen. ix. 20, 21.   [2] Ib. ix. 11, 15.   [3] Ib. vii. viii.

Again—In profane history, *Pul*, one of the last sovereigns of Assyria, and who, as king of Nineveh, subdued Israel in the reign of Menahem, is the Pul of the Hebrew Scriptures, who, with his people, repented at the preaching of the prophet Jonah.

So, also, the *Cambyses* of Persia, who added Egypt to his empire, is the same with the *Artaxerxes* of the Hebrew records.

And, finally, the city of Cadytus, mentioned by Herodotus, is identical with the Holy City of Jerusalem.

The truth is, that the Pagan notions of the abodes of the dead were derived from and were corruptions of, the *early inspired Patriarchal ages*. The learned Calmet, on this subject, observes: "The Hebrews thought and spake almost like the Greeks *before* Homer, Heziod, and the most ancient poets of this nation." Moses, for instance, speaks of "the *lowest* (שאול, sheol) hell."[1] Job says: "*Hell* (שאול, sheol), is naked before God."[2] And Solomon: that "*Hell* (שאול, sheol) and *destruction* are before the Lord."[3] Now, in all these passages, "Hell" is spoken of by these Jewish writers who preceded "the most ancient" Greek poets, as *the place* of the departed. It hence follows that, "from the Hebrews, this opinion passed to other people, and became disfigured by various figures of their respective invention. Thus the doctrine of the *Egyptians* respecting ᾅδης, (*Hades*), is given in the second book of Herodotus"—the oldest profane historian extant—"where we have the history of Rhampsi-

---

[1] Deut. xxxii. 22.   [2] Job xxvi. 5.   [3] Prov. xv. 11.

mitus, who, according to the opinions of the Egyptians, had visited the *infernal regions*, and returned safe to life." This " notion was variously embellished by the *Greek* poets ; and afterwards, being stripped by Plato of much of its poetic ornaments, was embodied by him in his philosophical system. And hence again, the *Latins* and other [heathen] nations at large, derived their phraseology in speaking of the state of the dead."

It results, therefore, that long anterior to all other, even the *remotest* nations of Pagan antiquity, the Hebrews had their *place of the departed*, which they denominated שאול, SHEOL ; and which the Septuagint and the New Testament writers who retained the same doctrine, translated by the corresponding Greek term ᾅδης, *Hades*. And from the Hebrews, these Pagan nations derived *their* place of the departed, to which they gave the name of *Hades, Orcus*, or *Inferi*. The following examples will serve to illustrate this :

1. The HEBREWS. True, their ideas of a future state were comparatively obscure. Their dispensation was but " the shadow of good things to come." [1] Still, the *place* for the repose of their pious dead, was designated by the phraseology common to the Old Testament of being "*gathered to their fathers*"—or " their people," etc., all of whom St. Paul declares " died in faith, not having received the promises," that is, in their fulness—their Heavenly Inheritance being held " *in reserve* for them"—" but beheld them *afar off*." Then, further. In the following passages, the DIFFERENT

[1] Heb. x. 1.

REGIONS into which their SHEOL was divided, are clearly indicated. Moses describes the justice of God thus : " A fire is kindled in mine anger, and it shall burn to the *lowest hell*," [1] (SHEOL). And David says : "Thou hast delivered my soul from the *lowest hell*," [2] (SHEOL.) On this last passage, Augustine observes : "We understand by it as if it were two worlds, an *upper* and a *lower*."

2. The SEPTUAGINT TRANSLATORS. The Greek word *Hades*, which occurs in all the places where we find the Hebrew word SHEOL, in the Old Testament, being of the same signification, must mean the same thing. And so,

3. The PAGAN WRITERS, POETS, etc. As to their traditionary *Hades*, *Orcus*, or *Inferi*, derived, as already stated, from the SHEOL of the Hebrews, and the HADES of the Septuagintists, Ulysses is represented as seeing the soul of Achilles, $\gamma\epsilon\theta\epsilon\sigma\acute{o}\nu\eta$, joyful, traversing the " $\alpha\rho\varphi\delta\epsilon\lambda o\nu\ \lambda\epsilon\iota\mu\omega\nu\alpha$," or the "amena vireta"—the *flowery plains* of Virgil ; but other souls—

" ——— $\alpha\chi\nu\upsilon\mu\epsilon\nu\alpha\iota,\ \epsilon\iota\rho o\nu\tau o\ \delta\epsilon\ \varkappa\epsilon\delta\epsilon\ \epsilon\varkappa\alpha\sigma\tau\eta$ "—
"all wailing with *unutterable woes*."

Eneas also, and the Sybil his companion, traverse the abodes of the departed :—

"Perque domus Ditis vacuas, et inana regna"—

" ——— the dismal gloom they pass, and tread
Grim Pluto's courts, the regions of the dead."

Here they view the different apartments of the wicked and the good :—

[1] Deut. xxxii. 22.   [2] Ps. lxxxvi. 13.

The gloomy *Tartarus,*
> "The seat of night profound, and punished fiends."

And the *fields of Elysium,*
> "The flowery plains,
> The verdant groves where endless pleasure reigns."

And finally—

4. Agreeably to the representation of the place and state of the righteous and wicked dead among the Hebrews, as consisting of the two great divisions of Sheol, is the account given of HADES in the New Testament. In the parable of the rich man and Lazarus, "Hell ($ᾅδης$, *Hades*) is represented as a vast region, which, as the receptacle of departed spirits in general, contained the soul of "Lazarus in Abraham's bosom," elsewhere called "Paradise" or "the third Heaven," i. e., where the pious dead were "gathered to their fathers" in a state of conscious blessedness with "the father of the faithful," or the *upper* Hades; and the soul of Dives in the *lower* Hades, or *Tartarus*. Accordingly, in this immeasurable region, the two abodes of the just and unjust are here represented as "*afar off*," and that between them "a *great gulf* is fixed," cutting off all possible communication as regards the two classes. Hence the language of Abraham to Dives: "They which would pass from thence"—i. e., from my "bosom" in the *upper* Hades or "PARADISE"—"to you, cannot; neither can they"—i. e., those who are "reserved" in the *lowest* Hades or *Tartarus*—"pass to us that would come from thence."[1] Thus much, then, as to this objection. But it is further alleged—

[1] Luke xvi. 19-26.

II. That the Hebrew word Sheol, and the corresponding Greek word Hades, in both Testaments, so far from denoting the place and state of the departed soul, simply means the *grave*. Thus Dr. Harbaugh, on the above words, says: "These are general terms, like the word *grave* and *eternity*, and are used to designate the future world, without any direct reference to the condition of its inhabitants, as happy or miserable," [1] etc. And he adds: "Heaven and Hell are in Hades; and yet"—alluding to the advocates of a separate place and state of the departed,—"with them Hades is to be a *third* place distinct from the two." [2] The importance of this subject is our apology for what follows. We remark then—

1. In regard to the *Hebrew* word SHEOL. Now true. There are a number of passages in which this word, at first view, may seem to signify the grave, as the repository of the *body*, rather than the place of the departed soul, and are hence translated *grave* in our English version. But we shall now proceed to show, that the Hebrew word קֶבֶר, KEBER, and *not* Sheol, is the proper word for "*grave*," or *Sepulchre;* and that our English translators should so have rendered it in all those places where the word Sheol is rendered by the word grave, it signifying the receptacle of dead bodies, the other word Sheol invariably denoting the abode of the *souls* of the departed, as already explained.

Of the passages above referred to, the following will suffice as a key to the import of the others.

---

[1] Harbaugh on Heaven, pp. 123, 124. [2] Ib.

In Gen. xxvii. 35, where the word שְׁאוֹל first occurs, Jacob says : "I will go down into the *grave* unto my son, mourning." Jacob, however, had supposed that his son had been devoured by wild beasts. Had he intended the joining his son in the grave, he would have used the word *Keber*, as in Gen. xxxv. 20 : "And Jacob set a pillar upon Rachel's *grave*," Keber. The above passage therefore should have been rendered—"I will go down to Hades, or Hell," i. e., to the place of departed spirits, "to my son, mourning." With this agrees the rendering of the Septuagint, as signifying that his *soul was "gathered unto his people."* (See also Gen. xxv. 8 ; xxxv. 29 ; Judges ii. 10.)

So also Job xii. : "If I wait, Sheol shall be my house." (verse 13). "They shall go down to the bars of Sheol, when our rest together shall be in the dust." (verse 16.) But Job also says, chap. vii. 9 : "As the cloud is consumed and vanisheth away, so he that goeth down to Sheol shall not come up again." Now, it is clear, that if the words "*house*" and "*dust*" in the above texts are to be taken, as some allege, that Sheol is to be interpreted of the *grave*, then the same inspired writer affirms that they who enter it shall *never leave* it. Such a view, however, can never be reconciled with the explicit declaration of Job, chap. xix. 25, 27 : "though worms destroy this body, yet in my flesh *shall I see God*, whom I shall see for myself," etc., which can only be by his *resurrection from* the grave. It is perfectly evident therefore that Job's meaning was, that he should "*rest*" in Sheol, as do the martyr "souls under the altar," till the bright morn of the "FIRST RESURRECTION," when the "dust" of his body would *leave* the "house" in which it had been so long reposing, and "*see* his Redeemer" as He is, not only, but "be made like unto Him." Hence his prayer in the midst of his deep affliction: "O that Thou wouldst *hide me*"—not in the grave, as in the English version—but "in Sheol;" and in the Septuagint Hades; "that Thou wouldst *keep me secret*, until thy wrath be past." (chap. xiv. 13).

Another. Psalm xxx. 3: "O Lord, Thou hast brought up my *soul* from Sheol: Thou hast kept me alive, that I should not go down to the *pit*." But, the "soul" does not go to the "grave," "pit," or "sepulchre," while the body does. David, therefore, under the figure of preserving his *body* from the pit or grave, and his *soul* from Sheol,—in the Septuagint Hades,—extols the Lord for his *deliverance* from bodily sufferings and from the hands of his malicious foes (See verses 1, 2). The same of Prov. i. 12; and Isa. xxxviii. 10. So of Psalm cxli. 7: "Our bones are scattered at the mouth of Sheol:" in our English version, "at the mouth of the *grave*." But the fact is, that here we have *no* mention of the grave at all. For the Psalmist is clearly speaking of persons massacred, whose *bones* were never in any grave, but which had been left to rot unburied, upon the surface of the earth, "*at the mouth* of Sheol" on this surface, as the entrance to Sheol, the place of the departed.

We now come to Hosea xiii. 14. This is the last and most important passage claiming our notice. "I will ransom thee from the power of Sheol: I will redeem thee from death. O death, I will be thy plagues: O Sheol, I will be thy destruction." In the English version, Sheol in both places is translated *grave*. But St. Paul, who quotes from this passage in 1 Cor. xv. 55, and applies it to the *resurrection*, translates Sheol by the Greek word Hades: "O death, where is thy sting?" Ποῦ σου, ἄδη, τὸ νῖκος: "O Hades, where is thy victory?" And he adds: "But thanks be to God, who giveth us the victory through our Lord Jesus Christ." (verse 57). In what way? Why, as he had argued in the context, by the *redemption* of the body from death, "the king of terrors,"[1] whose reign extends over the "grave;" and their "*ransom*" from the power of Hades (or Sheol), by the termination or destruction of that *intermediate state*, in which they had been held during the *interval* between death and the resurrection; and thus, by a *reunion* of body and soul, be transferred from the temporary and partial, to the eternal and consummate blessedness of "the world to come."[2]

We now pass to observe, that we might reasonably expect that the Greek word in the New Testament for *death* and the *grave*, would correspond with that of the Septuagint. Accordingly we find, first, that the word for death is not Hades, but Θάνατος (thanatos), as in Rev. xx. 13: "And Death (*thanatos*) delivered up the dead," etc. So, second, of the word grave, it is not Hades, but μνημειω (mnemeio), or its adjuncts, as in John xi. 17: "Lazarus had been in the grave (μνημειω) (mnemeio) four days." (See also

[1] Job. xviii. 14.   [2] Heb. ii. 5.

verses 31, 38) ; and chap. xii. 17, where it is said of Jesus that He "called Lazarus out of his *grave*," etc. And, as already stated, the word rendered "grave" in our English version in 1 Cor. xv. 55, "O *grave*, where is thy victory?" is a wrong translation. In the original it is ᾅδης, (Hades), the abode of departed spirits.

And finally, on this suject : Bp. Horsley translates Hosea xiii. 13, thus : "*Death*, I will be thy pestilence : *Hades*, I will be thy burning plague." It is evident, therefore, that the Greek word Hades, answering to the Hebrew word Sheol, is in the English version improperly rendered *grave*. And the Bishop justly observes : "no two words can be more distinct ; Hades is the mansion of the *departed spirit ;* the grave is the receptacle of the *dead body.*" But, another objection urged against the doctrine of the intermediate place and state of the departed is,

III. That it is *so nearly identical with the Papal doctrine of Purgatory,* as to be scarcely distinguished from it. Thus the writer in the Jewish Chronicle, says : "This doctrine has been the source of much corruption of Christian doctrine, and of many absurd notions and practices in the Christian Church : such are, the doctrines of purgatory, indulgences, prayers for the dead,"[1] etc. And Dr. Harbaugh says : "This idea continues with more or less authority even down to the present day, and is still held in respect, in one or other of its forms, in the Popish and Episcopal communions. Among the former it is held as *Purgatory ;* and among the

[1] Jewish Chron. April 1849, pp. 247.

latter, as a *place of detention* for the spirit, till the resurrection of the body—a kind of anti-chamber to Heaven and Hell, where the spirit undergoes some *necessary purification* for final reunion with the body and entrance upon its final state and abode. With some, the idea of *probation*, in a certain way, is also connected with this middle state," [1] etc. On this subject we observe,

1. The Papal doctrine of Purgatory teaches, that while "some few have *before* their death so fully cleared up their account with the divine Majesty, and washed all their sins in the blood of Christ as to go straight to Heaven at death; and that others who die in their guilt of deadly sin go straight to Hell;" a third class, viz., "those who do not die perfectly pure and clean, nor yet under the guilt of unrepented sin," it is alleged, "go to Purgatory," where they suffer certain undefinable pains, and the pains of a material fire, until God's justice is satisfied, or they are freed from these pains by the masses said for their souls." [2] And, in reference to Christ's "*soul*" being in "Hell," the Papists affirm that "He went not into the place of departed spirits, but into a region called *Limbus Patrum*, to manifest His glory to the saints who had departed *before* His advent, and to release them from their confinement," i. e., from Purgatory, "and take them to Heaven." [3]

Now, we here observe, first, that, in regard to the "Limbus Patrum" or Purgatory of the Romish Church, as the

[1] Harbour on "Heaven," p. 111.
[2] The Right Rev. Dr. Chaloner's Catholic Instructed. p. 176.
[3] Bp. Hobart's "State of the Departed." pp. 94, 95.

place whither Christ is said to have gone after death, being founded upon her interpretation of 1 Pet. iii. 19, where it is said that our blessed Lord "*went and preached unto the spirits in prison,*" etc., that is, the partially holy dead of the antediluvian world, and of the virtuous heathen: we insist that it is a gross perversion of what the apostle says on that subject. For, 1st. Christ's preaching, He declares, was to "the *disobedient* in the days of Noah," that is, the wicked antediluvians. But 2d. *How* did Christ preach to them? Was it *in person*? No: but "by His *spirit,*" "being put to death in the flesh, but quickened by the spirit, *by which,*" that is, by *His spirit,* " He went and preached to the spirits in prison." 3d. But *when* was this done? Was it while the Saviour's body was in the grave and His soul in Hell, ($ᾅδης$)? No, it was "*in the days of Noah,* while the ark was preparing." 4th. And to *whom* did "the spirit of Christ preach" in those days? Was it to the *souls* of the departed dead? No: it was to the *living,* to whom NOAH preached for the space of one hundred and twenty years,"[1] by the inspiration and assistance of CHRIST's spirit; and *whose* "spirits," or souls, having been separated from their bodies at the time of the flood, were, in Peter's time, those "*spirits in prison,*" that is, in the *intermediate* state between death and the resurrection spoken of Rev. xx. 5; whom he declares, 2 Pet. ii. 4, together with "the angels that fell, God hath delivered for chains under darkness, to be *reserved* unto the day of judgment and perdition of ungodly men."

[1] Gen. vi. 3; 1 Pet. iii. 20.

2. We remark on the other hand, As to the intermediate state being, as Dr. Harbaugh represents it, "a kind of *antichamber* to Heaven and Hell, where the spirit undergoes some necessary preparation for final re-union with the body, and entrance upon its final state and abode ;" or that it is in any way connected with "the idea" that it is a state of "*probation*," or in any degree "remedial," etc. : the true doctrine of that state is, that the condition of the departed, whether of the *saved* or the *lost*, in their respective places of abode between death and the resurrection, is an ABSOLUTELY UNCHANGEABLE condition of conscious happiness or misery, to be consummated only at the day of judgment, by a re-union of body and soul : not, mark, by a *simultaneous* resurrection of the just and the unjust, the former being "blessed with those who have a part in the first resurrection," *in the morning* of "that day ;" while "the rest of the dead"—i. e., the wicked dead—"live not again until the thousand years are finished"[1] *in the evening* of that "day."

We fully agree with this learned writer, as it respects the Romish doctrine of *purgatory*, that "the hint which led to it was received from the Pagan philosophy," glimmerings of which are to be found in the writings of "Homer and Virgil," and that it was nurtured by "the Platonic philosophical ideas of good and evil," to the effect that matter, being "essentially bad and spirit essentially good," producing "evil," the spirit might be "purified by a violent austerity and severe onset upon everything gross and material." Such

---

[1] Compare 1 Thess. iv. 16, with Rev. xx. 5, 6.

a theory as this, so congenial to "man's self-righteous spirit, it is easy to conceive might readily be adopted into the church, carried over the grave, and constructed into a purgatory." Accordingly we find ORIGEN, the learned presbyter and catechist of Alexandria, who flourished between A.D. 204 and 254, having "deduced from the eastern Platonism a philosophy *semi*-Pagan and *semi*-Christian," taught that "the fallen world is subject to a law of *restoration*, which is fulfilled in a long series of periods. Spirits pass successively through different states, till they are all purified;" a process by which He affirmed the *final* restoration or salvation of all fallen beings, angelic and human. "AUGUSTINE, however, afterwards took from it a hint for a *purifying abode after death*, which hint was, at a still later period, developed into a doctrine by GREGORY I., in the VIth century, who is considered as the father of the church's idea of purgatory."[1] We also agree with this writer, that this doctrine, with its kindred tenets—auricular confession, priestly absolution, works of supererogation, prayers for the dead, etc.—is a monstrous imposition, involving, as it does, a denial of the *sufficiency* of the merits of Christ, who "BY HIMSELF *purged our sins*, and is sat down on the right hand of God, there to make intercession for us."[2]

But we must demur to Dr. Harbaugh's statement, that the scriptural doctrine of the intermediate place and state of the departed in respect to either class as advocated in these pages, is in any way connected with, or that it in any sense

---

[1] Harbaugh on Heaven, pages 119-121. [2] Heb. i. 3.

involves, the idea of preparation in regard to man's final destiny in the eternal world, or that it is in any respect either disciplinary or remedial, in the sense that it is *probationary*. So far from this, there is nothing in that doctrine—as will be more fully shown in the sequel—which at all infringes upon the great cardinal truth, that "Christ also loved the church, and gave Himself for it, that He might *sanctify and cleanse it with the washing of water by* THE WORD"—not by the disciplinary or remedial process of a future state, but in the *present*—"that He might present it to Himself a glorious church, *not having spot, or wrinkle, or any such thing:*"[1] Ay, and that, too, as totally independent of the superadded purification of the soul by purgatorial fire! For He, by His *one offering* for sin, has *perfected for ever* them that are sanctified."[2]

And, as to a *probationary* state after death in regard to the unregenerate, we believe that it will consist, not in a change of character, but simply in the *mode* of existence; the final destiny of which, like that of the saints, *awaits* the second coming of our blessed Lord, when, appearing on His "GREAT WHITE THRONE" of judgment *at the close* of the millennial era,[3] the redeemed of the Lord will be admitted to their *eternal* inheritance in "the world to come;"[4] while the wicked "dead, small and great," then for the first raised and gathered from "the *sea*" and "*death*" or the *grave* and "hell," ($ἅδης$), "whose names were not found written in the

---

[1] Eph. v. 25-27.   [2] Heb. x. 14.   [3] Rev. xx. 11.
[4] Compare 1 Pet. i. 4-7, with Rev. xxi-xxii. Hebrew ii. 5.

book of life, together with him whose " name is DEATH" or with the DEVIL that deceived them, as the "last enemy that shall be destroyed," shall be cast into the lake of fire,"[1] which will be "*eternal.*"[2]

That the *character* of the departed between death and the resurrection respectively of the just and the unjust remains *unaltered*, will appear from the following : " It is appointed unto man once to die, and *after* that the judgment."[3] " Where the tree *falleth*, there it shall *be.*"[4] " Whatsoever thy hand findeth to do, do it with thy might : for there is no work, nor device, nor knowledge, nor wisdom *in the grave*, whither thou goest."[5] " But he that blasphemest against the Holy Ghost *hath never forgiveness*, neither in this life, neither in the life to come ; but is in danger of eternal damnation."[6] " For if we sin wilfully, *after* that we have received the knowledge of the truth, there *remaineth no more* sacrifice for sin, but a certain fearful looking for of judgment and fiery indignation, which shall destroy all God's adversaries."[7] These, and similar passages, must be decisive against the theory of a disciplinary, remedial, or probationary state, whether of the righteous or the wicked after death. Still we maintain that, between death and the resurrection, inasmuch as there is a separation of the body from the soul, the capacity of both saints and sinners for their final and eternal state

---

[1] Compare Rev. vi. 8, with Rev. xx. 7-15.   [2] Jude, verse 7.   [3] Heb. ix. 27.
[4] Eccles. xi. 3.   [5] Eccles. ix. 10.   [6] Mark iii. 9 ; Matt. xii. 31-32.
[7] Heb. x. 26-29.

of happiness or misery in "the world to come," *must await a re-union* of both AT the resurrection.

With these remarks kept in view as preliminary to the subject in hand, we now pass to a more direct inquiry as to what the Scriptures reveal of the ABODES OF THE RIGHTEOUS AND THE WICKED during the interval of the intermediate state between death and the resurrection. This will lead to a consideration of the Scriptural import and use of the terms under—

SECTION III.

Of Sheol—Tophet—Hinnom—Hades—Paradise—Tartarus—and Gehenna, etc.

Dr. Harbaugh, in speaking of the Hebrew word שְׁאוֹל, (Sheol), and the Greek word ᾅδης, (Hades), says: "They signify, in their primary sense, the *place of departed spirits*, without any reference at all to their condition, as happy or miserable. . . . The words Sheol and Hades are words of the same general import as the words *eternity* and the *grave*. We say, for instance, that one of our friends is gone to eternity; and, by saying so, we do not intend to express an opinion as to whether he has gone to a place of happiness or misery. We only say *in general*, that he has gone to eternity. So the ancients used the terms Sheol and Hades, without having their ideas at all defined as to place." They meant "the place and state of those who were out of sight, out of the way," and "to be sought for," etc. And he adds: "if the terms were intended to give a specific idea, it must be put into them by the context. Just as if, after speaking of a wicked man who died in some sudden and awful way, I say, he was called into a *dreadful* eternity, you at once understand me to mean that he went [immediately] to the place of the lost. If I say, of a good man, he has suffered much on earth, but now he has gone to eternity, you at once understand me to mean that he went [immediately] to the *inheritance* of the blest," [1] etc.

Now, it is on this hypothesis, that this learned Divine relies as the *basis* of his theory, in opposing the doctrine of an *intermediate* place and state of the departed between death and the resurrection. But we respectfully submit, that due consideration of the following passages:—Gen. xlii. 38; xliv. 29, 31; 1 Sam. ii. 6; and 1 Kings ii. 6, 9—will show that neither Sheol, *Hell*, nor Keber, the *grave*, are intended as distinct the one from the other, but, *a state of death*, which is expressed "under the *image* of a place of residence of the dead *collectively*. And for this place, taken in the gross, not as divided into the two separate lodgments of the spirit and the carcass, the word Sheol is used. As each dead body has its *separate* place in the grave, the only *general* place of residence of the dead collectively, is that of the *departed spirit*."

We allude to the above fact, simply as introductory to the remark, that "although the general name for the receptacle of departed spirits among the Hebrews was Sheol, and by the Septuagint translators and the writers of the New Testament

---

[1] Harbaugh on Heaven. p. 100.]"

Hades, yet that they all assigned *different abodes* in this vast region, to the righteous and the wicked, the one as a state of happiness, and the other of misery. To make this plain, our business will be,

I. To determine the import of the term שְׁאוֹל, Sheol. It signifies to ask, to crave, to crave as a loan.

Agreeably to " the first signification of its derivative, *to ask*, Sheol denotes a place which is an object of universal inquiry, the *unknown* mansion about which all are anxiously inquisitive.

" In the second acceptation of its derivative, Sheol is represented as a place of *insatiable craving*—e. g., " Hell (Sheol) hath enlarged herself, and openeth her mouth *without measure*." [1] " The proud man *enlargeth* his desire as Hell." [2] (Sheol).

" In the third meaning of the derivative of Sheol— *to demand or crave as a loan*, implying that what is sought for is to be rendered back ; it is to be understood, not simply as the region of departed spirits, but as the region that is to form their *temporary residence*, and from which, at some future time, they are to be rendered up : thus indicating the fact of an intermediate state of the soul between its departure from this world, and some future state of its existence."

We shall now proceed to show, that it is in this *latter* sense, as denoting the temporary residence of the spirits of the dead, that the Sheol of the Old Testament and the Hades of the New, are used. And that so far from their " signifying,

[1] Isa. v. 4.   [2] Habak. ii. 5.

in their primary sense, the place of departed spirits, without any reference at all to their condition as happy or miserable;" it will be seen that they express, in the most "specific" form, *the particular condition* of each, during the tenure of their temporary detention in that intermediate abode.

In support of the proposition here laid down, we quote the following from the writings of several of our most eminent Protestant divines, in proof that the *original* meaning of the word translated Hell, was no more than a hidden or *invisible place*, derived from the Saxon word Helen, to COVER OVER. The learned DR. DODDRIDGE observes: "Our English or rather Saxon word *Hell*, in its original signification, (though now understood in a more limited sense), exactly answers to the Greek word Hades"—[as the nearest to express the sense of the Hebrew word Sheol, which the Greek afforded]—"and denotes a *concealed or unseen* place; and this sense of the word is still retained in the eastern, and especially in the western counties of England," where, "to *hell over* a thing, is to *cover* it." [1] Dr. CAMPBELL, in a very learned dissertation prefixed to his "Translation of the four Gospels," says: "The term $ᾅδης$, (Hades), was anciently written $ἀΐδης$, (ab a priv. et $εἰδω$ video), and signifies *obscure, hidden, invisible*. To this word, *Hell*, in its primitive signification, perfectly corresponds. For at first, it denoted only what was *secret* or *concealed*. This word is found with little variation of form, and precisely in the same meaning, in all the Teutonic dialects," and he adds:

[1] Comment on Rev. i. 18.

"the term Hades implies, properly, neither Hell or the grave," i.e., in the sense in which these terms are popularly understood, "but *the place or state of the departed.*" "The word *Hell*," says Dr. ADAM CLARKE, as "used in the common translation, conveys *now*, an improper meaning of the original word; because the word Hell is only used," i.e., as popularly understood, "to signify the place of the damned. But as the word Hell comes from the Anglo-Saxon HELEN, to *cover over* or *hide*, hence the tiling or slating of a house is called, in some parts of England, (particularly Cornwall), *heling* to this day; and the covers of books (in Lancaster) by the same name. So the *literal* import of the original ᾅδης was formerly well expressed by it." [1] "The word *Hell*, in its natural import," says Bp. HORSLEY, "signifies only that *invisible place*, which is the appointed habitation of departed souls in the interval between death and the general resurrection." [2]

In the view, therefore, of this exposition of the *original* derivation and import of the Hebrew word Sheol, and its corresponding Greek word Hades, and which, in our translation is rendered by the English word Hell; we now observe, that, in *no* instance does it, either in the Old Testament or the New, as is alleged, denote the grave or sepulchre as the resting place of the inanimate body; but is, on the contrary, invariably expressive of *the intermediate place and state or condition of the soul, whether of happiness or misery.* In illustration, take the following passages :

[1] Clarke's Com. on Matt. xi. 22. [2] Horsley's Sermons. Vol. ii. p. 89.

First. From the OLD TESTAMENT, in which the word Sheol occurs.

2 Sam. xxii. 6: "The sorrows of *Hell* (Sheol) compassed me about; the snares of *death* prevented me," etc. In Ps. xviii. 4 and cxvi. 3, the word Sheol is used as synonymous with *death*, (פֶּה); and hence, "the *sorrows* and *pains* of death." The same terms are applied to Christ in Acts ii. 24. The obvious meaning therefore is, that the pains or sufferings endured by those who have departed from this life upon their entrance into Sheol, are employed to describe as in a figure, the *intensity* of David's trials and dangers from the hands of his enemies.

Job xxi. 13: "They spend their days in wealth, they go down quickly to Sheol." Job, in defending his innocence before his professed friends, reminds them that the wicked, who live in pleasure unwhipped of justice and die without pain, often drop *suddenly* into Sheol, free from any consciousness of the *horrors* that await them there.

Ps. lv. 15: "Let death seize upon them, and let them go down quick into Sheol." The Psalmist here refers to those *rebels against him* under Absalom, of whom it is said— 2 Sam. xviii. 7, 8, that "the wood *devoured* more on that day than the sword devoured:" And so, 20,000 of them suddenly descended into Sheol, the *intermediate* abode of wicked spirits. Of the same import is Ps. xxi. 17; lxxxviii. 4; lxxxix. 48: in each of which passages, as already shown, our English translators, though improperly, have substituted the word *grave*.

Eccles. ix. 10 : "Whatsoever thy hand findeth to do, do it with thy might ; for there is no work, nor device, nor knowledge nor wisdom in Sheol, whither thou goest." Here again, we have the substitution of the English word *grave* for Sheol. The passage, however, undeniably refers to the *soul*, and the close of its probation in this life, and of its *unalterably* fixed condition in Sheol, the place and state of the departed. Parallel to this is Ps. vi. 5 : "In *death* there is no remembrance of Thee ; in Sheol who shall give Thee thanks ? "

Job xxiv. 19 : " Drought and heat *consumeth* the snow waters : So Sheol those that have *sinned*." Here Sheol cannot mean the *grave*, as in our English version, for that is the receptacle alike of the *righteous* and the *wicked*. The passage clearly indicates the miserable state of the unregenerate in Sheol, the " *lowest Hell*," whose remembrance is perished from the earth like the melted " snow."

Job. xxvi. 6 : "Sheol is naked before Him, and destruction hath no covering." The word, "destruction," אֲבַד, *a-vad*, ABADDON—is expository of Sheol, it being a *proper name* applied to the Leader of the angelic revolt in Heaven, Rev. ix. 11, where he is called in Greek Ἀπολλύων, the DESTROYER. The passage affirms, therefore, that though the Devil and his angels, together with the lost " spirits in prison," are " cast down to Sheol or Hades, to be " reserved " there " for chains under darkness *unto* the day of judgment and perdition of ungodly men ; " yet that they cannot escape the *omniscient* eye of the omnipresent God. (See Ps. cxxxix. 8, 11). The same term is affixed to two other passages in connection with Sheol, viz., Prov. xv. 11; and xxii. 20, and in the same sense with the preceding.

Ps. ix. 18: "The *wicked* shall be turned into Sheol, and all the nations that forget God." It is in place in this connection to introduce the Hebrew word תֹּפֶת, TOPHETH, from *Toph*, which signifies, a drum. It was the term by which the Jews expressed the *place of final torments*, and was derived from the horrid custom of the idolatrous Jews in drowning the shrieks of their children, when offering them in sacrifice to the image of Moloch in the once beautiful valley of Hinnom, near Jerusalem, by the brook Kedron. During the reign of Josias, King of Judah, it had become so abominable, that they cast there the carcases of animals, and the dead bodies of criminals, where they were consumed by a *perpetual fire*. Hence their knowledge of the distinction, and belief in the difference, between Sheol as the *intermediate* place and state into which the souls of the wicked were lodged until their resurrection, and that of Tophet as the place of *final* misery.

The same holds true of their use of the Greek word, $\gamma\acute{\epsilon}\epsilon\nu\nu\alpha$, Gehenna, as denoting the region of *final* and *eternal* torments.

But, in as much as neither of these terms were known to be in use among the Jews until *after* the Babylonish captivity, it is denied by some writers, that they had any idea of, or belief in, a place and state of *future endless punishment* of the wicked. This circumstance has been made available, in no small degree, to the support of the ancient Origenic heresy of *Restorationism*, not only, but also of that of the more recently alleged *annihilation* of the souls of the wicked, by that class of Christianized materialists whose names are given in page 50. Both hypotheses are predicated on the ground, that the doctrine of man's IMMORTALITY WAS UNKNOWN to the inspired writers of the Old Testament.

The *fallacy* of these pretences, however, will appear from the fact of the existence and use among the Jews *before* the Babylonish captivity, of a term by which they expressed their knowledge of and belief in, a place and state of future endless torments. It is found in the following passage, Prov. xxi. 16: "The man that wandereth out of the way of understanding, *shall remain in the congregation of the dead:*" i. e., "IN CÆTU REPHAIM"—which word, "Rephaim," properly signifies *giants*, and in that sense is always rendered by the Septuagint translators by the words, gigantes, gegeneis, titanus, or asebeis, though it is generally, but improperly, taken for manes or mortui. Adhering therefore to the ancient rendering, the phraseology—"in the congregation," or assembly of giants, signifies those "giants" or rebels against God, of whom we read in Gen. vi.—those "*mighty men,*" or "*men of renown*" in "the old world," whose wickedness was so great, that it "repented and grieved God at His heart that He had made man;"[1] and, to take vengeance upon whom, all mankind, with every living creature, save those few admitted into the ark of the righteous Noah, were swept from the earth by the catastrophe of the flood, and "remain in the congregation of the departed" in Hades till the resurrection day.

[1] Gen. vi. 4-6.

Again. The phrase "*Cœtus Gigantum,*" or as it is in the Hebrew, *Cœtus Rephaim,* by the gloss of Rabbi Solomon on the passage, is rendered in "*Cœtu Gehenna,*" which is confirmatory of the interpretation of it as given above.

Another collateral passage may be found in that of Job xxi. 6: "Sheol is naked before Him, and destruction hath no covering." And to the same effect is Prov. xv. 11: "Sheol (Hell) and destruction are before the Lord," etc. Now, in both these places, as contra-distinguished from Sheol, which denotes the region of departed spirits, the Jews, as already stated,[1] take the word *Abaddon*, translated "*destruction*" in our English version, for Gehenna; that is, eliptically, for *Beth-Abaddon*, the house of destruction, which is the same with Cœtus Gigantum as above. The meaning therefore (as it is translated in the Latin Vulgate) is, "Gigantes genut sub aquis, et qui habitant cum iis. Nudus est infernes coram illo, (id est Deo) et nullum operimentum purditioni;" and which is agreeable to the Hebrew in Job xxvi. 6,—that *infernus*, or the place of perdition of the abode of the lost, *is naked and open* to the eye of God, from whom nothing is hid.

We would only add in conclusion on this view of the *locality* of Gehenna as the place of future torments, that it is the same with "*the lowest parts of the earth,*" prevalent in the belief of the Jews *before* the time of Christ, namely, that it was situated, as they were wont to term it, *under the waters*, and of which there are allusions in the sacred writings with-

[1] See page 103.

out number. Archbishop MAGEE, in his translation of Job xxvi. 5-6, renders the passage thus:

> "Dead things are formed
> From *under the water*, and the inhabitants thereof:
> *Hell* is naked before him,
> And *destruction* hath no covering (verse 5).
> The *seat of spirits* is naked before Him,
> And the *regions of destruction* hath no covering" (verse 6).

And he observes: "Here I take the *souls* of the dead, and the *inhabitants* of the place below the abyss of waters, to bear to each other the same proportion, that is to be found in the 6th verse to subsist between the *seat of spirits* and the *region of destruction:* those of the dead who are sunk in the lowest parts of Sheol, or *Tartarus,* being placed in the region of destruction, or the Gehenna of the *later* Jews."

The obvious inference, in reference to the above Latin Vulgate translation of Job xxvi. 5-6, is, that this passage is evidently to be understood of *the place* where the Rephaim or old giants, and their fellow inhabitants of the lost, mourn and wail with them in perdition, even the *infernus* which is under the waters.

So much, then, as to the knowledge and belief of the Jews in the doctrine of *immortality,* and of the *place* and *condition* of the lost, both *before* and after the Babylonish captivity.

And, as to the period *immediately following* that event, the 2d Book of Esdras, chap. iii.,—the Chaldee paraphrast, and other Jewish writings, furnish the most incontestible evidence, that the *name*, Gehenna, began to be in frequent use. Of this, the infamously cruel practises of the idolatrous Israelites, in offering their children in sacrifice to Moloch in the *Valley of Hinnom*, already adverted to, may be taken in proof. This practice occasioned that valley to become to posterity a name of execration, and to be applied *figuratively*, to denote the *place* of future endless punishment.

But, king Josias was not alone, in thus consecrating the Valley of Hinnom as a place of vengeance. JEHOVAH, Himself, appropriated it to a similar use, both before and after his time. The first instance was that of the destruction of the host of Sennacherib, king of Assyria, where 180,000 of their carcases were burned, as recorded in Isaiah, chap. xxx— " Through the voice of the Lord, shall the *Assyrian* be beaten down. For TOPHET is ordained of old ; yea, for the king it is prepared : He has made it deep and large ; the pile thereof is fire and much wood ; the *breath of the Lord* like a stream of brimstone doth kindle it." But, second. This was the place where the idolatrous Jews were slain and massacred by the Babylonish armies, when the city, Jerusalem, was taken and burned, and their carcases left, for want of room to bury them, to be meat for the fowls of heaven and the beasts of the field, according to the word of the Lord by the prophet Jeremiah, chaps. xvii,—xix : "The children of Judah have built the high places of Tophet, which is in the valley of the son of Hinnom, *to burn their sons and their daughters in the fire;* which I commanded them not, neither entered it into my heart. Therefore, behold, the days come, saith the Lord, that it shall no more be called *Tophet*, nor the Valley of the son of *Hinnom*, but the VALLEY OF SLAUGHTER. For, they shall bury in Tophet till there be no more place. And the carcases of this people shall be meat for the fowls of heaven and for the beasts of the field, and none shall fray them away."

Then, further. To the preceding acts of the Divine vengeance against sin, may be added that of the destruction of Sodom and Gomorrha, with the rest of the cities of the plain, by *showers of fire and brimstone from heaven*, and of which, down to this day, the lake Asphaltites, or the Dead Sea, is a standing monument. Nor can we close this catalogue of instances illustrative of God's *retributive* justice against sin, without adverting to one even *anterior* to that of the antediluvian world of the ungodly by the flood, spoken of by St. Jude, verse 6 : " And the *angels* which kept not their first estate, but left their own habitation, God hath *reserved* for everlasting chains under darkness"—that is, in the intermediate abode where they now are, and which is called by St. Peter, ταρταρώσας, *Tartarus*, (see the Greek), or " Hell "[1]—" UNTO the judgment of the great day."

We add a word or so in conclusion on this subject, in reference, first, to the Jewish sense attached to the word תֹּפֶת, Topheth. " Noldius considers this word as synonymous with מְדוּרָה the place of burning, or burning pit, *a lake of fire*." And second. St. Peter tells us that when God " condemned

[1] ii. Pet. ii. 4.

the cities of Sodom and Gomorrah with an overthrow," they were "made an *ensample*," or *pattern*, "unto those that *after* should live ungodly;" and he speaks of these as "the unjust," who, with the fallen angels, now in Tartarus, are "*reserved* unto the day of judgment to be punished,"[1] even that "day of judgment and perdition of ungodly men,"[2] who shall then "*suffer the vengeance of eternal fire.*"[3]

The following inferences, we submit, are logically deduced from the above facts: namely,

First. That the "Cœtus Gigantum," or the "Cœtus Rephaim" of the Jews *before* the Babylonish captivity, as denotive of "the congregation" or assembly of those antediluvian rebel giants who for their iniquities "perished by the flood,"[4] furnishes proof demonstrative of their *knowledge of* and *belief in*, a place of future eternal misery, as expressed in the passage from Job xxi. 16: "The man that *wandereth* out of the way of understanding, shall *remain* in the congregation of the dead." And,

Second. That the same doctrine was more distinctly set forth in the writings of the Jews *after* the Babylonish captivity, by the use of the terms Tophet and Gehenna, as already explained. We repeat: in analogy to those vile and abominable practises of things *visible* to the senses, such was the property of the Hebrew language, that the Jews came to regard them as figures of things *invisible*. Hence they looked upon this most execrable, revolting, and accursed

---

[1] ii. Pet. ii. 6, 9. [2] Ib. iii. 7.
[3] Jude, verse 7. [4] ii. Pet. iii. 6.

place of all places—the Valley of the son of Hinnom—as significant of *the place* of the lost. But we observe,

Third. That what is conclusive of this point, is, 1st, the evident allusion to the above practise of the Jews, and the use, doctrinally, to which they applied it, as drawn from our Lord's sentence of final condemnation of the wicked: "Go, ye cursed, *into everlasting fire*, prepared for the Devil and his angels;"[1] in which, He evidently refers to the *ultimate* destiny of those apostate angels now "reserved for chains under darkness" in Tartarus for that end. But we refer, 2d, and chiefly, to the following passage already noticed in 2 Peter ii. 4-9, where the apostle makes direct reference to three of the instances of God's judgments against the ungodly, as PATTERNS of the *endless punishment* of sinful men. He says: first—"For if God spared not the *angels that sinned*, but cast them down to ταρταρώσας, *Tarturus*" (not, mark, ἅδης, or Hell, as in our English version), "and delivered them to be reserved unto judgment for chains under darkness," i. e., in the region of Tartarus IN Hades—and second, "spared not *the old world*, but saved Noah the eighth person, a preacher of righteousness, bringing in the flood upon the world of the ungodly;" i. e., the Rephaim, for so the LXX. sometimes render it; and third, "turning *the cities of Sodom and Gomorrah* into ashes, condemned them with an overthrow, making them an example of such as should *after* live ungodly; and delivered just Lot . . . and to *reserve* the unjust unto the day of judgment," etc., "suffering

[1] Matt. xxv. 41-46.

the vengeance of eternal fire." (Jude, verse 7). It is here to be specially observed, that the word, "*example*," in the above passage, is synonymous with *pattern*—i. e. του κολασεος του μελλοτον ασιβειν—of the *punishment* of such at the final judgment-day. Nor of these only. For, besides that mention is made of the apostate "angels," the reference to "the old world" or the Rephidim as destroyed by the flood, makes them equally an "example" or pattern of the final *unending* "perdition" of the "ungodly."

Keeping in view, therefore, first, the obvious distinction, as has been shown, between the import of the terms Sheol and Hades, as denotive of the *intermediate place and state* of departed souls, good and bad, between death and the resurrection; and the terms "Cœtus Gigantum," "in Cœtu Rephaim, *before* and of Tophet or Hinnom (Gehenna) *after* the Babylonish captivity, as signifying the *future eternal* prison-house of the lost; we repeat: with these distinctions in view, we can readily understand "the mind of the Spirit" in that passage of the Apocalypse—"and DEATH" (or the Devil who has the power of death), "and *Hell*" (i. e., Hades), "and *whosoever* were not found written in the book of life, were cast into the lake of fire, which is the *second death*." On any other principle of interpretation, we deferentially submit it involves the absurdity of *Hell* being CAST INTO *Hell!* We now pass,

Second. To the much clearer light reflected on this subject in the pages of the NEW TESTAMENT.

We here remark in the first place, that, in exact

correspondence with the distinction made by the Jews in their use of the word Sheol, as denotive of an intermediate state of the soul between death and the resurrection; and of the terms Cœtus Gigantum, in Cœtu Rephaim, together with the words Tophet and Hinnom, to signify the *final place* of the lost; is that made by the New Testament writers, in the use and application of the two words, Hades and Gehenna. It will be found, that wherever the word Hades is properly translated HELL, the *place of departed spirits* is meant. And wherever the word Gehenna occurs, instead of being translated Hell, (as it is in our English version), it invariably denotes the *place of final punishment*. We must therefore carefully discriminate between these, in order to ascertain the true sense of the passages in which they occur.

I. Of the word, ἅδης, Hades. It is found eleven times in the New Testament. The first passage we shall consider is,

Acts ii. 27, 31. Here St. Peter uses the word Hades twice, in his quotation from Ps. xvi. 10: in which the prophet David speaks of the RESURRECTION of Christ: "Thou wilt not *leave* my soul in Hell, (Hades), neither wilt Thou suffer thine Holy One to *see* corruption." On this passage we lay down the following proposition, viz.:

1. That the "*soul*" of Christ, between His death and resurrection, *did not go* immediately to Heaven, that event not having transpired till after the *re-union* of His body and soul in His resurrected glorified humanity, at His ascension, which was *forty days* after.

We have already adverted to what is alleged by some writers, that in the Old Testament the term soul sometimes means the dead body; and they hence affirm that the signification of the above passage in reference to our blessed Lord is, 'Thou wilt not leave my *life*, or my *dead body*, in the grave,' etc. But, even admitting what is claimed of the term soul as above, yet we have shown that the word Nephesh in Deut. vi. 5, and in Ps. xvi. 10 quoted by St. Peter in Acts ii. 27, 31, and which he renders by the corresponding Greek word Psuche, is used in the sense of that *rational* faculty which thinks.

It is further to be observed, that the two passages, Ps. xvi. 10, and Acts ii. 27, 31, most explicitly recognize the *complex personality* of Christ, between death and the resurrection. The statement of St. Peter is a *literal* fulfilment of the prophecy of David, that while His *body* did not "see corruption," or become putrescent, as in the case of ordinary bodies; "His *soul* was not left in Hell" (Hades). It follows, that the soul of Christ, which was not in Hell *before* the crucifixion, nor *after* the resurrection, must have been in Hell during the interval *between* His death and resurrection. By the re-union of the two at the expiration of the third day, therefore, His complex personality was preserved *intact*. In further confirmation of the above it may be remarked, that if the terms Nephesh and Psuche do not denote the *rational soul* of Christ, it will follow,

(1.) That *all distinction* is lost, between the corporeal and spiritual nature of our Lord. It makes His body, which was not to "*see* corruption," the same as His soul, which was not to be "*left* in Hell," which would make a distinction without a difference. But this would be to entirely destroy the force of the passage. Such unmeaning tautology in the language of the inspired penman, therefore, cannot be admitted. The apostle evidently places the one part, the body, in *opposition to* the other part, the soul of Christ. Hence, " though the soul may, by a metonomy, be [sometimes] taken in Scripture for the body, yet it cannot be so understood, when it is placed in opposition to and in contradistinction from, the body, as in this text it is." Again,

(2.) If this passage relates *only* to the animal life or body of Christ, how are we to account for the *condition* of His soul in the interval between His death and resurrection? *What became of it?* But if it be admitted, as the text declares, that His soul *was* in Hell, (Hades), but not left there; and that His body *was* in the grave, but did not "see corruption," then all is clear. We have in this case a full account of *both parts* of His complex nature. Once more.

(3.) St. Peter affirms, that the *soul* of Christ, which is a distinct subsistence, as a part of His human nature, was to be *in* Hell, (Hades). But the term Psuche, (soul), cannot mean His body. It follows, therefore, on the hypothesis that the soul means the *animal* life, which has *no* distinct subsistence, that there was *no part* of His human nature in Hell, (Hades). The conclusion hence is, that the part of His human nature called the rational soul, *was in Hell*, (Hades). And, finally,

(4.) To affirm that the soul of Christ, properly so called, was not in Hades, in as much as His DEITY, which is omnipresent, does not admit of transition, is to *deny the existence of the human soul of Christ.* For, if Psuche means the animal life *only*, then, since there is no evidence of the existence, after death, of the animal or sensitive parts of our nature, it follows that Christ's soul at death became *extinct*, not only, but with the early heretic Appollinaris, it *denies* to Christ an intellectual or rational soul, in the place of which, he affirmed, was substituted the Word or Divinity. And so, the entire scheme of human redemption by the vicarious sacrifice of Christ as "GOD MANIFEST IN THE FLESH,"—"perfect God and perfect man"—*is swept away!* But if, on the other hand, the Scriptural doctrine is, that while the *dead body* of our Lord was really present in the *grave*, and His *soul* between death and the resurrection was really present in Hades, then all is clear.

That it *is* so, we shall now proceed to demonstrate, from St. Peter's quotation of Ps. xvi. 10, in Acts ii. 27, 31. The simple question to be determined, is,

Whither went the soul of Christ at the instant of death, if it did not go direct to Heaven?

An answer to this question depends solely upon the import, first, of the term Hades in Acts ii. 27, 31, and of Sheol in Ps. xvi. 10 ; and second, of the word Paradise, as intimately connected with the subject in hand. On these two words we observe,

I. In regard to the word Hades, that, wherever it occurs in

the New Testament, it has come to be popularly regarded as invariably denotive of the place of *future eternal torments* to the wicked at the instant of death. And this idea has become so extensively interwoven into the current theology of the day, that the veriest suggestion that it is an *error*, casts suspicion upon one's orthodoxy regarding the doctrine of the penal evil of sin and the punitive justice of God in the eternal punishment of the lost. If, however, it can be shown from Scripture, that this word Hades is *never* used to denote the *final* state or condition of the impenitent, but that it invariably points to a place and state *intermediate* between death and the resurrection, both of the just and the unjust, in which they await a conscious reunion of body and soul *in order to* their entrance into a state of consummate bliss or woe ; we repeat, if this can be shown from Scripture, it will fully confirm the articles of the orthodox faith in reference to the penal evil of sin, as an *infinite offence* in the sight of a Holy God, and the final subjection of the " ungodly" to the " vengeance of eternal fire." And so,

II. In reference to the word Paradise, which occurs in our blessed Lord's address to the penitent malefactor on the cross : "This day shalt thou be with me in *Paradise.*" [1] This term, it is alleged, is the same with "*the third heaven*" into which St. Paul " was caught up," and that it furnishes conclusive evidence, that the souls of Christ and the malefactor, *at the instant* of death, passed into a state of consummate blessedness at God's right hand in the "*highest heaven,*"

[1] Luke xxiii. 43.

"where the body of the Saviour now is." But if it can be proven from Scripture, that "Paradise" or "the third heaven" is entirely another place and state from the "*highest*" or *supernal* Heaven, it will follow, that neither Christ or the malefactor or any other of the righteous, enter *that Heaven* immediately at death.

These statements premised, we return to a consideration of the *import* of the terms Hades and Paradise, that we may determine the sense in which they are used and applied by the New Testament writers. What *we* affirm of "Paradise" and the "*third Heaven*," is, that while they are identical, i. e., that they refer to the *same* place and state of the departed in Christ, that place and state is in the *region* of Hades.

The words of St. Peter, Acts ii. 27, 31, and those of our Lord to the penitent thief, Luke xxiii. 43, will be considered together.

1. As to Acts ii. 27, 31, they relate, as we have seen, to the historical state or condition of our Lord for the short space of *three days*. During this interval, while His body *was in* the "sepulchre," it was not to decay ; and while His soul *was in* Hell, (Hádes), it was not to be left there. A *separation* of the soul from the body of Christ had taken place at the instant of death. But in the prophecy of David concerning Christ, the apostle tells us that "he spake of the *resurrection* of Christ," by which event His soul was to *leave* Hades, in order to be re-united to His raised body. And, according to our Lord's own prophecy respecting Himself,— "I will destroy this temple, and in *three days* I will raise it

again," [1] this resurrection transpired on the *third day* after His crucifixion. Now,

2. Let it be conceded, the *soul* of the converted malefactor *accompanied* the soul of Christ to "Paradise," or "the third heaven," whither St. Paul was "caught up;" it is nevertheless undeniable, that the malefactor *held a relation* to that Paradise, which our blessed Lord did not. This companionship of the soul of the malefactor with the soul of Christ, was limited to three days *only*. For, at the expiration of that period, Christ's soul *left* Paradise, in order to a *reunion* with His uncorrupted risen body, which, though "put to death in the *flesh*," yet was "quickened by the SPIRIT." [2] On the other hand, the *body* of the malefactor, like that of David, who "fell on sleep, and was laid unto (or with) his fathers," and whose "sepulchre remaineth unto this day," *has not yet* been raised from the dead.

We now submit the following argument, as demonstrative of the fact, that the *soul* of the malefactor, being *left* in "Paradise" at the time of the resurrection of Christ, was in a place and state entirely different from His, *after* that event. St. Peter, speaking of the resurrection of our Lord, represents Him, after "being seen of His disciples *forty days*, and speaking of the things pertaining to the kingdom of God," [3] as "being by the right hand of God *exalted*," [4] or "exalted at God's right hand." Now, St. Paul, speaking of Christ as our "HIGH PRIEST," says that He was "made *higher* than

---

[1] Mark xiv. 58. [2] 1 Pet. iii. 18.
[3] Acts i. 3. [4] Ib.—ii. 33.

the Heavens."[1] And, that these "higher Heavens" cannot be identical with "Paradise" or "the third Heaven" of the malefactor and of St. Paul, is clear from the fact, that when "the God and Father of our Lord Jesus Christ the Father of glory, according to His mighty power raised Him from the dead," He "set Him at His own right hand in the Heavenly places, *far above* all principality, and power, and might, and dominion, and every name that is named, not only in this world, but also in that which is to come, and hath put *all things* under His feet," etc. ; aye, "Paradise" and "the third Heaven" not excepted !

Our argument, then, demonstrative that the place and state into which the soul of the malefactor at death entered with Christ, differs from the "highest Heavens" to which He after forty days was "exalted," is simply this : It is presumed none will deny, that "the patriarch David's" soul was admitted at death to "*Paradise*,"—the same with "*Abraham's bosom*" or "*the third Heaven*"—as well as that of the penitent "thief." But St. Peter most explicitly declares, Acts ii. 34, that "David *is not ascended* into the Heavens :" that is, "the *highest* Heavens," "where the body of the Saviour *now* is." It follows, therefore, that *if* the "Paradise" of the malefactor be the same with the "highest Heavens far above all principality and power," etc., to which our Lord was "exalted" after His resurrection, then, in as much as king David, the sweet singer of Israel, and "the man after God's own heart" is not there, an immeasurably *higher* honor

[1] Heb. vii. 16.

was conferred upon the life-long flagitiously wicked though finally penitent thief, than upon the eminently pious and prophetically inspired ancestor of Christ !

The only way of escape from the dilemma here involved, therefore, we submit, is the following, namely : that the " Paradise" or " third Heaven" into which the *soul* of our divine Redeemer, together with those of David, St. Paul, and the regenerated malefactor entered at death, was in the *region* of the Sheol of the Old Testament and the Hades of the New. In other words, it was that *intermediate* abode of the pious dead, where patriarchs, prophets, apostles, and all who, having "died in the faith" of, and "fallen asleep in Jesus," "*rest in hope*" of the consummation of their final blessedness, at the bright morn of " THE FIRST RESURRECTION." [1]

The next passage in which the word Hades is found, is Luke xvi. 23, called the parable of the rich man and Lazarus—καὶ ἦν τοῦ ἅδης—"and in *Hell* (Hades), he lifted up his eyes, being in *torments;* and seeth Abraham afar off, and Lazarus in his bosom," etc. We have already alluded to the two abodes of the righteous and the wicked, as *located in* Sheol or Hades. That the same holds true of the Hades of this parable, is evident from the fact of the "*great gulf*" which supervenes between "the rich man" and "Lazarus," thereby cutting off all intercourse between the one " in torments" and the other in " Abraham's bosom."

And yet, we are by no means to infer, that Lazarus in "*Abraham's bosom*," is to be understood of his admission im-

---

[1] See on this, 1 Thess. iv. 13-17, and Rev. x. 4-6.

mediately at death into the "*highest*" or supernal "Heavens," "where the body of the Saviour *now is*," in contrast to Dives in the infernal regions, or *Tartarus:* for, remote as were the two places from each other, there is nothing in the parable to indicate, that the one was *higher* than the other. A "gulf" is not a chasm or abyss. A gulf separates a promontory, *in the same line* of the horizon. Tartarus *in* Hades, is not Gehenna *in* the abyss. And so, "Abraham's bosom," or "Paradise," or "the third Heaven" in Hades, is not the "*highest*" or supernal "Heaven." The terms *higher* and *lower* in reference to Paradise and Tartarus, therefore, are not to be taken in the absolute sense. This is evident from the fact as set forth in this parable, viz., that "the terms whereby motion from one place to another is expressed, are such as are never employed in designating motion *to* and *from* Heaven; but, always, when the places are *on a level*, or nearly so. Thus, Lazarus, when he died, (v. 22), is said— $\dot{\alpha}\pi\epsilon\nu\epsilon\chi\theta\tilde{\eta}\nu\alpha\iota$, to be 'carried away,' not $\dot{\alpha}\nu\epsilon\nu\epsilon\chi\tilde{\eta}\nu\alpha\iota$, to be carried up to 'Abraham's bosom.' It is the latter word, or one similarly compounded, that is always used when an *assumption* to Heaven is spoken of. Thus, St. Luke, when speaking of our Lord's ascension, says : $\dot{\alpha}\nu\epsilon\phi\epsilon\rho\epsilon\tau o$ $\epsilon\iota\varsigma\ \tau\grave{o}\nu\ o\grave{v}\rho\alpha\nu o\nu$—'He was parted from them, and *carried up* into Heaven;'[1] and St. Mark says of the same event, $\dot{\alpha}\nu\epsilon\lambda\acute{\eta}\phi\theta\eta\ \epsilon\iota\varsigma\ \tau\grave{o}\nu\ o\iota\rho\alpha\nu\acute{o}\nu$, that 'He was *taken up* into Heaven.'[2] But, where mention is made of passing from Abraham to the rich man, and inversely, the verbs employed

---

[1] Luke xxiv. 51.   [2] Mark xvi. 19.

are, $διαβῆναι$ and $διαπερῶσιν$, words which always denote motion on the *same ground or level*, as passing a river or a lake,' etc. And finally, when HEAVEN is spoken of as the termination *to* which or *from* which a passage is made, the word is invariably either in the first case $αναβαινο$, and in the second $καταβαινο$, or some word similarly formed, and of the same import." [1]

Still, it is urged that St. Peter, 2d Epist. chap. ii. 4, in speaking of "the angels that sinned," says that "God *cast them down to* Hell," (Tartarus), etc. Be it so. The angelic rebellion here alluded to, transpired *in the "highest"* or supernal "Heaven," which, placed in contrast with Tartarus in Hades, implies that their ejectment was from a higher to a lower region.

Again. We are reminded that in St. Paul's account of his rapture, he states that he was "*caught up* to the third Heaven," or "*into* Paradise," etc. Hence it is demanded, *if* "the third Heaven" and "Paradise" refer to one and the same place, how is this to be reconciled with the idea of their *location* in Hades? This may be explained by our Lord's declaration in reference to the "highest Heaven" where He now is: "*No man hath ascended up to Heaven*, but He *that came down from Heaven*," etc. And so, even "Enoch," of whom it is said, that "He was not, for God *took him*;"[2] and "Elijah" also, "who went up by a whirlwind *into* Heaven;"[3] with the above declaration of Christ before us,

---

[1] See Dr. Campbell's "Translation of the Four Gospels," on this Parable.
[2] Heb. xi. 3.   [3] 2 Kings ii. 11.

could not have been admitted into " the highest" or supernal " Heaven," any more than David, who " is not ascended into the Heavens." To *what part* of the aereal regions Enoch and Elijah were bodily translated, the Scriptures do not inform us ; but certain it is, that it could not have been *that* " Heaven where the body of the Saviour now is." And, in regard to St. Paul, the very doubt which he expresses as to whether he was " *in* the body or *out of* the body," during his rapture into " the third Heaven" or " Paradise," shows conclusively that he could not have ascended into " the *highest* Heaven."

And, in conclusion on this subject, as it is thought to be incongruous, to consider " the third Heaven" or " Paradise" at the same time the place to which our blessed Lord *went down*,—for He " descended into the deep"[1]—and the place to which St. Paul *went up ;* the explanation is, that, besides that up and down are mere *relative* terms, and consequently, that the same situation may be up or down according to its position relatively to other places to which a reference is tacitly made ; it is also to be observed, that the Greek words εος and εις as used by the apostle, do not necessarily denote either *up* or *down*, but that he was simply " *caught into* the third Heaven." Thus, we submit, the subject is cleared of all incongruity.

The fourth and fifth passages where the word Hades occurs, are Matt. xi. 23, and Luke x. 15. " And thou Capernaum, which art exalted to Heaven shall be thrust down

---

[1] Rom. x. 7.

to Hell," (Hades). The terms "Heaven" and "Hell" are here used *figuratively*, the former denoting the *highest* object, as illustrating the flourishing state of Capernaum; and the latter the *lowest*, when, as a punishment for her sins, she should be blotted out of the list of nations, to be no more seen; in allusion to the meaning of Hades, as an *invisible* place.

The sixth passage, is Matt. xvi. 18 : "πυλοι ἅδου, the gates of Hell (Hades) shall not prevail against it:" i.e., the Church. Here again, the word Hades is used *figuratively*, as denoting the place of the departed, which is represented in Isaiah, chap. xxxviii. 10, as a *spacious receptacle with gates*, as expressed by king Hezekiah : "I said, in the cutting off of my days, I shall go to *the gates of Hell*" (Sheol). The meaning is, that however the Church should be distressed or persecuted by the cruel machinations of the Devil, or by the hands of wicked men, all their combined powers, as here figuratively denoted by the phrase, "the gates of Hades," shall not be able to destroy her. In other words, as our blessed Lord declared of the collective body of the Redeemed, "Because *I* live *ye* shall live also," [1] as I hold in my right hand "the key of Death and of Hades," by my triumph over and final destruction of them, the Church shall *never die*, but live for ever.

The seventh place where the word Hades occurs, is 1 Cor xv. 55. "O Hades," (improperly rendered *grave* in our English version), "where is thy victory?" This passage has been already considered in a previous part of these discussions.[2]

[1] John xiv. 19   [2] See pages 88, 89.

The eighth place for this word, is Rev. i. 18 : "I have the keys—τον ἅδου—of Hades and of Death." In this passage, the Lord Jesus Christ is represented as having power over *Death*, to redeem the body from the grave, not only ; but as holding also "the keys of Hades," (Hell), the place and state of the departed souls of the saints who sleep in Him, and from which, in due time, He will *release* them, and re-unite them to their incorruptible bodies. This passage, therefore, clearly inculcates the doctrine of the intermediate place and state of the departed, in which the souls of men are "reserved" in conscious blessedness or woe, until every man, *in his own order*,[1] shall be raised "in the morning" or at close of[2] "the great judgment day."

Finally, the ninth, tenth, and eleventh places where this word is found, is Rev. vi. 8 ; xx. 13 ; and xx. 14. 1st. Rev. vi. 8 : "And I looked, and behold, a pale horse, and his name that sat on him was DEATH, and *Hell*, (Hades,) followed with him." 2d. Rev. xx. 13 : "And Death and Hell, (Hades) *delivered up* the dead which were in them." 3d. Rev. xx. 14 : "And Death and Hell were *cast into* the lake of fire. This is the second death." Three instances are here recorded of the most sublimely bold personifications. The first denotes that Hades is the receptacle of departed *spirits*, immediately after the body falls a prey to the dominion of Death. The second declares, that DEATH shall deliver up the *bodies*, and Hades the *souls*—not, mark, of the *righteous*, for they shall have shared with those who shall have "a part in

---

[1] 1 Cor. xv. 23.   [2] Compare Ps. with 1 Thess. iv. 13-17, and Rev. xx. 4, 5.

the FIRST RESURRECTION," and "over whom the second death shall have no power"[1]—but, "of the *wicked dead*," who lived not again " till the thousand years were finished."[2] And the third passage proves incontestably, that the word Hades (Hell) in neither passage, can possibly be synonymous with the word Gehenna. For, on such an hypothesis, as by "the lake of fire" into which Death or the Devil and Hades is finally "cast," is undoubtedly meant the place and state of *future eternal* torments, we should have the monstrous incongruity of Gehenna being "*cast into*" Gehenna!

We shall now pass to consider,

II. The New Testament use and import of this word, GEHENNA. In contradistinction to the signification of the term Hades, as employed by Christ and His apostles to denote the place and state of departed spirits, holy and unholy, between death and the resurrection; this word, Gehenna, the derivation of which has been already explained, was used by them invariably to designate the place and state of *future endless* punishments.

We find it, first, in Matt. v. 22. "But I say unto you, that whosoever shall say to his brother, thou fool, shall be in danger, $\gamma \varepsilon \varepsilon \nu \nu \alpha \ \tau o \upsilon \ \pi \upsilon \rho o \varsigma$, of *Gehenna*[3] (not Hell) *fire*." In this passage, evident allusion is made by our blessed Lord, to the *future consummate* punishment of the wicked in the place of final torments. Besides that it is drawn from its

---

[1] Rev. xx. 5, 6.   [2] Rev. xx. 5.

[3] In every instance where this word occurs, it has been invariably, but as we shall see, *improperly*, translated " HELL" in our English version.

analogy, as already explained,[1] to the burning of those victims offered in sacrifice to Moloch by the idolatrous Israelites in the valley of the son of Hinnom, it has an allusion also to the execution of those doomed to be burnt alive, according to the statutes recorded in Lev. xx. 14 and xxix. 9. The same word occurs in two other places of this chapter, viz., verses 29 and 30, both of which are to be understood in the same sense as the above.

The next passage is Matt. x. 28: "Rather fear Him who is able to destroy both soul and body in *Gehenna*" (not Hell). The punishment is here evidently made to depend on the re-union of body and soul, *at the resurrection* of "the rest of the dead that lived not again, until the thousand years are finished;"[2] and hence can only refer to the place of *final* misery.

This word also occurs twice in Matt. xxiii. 15, and 33: "Woe unto you, Scribes, Pharisees, Hypocrites! for ye compass sea and land to make one proselyte; and when he is made, ye make him twofold more the child of *Gehenna* (not Hell) than before." Verse 33: "Ye serpents, ye generation of vipers: How can ye escape the damnation of *Gehenna!*" (not Hell).

And twice again, in Mark ix. 43-46: "If thy hand or thy foot offend thee, cut it off: it is better for thee to enter into life maimed or holt, than having two hands or two feet to be cast into *Gehenna*" (not Hell), where their worm *dieth not*, and their fire *is not quenched*."

---

[1] See pages 104, 107-12.   [2] Rev. xx. 5.

Now, these passages clearly indicate that the place and state of *final misery* of the "ungodly" is intended. Hence our Lord's reference, in illustration of it first, to the *subjects*, as constituted in their complex personality of "both body and soul;" and second, to the *endless duration* of their misery, which He compares to the "worm," which continually preyed upon the dead carcases that were cast into the valley of Hinnom (whence *Gehenna*), and to the *perpetual fire* there kept to consume them.

The last place where this word occurs is in the Epistle of James, chap. iii. 16: "The tongue is a fire . . . a world of iniquity . . . and it is set on fire of *Gehenna*" (not Hell). Here, the malice, envy, hatred, and uncontrolable fury of "the tongue" of the unrenewed man is drawn from their analogy to like propensities among the finally damned in Gehenna.

This much, then, of our exposition and vindication,

First. Of the scriptural doctrine regarding the *intermediate* place and state or condition of the departed, both righteous and wicked, during the interval between death and the resurrection. As we have progressed, step by step, along the track of this intricate and imperfectly understood subject, and notwithstanding the comparative obscurity in which it was enveloped during the *early* patriarchal ages, we have, nevertheless, had the satisfaction to witness the gradual dissipation of those mists from the minds of the *later* patriachs and prophets until, through the clearer light reflected upon it by Christ and His apostles, the combined rays of the full sun-light of the inspired pages are collected into a focus, in the *last three* passages quoted from the Apocalypse.

And, unless our exegeses of the Scriptural phraseology relating to this subject can be overthrown, it will follow,

Second. That, inasmuch as the doctrine of the intermediate place and state of the departed, and their future resurrection, has been shown to be predicated of the original constitution of man as a *complex being* consisting of body and soul, as essential to the preservation, *intact*, of his entire personality in the future as well as in the present life ; and, also, that the intermediate state, whether of the righteous or the wicked, is neither *remedial, disciplinary*, nor *probationary;* we repeat, it will follow that the Scriptures affirm the *eternal blessedness* of the righteous, as consummated at their resurrection, not only ; but the equally certain *endless misery* of the wicked, as consequent of the same event.

The doctrine of the intermediate state, therefore, we maintain, furnishes a complete, and the *only* complete and unanswerable refutation of the modern heresies enunciated in the title page of this work, and especially of the alleged *annihilation of the souls of the wicked at or after death*, as advocated by Messrs. Miles Grant, Storrs, Colegrove, Hudson, Hastings, Himes, and others.

We now proceed to present,

II. AN HISTORIC VIEW, AS EMBRACING THE VOICE OF THE CHURCH, ANCIENT AND MODERN, IN RELATION TO THE DOCTRINE OF THE INTERMEDIATE PLACE AND STATE OF THE DEPARTED, ETC.

This doctrine, in these "last times," having been almost entirely excluded from the theological nomenclature both of the pulpit and the press, one can scarcely be surprised that it has come to be regarded, as we have said, either as of Pagan origin, or as identical with that fanciful invention of anti-christian Rome called Purgatory, and hence, that it is a novelty.

We now propose, however, to follow up the Scriptural argument on this subject as derived from the Old and New Testaments, by an exhibit of the *Historical* evidence of the fallacy of the above pretence, as derived from *the Voice of the Church*, ancient and modern. It will be seen, if we mistake not, that this doctrine of the intermediate place and state of the departed, as set forth in these pages, was thoroughly known to, believed in, and advocated by, ALL the Orthodox Christian writers of the purest age of the Church immediately following that of Christ and His apostles; and also by those Divines most eminent for their learning and piety, in the various branches of the Evangelical Churches of Christendom, since the period of the Continental and Anglican Reformation. We will begin,

I. With the writers of PRIMITIVE ANTIQUITY, or the age immediately following the close of the New Testament canon.

The *idea*, that the soul, immediately at death, passed to the *full enjoyment* of God's presence in "the highest" or supernal Heaven, as advanced by the followers of Valentinus, Basilides, and Marion, and subsequently by the Manichees, JUSTIN MARTYR held to be a *heresy*. Speaking of those who were called Christians, in his Dialogue with Trypho, he says (pages 307, 353): "They denied the *resurrection*, and held that as soon as they died, their souls were received into Heaven." And he adds (page 203), "That no souls die; but that the souls of *good* men remain in a better place, the souls of *bad* men in a worse, *expecting* the day of judgment." He wrote between A.D. 148—165.

And so, IRENÆUS, Bishop of Lyons, in A.D. 180, says: "That the *heretics* despised the formation of God (i. e., the body as formed by Him), and not receiving the salvation of the flesh, say, that as soon as they are dead, they *ascend* above the Heavens, and go to Him whom they call their Father." And having said that our Lord's soul went not to Heaven, but continued in the place of the dead till His resurrection, he adds: "This is sufficient to confound those men who say that their inward man (i. e., their souls), leaving the body here, ascends to the *super*-celestial mansions."[1] And then he gives the *orthodox* opinion thus: "It is manifest that the souls of the disciples of our Lord shall go into the *invisible* places appointed for them by God, *expecting* a resurrection; and then by receiving their bodies and rising with them, as our Lord did, shall come into the presence of

---

[1] Adv. Hær. lib. v. c. 31, page 491.

God."¹ He also speaks of the tradition of the Church thus : " The presbyters who were the disciples of the apostles say—Those that were translated (i. e., as Enoch and Elijah), were carried into *Paradise*, for that place is prepared for just men and such as have the Spirit, and there they remain, *till* the consummation, expecting or beginning immortality ; and that there shall be New Heavens and a New Earth ; and *then* they that are worthy of the celestial mansions shall go thither," etc.

TERTULLIAN also, Bishop of Carthage, in A.D. 207, having produced the same instance of the death of Christ and the continuance of His soul *apud inferos* till the resurrection of the body, positively concludes, " that Heaven is *open to none* while the earth remains" (i. e., in its present state) ; "the kingdom of Heaven being only to be opened at the dissolution" (not the annihilation) " of the world." ² And in his IVth book against Marion, he says : "The bosom of Abraham which is *higher* than the inferi, but *not so high* as Heaven, is that which gives refreshment to the souls of the just, *till* the consummation of all things produce the resurrection with a full reward." ³ And again. Having cited those words of the apostle—"And the very God of peace sanctify you wholly ; and I pray God your *whole spirit and soul and body be preserved blameless unto the coming of our Lord Jesus Christ*," says thus : "Here you see the *whole substance* of man designed for salvation, nor at any other

---

¹ Ib.   ² De Anima. c. iv.
³ Ib. v. c. 5 ; and c. xxxiv.

time but the appearance of our Lord, who is the key of the resurrection."[1]

NOVATIAN, of Carthage, in A.D. 252, holds the following language: "There is a place whither the souls of good and wicked men are carried, having some *foretaste* of their future judgment."[2]

CAIUS, a presbyter of Rome, says: "The just souls being celebrated by the angels placed over them, are led by them into a place of light called the bosom of Abraham, where the just from the beginning have been; where they are delighted with the vision of just fathers, *expecting*, after this place, their rest and everlasting habitation in Heaven."[3]

LACTANTIUS, in A.D. 320, observes: "Let no man think that souls are *forthwith* judged after death; they are held in one common custody till the time may come that the great Judge shall make trial of their merits,"[4] etc.

I will only add one more testimony to the above, from these ancient writers, that of

The eloquent CHRYSOSTOM, Archbishop of Constantinople. In his reply to the heresy of the Manichees, in A.D. 372, who affirmed that there is *no resurrection* of the body, and that the righteous had their full reward at the *instant* of death, etc., he replies, by conceding that the thief was indeed admitted to Paradise; but then he adds: "That Paradise *was not* the same with Heaven, for it contains not the good things which God hath promised to us;" and he concludes

---

[1] De Res. Carn, c. xlvii.   [2] De Trin. c. i.   [3] Apud Haschel. Note in Phot., p. 10.
[4] De Vit. Beat. Lib. vii. cap. xxi., page 717.

thus: "That if God promised the kingdom of Heaven, and only brought the thief into *Paradise*, He had not yet given to him the good things promised." [1]

From these brief extracts, derived from the writings of those Orthodox celebrities who flourished during the period emphatically and truly styled *"the golden age"* of the Church, therefore, we find them familiar with and advocating *all the main points* connected with the Scriptural doctrine of the intermediate place and state of the departed between death and the resurrection, and denouncing as heretical all those who opposed it.

And, it would be a matter of interesting inquiry, to trace, historically, the *departure* of the church from this doctrine at a comparatively early period, and of its loss as a fundamental truth, down to the era of the Reformation. Our limits, however, will only allow us to advert briefly to the *agent*, whose writings principally contributed to bring about that result. We allude to *Origen*, the renowned presbyter and cathechist in the school at Alexandria, who flourished between A. D. 204 and 254. History ascribes to this famous scholar and writer, first, that by his assertion of the inequality between the Father and the Son, he is regarded as the forerunner of the *Arian* heresy. Second. That his ambiguous and inadequate expressions concerning the work of redemption, in which he made but faint and indefinite mention of the incarnation, life, and sufferings of Christ, His sacrifice and satisfaction for His people, and the forgiveness of sins; together

---

[1] See on this subject, Dr. Whitby's Com. on ii. Tim. iv. 8, in a subsequent page.

with his resolute denial of the eternity of future punishments, he is looked upon as the father of *modern Universalists.* Third. His advocacy of the mutual relation of human power and divine grace, is claimed to have opened the way for the doctrine of the *Pelagians.* But chiefly, fourth, his substitution of the ALLEGORICAL or spiritualizing system of interpreting the Scriptures in the place of the LITERAL, has contributed, more than any other cause, to introduce into the expositions of the orthodox themselves, numberless phantasies totally subversive of evangelical truth.[1] It is to this circumstance that we are to trace *the loss* to the church, for so many centuries, of the primitive doctrine of the *intermediate place and state of the departed between death and the resurrection.* For, in order to introduce the souls of the saint and the sin-

---

[1] In proof of this statement in regard to ORIGEN, we quote the following extracts from the writings

(1.) Of MARTIN LUTHER. He says: "That which I have so far insisted on elsewhere, I here once more *repeat*, viz., that the Christian should direct his first efforts towards understanding the *literal* sense, (as they call it), which only is the substance of faith and of Christian theology, which *alone* will sustain him in the hour of trouble and temptation; and which will triumph over sin, death, and the gates of Hell, to the praise and glory of God. The ALLEGORICAL sense," he continues, "is commonly uncertain, and by no means safe to build upon; for as much as it usually depends upon *human opinion and conjecture only;* on which, if a man lean, he will find it no better than an Egyptian reed. Therefore, Origen, together with JEROME and similar of the fathers, are to be *avoided*, with the whole Alexandrian school, which, according to Eusebius, formerly abounded in that interpretation. For," he adds, "*later writers* unhappily following their too much praised and prevailing example, it has come to pass *that men make just what they please* of the Scriptures, until some accommodate the word of God to the most *extravagant absurdities;* and (as Jerome complains even in his own time) they extract from Scripture a sense *repugnant* to its meaning; of which offence, however, Jerome himself was also guilty." (Annot. on Deut. cap. i. folio. 55).

ner into a condition of *consummate* bliss or woe *at the instant of death*, this allegorical system of interpretation totally ignores the Scriptural doctrine of a *literal resurrection* of the body from the grave, alleging that the change to which it is subjected by that process is *purely spiritual,* in which state it is so assimilated to the soul as to become identical with it. This was the theory of the ORIGENIC SCHOOL of interpreters. And it was this heresy, as all the ancient writers above quoted term it, and *not* the doctrine of the intermediate state, that laid the foundation for the invention of the Papal dogma of *Purgatory.* This will appear from the fact, that in A. D. 240, ORIGEN himself, having borrowed his views from the

(2.) DR. MOSHEIM also, says that: "After the encomiums we have given to ORIGEN, . . . it is not without a deep concern we are obliged to add, that he also, *by an unhappy method*, opened a secure retreat for all sorts of errors, which a wild and irregular imagination could bring forth." And after noticing that he *abandoned the literal* sense, and divided the hidden [that is, the *allegorical* or spiritual] into moral and mystical, he adds:" A prodigious number of interpreters, both in this and succeeding ages, followed the unhappy method of Origen, though with some variations; *nor could the few,* who explained the sacred writings with judgment and a true spirit of criticism, oppose with any success *the torrent of allegory* that was overflowing the Church." (Mosheim's Eccles. Hist. Cen. iii. Sec. v. vi).

(3.) DR. MILNER, in his Church History, says : "No man, not altogether unsound and hypocritical, *ever injured the Church more than Origen did*. From the fanciful mode of allegory introduced by him, and uncontrolled by Scriptural rule and order, arose a *vitiated method* of commenting on the sacred pages ; (which has been succeeded by a contrary extreme, viz , a contempt for types and figures altogether) ; and in a similar way," he adds, " Origen's *fanciful ideas* of letter and spirit, tended to remove from men's minds all just conceptions of genuine spirituality. *A thick mist for ages* pervaded the Christian world, supported and strengthened by this *allegorical* manner of interpretation. The *learned alone* were considered for ages implicitly to be followed ; and the vulgar, *when the literal was hissed off the stage*, had nothing to do, but to follow *their authority* wherever it led them." (Milner's Hist. vol. i. p. 469.)

Platonic philosophy, and incorporated them into his own corrupt system, taught that the *souls*, at least of a portion of the dead, would pass to Heaven through the process of a *purgatorial fire*.

But let us now see what additional evidence in defence of the doctrine of the intermediate place and state of the dead, may be historically gathered,

II. From the writings of Evangelical Divines, alias the voice of the Church, SINCE THE TIME OF THE REFORMATION.

As it is presumed that the reader is more or less familiar with the *names* of the authors from whose writings we shall quote, we have concluded, instead of arranging them in chronological order, to reduce what they furnish on the subject in hand, to the *form* laid down in the following ANALYSIS; the advantage of which will be, that of presenting a *connected view*, doctrinally, of the details of the entire system technically designated the intermediate place and state of the dead.

Agreeably to this plan—though at the expense of a partial repetition of quotations here and there—it will be in place to adduce the above testimony in reference to,

1. The *origin* of this doctrine. As already observed, from the circumstance that the Greeks had their Hades and the Romans their *Orcus* or *Inferi;* it is alleged that the Jews derived their notions of a future state from Pagan writers, philosophers and poets. But, so far from this, as Moses,[1] and Job,[2] and Jacob,[3] and David,[4] and Solomon also,[5] had their

---

[1] Deut. xxxii. 22. Job. xxvi. 5. [2] —— [3] Gen. xxxvii. 35.
[4] Ps. xvi. 10; xxx. 3; xciv. 17. [5] Prov. xv. 11.

Sheol; the learned Calmet says: that "the Hebrews thought and spoke almost like the Greeks *before* Homer, Heziod, and the most ancient poets of this nation;"[1] and in this opinion he is supported by Bp. Horsley, who says that "Sheol is the only Hell of the Old Testament."[2] So also the learned Vitringa, who quotes Gen. xxxii. 35; Ps. xvi. 10; xxx. 3; and xciv. 17, as evidence that the Hebrews believed in "a place where souls, when freed from the body, were assembled," etc.; and that "from the Hebrews, this opinion passed to the other people,"[3] i. e., the Greeks and Romans. Hence *their* Hades, and *Orcus* or *Inferi*. The next article relates to,

2. The *import* of the word Sheol. On the passage, Gen. xxxvii. 35, Bp. Patrick observes: "that Sheol must signify the *state or place* of the dead, as it often doth." Lowth remarks: "The word Sheol cannot be understood of the *grave*, properly so called, because Jacob thought his son was devoured by wild beasts; but must be meant of the place where he supposed Joseph's *soul* was lodged."[4] And Archbp. Secker asserts: That "the translation [i. e. of Sheol] into the *grave*, is wrong; as if he meant to have his body by Joseph's. That could not be, for he thought him devoured by wild beasts. It means into the *invisible state*, the state of departed souls; and in this sense, it is said of several of the patriarchs, that they were "gathered unto their people,

---

[1] Calmet's Dict., Art. Hell., Eng. Ed. D. Oyly and Calson.
[2] Horsley's Com. on Hosea, p. 46.
[3] Vitringa, as quoted by Archbp. Magee on the Atonement, p. 346, et seq.
[4] Lowth on Is. xiv. 9.

Gen. xxv. 8 ; xxxv. 29 ; and of "all the generation" which lived with Joshua, that they "were gathered unto their fathers." VITRINGA also quotes this passage, and several others in the Old Testament, in which he says that the word Sheol ought not to be translated *grave*, but HELL, in the sense of a *receptacle* of departed spirits."[1] Another distinguished writer on this subject, Sir PETER KING, speaking of the phrase which so frequently occurs of being "gathered to their fathers," or "their people," says : that "they are to be understood of their being received to the assembly of good and pious souls as worshipers of the true God, who were admitted into covenant with Him, and lived and died in the observance of that covenant, as the old patriachs, the ancestors of the Jewish people did."[2]

3. Of the *original meaning* of the Greek word HADES, as found in the Septuagint and the New Testament. Instead of giving warrant to the *modern idea* of the Hell of future torments, we have already shown on the authority of Dr. DODDRIDGE, Dr. CAMPBELL, Dr. ADAM CLARKE, and Bishop HORSLEY, that it was used by the inspired writers to signify a hidden or *invisible place*, from the Saxon word Helan, to *cover over*. An entirely different word, viz., Gehenna, (and the same with the Jewish Tophet in the valley of the son of Hinnom), was employed by Christ and His apostles to signify the place of *final* torments. Hades (Hell), therefore, agreeably to its original signification, denotes the place and state

---

[1] Vitringa Com. on Isa. xiv. 9, p. 433.
[2] Peter's Crit. Dis. on the Book of Job, p. 381, 382.

of the departed *till* the resurrection, whether of the "just" or "unjust." Dr. CAMPBELL, in his very learned "translation of the Four Gospels," on the words Hades and Gehenna, maintains and vindicates the doctrine of an *intermediate state*, as indicated in the distinction respecting their import here insisted on.

4. As to the *translation* of the Hebrew word Sheol and the Greek word Hades, by the word *grave*, or *sepulchre*. The late Bishop HOBART, in his "treatise on the state of the departed," says that "the Hebrew word for grave is KEBER, the receptacle of the *dead body*, but *not* for the soul;" and that "the Hebrew Sheol *is never used for grave*, though it is sometimes translated by that word." And hence, he adds, "the Hebrew word for *soul*, Nephesh, is *never joined* with Keber, but with Sheol, the term denoting the abode of departed spirits."[1] And Bp. HORSLEY proves, in regard to several "texts in which the contrary may seem to have taken place, namely, the use of Sheol for Keber, to signify the repository of the *body*, rather than the mansion of the departed spirit," yet he adds that, "upon consideration it will appear that in every one of these, the thing to be expressed is never Hell, nor the grave, particularly, and as distinct the one from the other; but, *the state of death:* and this state is expressed under the image of a place of residence of the dead *collectively*. And, for this place . . . the word Sheol is used," etc. And to this he adds: "The grave is *no* general place, since every dead body has its *own* appropriate grave."[2]

[1] State of the Departed, p. 59.   [2] Com. on Hosea, p. 200.

And so, in reference to the Greek word Hades, Bp. Hobart says: "The expression sleep, or sleeping, so frequently applied in Scripture to the state of the dead, is evidently *metaphorical*, derived from the resemblance between a dead body, and the body of a person asleep. The *body* is said figuratively to '*sleep* in the dust of the earth,' expecting a resurrection at that day when the dead, small and great, shall be summoned to stand before God. Hence the words cemetery and dormatory, from the Greek and Latin words *κοιμάω* and *dormio*, to *sleep*, are applied to the receptacles of the dead."[1] And again, he says that "the authors of the Septuagint, except in a very few instances, have translated the Hebrew word Sheol, which occurs in about sixty places in the Old Testament, not by $\vartheta\alpha\nu\alpha\tau\sigma\varsigma$, death, by $\tau\alpha\varphi\sigma\varsigma$, the grave, by $\mu\nu\eta\mu\alpha$ or $\mu\nu\eta\mu\epsilon\iota\sigma\nu$, the sepulchre, but by Hades, the appropriate word for *the region of the dead, or the place of the departed*."[2] And finally, Bp. Horsley observes, that "no two things can be more distinct; *Hell* [Sheol or Hades] is the mansion of the departed spirit; the *grave* [Keber or $\tau\alpha\varphi\sigma\varsigma$] is the receptacle of the dead body."[3]

5. In reference to the *import* of the Hebrew word Nephesh, and the Greek word Psuche. Now, as it respects the first, *nephesh*, translated *soul*, it is conceded that it is sometimes applied to beasts, as in Gen. i. 24: "Let the earth bring forth the living creature," in Hebrews, the living soul, i. e., spirit, life, and respiration. But of the beasts it is said,

[1] State of the Departed, p. 32.   [2] Ib—p. 69.   [3] Com. on Hosea, p. 159.

"the *life*, (Heb. soul) of the flesh *is in the blood*," (Lev. xvii. 11). In this sense, therefore, the soul is the spirit, or *breath*, which is the principle of animal life, and as such, is common alike to *man*,[1] and *brutes*. This subtle element in the *brute*, however, is not *immortal*; for it is declared, Eccles. iii. 21, that "the spirit of the beast goeth downward to the earth." In other words, "the brutes," at death, "*perish*."[2]

Again. The same word, NEPHESH, in its application to *man*, is used to denote the *whole person*, both body and soul. The King of Sodom says to Abraham, Gen. xv. 21 : "Give me the *souls*, (nephesh), i. e., the *persons*, "and take the goods to thyself." (See also Gen. xii. 5).

It is also used to signify *death*, or a dead body, as in Numb. vi. 6 : "He shall come at no dead body," (Heb. dead soul—*nephesh*). See also Numb. ix. 6.

But it is also taken, and chiefly, to denote the more exalted part of man's nature, called the *rational*, *spiritual*, and *immortal* soul, or that thinking, reasoning faculty which, raising him immeasurably above the mere instinct of the lower orders of the animal creation, stamps him with "the *image* and *likeness* of GOD."[3] And hence, its employment in the Old Testament to express the emotions of desire, love, inclination, and the like, as in Deut. vi. 5 : "Thou shalt *love* the Lord thy God with all thy heart, and with all thy soul,"[4]

---

[1] See Ps. xxxiii. 19 ; vii. 5.   [2] Eccles. iii. 21.
[3] Gen. i. 26, 27. See on this, pages 43-47 of this Work.
[4] See also Gen. xxiii. 8 ; 1 Sam. xviii. 1 ; Prov. xxvii. 7 ; Deut. iv. 29 ; vi. 5 ; Ps. xxxiv. 4, etc.

(Heb. *nephesh*). In this sense it occurs also in Ps. xvi. 10: "Thou wilt not leave my soul (*nephesh*) in Hell" (SHEOL), etc. Bp. HOBART says on this passage: "Here soul is evidently used in the sense of the rational soul or *mind*, properly so called; that principle within us which thinks, and understands, and wills, and exercises the powers and faculties and propensities of our nature." And he then argues, that as St. Peter rendered the Hebrew word, NEPHESH by the corresponding Greek word PSUCHE, *soul*, in his quotation of this passage in Acts ii. 27, 31, "it will follow that he understood soul of the rational and *immortal* soul of Christ." And he then adds: "The following passage establishes the use of the word PSUCHE, or soul, to denote the rational or immortal part of *our* nature: 'Fear not them which kill the body, but are not able to kill the soul; (PSUCHE); but rather fear Him who is able to destroy both soul (PSUCHE) and body in Hell,' GEHENNA; (not HADES, Matt. x. 28); that is, to punish in the torments of Gehenna the *spiritual and immortal* part of man as well as his corporeal nature."[1] The same word PSUCHE occurs in Matt. xi. 29; xxvi. 38; John xii. 27, etc.

Bp. BURNET observes on Ps. xvi. 10, and Acts ii. 27, 31, that on the hypothesis that soul is to be taken as synonymous with animal life or dead body, then "there will be *no opposition* in the two parts of this period; the one will be only a redundant repetition of the other. Therefore it is much more natural to think, that this other branch of Christ's *soul*

---

[1] State of the Departed, pp. 42, 43.

being left in Hell, must relate to that which we commonly understand by soul." [1]

Bp. Pearson, on the words, "Thou wilt not leave my *soul* in Hell," says: "From this place, the article (of the descent into Hell) is clearly and infallibly deduced thus: If the soul of Christ were left in Hell *at* His resurrection, then His soul was in Hell *before* His resurrection. But it was not there before His *death*; therefore, upon or after His death and before His resurrection, the soul of Christ descended into Hell . . . We must therefore confess from hence, that the soul of Christ was *in* Hell; and no Christian can deny it, saith St. Augustin, it is so clearly delivered in this prophecy of the Psalmist, and application of the apostle." [2]

Sir Peter King gives the same view of the opinions of the Christian fathers. "They apply this action of our Saviour's to His soul *alone*, employing for that end the text of the apostle cited by him from the Psalmist, on which this article is principally founded, viz., Acts ii. 27. By the soul of Christ, which God would not leave in Hell, they understood the *rational* part of man, that spirit which distinguishes him from the brute, and subsists after its disunion and departure from the body." [3] And Bp. Pearson on this subject says: "If the fathers had proved only that the *animal* soul of Christ had descended into Hell, they had brought no argument at all to prove that Christ had an *human intellectual* soul. It is, therefore, certain that the Catholic fathers, in

---

[1] Burnet's Expos. of the Articles. Art. iii.
[2] Bp. Pearson on the Creed. Art. iii. Oxford Ed. pp. 358-360.
[3] History of the Apostles' Creed. Descent into Hell.

their opposition to the Apollinarian heresy, did declare, that the intellectual and immortal *soul* of Christ descended into Hell.

Bp. HORSLEY, on this passage, and on the words in the Creed, "He descended into hell ;" and Dr. CAMPBELL, in his critical notes, vindicate the same construction of it.

Dr. DODDRIDGE paraphrases the words thus: "I am fully satisfied, that Thou wilt not leave my *soul*, while separated from the body, in *the unseen world*." And in opposition to the opinion of Whitby and the learned Parkhurst, (though both are strong advocates for an intermediate state), that the passage should read: "Thou wilt not leave my *life in the grave*," on the ground that *Hades* should be understood of the grave; he observes in a note: "as PSUCHE, which is the word here used, can hardly be considered to signify a dead body, and HADES is generally put for the state of *separate spirits*, the version here given seemed preferable to any other." Finally,

Dr. ADAM CLARKE interprets the same words, Acts ii. 27, 31, of "the *soul* of Christ not being left in *the state* of separate spirits."

We now pass to consider what these writers say in regard to—

6. *Locality*, as applied to the *soul*. On this subject, Bp. HOBART remarks: "In reasoning upon it the principle will be assumed, that, with the existence of all created spirits, is essentially connected the idea of locality. They *must exist in some place*." [1]

[1] State of the Departed, p. 31.

Bp. Pearson observes: "As the sepulchre is appointed for our flesh, so there is another receptacle, or habitation, or mansion, for our *spirits*. From whence it follows, that in death, the soul doth certainly pass by *a real motion* from that place in which it did inform the body, and is translated to that place, and into that society, which God, of His mercy or justice, hath allotted to it."[1] And,

Bp. Horsley states, that, "the soul existing after death, and separated from the body, though of a nature immaterial, *must be* in some place." For, he adds, "it is hardly to be conceived, that any *created* spirit, of however high an order, can be without locality."

Then further. Immediately allied to this subject, is that,

7. Of the *consciousness* of the soul, wherever located, as illustrated by the Scriptural term "*sleep.*" I here quote first, from the renowned Martin Luther's remarks on Gen. xxvi. 24: "And the Lord appeared unto him, (Isaac) that same night, and said, I am the God (God's) of *Abraham* thy father; fear not, for I am with thee, and will multiply thy seed for my servant Abraham's sake." On this passage he says: "To this consideration, (that of blessedness in the future life,) that phrase also has reference—'for my servant's sake.' For how should Abraham be the servant of God *after* his death? Nay, assuredly, *he is yet* serving God, as Adam, Abel, Noah, serve Him. And this must be carefully observed, that Abraham is *living, serving* God, *reigning* with Him. But what sort of life that is—whether he be sleeping

---

[1] Com. on the Creed. Art. v.

or waking, is another question. In what way the soul *rests*, it is not for us to know: one thing is certain, that it is *alive*."

There seems, however, some confusion of mind on the part of Luther, in tracing the *analogy* between the state of " men entranced," and of those " in natural sleep," and that of a dead body, and of a soul in a *future* state. In the former instances, soul and body are *united*. In the latter, they are *separated*. A man when in a trance or in natural sleep, undergoes a sort of *metaphysical* death. But when the soul leaves the body, the latter is subjected to an *organic* death. As Daniel says—"it *sleeps* in the dust of the earth,"[1] in a state of " insensibility." This, however, does not hold true of the *soul*, " whether *in* the body or *out of* the body : " for, in either case, the soul is " alive," and active. Then again. Even in the instance of an organic death, or " sleep," there is a *germ* of life, which, when " quickened " by the resurrection power of God, shall " *awake*"[2] it again to life, in analogy to that of awaking from a state of metaphysical death, or natural sleep, by the continued operations of those organic functions of life, the throbbing heart, the beating pulse, the respiring lungs. Now, Luther says truly, when speaking of *natural* sleep, " it cannot be said, this man is *dead* ; but while asleep or dreaming, he is *yet* alive, all the world will allow." But he then adds : " Yet I am not conscious that I am alive, while asleep. For neither any of the senses nor reason itself performs its office." How then, we

[1] Dan. xii. 2. [2] Dan. xii. 2.

deferentially submit, came Luther to know when awake, that, as he says,—"often *in my sleep* I believe myself in Hell, in Heaven, at Venice, or any where else?" Surely this furnishes the most indubitable evidence of the soul's *consciousness*, whether asleep or awake.

This eminent Reformer, however, speaks more to the point when he says—"What then shall we suppose to be the *nature* of this rest or life of the soul?" and he refers by way of illustration to Isaiah xxvi. 20,—"'Come, my people, enter into thy chambers, and shut the door about thee : *hide thyself as it were for a little season*, until the indignation be overpast.' And also chap. lvii. 2.—'He shall *enter into peace :* they shall *rest* in their beds, each one walking in his uprightness ;' and that too, much more peaceably than those that are merely asleep. They too rest, and *because* of that rest, men are never more alive than when they are *asleep :* for the life of men awake is full of cares, sorrows, toils, sickness ; but *bodily sleep* changes and overpowers diseases ; as the disciples say in St. John xi. 12—'Lord, if he [i. e., Lazarus] sleep, he shall do well.' We may truly say then, that while we are asleep, *we are most alive;* for the *vital spirits* are then most powerful," etc.[1]

Bp. Hobart says : "The term sleep, applied to the state of the dead, denotes not *unconsciousness*, but a freedom from the cares and labors of life ; and as it respects the righteous, expresses comparative enjoyment, rest, security, felicity. It is a phrase by which, in all languages, the state

---

[1] See Investigation of Prophecy, vol. iii. pp. 87, 88. London.

of the dead is denoted. And yet the popular belief among all nations, assigned *consciousness* and *activity* to the departed.

"In the SHEOL or Hell of the prophets Isaiah and Ezekiel, the departed monarchs *rise* from their thrones to meet and hail the kings of Babylon and Egypt.

"In the HADES or Hell of Homer, Ulysses, having trod 'the downward melancholy way,' *converses* with the shade of his mother, and the 'forms of warriors slain.'[1] And Virgil represents Æneas, in 'facibus orci,' in the jaws of Hell, in the entrance of Orcus, or the receptacle of the dead, as encountering 'variarum monstra ferarum,' of various forms unnumbered spectres. And having passed the bank 'irremeabilis undæ,' of the 'irremeable flood,' he *holds converse* with the shades of the dead.

> ".   .   .   .   juvat usque morari
> Et conferre gradum et veniendi posere causas."

> "The gladsome ghosts—
> Delight to hover near, and long to know
> What business brought him to the shades below."

The Bishop then argues, that though "there may be a metaphysical difficulty as to *how* the soul can exist in an incorporeal state," yet, as GOD, who is a spirit, exerts an infinite intelligence and activity, independently of material organs," so the "*soul*" also may "thus act." And he adds, in reference to natural sleep: "while the *body* is locked in the benumbing embrace of sleep, the *soul* wakes, the soul is active,

[1] Odyss. xi.

the soul dreams. And may there not be dreams in the sleep of death!"

"To die, to sleep—
To *sleep!* perchance to *dream.*"[1]

But, these writers have also somewhat to offer, on the subject of,

8. The *locality* of Sheol, or Hades, (Hell). It will be of service by way of introduction to what is to follow, to recite the Pauline references made to Acts ii. 27, in relation to the *soul* of Christ as being in Hades, (Hell). St. Paul represents it as a *descent.* Having said, Ephes. iv. 9, that our blessed Lord "descended into the lower parts of the earth," he warns us thus : Rom. x. 6, 7 : "Say not in thine heart, . . . who shall descend into the deep? that is, to bring up Christ again from the dead." Now, the argument of the apostle here is, that as "He that *descended,* is the same also that *ascended* far above all heavens," etc., (Eph. iv. 10), so whether in "the lower parts of the earth," or "far above all heavens," (though under different conditions of His complex humanity), His body and soul were alike *in both places.* As to the motion of. His "descent into the lower parts of the earth," while His body was in the *grave,* His soul was in *Hades.*

On this subject, Bishop HORSLEY observes: "It is evident that this (the place to which our Lord descended) must be some place *below* the surface of the earth ; for it is said that He 'descended,' that is, *went down* to it. Our Lord's

---

[1] State of the Departed, pp. 32, 35.

death took place upon the *surface* of the earth, where the human race inhabit; this, therefore, and *none higher*, is the place from which He 'descended;' of consequence, the place to which He went by descent was below it, and it is with relation to these 'parts' *below* the surface, that His rising to life on the third day must be understood. This was only a return from the *nether regions*, to the *realms of life and day*, from which He had ascended—*not* His ascension into Heaven, which was a subsequent event." And to this the Bishop adds, that "the writers of the Old Testament speak of such a common mansion in the *inner parts of the earth;* and we find the same opinion among the heathen writers of antiquity that it is more than probable it had its rise in the earliest patriarchal revelation than in the imagination of men, or in poetic fiction.[1]

Bishop LOWTH says: "A sort of popular notion prevailed among the Hebrews, as well as among other nations, that the life which succeeded the present was to be passed *beneath the earth:* and to this notion even the sacred prophets were obliged to allude occasionally, if they wished to be understood by the people."[2]

Bishop HOBART remarks: "This popular opinion, that the receptacles of departed souls were under the earth, arose from the use of the word "*descended,*" in reference to the passage of Christ into the place of departed Spirits."[3] The next point relates to

---

[1] Horsley's Sermons, vol. ii.   [2] Lowth on Hebrew Poetry, vol. i., page 163.
[3] State of the Departed, page 71.

9. The *division* of SHEOL or HADES *into two regions.* On this subject, Archbishop SECKER observes: That "the most common meaning, not only among the heathen, but Jews, and the first Christians, of the word (SHEOL or) HADES, translated Hell, was, in general, that invisible world, one part or another of which, the souls of the deceased, whether good or bad, inhabit." "In what part of space, or of nature that receptacle is, in which the souls of men continue from their death till they rise again, we scarce know at all; excepting, that we are sure it is divided into two extremely different regions, the dwelling of the *righteous,* called in St. Luke '*Abraham's bosom,*' where Lazarus was; and that of the *wicked,* where the *rich man was;* 'between which there is a great gulf fixed.' And we have *no* proof that our Saviour went on any account to the *latter:* but since he told the penitent thief that he should that day be with Him in Paradise, we are certain that He was in the *former,* where they, which die in the Lord, rest from their labors and are blessed, *waiting* for a still more perfect happiness at the resurrection of the last day."[1]

The famous Bishop BULL also says: "The souls of all the faithful, immediately after death, enter into a place and state of *bliss,* far exceeding all the felicities of the world, though short of that most consummate perfect beatitude of the kingdom of Heaven, with which they are to be crowned and rewarded in the *resurrection.* And so, on the contrary, the souls of the wicked are, presently after death, in a state of

---

[1] Lecture on the Catechism, page 9.

very *great misery;* and yet dreading a far greater misery at the day of judgment."[1]

10. The *location of Paradise* is the next subject in order. As this place was that in which the Redeemer declared that the penitent malefactor should be with Him on the day of His death, it will be interesting to trace the opinions of the learned as to its situation. We quote first from

Bishop HORSLEY. He remarks thus: "Paradise was certainly some place where our Lord was to be *on the very day* on which He suffered, and where the companion of His sufferings was to be *with* Him. It was not Heaven; for to Heaven our Lord ascended not till (forty days) *after* His resurrection, as appears from His own words to Mary Magdalene.[2] He was not therefore in Heaven on the day of His crucifixion. And, where HE was not, the *thief* could not be with Him. It was no place of *torment,* for to any such place the name of Paradise never was applied. It could be no other than the *region of repose or rest* (i. e., Sheol or Hades—Hell), where the souls of the righteous abide in joyful hope of the consummation of bliss."[3]

Dr. CAMPBELL, in his explanation of the parable of the rich man and Lazarus, observes: "The Jews did not indeed adopt the *Pagan* fables on this subject, nor did they express themselves entirely in the same manner; but the general train of thinking in both came pretty much to coincide. The Greek Hades ($ἅδης$) they found well adapted to ex-

---

[1] Bishop Bull's Works, vol. i., pages 102, 103: See also pages 126, 127.
[2] John xx. 17; Acts i. 3.   [3] Horsley's Sermons. Vol. ii. p. 91.

press the Hebrew Sheol. This they came to conceive as including different sorts of habitations for spirits of different characters. And though they did not receive the terms Elysium or Elysian fields, as suitable appellations for the region peopled by good spirits, they took instead of them, as better adapted to their own theology, the garden of Eden, or PARADISE, by which the word answering to garden, especially when applied to *Eden*, had commonly been rendered by the Seventy. To denote the same state, they sometimes used the phrase, "*Abraham's bosom*," a metaphor borrowed from the manner in which they reclined at meals." . . .
' According to this explication, Lazarus and Dives were *both* in HADES, though in very different situations; the former in the mansions of the happy; the latter in those of the wretched.

Dr. ADAM CLARKE, who interprets the passage in Acts ii. 27—"Thou wilt not leave my soul in HADES" (Hell), of the soul of Christ not being left in the state of separate spirits, on the subject in hand, remarks: That "the garden of Eden," mentioned Gen. ii. 8, is called from the Septuagint the Garden of Paradise. Hence the word has been translated into the New Testament, and is used to signify a place of *exquisite delight*. The word Paradise is not Greek, but is of Asiatic (Persian) origin. In Arabic and Persian, it signifies a garden, a vineyard, *the place of* the blessed. Our Lord's words intimate that this penitent thief should be immediately taken to the abode of the spirits of the just ;" i. e., of course, where Christ was, "in HADES, or Hell; where they should enjoy the presence and approbation of the Most High."[1]

Dr. WHITBY considers Paradise as "the place into which pious souls, *separated* from the body, were immediately received."[2]

Dr. DODDRIDGE also speaks of Paradise as the abode of happy spirits when *separated* from the body; that garden of God which is the seat of happy spirits, in the *intermediate* state, and during their separation from the body."[3]

Dr. MACKNIGHT states, that "the name Paradise was also given to the place," i. e., HADES, "where the spirits of the just, after death, reside in felicity *till the resurrection*, as appears from our Lord's words to the penitent thief."[4]

But, if Paradise, as an abode of *happiness* to departed spirits, is located in HADES, or Hell, this latter place being an *enemy* from which Christ is to redeem them—"I will *redeem* them from the power of (not the *grave*, as in our English version) but SHEOL or HADES (Hell); the question is, How are these apparently conflicting statements to be reconciled? Bishop HORSLEY replies thus: "The state of the departed saints, while they continue there," i. e., in SHEOL, "is a condition of *unfinished* bliss, in which the souls of the justified would not have remained for any time (if indeed they had ever entered it), had not sin introduced death. It is a state, therefore, consequent upon death; consequent, therefore, upon sin, though *no part of the punishment* of it. And the resurrection of

---

1. Com. on Luke xxiii. 43.
2. Com. on Luke xxiii. 43.
3. Doddridge on Luke xxiii. 43.
4. Com. on ii. Cor. xiii. 4.

the saints is often described as an *enlargement* of them by our Lord's power, from confinement in a place, not of punishment, but of *inchoate* enjoyment only. Our Lord will 'break the gates of brass, and cut the bars of iron in sunder,'[1] and set at liberty 'the prisoners of hope.'[2] And when this place (i. e., SHEOL or HADES, Hell) of safe keeping is *personified*, it is, consistently with these notions of it, represented as one of the enemies which Christ is to *conquer*." We now pass to

11. The *location of Tartarus*. On this subject, as distinguished from the situation of Paradise, Dr. LOWTH observes: "That the place where the *wicked*, after death, were supposed to be confined, was believed, from the destruction of the old world by the deluge, the covering of the asphaltic vale with the Dead Sea, etc., to be situated *under the waters*." To this "idea," which certainly very naturally accounts for the popular belief on the subject, "there are allusions in the sacred writings without number."[3] And hence, Dr. CAMPBELL says: "To express the unhappy state of the wicked in the intermediate state, they (i. e., the apostles) do not seem to have declined the use of the word TARTARUS. The apostle Peter says of *evil angels*, that 'God cast them down to Hell (*Tartarus*), and delivered them for chains under darkness, to be *reserved* unto judgment.'[4] So it stands in the common version, though neither GEHENNA nor HADES is in the original. . . . The word is *Tartarus*,

[1] Ps. cxvii. 16.
[2] Zech. ix. 12.
[3] Lowth's Lec. on Heb. Poetry, vol. 1.
[4] ii. Pet. ii. 4.

which is, as it were, the *prison* of HADES, wherein criminals are kept *till the general judgment*. And as in the ordinary use of the Greek word, it was comprehended under HADES, as a part, it ought, unless we had some positive reason to the contrary, by the ordinary rules of interpretation, to be understood so here. There is, then, no inconsistency in maintaining that the rich man, though in torments, was not in *Gehenna*, but in that part of HADES called *Tartarus*, where we have already seen that the spirits *reserved* for judgment are detained in darkness."[1] And,

12. In reference to the location of GEHENNA, as distinguished from Tartarus *in* HADES (Hell), Archbishop MAGEE gives a new rendering to the passage in Job xxvi. 5, 6 : " Hell [SHEOL] is naked before Him, and destruction hath no covering," thus : " The souls of the dead tremble ; [the places] below the waters, and their inhabitants" (verse 5). "The seat of spirits is naked before Him, and the region of destruction hath no covering." And he adds : " Here I take the *souls* of the dead, and the *inhabitants* of the places below the (abyss of waters) to bear to each other the same proportion, that is found in the next verse to subsist between *the seat* of spirits, and the *region* of destruction : those of the dead who were sunk in the *lower* parts of SHEOL,[2] being placed in the region of destruction or the GEHENNA of the later Jews. So that the passage, on the whole, conveys this—that nothing is, or can be, concealed from the all-seeing

---

[1] Com. on the Parable of the Rich Man and Lazarus. Luke xxiii. 43.
[2] See Deut. xxxii. 22 ; Job xxvi. 5, 6 ; Prov. xv. 11.

eye of God; that the souls of the dead [in Tartarus] tremble under His view, and the shades of the wicked sunk to the bottom of the abyss, can even there find *no* covering from His sight."[1]

13. On HADES, or "HELL," in "*the Apostles' creed.*" This creed, though doubted by some to have been compiled, as others allege, by the apostles themselves, yet is generally received by all Evangelical Christians, as containing a true exposition of the primitive faith. In it occurs that important and much litigated phrase concerning our blessed Lord— "*He descended into Hell.*"

Archbishop SECKER on this sentence remarks: "The most common meaning, not only among the heathen, but Jews, and the first Christians, of the word HADES, here translated Hell, was in general that *invisible* place, one part or other of which, the *souls* of the deceased, whether good or bad, inhabit."[2]

Bishop HORSLEY observes: "That these words of the creed, 'He descended into Hell,' declare what was done by His (Christ's) rational soul in its *intermediate* state." And on the passage in Acts ii. 27, upon which the article of the creed is founded—"Thou wilt not leave my soul in Hell," etc., he says: "From this text, if there were no other, the article, in the sense in which we have explained it, is clearly and infallibly deduced; for *if* the soul of Christ were not left in Hell *at* His resurrection, then it was in Hell *before*

---

[1] Dissertation on the History of the Book of Job.
[2] Lecture on the Catechism. Lec. 9.

His resurrection. But it was not there either *before* His death, or *after* His resurrection, for that never was imagined: therefore, it descended into Hell after His death, and before His resurrection; for as His flesh, by virtue of the Divine promise, saw no corruption, although it was in the grave, the place of corruption, where it remained *until* the resurrection; so His soul, which, by virtue of the same promise, was not left in Hell, was in Hell where it was not left, until the time came for its *reunion* to the body for the accomplishment of the resurrection. Hence it is so clearly evinced, that the *soul* of Christ was in the place called Hell, 'that none but an infidel,' saith Augustine, can deny it.'"[1]

Bishop BULL also, in his defense of the Nicene Faith, has a sermon on "the middle state of happiness and misery," in which he says: "All good men, without exception, are, in the whole interval between their death and resurrection, as to their *souls*, in a very happy condition; but after the resurrection they shall be yet more happy, receiving then their *full reward*," etc. "On the other side, all the wicked, as soon as they die, are very miserable as to their *souls*, and shall be yet *far more* miserable both in soul and body after the day of judgment, proportionably to the sins committed by them here on earth. This is the plain doctrine of the Holy Scriptures, and of the Church of Christ in its first and best ages, and this we may trust to."[2]

And so, the third of the xxxix articles of the ANGLICAN AND AMERICAN EPISCOPAL CHURCH, "As Christ died and was

[1] Horsley's Sermons, vol. ii. p. 88.   [2] Bp. Bull's Works, vol i. pp. 126, 127.

buried, so also it is believed He went down into *Hell,"* (Hades).

Bp. HORSLEY again remarks: "The terms in which the REFORMERS in this article state the proposition, imply that Christ's going down into Hell is a matter of no less importance to be believed, than that He died upon the cross for men;" and that "it is no less a plain matter of fact, in the history of our Lord's life and death, than the burial of His dead body." [1] And,

In the PRESBYTERIAN "CONFESSION OF FAITH," the Apostles' Creed is inserted entire on pages 347 and 348. And, on the article "He descended into Hell," it adds in a note thus: "i.e., continued in the *state* of the dead, and under the power of death, until the *third day*." This is also the language of the answer to the 50th question, in the "Larger Catechism," to which is added the following— "which hath been otherwise expressed in these words, 'He descended into *Hell*,'" [2] (Hades).

14. As it respects the *General Doctrine* of the intermediate state. Dr. MAGEE, with great force of argument, maintains the existence of a *region* for the abode of departed spirits, and of an intermediate state of the soul between its departure from this world and some *future* state of its being.[3]

Bp. HORSLEY maintains the position, that Christ descended into Hell, properly so called, to the *invisible* mansion of

---

[1] Horsley's Sermons, vol. ii. p. 87.

[2] Conf. of Faith, p. 177.

[3] See Discourse and Dissertation on the Doctrines of the Atonement and Sacrifice, note, p. 346, et seq.

departed spirits, and to that part of it where "the souls of the faithful, after they are delivered from the burden of the flesh, are in joy and felicity." [1] In the notes in his Commentary on the book of the prophet Hosea, the same doctrine is advanced.

Bp. HORNE, in his Commentary on Ps. x. 16, maintains the doctrine of the place of departed spirits. He says: "Although our mortal part must see corruption, yet it shall not be finally left under the power of the enemy; but shall be raised again and *reunited* to the old companion of the soul, which exists meanwhile in secret and undiscoverable regions, there waiting for the day when its REDEEMER shall triumph over corruption in His *mystical*, as He has already done in His *natural* body."

Sir PETER KING, in his "Critical History of the Apostles' Creed;" and Bp. NEWTON, the author of "Dissertations on the Prophecies, in the VIth volume of his works, both advocate this doctrine of an *intermediate* state.

Dr. WHITBY also, in many parts of his Commentary, and particularly on 2 Tim. iv. 8, advances many arguments from Scripture, to prove that the final and complete happiness of the righteous does not take place until *after* the judgment at the great day. He considers the immediate ascent of the soul to Heaven at death as a *heresy*, contradicted by Scripture, and by the faith of the primitive ages. And he quotes numerous passages from the fathers, to prove that the souls of good men remain till the day of judgment, in a

---

[1] Horsley's Sermons, vol. ii. p. 91.

certain place called *Heaven*, (i. e., what St. Paul calls "the *third Heaven*," and which has been shown to be identical with "Paradise," etc., located in Sheol or Hades), *expecting* the day of judgment and retribution.

The learned BINGHAM, speaking of the sense of the primitive church on this subject, says: "The soul is but in an imperfect state of happiness till the resurrection, when the *whole man* shall obtain a complete victory over death, and, by the last judgment, be established in an endless state of consummate happiness and glory." [1]

Dr. WHATELY and Dr. NICHOLS, in their respective Commentaries on "the Book of Common Prayer," assert the same doctrine; the latter interpreting the descent into Hell, of Christ's descent into *the place* of separate spirits.

Dr. HAMMOND says: "It is certain that some means of bliss, which shall, at the day of judgment, be vouchsafed the saints, when their bodies and souls shall be reunited, is not *till then* enjoyed by them." [2]

Dr. WALL goes on at considerable length, into a statement of the doctrine of the *intermediate* state, and of the opinions of the primitive Christians on this point.

Dr. DODDRIDGE, in several passages of his Commentary, shows his belief in this doctrine. He paraphrases on the text, Acts ii. 27,—"Thou wilt not leave my *soul* in Hell, while separated from the body, in *the unseen world*." And in a note, he observes, that "ᾄδης, (Hades, Hell), is generally put for the *state* of separate spirits," into which he considers Christ descended.

---

[1] Christian Antiq. Book xv. ch. iii. sec. 16.
[2] Hammond's Annotations on ii. Tim. i. 16.

The late JAMES P. WILSON, D. D., a distinguished clergyman of the Presbyterian Church, in a note on "Ridgeley's Body of Divinity," states that the Hebrew and Greek words [Sheol and Hades] translated *Hell*, (Ps. xvi. 10 ; Acts ii. 27), " are each taken for the *invisible world*, or separate state of the good as well as evil, both in the Old and New Testaments; and this was thought by the Jews and Gentiles to be *under the surface*." "Christ's descent into Hell," he observes, " therefore means, that His *soul*, when separated from the body, was immediately with the separate spirits who are *happy*, and so said to be in *Paradise*. But," he adds, " whether *above* or *below* the surface, is unimportant." [1]

It is evident from his Commentary on Matt. xi. 23, and on Acts ii. 27, that Dr. ADAM CLARKE considered that there is a *separate place and state* of the departed spirit between death and the resurrection. His criticism on the deriviation and import, originally, of the word Hell, from the Anglo-Saxon word Helan, to *cover over*, as opposed to the modern sense attached to it, shows that he understood it as a state and place entirely distinct from the *Gehenna* of future and eternal torments. And finally,

That this doctrine was advocated by the Rev. JOHN WESLEY, the founder of Methodism, is evident from his " Notes on the New Testament,"—Acts ii. 27 ; Rev. i. 18 ; vi. 8 ; and xx. 13, 14. For example : On Rev. i. 18,— " I have the keys of Hell and of Death," he observes, " that is, the *invisible world ;* the body abides in death, and the soul

---

[1] See Ridgeley's Body of Divinity. Am. Ed. Vol. ii. pp. 440, 441, and notes

in Hades." Again, Rev. xx. 13 : "and Death and Hell gave up the dead that were in them," etc, he explains : " Death gave up all the bodies of men, and Hades (Hell), the receptacle of separate souls, gave them up to be *reunited* to their bodies."

15. *Expositions of Particular Passages.*

(1.) Isaiah xiv. 9 : " *Hell* (Sheol) from beneath is moved for thee." The elder LOWTH remarks on these words, thus : "The Hebrew word Sheol, which our translators render Hell, or [improperly] the grave, signifies the state of the dead *in general*, and is indifferently applied to the good and the bad."

(2.) Ezekiel xxx. 8 ; and xxxi. 15, 16 : (which see) The same writer, in his Commentary, considers the prophet in these passages, as furnishing a poetical description of the *infernal regions*, where the spirits of deceased tyrants, with their subjects, are represented as coming to meet the king of Egypt, and his auxiliaries, upon their arrival to the same place : Hell here signifies the *state* of the dead."

Dr. MAGEE observes : that " this poetic imagery of Isaiah must be allowed to indicate amongst the Jews, the existence of a popular belief that there was a region for departed *souls* called Sheol, in which the Rephaim or *manes* took up their abode." He also furnishes us with an analysis of their opinions, (as given in detail by Vitringa, in opposition to Bp. Lowth's view, that the word Sheol in these passages means the grave), in which he says : "That the *souls* of men, when released from the body by death, pass into a vast subterranean region, as a common receptacle, but with different mansions, adapted to the different qualities of its inhabitants: and that here, preserving the shades and resemblances of the living, they fill the *same characters* that they did in life: and, that this entire region was called by the Jews Sheol, [the Greek word corresponding to which is Hades,] and by the Latins *Inferi*." [1]

(3.) Matt. xvi. 18. "On this rock I will build my church: and the *gates of Hell* shall not prevail against it." The learned Dr. PARKHURST remarks on this promise of our Lord, that, "it seems to be that His church on earth, however persecuted and despised, *shall never fail* till the consummation of all things, and should then, at the resurrection of the just, *finally triumph* over death and the grave." [2]

Dr. DODDRIDGE gives the same construction to this passage, and observes: "It is most certain that the phrase παλαι αδου, does generally, in the Greek writers, signify the entrance into the *invisible world*."

Dr. CAMPBELL, in his " Preliminary Dissertation" prefixed to his translation of the " four Gospels," and Dr. WHITBY on this text, prove, at great length, that the expression, " the gates of Hades, denotes, both among the Jewish and Christian writers, the *invisible world*," and they establish the construction of the text already given.

(4.) Acts ii. 27, in *connection* with Ps. xvi. 10. See on this, the quotation from the Rev. James P. Wilson's note to Ridgeley's Body of Divinity, page 164.

---

[1] Magee on the Atonement and Sacrifice, p. 346, et seq.
[2] Parkhurst's Greek Lex., Art. *Hades*.

On the same, *separately*. See Dr. DODDRIDGE's paraphrase, page 156 and 163. Also the Rev. John Wesley and Dr. ADAM CLARKE, on this and the collateral passages, together with Bp. HORNE, on Ps. xvi. 16.

We have in a previous page, adduced the evidence, that if we *deny* the descent of the soul of Christ, properly so called, into Hades, we relinquish the principal argument in support of the doctrine of the *real incarnation* of our Lord, against the heretics, ancient and modern, who have impugned it. On this subject, Bp. PEARSON observes : " The true doctrine of the incarnation, against all the enemies thereof—Apollinarians, Nestorians, Eutychians, and the like, was generally expressed by declaring the *verity of the soul of Christ really in Hell*," i. e., as set forth in the above passage ; and the *verity of His body*, at the same time, *really present in the grave*." [1]

(5.) Hebrews xi. 40.—" God having provided some better thing for us, that they *without* us should not be made *perfect*." Dr. MACKNIGHT, in his note on this passage, remarks : " The apostle's doctrine, that believers are all to be rewarded together, and at the same time, is agreeable to Christ's declaration, who told His disciples that they were not to come to the place He was going away to prepare for them, TILL He returned from Heaven, to carry them to it. (John xiv. 3.) . . Further. That the righteous are not to be rewarded, TILL ' the end of the world,' [not $\varkappa o \sigma \mu o s$, earth or globe, but $\alpha\iota\bar{\omega}\nu\omega s$, *age*, or *dispensation*], is evident from Christ's words," Matt. xiii. 40, 43.

---

[1] Pearson on the Creed. Vol. ii. p. 306.

Bp. Hobart says: "In like manner, St. Peter hath told us, that the righteous are to be made glad with their reward, 'AT the revelation of Christ,' (1 Pet. iv. 13), when they are to 'receive a crown of glory that fadeth not away.' (1 Pet. v. 4.) John also tells us, that '*when* He shall appear, we shall be made *like unto Him*, for we shall see Him as He is.'" (1 John iii. 2). So also Dr. Whitby's note on 2 Tim. iv. 8, which see. Bp. Hobart adds: "This determination, *not* to reward the righteous ancients without us, is highly proper: because the power and veracity of God will be most illustriously exhibited in the view of angels and of men, by raising the whole of Abraham's [believing] seed from the dead *at once*, and by introducing them into the heavenly country *in a body*, after a public acquittal at the judgment, than if each were made perfect *separately*, at their death."[1]

Dr. Doddridge on this text remarks: "The apostle refers this perfection, which the saints of the Old Testament do not *now* enjoy, but which they shall inherit with us, to the glory of the heavenly state, interpreting the words, 'they without us might not be made perfect,' of God's purpose of bringing all His children together to the *full consummation* of their hopes in Christ Jesus His Son, AT THE TIME of His final and triumphant appearing."

Dr. Whitby, in harmony with the primitive fathers, also maintains from this passage, that the souls of the Old Testament saints, as well as those who have died under the Christian dispensation, are not "exalted to the *highest* heavens,"

---

[1] State of the Departed, pp. 21, 22.

and that they "had not received their *full* reward; yea, that they were not to expect it *till* the day of judgment." And,

The Rev. JOHN WESLEY, in his Notes on this passage, observes: "Though they, (the Old Testament saints) obtained a good testimony, yet *did not* receive the great promise, the Heavenly inheritance,—'God having provided some better thing for us,' namely, everlasting glory,—'that they without us should not be made perfect;' that is, that we might all be perfected *together* in Heaven." Finally,

(6.) On Rev. i. 18; vi. 8; xx. 13, 14, we have only to add to the expositions of them already given, (which see), that Dr. DODDRIDGE considers the word *Hell*, (Hades), in all of them, as denoting the *separate state*. And Dr. THOMAS SCOTT unequivocally avows its existence. His comments are as follows: "The grave and separate state," [i. e. Keber, or Taphos, and Sheol or Hades], "represented as *two persons*, will be cast into the lake of fire: that is, they shall subsist *no longer*, to receive the bodies and the souls of men."

We add in conclusion to the above quotations, one more,

(16.) On the subject of *the Romish doctrine of Purgatory*. The sermon of Bp. BULL, (from which Dr. DODDRIDGE quotes with approbation), in which he establishes this doctrine of a place and state of departed souls, contains a refutation of the Papal dogma of Purgatory, and shows the *entire difference* between it and the doctrine which he advocates of an intermediate state. After presenting a view of the faith of the primitive Church on this point, he says:

"From what has been said, it appears that the doctrine

of the distinction of the joys of Paradise, the portion of good souls in that state of separation, from that yet fuller and most complete beatitude of the Kingdom of Heaven, after the resurrection, consisting in that clearest vision of God, which the Holy Scriptures call seeing Him 'face to face,' is far from being *popery*, as some have ignorantly censured it; for we see it was the current doctrine of the *first and purest* ages of the Church. I add, that it is so far from being popery, that it is *directly* the contrary. For it was the popish convention of Florence," [in the xvth century], "which *first* boldly defined against the sense of the primitive Christians, that those souls, which, having contracted the blemish of sin, are, either in their bodies or out of them, purged from it, do presently go into Heaven, and there clearly behold God himself, one God in three Persons, as He is. And this decree they made, partly to establish their superstition of prayer to the saints deceased, whom they would needs make us believe, to see and know all our necessities and concerns *in speculo Trinitatis*, in the glass of the Trinity, as they call it, and so to be fit objects of our religious invocation; but chiefly to introduce their *Purgatory*, and that the prayers of the ancient Church for the dead might be thought to be founded on the supposition, that the souls of some faithful persons, after death, go into a place of grievous torment." [1]

We here bring to a close our Scriptural and Historical exhibit of the doctrine of an intermediate place and state of

[1] Bp. Bull's Sermons. Vol. i. p. 114.

the dead, both of the righteous and the wicked, between death and the resurrection. It is founded, as has been shown, upon the apostle Peter's statement, that the "INHE-RITANCE," which God has provided for His saints collectively, is an inheritance "*reserved in Heaven* for them ;" and hence that, as such, they cannot be admitted to its full, complete, and perfect possession and enjoyment at the instant of death. Also, that the same holds true of the apostate angels and ungodly men, who are declared to be "*reserved for chains under darkness* against (or unto) the day of judgment." It follows, inevitably, by implication, that—unless *man*, like "the brutes that perish," was created *mortal*, and is subject to *annihilation* at the instant of death, or after—while his *body* "sleeps in the dust of the earth ;" his *soul*, whether in a justified or condemned state, must pass into a condition of *conscious* existence somewhere, to await his *final* consummated destiny of bliss or of woe.

Against the modern heresy of the *annihilationists*, as built upon the alleged hypothesis that man, being created *mortal*, and hence that the soul only is the man, or person ; and that the soul, falling under the original penalty of sin, dies or becomes *extinct* at the instant of death ; we claim to have demonstrated in Section I, that man was created a *complex* being, his proper personality consisting of his being constituted of body *and* soul. Also that, in order to preserve intact man's proper personality as a complex being in the present and future life, a *resurrection* awaits his body after death, while his soul, being then *reunited* to the body, he enters upon his *final* destiny of happiness or misery.

It was further shown, that, consequent of the fact of the *reservation* of the inheritance of the saints till the resurrection morn, and also of lost angels and men till the judgment day, is the Scriptural doctrine regarding the *local habitation* occupied by each, during the intervals of their entrance upon their respective final or eternal states. Having therefore produced the Scriptural evidence, in Section II. of the *existence* of a separate place and state of the souls of men after death; accompanied with a refutation of all the popular arguments urged against it: Section III. was devoted to a critical exegesis of *all the terms* employed in the Old and New Testaments respecting them. It was there shown, that while the Hebrew word SHEOL and the Greek word HADES, were used by the Jews, by the Seventy, and by Christ and His Apostles, to denote *the abode of departed souls generally;* (the Hebrew word for *grave* being KEBER, and *never* SHEOL; and the Greek word for *grave* being TAPHOS, and *never* HADES); yet that the *region* denoted by these terms was divided into two apartments; the one, the abode of the *happy*, designated by the early patriarchs as being "gathered unto their fathers," or "to their people;" and by the later Jewish writers, by the terms "Paradise"—"Abraham's bosom"—"the third Heavens," etc. The other, the abode of the *lost*, being denominated by the Jewish writers *before* the Babylonish captivity, "the congregation of the dead," or "Cœtus Gigantum," or "in Cœtu Rephaim;" and by those *after* that period, by the terms TOPHET and *Tartarus*. While, on the other hand, the Hebrew and Greek word used to signify the place and state of *final torments*, was in *no* instance either Sheol or Hades, but GEHENNA.

We submit, therefore—and this is our apology for dwelling thus at length on this subject—that a Scriptural answer to the question, WHERE IS HEAVEN? necessarily involves an inquiry into, and a determination of, *the place and state or condition* of the departed between death and the resurrection. For, unless what we have said regarding it can be proven fallacious, then, the "Heaven" *in* which the "reserved inheritance of the saints" is, can neither be "Paradise," nor "Abraham's bosom," nor "the third Heaven." And this brings us to a direct examination of the *main subject* of Part I. in these inquiries, under—

CHAPTER III.

"An Inheritance . . . Reserved in Heaven."

QUESTION.

In what Heaven is the Deferred Inheritance of the Saints Located?

FAITH IN THINGS UNSEEN.

> " I have seen
> A curious child, that dwelt upon a track
> Of inland ground, applying to his ear
> The convolutions of a smooth-lippéd shell,
> To which, in silence hushed, his very soul
> Listened intently ; and his countenance soon
> Brightened with joy ; for, murmuring from within
> Were heard, sonorous cadences ! whereby
> To his belief, the monitor expressed
> Mysterious union with its native sea—
> E'en such a shell the universe itself
> Is to the eye of Faith."—*Wordsworth.*

DR. HARBAUGH on this subject, thus expresses himself : "The world of eternal blessedness and glory, called—in respect to its locality— HEAVEN, is alluded to in the Scriptures under a great variety of names, which designate it *as a locality*. It is the Heaven of heavens—it is our Father's House— it is the throne of God, to which the earth is a footstool—it is the Holiest Place—it is the City of God, the New Jerusalem—it is the Paradise of God—the Inheritance of the saints in light—it is the place to which Christ has gone; the place which He has prepared for His saints, and where it is His will that they shall be with Him to behold His glory, the glory which he had with the Father before the world was. It is a place far above all heavens—far above all principalities and powers, and above every name that is named. It is the place where God, the blessed and only Potentate, dwells in light which no man can approach unto—the glorious central presence of Him of whom the Shekinah itself is but a shade," [1] etc.

Now, it is, we deferentially submit, by a confounding of things which differ, when treating of this momentous subject—and of which the above is an illustration,—that has produced in the minds of the devoutly pious so much of confusion and perplexity, in regard to any just conceptions of the *locality* of that place of Heavenly blessedness to which their faith and hope aspires. Here we have, for example, the saints of God, at the instant of death, admitted to that "place to which Christ has gone," and " where God the blessed and only Potentate dwells," "far above all heavens," etc., when we are expressly told that " *no man can approach unto*" God, and that "*no man hath seen, nor can see*" [2] Him, in " *the Heaven of heavens.*" This class of writers obviously overlook the distinction instituted by the apostle Peter, between "the *inheritance* of the saints" and "*heaven.*" The

[1] Harbaugh on Heaven, pages 125-126. [2] Tim. vi. 16.

inheritance is spoken of as being "IN Heaven." Clearly, therefore, the inheritance is one thing: Heaven, another. The idea of locality belongs to the "*inheritance,*" which floats amid some one or other of "the Heaven of heavens" of infinite space. Hence, in order to determine the question, In which of these heavens the "reserved" inheritance of the saints is located, we must fix upon THE Heaven "*in*" which it is said to be.

Let it be observed, then, that the terms, atmosphere, air, and heavens, are often used without any definite idea as to their nature or import. They are, however, all resolvable into the same thing. For instance. We speak of an æronaut, who is raised to the distance of one, three, or five miles from the earth, that he has ascended so far into the *atmosphere, air,* or *heaven.* And, could the intrepid voyager continue his upward flight for myriads of miles beyond the most distant star, either phrase would be equally applicable to the boundless region which surrounded him.

And yet, these terms have a meaning appropriate to each, and are divided into *distinct regions,* adapted to the existence of those orders of living creatures, or beings, as the case may be, which is best adapted to the manifestation of the glory of Him who created them. This accounts for the fact that the apostle Paul, ii Cor. xii. 2, speaks of at least *three separate and distinct heavens.* It will repay us to examine, briefly, what light may be gathered from the Scriptures regarding them.

1. There is the *lower,* or *sublunary Heaven, air,* or *atmosphere,* or that respirable fluid which BEGIRTS OUR EARTH, and

which reaches scarcely more than *fifty miles* beyond its surface. In this Heaven may be seen the clouds, meteors, etc., together with those living creatures mansioning therein, as the *fowls* of Heaven.[1] Then also, in this same sublunary heaven, dwell those *invisible* beings, the satanic "prince of *the power of the air*, who worketh in the children of disobedience,"[2] together with those demoniacal "spirits" who do his bidding amid "the principalities and powers and spiritual wickedness in high places," called "the *rulers of the darkness of this world.*"[3] Then there is,

II. The *starry Heavens*, or stellar universe. Philosophically, this is the same as the other, only rarified to a vastly higher degree. Indeed, it is so attenuated, that, stretching throughout the whole region of the stars, it is powerless in absorbing the light of the sun, distant from the earth 95,000,000 of miles, and producing no effect except upon the light of the stars, after a progress of millions of millions of miles.[4] And, according to St. Paul's enumeration, there is,—

III. "*The third Heaven.*" This is the same with the "Paradise," to which he was "caught up," (or rather caught away), during his rapture. As to this region, the language of the apostle, Eph. iv. 9,—"Now that He (i.e., Christ) ascended, what is it but that he also descended first into the lower parts of the earth," clearly indicates, as has already been shown, where we are to look for it. It teaches us that, as

---

[1] Consult Job xxvi. 8; Gen. i. 20; xxvii. 28; James v. 8. [2] Eph. ii. 2.
[3] Eph. vi. 12. [4] Consult Gen. i. 14-19; Deut. ix. 19.

to the *motion* of Christ's " descent into the lower parts of the earth," while His body was in the sepulchre, His soul was in " Paradise," where the penitent thief was joined with Him, that is, " in *Hell*," (Hades). For, as our Lord's death took place upon the surface of the earth, this must have been the place whence He descended into the region *below* it. His ascent, therefore, must have been from the nether regions, Sheol or Hades, to the realms of light on the third day. It follows, hence, that we are not to look for " the third Heaven," either in the sublunary or the steller heavens of space.

Nor will it avail, in reference to St. Paul's statement of being " caught up into the third Heaven," and being " caught up into Paradise," to allege, as some writers do, that these are two distinct places. The hypothesis on which this is affirmed to rest, is, that the apostle " speaks of two distinct visions ; " and hence that "the scenes in these visions—the third heavens and Paradise—are not necessarily the same," etc. True, his words are, " I will come to visions and revelations," in the plural. But the question is, had he more than *one rapture ?* If not, the one rapture may admit of *many visions*, like the *one " dream "* of Nebuchadnezzar.[1] Besides, why limit St. Paul's visions to *two* only ? For he says : " Lest I should be exalted above measure through the *abundance* of my revelations," etc. ; an expression, surely, which implies many more than two. So much, then, for the confounding of the rapture, with the visions and abundance of revelations of which *it* was the occasion.

[1] Dan. ii. 1, et seq.

The same reasoning will apply to the confusion produced by those expositors—Dr. Whitby, Bp. Bull, Dr. Doddridge, Dr. Campbell, and others—who confound "*the Paradise of God,*" Rev. ii. 7, with "*the Holy City,* or *New Jerusalem,*" Rev. xxi. 2, 10. For, this latter, unlike "Paradise," or "the third Heaven," into which St. Paul says he was "caught up," St. John explicitly declares that he "saw coming down from God *out of* Heaven."

Here then we have, first, the *sublunary* Heaven, or that which surrounds our earth. Second, the *starry* or steller Heaven, in which float the sun, moon, and stars. And third, "Paradise," or "*the third Heaven,*" the Sheol or Hades of the Old and New Testaments, where "rest" those who "sleep in Jesus," in expectancy of "a part in the first resurrection."

But, we now observe, that in addition to these three Heavens, the Scriptures speak of another, under the appellation of,

IV. "THE HEAVEN OF HEAVENS." Now, this phraseology, which involves the idea of comparison, clearly indicates that region of infinite space which, in its relation to the others, is entitled to the denomination of the "*highest,*" *supernal*, or *empyreal* Heaven, in the same sense in which the uncreated and eternal "I am," is declared to be the "GOD *of gods*"—"LORD *of lords,*" etc.

Our first remark on this subject, is, that the Scriptures in numerous places associate God, Christ, angels, and the redeemed, with this word, "*Heaven.*" Not, however, as we shall see, that they are all represented as bearing *the same relations* to that Heaven. It is by neglecting to properly discriminate between these relations, and the *adaptedness* of the Heavenly spheres to their respective natures, conditions, prerogatives, and the like, which has produced so much confusion in the popular mind, in regard to *the* " Heaven *in* " which is "reserved" the promised "Inheritance of the saints."

We observe, then : as it respects " the Heaven of heavens," or that infinite space which surrounds and encompasses all others, Moses speaks of it thus :—" Behold, the Heaven, and the Heaven of heavens, is the Lord's thy God."[1] The boundless extent of this Heaven of heavens is indicated in the words of the prophet Jeremiah : " If the Heaven above can be measured,"[2] etc. Now, let us take into view that declaration,

1. " GOD IS A SPIRIT." As such, of Him it is affirmed, as " the blessed and only Potentate, the King of kings and the Lord of lords, who only has immortality," that " *no man*" can approach unto ; whom *no man* hath seen nor can see." We are however reminded that of Moses and Aaron, etc., it is said, that they " *saw* the God of Israel." But to this it may be replied, that the inspired Lawgiver explains—" And the Lord *spake* unto you out of the midst of the fire ; ye *heard the voice* of the words, but saw *no* similitude : *only* ye heard a voice."[3] The Scriptures therefore declare in the most explicit terms, that as God, the Eternal Spirit, in His

[1] Deut. x. 14 ; Ps. cxv. 16.   [2] Jer. xxxi. 37.
[3] Deut. iv. 12.

indivisible, incorporeal essence, *has never been approached by mortals*, so, throughout eternal ages, He *never can or will be*.

Nor can we assign to God as an Infinite Spirit, a *local habitation*. Does Job demand, "Is not God in the *height* of Heaven?"[1] And does he declare, that "He walketh in the *circuit* of Heaven?"[2] David calls upon us to "extol Him that *rideth* upon the Heaven."[3] While Jehovah himself demands, "Do not I *fill* Heaven and Earth?"[4] Hence the exclamation of the Psalmist: "Whither shall I go from Thy Spirit? or whither shall I flee from Thy presence? If I ascend up into *Heaven*, Thou art there; if I make make my bed in *Hell* (SHEOL), Thou art there also; if I take the wings of the morning, and dwell in the *uttermost parts of the sea*, even there shall Thy hand lead me, and Thy right hand shall hold me; and if I say, surely the *darkness* shall cover me; even the darkness shall be light about me. Yea, the darkness hideth not from Thee; but the night shineth as the day: the darkness and the light are both alike to Thee."[5] Yea, "He dwelleth in the uttermost parts of the sea."[6] Hence, of this Infinite Spirit it is declared, that it is "He that *buildeth His stories*" (marg., spheres or ascensions) "in the Heavens,"[7] piling up, so to speak, heaven upon the top of heaven; His presence everywhere; His circumference nowhere.

1 Job xxii. 12. 2 Ib. v. 14. 3 Ps. lxviii. 4. 4 Jer. xxiii. 24.
5 Ps. cxxxix. 8—12. 6 Ib. lxviii. 4. 7 Amos ix. 6.

WHERE IS GOD?

Where is He? Ask His emblem,
　　The glorious, glorious sun,
Who gilds the round world with his beams
　　Ere the day's long course has run.
Where is He? Ask the stars that keep
　　Their nightly watch on high:
Where is He? Ask the pearly dews,
　　The tear-drops of the sky.

Where is He? Ask the secret founts
　　That feed the boundless deep;
The dire simoon, or the soft night breeze
　　That lulls the earth to sleep.
Where is He? Ask the storm of fire
　　That bursts from Ætna's womb;
And ask the glowing lava flood,
　　That makes the land a tomb.

Where is He? Ask the maelstrom's whirl,
　　Shivering tall pines like glass:
Ask the giant oak, the graceful flower,
　　Or the simplest blade of grass.
Where is He? Ask behemoth,
　　Who drinketh rivers dry;
The ocean king, leviathan,
　　Or the scarce seen atom fly.

Where is He? Ask the awful calm
　　On Mountain tops that rest;
And the bounding, thundering avalanche,
　　Rent from their ragged crests.

Ask the wide wasting hurricane,
   Careering in its might;
The thunder crash, the lightning blaze,
   Earth all convulsed with light.

Where is He? Ask the crystal isles
   On arctic seas that sail;
Or ask from lands of balm and spice,
   The perfume breathing gale.
Where in the universe is found
   That presence-favored spot?
All, all proclaim His dwelling place,
   And say,—WHERE IS HE NOT."   *Anon.*

And *there*, where "He has set His glory above the earth and the heavens,"[1] it is said, that "the Heavens do rule,"[2] an expression denotive of Him who governs all worlds. And He declares, "Heaven is my throne, and the earth is my footstool;"[3] while St. Paul speaks of the throne of the Majesty *in the Heavens.*"[4]

And if it be asked—Is God, as an Infinite Spirit, seated on a *material* throne? The reply is, that this cannot be said of Him as such. And hence, if there were no other medium of attaining a knowledge of Him, the words of Job— "Behold I go forward, but He is not there; and backward, but I cannot perceive Him: on the left hand, where He doth work, but I cannot behold Him; He hideth Himself on my right hand, that I cannot see Him;"[5] would forever have

---

[1] Ps. viii. 1; cxiii. 4; cxlviii. 13.   [2] Dan. iv. 26.
[3] Isa. lxvi. 1.   [4] Heb. viii. 1.
[5] Job xxiii. 8, 9.

holden true in regard to *all* created intelligences, whether angelic or human. No: the Eternal God, as an *infinitely spiritual* Being, can only make himself known to His creatures, by a MANIFESTATION of Himself through His works. These works of God embrace the vast fields of creation, and Providence, and Grace. Through the first, "the invisible things of the eternal power and Godhead are clearly seen, being understood by the things that are made."[1] Through the second, we read, that "He is the Governor among the nations,"[2] and that "He satisfieth the desire of every living thing" in air, and earth, and sea.[3] But, in an especial manner, third, has God, "according to His eternal purpose"[4] and for "His own glory," been pleased to manifest Himself,

2. In a DIVINE PERSON INCARNATE—the Lord Jesus Christ. In Christ, therefore, we have, as it were, the *shrine* of the otherwise invisible Deity, that He might thereby "*make all men see* what is the fellowship of the mystery, which, from the beginning of the world hath been hid in God, who created all things by Jesus Christ: to the intent, that now unto the principalities and powers in heavenly places, might be known BY THE CHURCH, the manifold wisdom of God."[5]

Thanks, eternal thanks therefore to the Grace of the Infinite "Majesty in the Heavens" supernal, ours is not an "unknown," but a manifested God—"GOD MANIFEST IN THE

---

[1] Rom. i. 20.   [2] Ps. xxii. 28.   [3] Ib. civ. 14, 21; 25; cxlv. 16.
[4] Eph. iii. 11.   [5] Eph. iii. 9, 10.

FLESH :"[1] And also that, "in the heavenly places" of that *infinite space* which encircles all the heavens, there are "principalities and powers" innumerable!

"PRINCIPALITIES." Aye, and they are *material*. They comprehend those worlds on worlds, which, like so many sparkling diamonds under the feet of the Infinite "Majesty," make up "as it were the body of Heaven in its clearness"— Yes, we repeat: God's great mosaic work of the material universe, that shine in resplendent glory both in the sublunary and stellar regions.

"POWERS." Aye, even that "*innumerable company of angels*," whose "train fills the temple" of Him who "dwelleth in light which no man can approach unto."[3]

Nor can these "angels" be *purely spiritual* beings. None but God himself can be possessed of *pure* spirituality. They are *created* beings; and creation forms the great and impassable BOUNDARY LINE between the Infinite and the finite. Hence David says of "the Most High," "Who maketh His angels *spirits*, His ministers *a flame of fire*." Here, the terms "angels" and "ministers" are used interchangeably to denote the *same* beings; while that of "spirits" refer to their *intellectual*, and that of "flames of fire" to the *corporeal vehicle* through which they exercise their functions on such occasions of their manifestations as God may please. This angelic corporiety, however, being of a far more refined and exalted nature than that of the human, renders them imperceptible to

---

[1] Acts xvii. 23; 1 Tim. iii. 16.

[3] On these sublime passages, consult Nehem. ix. 6; 1 Kings xxii. 19; Isa. vi. 1-3; 1 Tim. vi. 15, 16.

our grosser natural vision, except in those instances in the sacred records where it has been so intensified as to enable men to perceive them.

But it is urged against this view, that our Lord says: "Despise not one of these little ones; for in Heaven their angels do always behold the face of My Father, which is in Heaven."[1] To this we reply, that it is the "*angels*," who "are sent forth" to them as "ministering spirits," who are said "always to behold the face of their Father in Heaven," and *not* the "little ones." It is on the above passage upon which is founded the popular idea of a transformation, in Heaven, of the *human* into the *angelic* nature. But the words of the poet—

———"I would be an angel," etc.

is a misnomer. The Scriptures no where teach, that the human shall ever be *changed into* the angelic. This would be to totally destroy *all distinction* between the two orders of beings, which cannot be. The passage which declares that, in the resurrected state, the saints shall be "*equal unto* the angels,"[2] is to be understood, *not* of the change of the human into the angelic, but, that they shall be "equal unto" them as it regards both their intellectual and corporeal *functions*.

Here then we have, so to speak, an inspired photographic picture of the innumerable *material* "principalities" of the stellar universe "IN the heavenly places," above and over

[1] Matt. xviii. 10.   [2] Luke xx. 36.

which, "upholding all things by the word of His power,"[1] sits enthroned, in ineffable glory, "THE MAJESTY in the heavens," adored, worshiped, and served, not by *human*, but by that angelic "host," who, though of a higher condition than man's in his fallen sinful state, (for man was created, for " a little season, lower than the angels"[2]) are nevertheless *corporeal* beings. And hence, the adaptation of their natures to those *material* "principalities" through which, as the "powers" thereof, they continually roam.

THE HEAVENLY PRINCIPALITIES.

" Bright diamonds in yon blue expanse,
    Immeasurably broad !
Attendants on night's cooling shade,
    Ye speak your MAKER—God !

Shedding around the traveler's path
    A faint, yet welcome light ;
And casting o'er this spacious earth
    The requiem blush of night.

Yes ! while all nature sleeps in peace,
    Ye shoot a kindly ray ;
To show some pilgrim, all forlorn,
    His solitary way !

And ye, like Heaven-born modesty,
    Do shun the glare of day ;
Nor are ye seen while yet the sun
    Emits his powerful ray.

---

[1] Heb. i. 3.   [2] Ps. viii. 5; Heb. ii. 7, 9. See on this, pp. 34-37.

Ye gems of yon ethereal sky,
  (Fix'd by a hand Divine),
Teach me to raise my thoughts on high,
  Where Heavenly glories shine.

Oh! may I seek, and seeking, find,
  By ardent, earnest prayer,
JESUS, the Prince of grace and peace,
  'THE BRIGHT AND MORNING STAR.'"

Aliquis.

THE HEAVENLY POWERS.

"Ye angels who stand round the throne,
  And view my IMMANUEL's face,
In rapturous songs make Him known,
  Tune, tune your sweet harps to His praise.
HE formed you the spirits you are,
  So happy, so noble, so good;
While others sunk down in despair,
  Confirmed by HIS power, ye stood."   *Watts.*

But, we now pass from these "principalities and powers," to resume the subject as connected with the Lord Jesus Christ—"GOD MANIFESTED IN THE FLESH."

THE INCARNATION.

"O, wonder-working God,
  What germs of life are Thine!
That THOU shouldst lodge in this poor clod,
  And make its substance Thine!"

THE PRESENCE OF THE LORD.

1 Kings xiv. 11, 12.

The whirlwind rides on the wings of the storms,
The rush of its light the blue heavens deforms,
The forests are broken before its career:
'Tis the *power of the Lord*, but the Lord is not there.

The earthquake is rending the mountains and rocks,
The valleys are trembling before its wild shocks;
'Tis the *arm of the Lord* that is bared in His might,
But the Lord remains hid in pavilions of light.

The fiery-eyed lightnings are flashing afar,
The thunders are pouring their peals through the air;
'Tis the *shout* of His anger, the *glance* of His sword,
But Jehovah is absent—still comes not the Lord.

Yet hark ! He's REVEALED—there's a voice still and small, [1]
Comes forth from the desert, and whispers to all,—
Bow down to the dust, and give ear to His word,
For JEHOVAH is present—THE MANIFEST GOD !" [2]

This subject has to do with the LORD JESUS CHRIST, in connection with what Holy Scripture reveals of—

HIS RELATIONS TO THE HEAVENS.

A proper understanding of this matter, is indispensable to a determination of THE Heaven *in* which the promised "inheritance of the saints" is located. It involves a consideration of the relations of our blessed Lord to the Heavens, both in His pre-existent and in His incarnated states; and

---

[1] See Isa. xlii. 2. [2] Altered from the original.

also in reference to the latter, both to His suffering and His risen glorified Humanity.

FALSE PHILOSOPHY—AN APPEAL.

> " Here begin
> Thy search, Philosopher, and thou shalt win
> Thy way deep down into the soul. The light
> Shed in by God shall open to thy sight
> Vast powers of being ; *regions left untrod*
> *Shall stretch before thee,* FILLED WITH LIFE AND GOD :
> And faculties come forth, and put to shame
> Thy vain and curious reasonings."
>
> R. H. Dana.

1. First, then : Of our Lord's *pre-existent* relations to the Heavens. As has been said, " the *invisible* things" that appertain to the " eternal power and Godhead," relate to the GOD TRIUNE, in His ineffable spiritual essence. Hence of Jesus, as the *second* person in the adorable Trinity, the inspired Solomon, who appropriates to Him the title of " wisdom," in speaking of His *pre-existent* relation to the Father, represents Him as saying : " The Jehovah possessed me in the beginning of His way, before His works of old. I was set up from everlasting, from the beginning, or ever the earth was. When there were no depths I was brought forth . . while as yet He had not made the earth, nor the fields, nor the highest parts of the dust of the world. When He prepared the Heavens, *I was there;* when He set a compass upon the face of the deep," etc., . . . " then was I by Him, as one brought up with Him, and I was daily His de-

light, *rejoicing always before Him.*"[1] Agreeably to this representation, John the Baptist testified of Him: "No man hath seen God at any time; the only Begotten Son, which is *in the bosom* of the Father, He hath REVEALED Him."[2] And so also, Jesus Himself speaks of "the glory which He had with the Father *before* the world was."[3] And again: "*Before* Abraham was, I AM."[4] And again: "I and my Father *are one*"[5]—as the Athanasian Creed has it—"God *of* God, light *of* light, very God *of* very God, Begotten, not made, being of one substance with the Father, *by whom* (i. e., Jesus Christ) all things were made,"[6] etc.: and hence, declared by St. Paul to be "the brightness of the Father's glory, and the express image of His person,"[7] "in whom *dwelt all the fulness* of the Godhead bodily."[8]

Such, then, was the Lord Jesus Christ, when enthroned *with* the Father above, and over, and amid those "principalities and powers *in* the Heavenly places," in His pre-existent state. But,

2. "The fulness of the time" at length came, when, "according to the eternal purpose which God purposed in Christ Jesus our Lord" concerning His taking upon Himself the *limitations of creaturehood* as "the woman's promised seed,"[9] He "sent forth His Son, made of a woman, made under the law, that He might redeem them that were under the law."[10] This involved a change in the THEATRE OF ACTION on the part of Jesus as "God manifest in the flesh," in His *suffering*

[1] Prov. viii. 22-31. [2] John i. 18. [3] Ib.—xvii. 5. [4] Ib.—viii. 57, 58.
[5] Ib.—x. 30. [6] See Athanasian Creed. [7] Heb. i. 3.
[8] Col. ii. 9. [9] Gen. iii. 15. [10] Gal. iv. 4.

Humanity. Hence His descent from the "highest" or empyreal Heaven, into the circumambient or sublunary Heaven and earth, concerning which He declares: "*I came down from* Heaven, not to do mine own will, but the will of Him that sent me."[1] And so we read: "The Word Λογος, (God) was made flesh, and *dwelt among us*, and we beheld His glory, the glory as of the only begotten of the Father, full of grace and truth."[2] But we must go on to observe,

3. That the great work of Christ's "one offering of Himself for sin"[3] upon the cross, whereby He "perfected for ever them that are sanctified,"[4] being accomplished, on the fortieth day after His resurrection, He again *returned*, in His glorified Humanity, into the "*highest*" or *empyreal Heaven*.[5] Yea, and there He must *remain*, "until the times of restitution of all things which God hath spoken by the mouth of all His holy prophets, since the world began."[6]

It is quite superfluous to remark, that the *Humanity* of the Lord Jesus had *never before* been in this "highest" Heaven. But now, He takes His seat, not, mark, on His own, but on His *Father's* throne, at His right hand.[7] And that for the purpose, not to reign as a king, but to continue His official work as an "High Priest over the house of God" to "MAKE INTERCESSION for us; thenceforth expecting,"—i. e., from the time of His ascension till He come again,—"TILL He make His enemies His footstool,"[8] by "dashing them to

---

[1] John vi. 38. [2] Ib.—i. 14.
[3] Heb. x. 14. [4] Ib. x. 14. [5] Compare Acts i. 9, with chap. iii. 21.
[6] Acts iii. 21. [7] Heb. i. 3; viii. 1. [8] Ps. cx. 1; Heb. 13.

pieces like a potter's vessel."¹ But, "we see not yet all things put under Him."²

At this point, therefore, we reach the question which principally concerns us in this connection. It respects—

THE LOCATION OF THAT INHERITANCE OF THE SAINTS WHICH IS DECLARED TO BE "RESERVED IN HEAVEN FOR THEM."

The question is this: "Are we to look for it in that "highest" or empyreal Heaven, "where," as Dr. Harbaugh affirms, "the body of the Saviour *now* is?" This, we have said, is the popular view. But, let us see.

On this subject it is to be observed, that the "DOMINION" over the earth and over all species of the lower order of creatures which was conferred upon man in his state of innocence, but which he forfeited by sin, though in the purpose of God it is to be *restored*, yet that restoration is an event of the future. Down to the present time, "the whole creation groaneth and travaileth together *in pain*." And not only the creature, "but we ourselves also, which have the first-fruits of the Spirit, groan within ourselves, *waiting* for the adoption, to wit, the REDEMPTION OF OUR BODY."³

But, this cannot be, until Christ shall have again *returned from* the highest or supernal Heaven, to this sublunary earth and Heaven. And, when He thus returns, it will be for a *two-fold* purpose. The *first* in order will be, to raise the dead who "sleep in Him, and change and translate those living saints who shall remain unto His coming."⁴ The *sec-*

1 Ps. ii. 9.   2 Heb. ii. 8.
3 Rom. viii. 21, 22.   4 1 Thess. iv. 13-17.

ond, the Lord's descent from "the air" with His risen and raptured saints,[1] which will be in answer to the prayer of those martyr-"souls under the altar," whom St. John heard "crying with a loud voice and saying, How long, O Lord, holy and true, dost thou not avenge our blood on them that dwell on the earth"—to "make His enemies His footstool," by bringing destruction upon the LAST ANTICHRIST, St. Paul's "man of sin and son of perdition," or the MAN-GOD, together with his confederated atheistic hosts, whom the LORD will consume with the spirit of His mouth, and destroy by the brightness of His (Gr. $\pi\alpha\rho o\upsilon\sigma\iota\alpha$ personal) coming."[2]

It is necessary, however, in this connection, to advert to another momentous event. We are told that, although in the overthrow of the confederated hosts of the last Antichrist, "the slain of the Lord shall be *many*,"[3] yet that some shall *escape*.[4] These will embrace both Jews and Gentiles.[5] The event to which we now allude, is, their *conversion* to Christ. First. Of the JEWS it is declared that, immediately after the destruction of their persecutors, "The Lord will pour upon them the spirit of grace and of supplications." Nor this only. For, being now *personally* manifested to them, it is declared that, "they shall *look upon me* whom they have pierced, and mourn,"[6] etc. Thus, as Isaiah predicts, "a nation shall be born at once;"[7] and that, after the example or pattern of St. Paul, whose conversion as a

---

[1] See Zech. xiv. 4, 5; and Rev. xix. 11-14.
[2] Consult on this Zech. xiv. 1-3; 2 Thess. ii. 3-8; Rev. xix. 11-14, and vs. 15-21.
[3] Isa. lxvi. 16.   [4] Zech. xiv. 2; and verse 16.
[5] Zech. xiv. 2. Isa. lxvi. 19.   [6] Zech. xii. 9, 10.   [7] Isa. lxvi. 8.

Jew, and as "one born out of due time," [1] was effected by no other and by no less an agency than the *personal* manifestation of Christ to him.[2] So, second, it is predicted, that "the *Gentiles* shall come to *their* light, and kings to the brightness of *their* rising." [3]

Thus, then, through the medium of the *moral* and *supernatural* agencies of the manifested God, will be effected the conversion of all nations to Christ, both Jewish and Gentile, as introductory to the establishment of that MILLENNIAL ERA of peace, prosperity, and blessedness to the saved of the nations, so graphically depicted in the writings of the Old and New Testament prophets. The following must suffice by way of illustration. The Lord by the mouth of the prophet Isaiah, says: "Lift up thine eyes round about, and see: thy sons" (i. e., the ten Tribes of Israel, *Judah* having already been gathered) "shall come from afar," (i. e., Assyria), "and thy daughters shall be nursed at thy side. Then shalt thou see, and flow together," (i. e., Judah and Israel shall be *united* into one nation), "and thine heart shall fear and be enlarged."—In what way? "Because the abundance of the sea shall be *converted* unto thee; the forces" (marg. Wealth) "of the Gentiles shall *come* unto thee." . . . "For, the nation and kingdom that will not serve thee, shall *perish;* yea, those nations shall be *utterly* destroyed." . . . "The sons also of them that afflicted thee shall come *bending* unto thee; and all that despised thee shall *bow themselves down* at the soles of thy feet; and they

---

[1] 1 Cor. xv. 8.   [2] Acts ix. 3–6.   [3] Isa. lx. 1–7, and following chapters.

shall call thee THE CITY OF THE LORD, THE ZION OF THE HOLY ONE OF ISRAEL." [1]

In this way, therefore, *and in none other*. shall that "FIRST DOMINION," lost by the sin of the "first Adam," be restored by the triumphs over sin of "the second Man, the Lord from Heaven,"[2] to Judah and Israel, and to the saved of the Gentile nations, having Jerusalem as the METROPOLIS of the Millennial Earth, subject to the rule over them of Christ as their KING, together with His *co-reigning* risen and glorified saints, whose SEAT or CAPITAL of universal Empire will be "*in the air.*" [3]

ON THE MILLENNIUM.

"A light to lighten the Gentiles,
And the glory of His people Israel."

"O'er the green earth, long benighted,
Truth shall, like a morning star,
Smile on lands for ages slighted,—
Shed its radiance wide and far.

Watchmen say, the morning cometh,
Lo! it gilds the mountain peaks;
Moral Spring in beauty bloometh,
Lustre all the orient streaks.

In His chariot, 'love-paved,'
Jesus shall to Earth descend;
Millions of the *heathen* saved,
Lowly at His footstool bend.

---

[1] Isa. lx. 5, 12, 14. [2] Compare Mic. iv. 8, with Dan. vii. 14; and 1 Cor. xv. 47. [3] 1 Thess. iv. 16, 17.

Lines on the Jewish Restoration.

Verdant isles in either tropic,
   On the mild IMMANUEL call;
Grace and Mercy all their topic,
   Rich, and full, and free for all.

All the penal curse repealed,
   Love and Light and Truth abound;
Nature's bitter waters healed,
   All the Earth is holy ground.

Days, by sages long predicted,
   Triumphs of atoning blood;
Jews, by Aaron's rod depicted,
   Dried and withered, seem to bud.

All along the 'vale of vision,'
   Gales of quickening mercy blow;
Jews, a by-word and derison,
   All their ancient glory show.

Yes, a nation long forgotten,
   As the corpse returned to clay;
Bones dry up, and bodies rotten,
   Shall be *born within a day*.

Open the Prophetic Volume!
   He that runs may surely read;
God has by a promise solemn,
   Israel's grafting in decreed.

By the flaming cross revealed,
   By the truth-inspiring Word,
By the Gospel ages sealed,
   Jacob's race shall be restored!

Salem shall, in ancient splendor,
    Lift her consecrated towers ;
God, her glory, hope, defender,
    Clothe her wilderness with flowers.

Yes, of what the Lord hath spoken,
    Not a tittle e'er shall fail ;
'Tis God's word, and by this token,
    Israel's restoration hail !

He who on the cross was smitten,
    Jacob's outcasts shall redeem ;
'Tis in Heaven's volume written,
    They shall *weep and turn* to Him.

Though they suffer partial blindness,
    ' God shall take away the vail ;
From His lips the law of kindness,
    Shall His ISRAEL'S PARDON SEAL.' "

Joshua Marsden.

But, this restoration of " the first dominion" to Judah and Israel and the Gentile nations during the Millennial era, however it may be regarded as *a* restoration, yet it is not that

"FINAL INHERITANCE OF THE SAINTS,"

—identical with " the New Heavens and the New Earth," *to* or *upon* which, St. John " saw the Holy City" or the " New Jerusalem coming down" or descending from God out of Heaven—which St. Peter declares is *"reserved in Heaven for them."* This will appear from the fact, that, maugre the prophetic descriptions given of the prevalence of universal righteousness, peace, prosperity, blessedness, and glory of the

Millennial state of the Church, it is no where described as an absolutely indefectible state of grace. So far from it, the prophet Isaiah (chap. lv. 20), declares that "the child shall die an hundred years old ; but the sinner, being an hundred years old, shall die and be accursed :" or, which, more literally rendered, may read thus—" The *child* of an hundred years old, being a *sinner*, shall *die* and be *accursed*." That is, in analogy to the summary act of judgment inflicted upon Ananias and Sophira of Apostolic times ; sin and its consequences during that era will not be permitted generally to propagate. Nevertheless, a general apostacy, occasioned by the tendencies thereto as above during the Millennial era, will—as we shall see presently—transpire *at the close* of that era. Indeed, we advance a step further on this subject. Even "the Inheritance of the saints," IN ITS FULNESS, does not hold true as it regards the risen and raptured saints of "THE FIRST RESURRECTION." For, there will be an " *end*" to the peculiar form of their reign over the Millennial period of the saved nations in the flesh, when Christ will "*deliver up* that kingdom to God, even the Father, that He may be ALL IN ALL." [1] During that era, Christ shall not yet "have put *all* enemies under His feet." [2] But, having "reigned a thousand years," [3] *then* " the *last enemy* to be destroyed" by Him, namely, "DEATH," or he that has had " the power of death," even that " old dragon or serpent which is the Devil and Satan," [4] having been incarcerated " in the bottomless

---

[1] 1 Cor. xv. 24–28.   [2] Ib.—verse 25.   [3] Rev. xx. 4.
[4] Compare Rev. xii. 9, and xx. 2.

pit" at the *commencement* of that period, [1] but released at the *close* of it for "a little season;" [2] and having gone forth " to deceive the nations which are in the four quarters of the earth, Gog and Magog, to gather them to battle . . . against the camp of the saints and the beloved City;" THEN, we repeat, " fire comes down from God out of Heaven and devours them; and the Devil that deceived them is cast into the lake of fire and brimstone, where the beast and the false prophet are"—not, mark, to be *annihilated*,—but, to " be *tormented day and night* FOR EVER AND EVER."[3]

And, blessed be God! This is the LAST APOSTACY, that shall mark or mar the history of man! Expositors have been greatly perplexed—but so far as we can see without just cause—to account for it. Its magnitude—being in " number as the sand of the sea" and " covering the breadth of the earth," seems, to a superficial observer, incompatible with the declared prevalence of universal righteousness in the earth during the Millennial era. This, however, we submit, arises from overlooking the facts following, namely, first, that this apostacy transpires at the *loosing* of Satan at the close of that era. Second. That it takes effect, not among the JEWS; for, with them, at the time of their restoration and conversion, God had made a covenant that they "*should not again* depart from His ways;"[4] nor yet of those of the truly regenerate among the *Gentile* nations, who together constitute " the camp of the saints and the beloved city."[5] But

---

[1] Rev. xx. 1–3.   [2] Ib.—verse 3, 7.   [3] Ib.—verses 9, 10.
[4] Isa. liv. 10.   [5] Rev. xx. 9.

they are those of Gentile nations of whom it is said, "the nation and the kingdom that *will not serve thee*," (i. e., the united tribes of Judah and Israel), "*shall perish*; yea, those nations shall be utterly destroyed."[1] Now, these Gentile nations, all of whom, during the thousand years that shall have elapsed, having retained the *names* by which they were originally designated, have so multiplied, that they are said to extend over "the *four quarters* of the earth;"[2] and, being brought under the influence of that *Satanic* deception to which they will be exposed at the expiration of that period, and which was held under restraint *during* that interval,[3] will now prove effectual in drawing them off from their *feigned* allegiance to Christ, and will constitute that stupendous MAGOGEAN CONFEDERACY, that shall "compass the camp of the saints and the beloved city."[4]

But, their assault is in vain. Instantly, "*fire* comes down from God out of Heaven, and *devours* them."[5]

And now, being numbered among "*the rest of the dead that lived not again until the thousand years were finished*,"[6] Christ appears on His GREAT WHITE THRONE"[7]—not, observe, as though this were a *third* coming, but, as forming the last or closing act of the second in *continuation*. For, it is expressly declared that "HE MUST REIGN," i. e., during the thousand years that are comprehended under His SECOND coming, 'TILL *He has put all enemies under His feet*," the *last* of whom, as we have seen, is "DEATH."[8]

---

[1] Isa. lx. 12. [2] Rev. xx. 8. [3] Comp. Rev. xx. 1-3, with verses 7, 8; Isa. lxv. 20.
[4] Rev. xx. 9. [5] Ib. verse 9. [6] Ib. verse 5. [7] Ib.—verse 11.
[8] i. Cor. xv. 24-26.

"The end," therefore, that is, "of the thousand years," having "come,"[1] *preparatory* to Christ's "delivering up the" Millennial "kingdom to God, even the Father, that He may be all in all;" "the dead, small and great," from "the *sea*," and "*death*" or the grave, and "*hell*," (HADES), "deliver up the dead which were in them," who, "standing before God, are judged, every man (i. e., of these raised *wicked* dead) according to his works." These, together with "DEATH," or "the Devil who had the power of death," "and HELL, (HADES), and whosoever were not found *written* in the Book of Life, are" (not *annihilated*, but) "cast into the lake of (GEHENNA) fire."

Having therefore at length settled these preliminaries, which, as has been shewn, are indispensable to a proper exposition of the *main* subject of our inquiry, we are prepared to pass to—

[1] i. Cor. xv. 24-28.

CHAPTER IV.

"An Inheritance ... in Heaven."

The Heaven in which is located the Final Inheritance of the Saints.

THE STUDY OF HEAVEN.

" The rill is tuneless to his ear who feels
   No harmony within : the South wind steals
   As silent as unseen among the leaves.
   Who has no inward beauty none perceives,
   Though all around is beautiful.   *R. H. Dana.*

" For what though the mountains and skies be fair,
   Steeped in soft blue of the summer air?
   'Tis the soul of man, by its hopes and dreams,
   That lights up all nature with living gleams."
                                   Felicia Hemans.

THE BETTER LAND.

" I hear thee speak of the better Land,
   Thou call'st its children a happy band.
   Mother, oh ! *where* is that radiant shore ?
   Shall we not seek it and weep no more ?
   Is it where the flower of the orange blows,
   And the fire-flies glance through the myrtle boughs ?
   — *Not there, not there,* my child.

Is it where the feathery palm-trees rise,
And the date grows ripe under summer skies?
Or midst the green islands of glittering seas,
Where fragrant forests perfume the breeze?
And strange, bright birds, on their starry wings,
Bear the rich hues of all glorious things?
—*Not there, not there,* my child.

Is it far away in some region old,
Where the rivers wander o'er sands of gold?
Where the burning rays of the ruby shine,
And the diamond lights up the secret mine,
And the pearl gleams forth from the coral strand—
Is it there, sweet Mother, that BETTER LAND?

' Eye hath not seen,' my gentle boy !
' Ear hath not heard' its deep songs of joy !
Dreams cannot picture a world so fair—
Sorrow and death do not enter there :
But ' THE NEW EARTH AND HEAVEN' beyond the tomb,
—*It is there, it is there,* my child."

Felicia Hemans.

WE have now shewn, first, that "Paradise," "the third heaven," or "Abraham's bosom," as the abode of saintly souls between death and the resurrection,—that unseen, intermediate state,—is not the *final* "Inheritance of the saints in light." And also, second, that the "Heaven" *in* which that "Inheritance" is located, is not the "*highest,*" supernal, or empyrial Heaven. So further, third, that the Millennial era of blessedness to the saved nations in the flesh, nor the resurrected and glorified saints who rule over the earth as "joint-heirs with Christ" for a thousand years, do not constitute that "Inheritance" IN ITS FULNESS.

It hence results, that, as an object of the faith and hope of the true saints of God in all ages, both dead and living, that "Inheritance is still held in "*reserve*" for them.

The question, therefore, which remains to be determined, is,

IN WHAT PORTION OF THE INFINITE EXPANSE OF "THE HEAVEN OF HEAVENS," ARE WE LO LOOK FOR IT?

Even at the expense of presenting a view that may be thought a novelty, we reply, that it is not

—"Far away in some region old:"

but that it is to be found in that SUBLUNARY WORLD, which, though in the popular apprehension is doomed to be *totally obliterated* from the other portions of God's handiwork, is nevertheless called in Scripture—"THE NEW HEAVENS AND EARTH WHEREIN SHALL DWELL RIGHTEOUSNESS."—(2 Peter iii. 11).

What we deferentially maintain on this subject, is, that it is to *this* "New Heavens and Earth"—τὴν οἰκουμένην τὴν μέλλουσαν—"world (or *habitable earth*) to come,"[1] to which St. Paul alludes when, in his address to the Hebrews, he says: "Knowing in yourselves, that ye have IN Heaven, a better and an enduring substance,"[2] etc.

Let us then turn back, the while, to take a glance at that stupendous event which immediately follows the *final* destruc-

[1] Heb. ii. 5. [2] Ib. x. 34.

tion, by the "conqueror,"[1] the Lord Jesus Christ, of His "last enemy, DEATH." Thus we read: "And I saw A GREAT WHITE THRONE, and HIM that sat upon it, from whose face the earth and the heavens *fled away*, and there was found no place for them."[2]

A most unpropitious beginning, perhaps the reader will exclaim. Why, does not this very passage teach, that "the heavens and the earth which *are now*," and which for 6,000 years have been "kept in store, reserved unto fire against the day of judgment and perdition of ungodly men," will then be *annihilated?*

But, this difficulty to the contrary notwithstanding, with the reader's indulgence, we shall proceed to adduce the evidence, that the *present* "Heavens and earth," so far from being annihilated by that "fire from God out of Heaven" which is to "consume" the apostate apocalyptic "Gog and Magog" army, they will constitute the material or basis *out of which*, in analogy to the raised body from "the dust of the earth," or to the fabled ashes of the Phœnix, will spring forth a "NEW HEAVEN AND A NEW EARTH." Whether we believe it or not, the Scriptures clearly reveal a *renascency*, or regeneration, not only of the slumbering dead, but also of the "Heavens and earth that are now." The latter is no more a matter of impossibility with God, than the former. Of this we are certain: that neither *fire*, nor any other natural agent, can destroy, in the sense of *annihilating* matter. True, the original form of it may be *changed*, nothing

[1] Rev. vi. 2.   [2] Rev. xx. 11.

more. And so, as to the effect of the last universal conflagration of the present earth and heavens, it reaches only to the *elements* of which they are constructed. These "elements," we read, "shall melt with fervent heat;" "shall be dissolved;" "shall be *changed*," etc. That is, the *present* "fashion," scheme, or form of this earth, "shall pass away:" but, like gold in the furnace, it will only be to *purify* it from the alloy or curse of sin.

Again. If, as St. Paul declares, Rom. i. 20, "the invisible things of God from the creation are clearly seen, being understood by the things that are made, even His *eternal* power and Godhead," then it is reasonable to infer, that, under the direction of infinite wisdom, they will be made, as they were originally designed, ultimately to subserve His highest glory, and the greatest good of the universe, *ad infinitum*. But, their annihilation, as such, would be totally subversive of these high, and holy, and benevolent ends. We hence argue that, judging from the apostle's statement, the *reflection* of "the invisible things of God" as connected with "His eternal power and Godhead" through the medium of "the things that are made," is as true of the earth *after* the curse denounced against it on account of man's sin, as in its primeval state. This consideration alone, we submit, goes far to argue its PERPETUITY.

And further. That this representation, though among the some of the *last* "*things* that are hard to be understood," and which "those that are unlearned and unstable wrest, even as they do the other Scriptures," is not "a cunningly devised fable," will appear, unless we greatly err, from what St. Peter says in reference to the *final destiny* that awaits the present Heavens and earth. He had just been speaking of those "scoffers" whom he predicted would appear "in the last days," and demand, "walking after their own lusts, *Where is the promise of Christ's coming?* for since the fathers have fallen asleep, all things continue as they were from the beginning of the creation." And he then adds: " For of this they are willingly ignorant, that by the word of God, the Heavens were of old, and the earth standing out of the water and in the water: whereby the world that *then* was, being overflowed with water, *perished:* but the heavens and the earth which *are now*, by the same word are kept in store, RESERVED UNTO FIRE," etc. "Nevertheless," he continues, "we, according to His promise, look for NEW HEAVENS AND A NEW EARTH, WHEREIN DWELLETH RIGHTEOUSNESS."

Now here, it is evident that St. Peter does not speak of three separate and distinct earths, but of the *same* earth under three separate and distinct states or conditions. First. He directs us, "*ὁ τό τε κόσμος,*"—that is, to the earth as it existed *before* the flood, called "the old world," or "the earth that then was," and which he tells us "*perished* with water." But, it was not *annihilated*: for he points us to it, second, "*οἱ δε νῦν οὐρανοὶ καὶ ἡ γῆ*"—that is, as the earth that has existed *since* the flood—"the earth and the Heavens which *are now.*" And from this he proceeds directly to speak, third, "*καινοὺς δέ οὐρανοὺς καὶ γῆν* καινὴν—that is, of "the new heavens and earth,"[1] which are still *future*.

And, we now observe that, as though to remove all doubts as to the perpetuity of the *same earth* in passing through these successive transformations, the apostle, as he stands 'looking for and hasting unto the coming of the day of God," he speaks of it as that day "*wherein* the heavens, being on fire, shall be dissolved, and the elements shall melt with fervent heat,"[2] etc. Then in verse 7, he says, that "the Heavens and the earth which are now, are kept in store, *reserved* unto fire against (or unto) *the day of judgment*," etc. But, that this "day of judgment" and "day of God" above spoken of refer to the *same period;* and that, so far from its being limited to a natural day of twenty-four hours, as is generally supposed, it spans the *whole space* assigned to the Millennial era, he adds,—"But, beloved, be not ignorant of this one thing, that one day is with the Lord as a thousand years, and a thousand years as one day," (verse 8). Hence, speaking of "the day of God" towards which he was then "looking and hastening," from the point of time when it should commence its course, the *period*, during which "the Heavens and the earth that are now" were to be "reserved unto fire," was the above "THOUSAND YEARS." And, to remove all doubt, and avoid the otherwise insalutary effects, on the part of his brethren, that might arise from this long delay of their deferred hopes of the promised "Inheritance," he adds: " The Lord *is not slack* concerning His promise, as some men

---

[1] ii Pet. iii. 3-6, and verse 13. [2] Ib., verse 12.

count slackness," as for example, those "scoffers" who demand, "where is the promise of His coming?" for, notwithstanding this long delay in *man's* account, what the LORD hath promised concerning "the new heavens and earth wherein shall dwell righteousness" eternal, He will most surely perform.

With the above exposition, therefore, of the import of the phraseology, "day of God" and day of judgment" kept in view, they will be found to exactly harmonize with the expression in reference to that period, to wit: "Wherein"—that is, *within* which "day,"—"the heavens and the earth, being on fire, shall be dissolved," etc. In other words, in as much as this "day of God" and "day of judgment," being *identical* with the "thousand years," (six times repeated in Rev. xx. 1–6), has its morning and its evening; so, the renascency or renovation of "the heavens and the earth" by "fire," will be a *progressive* process, its first stage adapting it to the MILLENNIAL era, the last to the *eternal* state.

As this is an important and much litigated point, we submit the following in defence of the position here assumed—

In the prophecy of Isaiah, chap. lxv. 17, and lxvi. 22, mention is made of *a* "new Heaven and a new earth." But, that the physical change then effected by this renascency is *partial* only, is evident from Isa. lxv. 18: "For I will create Jerusalem a rejoicing, and her people a joy." That is, the change effected in the *salubrity* of the atmosphere and the *fruitfulness* of the earth compared with the present will be so great and marvellous, as to entitle them to the appellation of a "*new heavens and a new earth*," in the possession and enjoyment of which God's "people" will rejoice. But, that this change will be partial only, in chap. lxvi. 22, the prophet, speaking of the same "new heavens and earth," says: "And it shall come to pass, that from one new moon to another, and from one Sabbath to another, shall all flesh come to worship before me, saith the Lord." To this the prophet adds, (verse 23), "And they shall go forth, and shall *look upon the carcasses* of the men that have transgressed against me: *for their worm shall not die*, neither shall their *fire be quenched;* and they shall be an *abhorring* to all flesh."

Now turn to "the new heavens and the new earth" state spoken of by St. Peter, 2 Epist. chap. iii. 14, and by St. John, Rev. xxi. 1, 5. This latter, as St. Peter has it, is "according to God's *promise*," of which, there is none other in the Scriptures, except that derived from Isaiah above as its earnest or type. Comparing the two, it would be superfluous to say, that the above description of the Millennial "new heavens and earth" state is *totally incompatible* with that of St. Peter, and as more elaborately described by St. John. The revelator says of it: "And God shall wipe away all tears from their eyes; and there shall be no more death, neither sorrow, nor crying, neither shall there be any more pain: for *the former things*"—that is, the *state* of "the new heavens and earth" of Isaiah during the Millennial era—"*are passed away*," in order to give place to the condition of the promised "Inheritance of the saints" IN ITS FULNESS.

It follows, therefore, that this latter state *only*, of "the new heavens and earth" of St. Peter and St. John, will constitute their *final* renascency or renovation by "fire." This accomplished, and "the redeemed of the Lord" will be furnished with that "INHERITANCE," which, as St. Peter declares, "shall not fade away;" even that "better country," "the Heavenly;" and the same with that "*kingdom prepared*" for those who were chosen in Him, *from before* [1] *the foundation of the world;*" that "city which hath foundations," [2] whose "builder and maker is God;" together with those "many mansions" among "the principalities and powers" suspended and upheld by Almighty power "IN the Heavenly places" of infinite space; and, in the joyful anticipation of which, beholding it as "*a far off*," all the old patriarchs and prophets and apostles and saints "*died in faith*," "not accepting deliverance" from their sacrifices and sufferings by inglorious compromises with their persecutors, "*that they might obtain* A BETTER RESURRECTION." [3]

THE HEAVENLY BLESSEDNESS.

No sickness there,
No weary wasting of the frame away:
No fearful shrinking from the midnight air,
No dread of summer's bright and fervid ray.

No hidden grief,
No wild and cheerless vision of despair:
No vain petition for a swift relief,
No tearful eye, or broken heart, are there.

[1] Compare Matt. xxv. 34, with Eph. i. 4. [2] See Rev. xxi. 19-27.
[3] See Heb. xi.

Glory of the Better Land.

Care has no home,
Within that realm of ceaseless praise and song—
Its tossing billows break and melt in foam,
Far from the mansion of the saintly throng.

The storm's black wing,
Is never spread athwart celestial skies;
Its wailings blend not with the voice of spring,
As some poor flowret fades and dies.

No night distils
Its chilling dew upon the tender frame;
No morn is needed there! the light which fills
The land of Glory, from its MAKER came.

No parted friends,
O'er mournful recollections have to weep—
No bed of death sundering love attends,
To watch the comings of a pulseless sleep!

No withered flower,
Or blasted bud celestial gardens know!
No scorching blast, or fire's descending shower,
Scatters destruction like a ruthless foe.

No battle-word
Startles the sacred hosts with fear and dread!
The song of peace, creation's morning heard,
Is sung wherever angel footsteps tread!

Let us "depart,"
If Home like this await the weary soul!
Look up, thou stricken one! thy wounded heart
Shall bleed no more at sorrow's stern control.

> *With* FAITH *our guide,*
> White robed and innocent to tread the way,
> Why fear to plunge in Jordan's rolling tide,
> And find th' "INHERITANCE" OF ETERNAL DAY.—*Anon.*

In further confirmation of the doctrine here set forth regarding the future locality of the saint's "Inheritance," we adduce the following in proof of—

THE ETERNAL PERPETUITY OF THE PRESENT EARTH AND HEAVENS.

That this will be, we select from Holy Scripture, the following declarations regarding the present earth and heavens in their regenerated state. The inspired Psalmist, in speaking of man as he whom God created, says, that he was "made" only "a little season lower than the Deity," [1] and that he "crowned him with glory and honor," and "made him," (i.e., as the "*first Adam*") "to have DOMINION over the works of His hands," etc. Now, undeniably, allusion is here made to the *original* "Dominion" delegated to Man in innocence over the earth, and of all things in air, and earth, and sea.[2] And, although his forfeited earthly lordship was not restored in the person of Noah, as the father of "the world that is now;" yet, as "the old world" emerged from its baptism in the flood, the prismatic-colored bow in the clouds "which spanned the vaulted Heaven, was the token and pledge of a *covenant* between God and him," that there should "*no more be a flood to destroy the earth.*"[3] In virtue of this "covenant," therefore, even in man's *lapsed* state, the inspired David declares: "The

---

[1] See on this, Dr. Clarke's translation, p. 44 of this work.
[2] Gen. i. 26–28.   [3] Ps.—ix. 9–17.

Heaven, even the heavens are the Lord's; BUT THE EARTH HAS HE GIVEN TO THE CHILDREN OF MEN.'[1] And, that this promise extends *beyond* the earth's future baptism by "fire," the Psalmist assures us, that "the world is established, *that it cannot be moved.*"[2] And so also, among the beatitudes of our blessed Lord's sermon on the mount, is this: "Blessed are the *meek*, for they shall *inherit* the earth."[3] This is a quotation from Ps. xxxvii. 11, in which the Psalmist also says of those who "*wait* upon the Lord," that "they shall *inherit* the earth;" and that "the righteous shall inherit the land, and dwell in it FOR EVER."[4] The prophet Isaiah also declares the same thing: "Thy *people* also shall be all righteous; they shall *inherit* the land FOR EVER,"[5] etc. For this reason St. Paul tells us, that when God made His covenant with faithful Abraham, He constituted him "THE HEIR OF THE WORLD"[6]—i. e., "the world,"—($\tau \grave{\eta} \nu$ οἰκουμένην τὴν μέλλουσαν—*habitable earth*) "to come," of which he speaks in Heb. ii. 5. And finally, the same apostle sums up the whole in that notable *title deed* given to the "children of faithful Abraham"—"Whether Paul, or Apollos, or Cephas, or *the world*, ($\kappa o \sigma \mu o s$), life, or death, or things present, or *things to come*, ALL ARE YOURS, and ye are Christ's, and Christ is God's."[7]

And now, in as much as those to whom these "great and precious promises" belong, from "the righteous Abel" down to the last departed saint, together with those among the living

---

[1] Ps. cxv. 16.   [2] Ib—xciii. 1; cxvi. 10.
[3] Matt. v. 5.   [4] Ps. xxxvii. See also verses 9, 22, 34.
[5] Isa. lx. 21.   [6] Rom. iv. 13.   [7] i. Cor iii. 22, 23.

who follow in their footsteps, have never yet realized a verification of them; we shall proceed to adduce the *direct* Scriptural proof,—

THAT THE PRESENT HEAVENS AND EARTH, OR THIS SUBLUNARY WORLD, IN ITS FINAL RENOVATED STATE, IS DESTINED TO CONSTITUTE THE ETERNAL INHERITANCE AND ABODE OF THE SAINTS.

As we have seen, great and glorious as are the things described of the Millennial state of the church; connected though it will be with the direct "reign" over it of Christ, and His risen and raptured saints; yet that state falls infinitely short, both in degree and duration, of their restored " Inheritance " IN ITS FULNESS. True, with Jerusalem, " the city of the Lord," the " place of His sanctuary," where He " will make the place of His feet glorious," as the *metropolis* of the Millennial earth ; and Christ and His co-reigning saints,—after the pattern of the things adumbrated by the typical ladder of Jacob—will hold uninterrupted intercourse with the saved nations in the flesh from their seat or CAPITAL of legislation and government " *in the air ;* " one is ready to conclude, that this were enough to reach the most enlarged aspirations of the redeemed. Nevertheless, if what the Scriptures *reveal* to the eye of faith in regard to the final or eternal state of Heavenly Blessedness, is to be the standard of our available conceptions of it ; (however, we may yield to human aspirations the credit, in these premises, of being measured by a consciousness of ill deserts in the conferment upon the redeemed of anything *beyond* the Millennial state of the church); then is it our privilege, not only, but we are in duty bound to aggrandize the love, mercy, and grace of God in Christ, in contrasting with that state,

"THE GLORY THAT EXCELLETH."

This we hold to be true of that "better country, even an Heavenly," or "the new heavens and new earth," together with that "Holy City, new Jerusalem," which St. John "saw coming down from God out of Heaven" unto it, and the "many mansions" appertaining thereto. These unitedly, form but different appellations of the aggregate of that "Inheritance, incorruptible, undefiled, and that fadeth not away," which St. Peter declares is "reserved in Heaven for us."

But it will doubtless be urged, that the old prophets, in speaking of the MILLENNIAL KINGDOM of the Messiah, as the "son of David" who is to "sit upon His throne,"[1] and which is to be "set up by the God of Heaven in the days of the kings" of the four Gentile monarchies, declare that it shall never be destroyed," nor "be left to other people;" but that "it shall break in pieces and destroy all these kingdoms," and that it "shall stand for ever."[2] And again: that "the *saints* of the Most High shall take the kingdom and possess the kingdoms for ever, even for ever and ever."[3] Also, that, to the same purport, was the declaration of the angel to Mary concerning her son, JESUS: "He shall be great, and shall

---

[1] Acts ii. 30.   [2] Dan. ii. 44.   [3] Ib—vii. 18.

be called the son of the Highest; and the Lord God shall give unto Him the *throne* of His father David; and He shall reign over the house of Israel for ever; and of His Kingdom, there shall be no end." [1]

In reply to the above, we observe, that it would be superfluous to admit what no one denies, that this kingdom of Christ and of His saints is to be located ON THIS EARTH. We admit also, that the phraseology applied to express the duration of this kingdom—that there is to be "*no end*" to it, that it is to "*stand forever, even for ever and ever,*" etc., are employed by the Holy Spirit to denote the eternity of its existence. And, having demonstrated, as we deferentially claim, the eternal perpetuity of the present earth and heavens when renovated by the *post*-millennial "fire," what we maintain is, that it is to constitute the *theatre of action* of the eternal kingdom. In other words, we have no authority to affirm, that it is ever destined to be removed to some other sphere, e. g., to some orb in the "highest," supernal, or empyreal "Heaven." In illustration and in confirmation of this, we remark,—

First. That, in perfect harmony with the above representation, He of whom it is said: "The High and Lofty One who inhabiteth eternity," [2] and "whose goings forth have been from the days of eternity;" [3] it is also declared of Him, that "the Lord is the true God, the living God, and the King of eternity;" [4] or "the "everlasting King." It follows, there-

---

[1] Luke i. 32, 33.
[2] Isa. lvii. 15.
[3] Micah v. 2.
[4] Jer. x. 10.

Christ's Kingship and Kingdom Eternal.

fore, that if God is an ETERNAL KING, then His kingdom must be ETERNAL also. Aye, and this holds true, even though the kingdom itself has not always existed in *visible* form. The obvious meaning is, that it existed from eternity as one of "the deep mysteries of the will"[1] of HIM who, "knowing the end from the beginning," accounteth of "things that are not as though they were."[2] It is hence associated in the New Testament with numerous passages, denotive of the *eternity* of its existence. The saints, for example, "according to the faith of God's elect, and the acknowledgment of the truth which is after godliness," are said to be "called unto His *eternal* glory by Christ Jesus,"[3] "in hope of *eternal* life, which God, who cannot lie, promised before the world began."[4] And those who are thus "called," it is to the end that they "might receive the promise of an *eternal* inheritance;" which inheritance is none other than that "House" with "many mansions,"—"the New Heavens and New Earth wherein dwelleth righteousness,"—"*eternal* and IN the heavens."[5]

But, in the next place, it is to be specially observed, that in accordance with "the eternal purpose which God purposed in Christ Jesus our Lord," this "eternal inheritance," "House," or "Kingdom," was in due time to be *manifested* to the saints, in, through, and by, the Lord Jesus Christ as THE GOD-MAN. Hence saith He, "to this end was I born, and for this purpose came I into the world."[6] And so, IF

---

1 Eph. i. 9. 2 Isa. xlvi. 10. 3 i Pet. v. 10.
4 Titus i. 2. 5 ii Cor. v. 1. 6 John xviii. 37.

THEY WOULD, at His *first* coming in the flesh, Jesus would *then* have commenced His visible Messianic "reign over the house of Jacob for ever."[1] But, though "He came to His own" world, "His own" people, the Jewish nation, "*received Him not.*"[2] They "rejected the Prince of glory," not only, but they "crucified" Him! And, mark: Jesus was crucified as a King—"the KING OF THE JEWS!"[3] And therefore the second *deferment* of the Eternal Kingdom in its outward and visible form, until the time come when they shall say, "Blessed is He that cometh in the name of the Lord."[4]

That event, however, though nigh at hand, is not yet. It still forms the burden of that prayer taught by our blessed Lord to the Church, "*Thy kingdom come*: Thy will be done *in* earth, as it is done *in* heaven."[5]

It is however to be observed in this connection, that the above prayer, when answered, will only manifest the "Kingdom" in its *Millennial* form. In other words, it will be the eternal kingdom developed *in part* only. The Millennial period of the Kingdom is limited. "*A thousand years*"— whether understood of natural or prophetico-symbolical time, which latter would extend said period to 365,000 years, is unimportant—is assigned to the "reign" of Christ and the co-heir partners of His throne, the risen and raptured saints, during that particular form of its manifestation. A *change*, therefore, awaits it. But, in whatever this change in its external normal form of manifestation may consist, it by no means argues a termination of its existence as such, or

---

[1] Luke i. 33.   [2] John i. 11.   [3] Matt. ii. 2; xxvii. 11, 37.
[4] Matt. xxiii. 39.   [5] Ib.—vi. 10.

of a transfer of its locality to some remote orb in infinite space.

In regard to this latter point, we beg to ask, *Why should it be?* True, in the Scriptures, the earth we inhabit, is often contrasted with "the principalities and powers IN the heavenly places" in an *odious* sense. When man fell, the sentence was pronounced, "cursed is the ground for *thy* sake." And as a part of the token of this curse, it was declared, "thorns also and thistles shall it bring forth to *thee;* and *thou* shalt eat the herb of the field; in the sweat of thy face shalt thou eat bread, till thou return to the ground. . . . for dust thou art, and unto dust shalt thou return."[1]

It hence turns out, that, in the popular view, men have come to imbibe the most contemptuous notions of this portion of the Creator's works! But wherefore, pray, is it thus spoken of? Was it *originally* created so worthless a thing, as to warrant our scorn, and to appear unworthy of man? So far from it, "God saw everything that He had made, and, behold, *it was very good.*"[2]

Besides. Has not the Eternal God Himself, IN OUR NATURE, condescended to bestow an *infinite honor* upon the earth and upon man, by descending from the "highest" or empyreal "Heaven," and mingling with its sinful and guilty inhabitants in sorrow and suffering, aye, even unto death, that they "might be *raised* to glory, honor, and immortality, eternal life?"[3] Wherefore, then, it may be demanded,

---

[1] Gen. iii. 18, 19.   [2] Gen. i. 31.   [3] Rom. ii. 7.

"should it be thought a thing incredible," as though it were degrading to "the Son of God," that, having selected this earth from among the numberless worlds of the universe as the theatre of His *humiliation* for *man's* sake, He should choose the same earth as the theatre for the display of His and the saints' RESURRECTED GLORIFICATION for His OWN sake?

Take, in illustration, a view of this subject in the abstract. Regard this our planet, as it were, from some point in infinite space, in common with others of the innumerable "principalities and powers IN the heavenly places," with the curse of sin purged from it, and that it is restored to a condition and beauty and glory vastly transcending that in which it first emerged from the hand of its Creator. Would it not be looked upon, under such circumstances, as well entitled to be numbered among the *celestial spheres*, as any other planet in the universe? Could we conceive of any other idea regarding it, but that it was equally entitled to form *a part* of that brilliant galaxy of worlds on worlds, amid which the angelic hosts now do God's bidding in the boundless expanse of the "highest" or supernal Heaven? Yea, more. Might we not expect that, instead of finding this earth invariably contrasted with and opposed to those spheres IN the "Heaven of heavens" that have not passed under the shock of sin, that there were at least some intimations given of its forming *a part* of what is included under the appellation of the "Heavenly principalities?"

Let us here then recall to mind that apocalyptic declaration of the Lord Jesus, Rev. xxi. 5: "BEHOLD, I MAKE ALL

THINGS NEW!" Aye, whereas sin was overruled as the *occasion* of the curse, in these words we are taught to look forward to the creation of "a new earth," that is, as has been already shown, *a new state* of this earth. Nothing, we maintain, can be more evident than that in 2 Peter iii., the apostle speaks of three distinct states or conditions of the *same* earth, growing out of two separate and widely different changes. He first speaks of "the old world" in its original state as having been "overflowed with *water*," and which he tells us "*perished*"—not that it was *annihilated*, and another planet substituted in its place;—but that the earth, as it was in its primeval and antediluvian form, underwent a wonderful alteration by being subjected to the *action* of the universal flood. The apostle then passes on to speak of "the heavens and the earth which are now," i. e., the *same globe*, but changed; respecting which he states that they are *reserved unto fire*," under the *action* of which, although "the heavens shall pass away with a great noise, and the elements shall melt with fervent heat, and the earth also, and the works that are therein shall be burned up," etc., yet that they shall be—not *annihilated*, but—"dissolved," "changed," etc., that is, from their *present form*. And so, when that "fire" shall have done its work, (and we know that it is the property of fire to *purify* matter, not annihilate it), St. Peter adds, that we are to "*look*, according to God's promise, for NEW HEAVENS AND A NEW EARTH, wherein shall dwell righteousness."[1]

---

[1] ii Peter iii. 13.

The conclusion, therefore, legitimately drawn from these apostolic statements, is, that *when* this second stupendous renascency or regeneration by "fire" shall have passed over the present earth, it will to all intents and purposes constitute a fulfillment of the words of Jesus, "Behold, I make all things new." Yes, it will be that "*restitution of all things*," full, complete, everlasting, "which God hath spoken by the mouth of all His holy prophets since the world began." [1]

Well then, will not "the new Heavens and earth," thus regenerated by "*fire*," and restored to its place among the *unsinning* "principalities and powers IN the Heavenly places," in every way be *fitted* for the display of the glory of the resurrected Humanity of Jesus and of His redeemed saints in His kingdom throughout eternal ages?

That it will be so, is undeniable, if we can adduce from Holy Scripture the evidence, that they speak of "the Kingdom of God" in this *last form* of its manifestation under such conditions, as to inevitably force us to consider this earth as *the seat* of that kingdom. Take then the following. Our divine Lord says: "Blessed are the *poor in spirit*; for *theirs* is the kingdom of Heaven." [2] Now, place this beside the following: "Blessed are the *meek*; for *they* shall inherit the earth." [3] According to the popular idea, Christ in the *former* passage, refers, not to any one of "the principalities and powers IN the Heavenly places," neither to this earth; but to some remote and undefined region of spiritual ecstacies

[1] Acts iii. 21.   [2] Matt. v 3.   [3] Ib—verse 5.

in the "higher" or empyreal Heaven "where the body of the Saviour *now* is." But, on this hypothesis it may be demanded, in what sense are we to understand the *latter* text ? Surely, "the poor in spirit" and "the meek," refer to the *same class*. Are they then to be understood as having been led by our blessed Lord, to have anticipated a future state of the Heavenly Blessedness in *two separate and distinct regions*, the one in the supernal Heaven and the other on earth? Nay verily, and the only possible way, unless we greatly err, by which to harmonize both passages, is, by considering our Lord as having used the above phraseology interchangeably, as denoting, *unitedly*, that "inheritance incorruptible, undefiled, and that fadeth not away," spoken of by St. Peter as that new Heavens and new earth wherein shall dwell righteousness "eternal, and which he declares is reserved IN Heaven for them.

We are now drawing this important part of the subject in hand to a close. As already intimated, the session of the saints with Christ "in the air," as co-rulers over the saved nations in the flesh on earth during the Millennial era, *does not* constitute "the new heavens and earth" state of the redeemed. This is evident from the fact, that "the dead who sleep in Christ" at the time of "the first resurrection," together with the "living saints who remain until He come," are "*caught up* in the clouds to meet Him *in the air*."[1] Whereas the revelator St. John tells us, when speaking of "the Holy City, new Jerusalem,"—and which he so

---

[1] i Thess. iv. 13-17.

elaborately describes in the xxist and xxiid chapters of that book—that he "saw it *descending from God out of Heaven*" to "the new Heavens and new earth"¹ of which he speaks, chap. xxi. 1.

It follows, therefore, that "the Holy city, new Jerusalem," which is declared in this passage to come down out of the "highest," supernal, or empyreal "Heaven," cannot in any consistency be said at the same time to be *in* that Heaven. True, it, together with "the new heaven and earth" to which it descends, are *enfolded* within the boundless realm of "the Heaven of heavens." But, it is the *sublunary*, or first or lower Heaven, from which the demoniacal spirits that have so long occupied it as "the principalities and powers and spiritual wickedness in high places," together with every unclean and ravenous bird, and all those diabolical agencies of nature under the curse, both physical and moral, that have so often lashed it into fury, *are now cast*; and, "IN" its serene, and purified, and blissful expanse, now floats "THE NEW EARTH," which, having also passed through the fiery ordeal of "the great day of the Lord," is now transferred to the *full possession* of the whole redeemed family of the Lord "out of every kindred, and tongue, and nation, and people," under the wide-spread heaven, as their long-promised "ETERNAL INHERITANCE."

And, in conclusion, when this *final* change in the earth and heavens shall have taken place, then shall be verified, in its most enlarged sense, that prophecy—"All the earth shall be *filled* with the glory of the Lord."¹ The old heavens and

[1] Numb. xiv. 21.

earth as they were under the curse of sin shall have "passed away as a scroll,"[1] to come in remembrance before God no more for ever.[2] Then shall the entire universe of angels and of the redeemed shout aloud—"Behold, *the tabernacle of God is with men, and He will dwell with them*, and they shall be His people, *and God Himself shall be with them,* AND BE THEIR GOD."[3] Then, there shall have been "delivered up" the Millennial "Kingdom to God, even the Father, that He may be ALL IN ALL." Then, that which cannot be said of the enthronement of Christ and His saints "in the air" during the Millennial era, shall be verified: "*The throne of God* AND *the Lamb*," in undistinguished unity, shall be established in the newly descended "Holy City, New Jerusalem," as the CAPITAL of universal empire in "the new Heavens and earth," or HABITABLE "WORLD TO COME" spoken of by St. Paul, Heb. ii. 5. Finally. Then "shall God have wiped away the tears from all faces; and there shall be no more death, neither sorrow nor crying; neither shall there be any more pain: for the former things are passed away."[4]

Blessed be God! No: no more a Devil to tempt: no more a sinful and enchanting world to allure: no more easily besetting sins to harass!

HOME IN VIEW.

"As when the weary traveler gains
    The sight of some o'erlooking hill,
His heart revives, if 'cross the plains
    He sees his home, though distant still:—

[1] Rev. vi. 14. [2] Rev. xxi. 11.
[3] Rev. xxi. 3. [4] Rev. xxi. 4.

While he surveys the much-loved spot,
  He slights the space that lies between;
His past fatigues are all forgot,—
  Because his journey's end is seen.

Thus, when the Christian pilgrim views
  By faith, his mansions in the skies,
The sight his fainting strength renews,
  And wings his speed to reach the prize.

The thought of home his spirit cheers,
  No more he grieves for troubles past,
Nor any future trial fears,
  So he may safe arrive at last.

'Tis there, he says, I am to dwell
  With Jesus, in the realms of day,
Then shall I bid my cares farewell,
  And He shall wipe my tears away.

Jesus, on Thee our hope depends,
  To lead us on to Thine abode;
Assured our Home will make amends,
  For all our toil while on the road."—*Newton.*

Say, then, ye who profess to have been "begotten again unto a lively hope by the resurrection of Jesus Christ from the dead, to an inheritance incorruptible, and undefiled, and that fadeth not away," as "reserved in Heaven for you," can your utmost aspirations grasp a higher, a holier, or a more sublimely glorious and eternal Home than this?

May the Holy Spirit, the only infallible "Teacher," "Guide," and "Comforter," "take of the things that are Christ's and make them known to us," for His name's sake. Amen.

END OF PART FIRST.

PART SECOND.

What is Heaven?

CHAPTER V.

"An inheritance incorruptible, and undefiled, and that fadeth not away."

SECTION I.

The adaptation of the Inheritance of the Saints, to the nature of the Resurrected Body.

INTRODUCTORY REMARKS.

HEAVEN.

"O scenes surpassing fable, and yet true,
Scenes of accomplished bliss!"

"Where the rivers of pleasure flow o'er the bright plains,
And the noon-tide of glory eternally reigns!"

"We speak of the realms of the blest
Of that country so bright and so fair,
And oft are its glories confest,
But what must it be to be there?"

> We speak of its pathways of gold,
>   Of its walks decked with jewels so rare,
> Of its wonders and pleasures untold—
>   But what must it be to be there?
>
> We speak of its freedom from sin,
>   From sorrow, temptation, and care,
> From trials without and within,
>   But what must it be to be there?
>
> We speak of its service of love,
>   Of the robes which the glorified wear,
> Of the Church of the first-born above,
>   But what must it be to be there?
>
> Do Thou, Lord, 'midst sorrow and woe,
>   Still from my Home, my spirit prepare,
> And shortly I also shall know,
>   And feel what it is to be there!

HAVING, in the preceding pages, discussed the nature of the resurrected bodies of Christ and of His saints; we now proceed to consider the *adaptation* of the "Inheritance" of future Heavenly Blessedness to that state.

The theory that alleges of the dead body, that when it is raised, it is so completely divested of all corporeity as to be transformed into a *purely spiritual* entity, can be consistently maintained on no other hypothesis than that the *soul only* is the man, or the PERSON. And, it is this theory that forms the basis of the current sentiment regarding the future state or condition of happiness of saints who are departed this life, viz., that they are *immediately* at death, introduced into their final abode of consummated bliss. For, agreeably to this theory, its advocates affirm that this spiritual resurrection, taking place *at the moment* of the release of the soul from the body, it speeds its flight on angelic wings to a remote point in infinite space somewhere above the stars, where God the Infinite Spirit, and holy angels, and " the body of the Saviour now is," to bask in the sunshine of supreme, ecstatic, and eternal enjoyment in what is called " Heaven."

Now, that the soul, when separated from the body at death, is eligible to a *local* habitation, we admit. But, as the reader will have seen, the difference in the premises between the above theory and that maintained in this treatise is, that the souls of departed saints occupy a place and state *intermediate* to that of death and the resurrection, called Sheol or Hades, indiscriminately known in Scripture under the appellations of " Paradise," " the third heaven," or " Abraham's bosom."

This view, it is obvious, rests upon the ground of man's *actual* personality as a complex being, constituted, as St. Paul affirms, of " spirit, soul, and body" [1] conjointly ; and the necessity thence arising, that, in order to preserve that personality intact *after* death, there must be a *literal* or corporeal resurrection of the body from the grave, and its RE-UNION to and with the soul, in order to its entrance upon a condition of *consummate* Heavenly Blessedness.

[1] i Thess. v. 23.

Then further. The corporeal and the spiritual in man, cemented together during natural life by the most intimate, though to us inscrutable bonds, were equally susceptible of influences from both physical and moral causes; and hence, by their *joint* companionship in the pursuit of virtue or of vice, form that character which follows them to the eternal world. Enlightened reason, therefore, will be found to coincide with Scripture, in requiring the adaptation of the *physical* constitution of the future state to the *corporeal* as well as to the spiritual nature of man. It is clear that, on any other hypothesis, as we have said, it is only *one-half* of the man that enjoys the happiness of Heaven or the miseries of Gehenna torments. In harmony with the sentiment above indicated, therefore, we introduce the reader to the subject following, in—

SECTION II.

ON THE PHYSICAL NATURE OF THE FUTURE "INHERITANCE OF THE SAINTS," AS CONTRADISTINGUISHED FROM THE "HEAVEN" IN WHICH IT IS SAID TO BE.

On this subject we must premise, that we are to look to *a violation of the legitimate Laws* of Scriptural interpretation, viz., the literal, natural, or grammatical, for all those vague, visionary, and confused conceptions as to *what* Heaven is, so prevalent in the theological nomenclature of the present day. This has arisen from the circumstance, that, from their familiarity with the phraseology of Scripture on this subject, expositors, at least for the most part, have been betrayed into a sort of ready, and to a great extent, unconscious acquiescence to the dogmas of the ORIGENIC school of Biblical hermeneutics, without stopping to inquire into the soundness of the *principles* of exegesis, which controlled the interpretations of that writer.[1] This will be found, if we mistake not, to hold true in an especial manner, in its application to the subject in hand. Let us proceed to consider it, in reference to the question—

WHAT IS HEAVEN?

As a guide to enable us to ascertain the *source* whence the popular views regarding Heaven originate, they are to be traced, we submit, to the phraseology, "kingdom of heaven" —"kingdom of Christ"—"kingdom of God"—"kingdom of the Son of Man," etc. Now, the terms here employed have come generally to be regarded as denoting the constitution of the Church under this dispensation as a PURELY SPIRITUAL KINGDOM, which Christ came to establish at His first appearing in the flesh, and over which He now reigns as King, and is for ever so to reign. In proof of this, we are referred,

First, to that notable declaration of our Lord—"*My kingdom is not of this world*,"[2] etc. The difficulty in reaching the import of this passage, lies in the Greek word $\varkappa o\sigma\mu o\varsigma$, (world), and $\nu\upsilon\nu$ (now). The $\varkappa o\sigma\mu o\varsigma$ or world here, evidently means the aggregate population of the earth. But, there is another Greek word mistranslated "world," viz., $\alpha\iota\omega\nu$, in the passage, "Lo I am with you alway, even unto

---

[1] See on this subject, pages 135-137 and Note. [2] John xviii. 33-37.

the end of the ($\alpha\iota\omega\nu o\varsigma$) *world.*" It should have been age or dispensation. And so, $\varkappa o\sigma\mu o\varsigma$ refers to the *people;* $\alpha\iota\omega\nu o\varsigma$ to the age or *period* of time when the people lived. The passage in question was Christ's reply to Pilate, " Art thou the king of Jews ?" and when our Lord said, " My kingdom is not of this world," and also added, " but ($\nu\upsilon\nu$) *now* is my kingdom not from hence ;" and Pilate asked Him the second time, " Art Thou a king, then ?" Jesus answered him, " Thou sayest (truly) that I am a king :" that is, it is so ; *I am a king:* for, " to this end was I born, and for this cause came I into the ($\varkappa o\sigma\mu o\varsigma$) world," etc., i. e., to the Jewish and Gentile world, " that I should bear witness unto the truth." And, for this reason, as Peter and John declare, " both Herod and Pontius Pilate, with the Gentiles and people of Israel," conspired to put Him to death. Proof enough, this, surely, that " Christ's kingdom was *not* of this world," that is, it was not composed of men (the collective body of mankind) $\nu\upsilon\nu$—" *now*" dwelling on the earth ; for *if* this were so, " then would my servants *fight,* that I should not be delivered to the Jews :" but, in as much as " My kingdom is not ($\nu\upsilon\nu$) now from hence"—that is, does not now take its *commencement* ($\dot{\varepsilon}\nu\tau\varepsilon\tilde{\upsilon}\theta\varepsilon\nu$) from hence, or from this point of time, it is still future. In a word, it is as though our Lord had said to Pilate—" My kingdom" is not *of* the " generation of vipers," Jewish and Gentile, *of this age:* nevertheless, though not of this $\varkappa o\sigma\mu o\varsigma$, it will, at " the set time," be ON THIS EARTH, agreeably to the declaration of the prophet Daniel, chap. vii. 27, that " the kingdom, and dominion, and greatness" of the kingdom of Messiah, when "set up,"[1] will be "under the whole heaven:" and also of St. John, Rev. xi. 15, that "the kingdoms of this (κνσμος) world are (or will) become the kingdoms of our Lord and of His Christ."

Again Did our Lord say, "'My kingdom is not of this κοσμος, physical world?' He also said of His disciples, 'Ye are not of this world, κοσμος.' (John xv. 19.) The two propositions are identical. Now, if the first one proves that Christ's kingdom shall never be literally on the earth, then the second proves that the disciples to whom he addressed these words were not then literally on the earth, because neither were of the κοσμος. This clearly shows the imbecility of the objection. On the other hand, if it be true that while the disciples 'were not *of* this world,' (John xvii. 16,) they might remain *in* it, (John xvii. 25;) it is also true, that the *kingdom* is not of this world, and yet shall be *in* it; for what may be said of Christ and his disciples, can also be said of His kingdom . . . Christ's kingdom," therefore, "in its origin, form, spirit, economy, nature, and object, is not in any of these respects like the kingdoms of the earth, such as Cæsar's." The point herein advocated "affirms the truth of the anticipation of the saints who are now disembodied." Rev. v. 10 : "WE SHALL REIGN ON THE EARTH."[2]

But, out of several other passages adduced in support of the popular view as above, it must suffice that we refer,

---

[1] Dan. ii. 44.   [2] Christocracy. Demarest and Gordon, p. 196.

Second, to the following: "If I cast out devils, (demons) by the Spirit of God, then the kingdom of God is come unto you."[1] From the present tense of this text, it is alleged that the kingdom of Christ was *then* "set up." All that is necessary to say by way of reply, is this: these words were spoken in the very same year in which the kingdom of God was declared to be "nigh," as "at hand," and as "even at the doors," etc.; and also about the time when the disciples were taught to pray—"Thy kingdom come," which clearly show that it was still *future*. Nor was this prayer answered by the setting up of the kingdom at any time *before* the crucifixion, nay, nor *after* the resurrection. For, to the question propounded by the disciples to the risen Saviour, "Lord, wilt thou *at this time* restore the kingdom to Israel?" He said unto them, not, observe, the kingdom will never be restored, but—"it is not for *you* to know the times or seasons which the Father hath put in His own power."[2] It is evident, therefore, that this passage must be understood of the kingdom of God *in* "*mystery*"[3]—as set forth in the parables of the sower and his seed, of the husbandman, of the ten pounds, and of the drag-net, etc.—to "take out of (or from among) the Gentiles a people for Christ's name,"[4]—which is to prepare the way for its *final* establishment in the earth.

In view of the importance of a proper understanding of this subject, however, we remark,

1. That while it is admitted that the Church of Christ as at present constituted, is "built up a spiritual house, to offer

---

[1] Matt. xii. 28. [2] Acts i. 7. [3] Mark iv. 11. [4] Acts xv. 14.

up spiritual sacrifices" to God, in that it is formed of those who "are called, and justified, and sanctified in the name of the Lord Jesus and by the Spirit of our God,"[1] and hence, "is not of this world" but from Heaven, as having God for its author; yet, as a *visible* Church among men, the spiritual is united to or with the physical, the *body* of the believer being made "the temple" for the indwelling "of the *Holy Ghost*."[2] Such, therefore, "walk by faith and not by sight,"[3] proving thereby that "the kingdom of God" in mystery consisteth "not of meat and drink, but of righteousness, and peace, and joy in the Holy Ghost."[4] It follows, that in the Christian Church as at first constituted, and as it must ever remain, we have the corporeal *joined with* the spiritual, in all the true followers of Christ. This union is illustrated by that of the branches to the vine,[5] of the building to the foundation, and of the members of the body to the head,[6] etc. And finally, St. Paul takes in the *entire personality* of the believer as a complex being in the words—"I pray God your whole spirit, and soul, and body, be preserved blameless, unto the coming of our Lord Jesus Christ."[7] But we observe,

2. That, in reference to the distinction above indicated, between the kingdom of God in mystery and the same kingdom in its *future manifestation*, the meaning is, that the present is the dispensation of the Holy Spirit[8] for the *ingathering* of the loyal subjects of Christ's coming kingdom,

---

[1] i Cor. vi. 11. [2] 1 Cor. iii. 16. [3] 2 Cor. v. 7. [4] 1 Rom. xiv. 17.
[5] John xv. 1–5. [6] 1 Cor. iii. 9. [7] 1 Thess. v. 23. [8] John xiv. 15–17; 25, 26.

through the work and reign of grace in the hearts of all who are "taken out of (or from among) the Gentiles to the praise of His name."[1] Hence, not *until* Christ receives that kingdom from the hand of the Father—as depicted in the parable of the nobleman who "took his journey into a far country to *receive a kingdom and to return*"[2]—can "the consecrated host of God's elect" hail their now absent Lord and King with the acclaim—"Blessed is He that cometh in the name of Lord,"[3] or receive from Him the welcome, "Come ye blessed of my Father, inherit the kingdom prepared for you from before the foundation of the world."[4] Finally, on this subject, we remark,

3. If to the above it be objected that our blessed Lord declares, "flesh and blood cannot inherit the kingdom of God, neither can corruption inherit incorruption :"[5] our reply is, that, inasmuch as this objection is founded on the fallacious theory that the soul only is the man, or person, and hence ignores the doctrine of a *literal* resurrection of the body after death ; it arises, we submit, from a total misapprehension of the *nature* of the resurrected state. The impossibility of "flesh and blood inheriting the kingdom of God," evidently refers to the present body as "*vile*," polluted by sin, and subject to death ; and not to the same body as *raised* and changed. For, as we have shown, "the blood, which is the (animal) life" in man in this state, and which, when congealed causes death ; in his spiritualized

---

[1] Acts xv. 14.   [2] Luke xix. 12.   [3] Matt. xxiii. 39.
[4] Ib.—xxv. 34.   [5] 1 Cor. xv. 50.

resurrected state, forms no longer *a part* of his corporeal nature." "Death is then destroyed." It is "swallowed up in victory." "Corruption puts on incorruption." The body thenceforward "dies no more. Death has no more dominion over him."[1] This is undeniable, if our blessed Lord spake truly when He said, " I AM THE RESURRECTION AND THE LIFE ; whosoever believeth in me, though he were dead, yet shall he live : and whosoever believeth in me *shall never die.*"[2] And, as to the nature of the resurrected state, the "blood" being no longer the basis of man's organic life, being rendered immortal by the resurrecting power of Christ ; although the transformation which then takes effect upon the body of man, both in kind and degree, is inscrutable to us, yet we have the assurance that when He comes again the second time, " He will *change* our vile bodies, and fashion them LIKE UNTO HIS OWN GLORIOUS BODY ;"[3] aye, and that in such manner as that we shall be made partakers " of His flesh and of His bones."—(See Eph. v. 30.). It is hence in place here to allude to the declaration of Job—" In my flesh shall I see God."[4] These statements, therefore, when taken together, are expository of the nature of man's resurrected organic state, of which our Lord's declaration to His apostles after His own resurrection is the key : addressing Himself to them, He says—" Handle me and see : for *spirit hath not* flesh and bones, AS YE SEE ME HAVE."[5] Stronger language than the above, in affirming the *actual*

---

[1] Rom. vi. 9.   [2] John xi. 25.   [3] Phi.ipp. iii. 21.
[4] Job xix. 26.   [5] Luke xxiv. 39.

corporeity of the risen bodies both of Christ and His saints, cannot be conceived.

With these preliminaries in view, we now pass to a more direct elucidation of the subject in hand. This relates to,

THE PHYSICAL CONSTITUTION OF THE FUTURE "INHERITANCE OF THE SAINTS," AS CONTRADISTINGUISHED FROM THE "HEAVEN IN" WHICH IT IS SAID TO BE.

The apostle Peter represents the believer as "begotten again unto a lively hope, by the resurrection of Jesus Christ from the dead, to an inheritance incorruptible, and undefiled, and that fadeth not away, reserved in Heaven for them."

Now, nothing can be more evident, as already stated, than that the inheritance here spoken of is one thing, and that Heaven is another. The inheritance is explicitly declared to be "IN Heaven." They are as absolutely distinct the one from the other, as are the planets from the Heaven of infinite space in which they float. It would be an absurdity to speak of an inheritance as being "*in*" an inheritance. On the other hand, in view of the doctrine of the intermediate state between death and the resurrection, where the believer, having "died in faith" of the promised inheritance at the resurrection morn, and where he "rests" in joyful expectation of its final conferment, it is perfectly consistent to speak of it as "*reserved in* Heaven" for him.

It follows, of course, that this inheritance, in its nature and properties, differs from the Heaven in which it is said to be, just as the orbs of the solar system differ from the æreal region in which they are suspended. Let it be observed, then, that in whatever consists the nature and properties of this inheritance which is the object of the believer's faith and hope, there must necessarily exist a *homogeneity* between them, and the nature and properties of man's resurrected corporeal being.

Now, of this "INHERITANCE," as made up of the various parts that appertain to it, the Scriptures abound in the most sublimely graphic descriptions. Take the following in illustration.

1. In its TERRITORIAL aspect, it is called, "*a country.*" As such, it is spoken of as that "better country," that is, a heavenly,"[1] because it is "*in* Heaven." And so, the country and the heaven combined, constitute that "New Earth and new Heaven wherein dwelleth righteousness."[2]

2. It is also called *A Kingdom*. As such, it is declared to have been "prepared from *before* the foundation of the world."[3] It is described as universal in its extent, being that "kingdom and dominion and greatness of the kingdom under the whole heaven," which in Daniel's prophecy is to "be given to the people of the saints of the most High," and which they are to "take and possess for ever and ever."[4] Its boundaries, therefore, extending "from sea to sea, and from the rivers to the end of the earth,"[5] will be commensurate with the entire "country" mentioned above. Then there is connected with this "Kingdom,"

[1] Heb. xi. 16.   [2] ii Pet. iii. 13.
[3] Matt. xxv. 34. See also John xvii. 24; Eph. i. 4.
[4] Dan. vii. 22, 27.   [5] Zech. ix. 10.

3. *A City*, which hath foundations, whose Builder and Maker is God."[1] This is the same with that "*Holy City, new Jerusalem*," which St. John "saw coming down or descending from God out of Heaven" to the earth.[2] As shown in vision to the prophet, it is thus described :—" And I John saw the Holy City, new Jerusalem." . . . " One of the seven angels came unto me, and carried me away in the spirit to a great and high mountain, and showed me that Great City, the Holy Jerusalem" . . . " having the glory of God: and her light was like unto a stone most precious, even like a jasper stone, clear as crystal ; and had a wall, great and high ; and had twelve gates, and at the gates twelve angels, and names written thereon," etc., (i. e., the gates), " which are the names of the twelve tribes of Israel : on the east three gates ; on the north three gates ; on the south three gates ; and on the west three gates. And the wall of the city had twelve foundations, and in them the names of the twelve apostles of the Lamb. And he that talked with me had a golden reed (in his hand) to measure the city, and the gates thereof, and the wall thereof. And the city lieth four square, and the length is as large as the breadth : and he measured the city with the reed, twelve thousand furlongs. The length, and the breadth, and the height are equal. And he measured the wall thereof, a hundred and forty and four cubits, according to the measure of a man, that is, of an angel. And the building of the wall was jasper, and the city was pure gold, like unto clear

---

[1] Heb. xi. 10, 16.   [2] Rev. xxi. 2, 10, compared with verse 1st and 3rd, etc.

glass. And the foundations of the wall of the city were garnished with all manner of precious stones. The first was a jasper; the second, sapphire; the third, a chalcedony; the fourth, an emerald; the fifth, sardonyx; the sixth, sardius; the seventh, chrysolite; the eighth, beryl; the ninth, a topaz; the tenth, a chrysoprasus; the eleventh, a jacinth; the twelfth, an amethist. And the twelve gates were twelve pearls; every several gate was a pearl. And the street of the city was pure gold, as it were transparent glass. And I saw no temple therein; for the Lord God Almighty and the Lamb are the temple of it. And the city had no need of the sun, neither of the moon, to shine in it: for the glory of God did lighten it, and the Lamb is the light thereof."[1]

"And he (the angel) shewed me a pure river of water of life, clear as crystal, proceeding out of the throne of God and the Lamb. In the midst of the street of it," (i. e., the city), "and on either side of the river, was the Tree of Life, which bear twelve manner (or kinds) of fruits, and yielded her fruit every month; and the leaves of the trees were for the healing of the nations."[2]

For, "the nations of them which are saved shall walk in the light of it: and kings do bring their glory and honor into it. And the gates of it shall not be shut at all by day: for there shall be no night there."[3] Then, further—

4. In this "better country" or "kingdom," which our blessed Lord calls "His Father's House," He tells us "are many *Mansions*." And finally,

[1] Rev. xxi. 2, 10, and verse 10-23.   [2] Ib.—xxii. 1, 2.
[3] Ib—xxii. 24, 25, and verse 26.

5. Taking the whole collectively—the "country," "kingdom," "city," and "mansions"—the apostle Paul places them among "the PRINCIPALITIES IN the Heavenly places."

As it regards the question of the *literality* of these magnificent representations, unless, as the great Luther says, by following the allegorical interpretations of Origen, we are at liberty to "make just what we please of the Scriptures,"— (and of whom Dr. Milner the Ecclesiastical historian, when speaking of his theory, says: "No man ever injured the church more than he did)"[1] the most tortuous efforts to construe and apply them figuratively, must prove totally unavailing in giving their true sense. On the other hand, if taken as literally as when we speak of any other of the countless orbs scattered through the ethereal expanse of "the Heaven of heavens," then we have an intelligent and consistent view of the *adaptation* of the physical constitution of "the new heavens and earth," to the complex corporeal and spiritual nature of man in resurrection glory.

As it needs no further argument to prove that the "better country, even an Heavenly," together with its appurtenances, "the Holy City, new Jerusalem," and the "many mansions," constitute the *final* abode of the saints, and of which Jesus, as the omnipotent Restorer of all things, is the architect; so we are assured that, by A TITLE-DEED, sealed "by an oath of twofold immutability in which it is impossible for God to lie,"[2] "the heirs of promise" shall at last be admitted to its full and eternal possession and enjoyment, as that "Inheritance

---

[1] See pages 136, 137.   [2] Heb. vi. 16-20.

incorruptible and undefiled, and that fadeth not away," now "reserved in Heaven for them.".

O MOTHER DEAR, JERUSALEM.

O mother dear, Jerusalem,
    When shall I come to thee?
When shall my sorrows have an end?
    Thy joys when shall I see?
O happy harbor of God's saints!
    O sweet and pleasant soil!
In Thee no sorrow can be found;
    Nor grief, nor care, nor toil.

No dimning cloud o'ershadows thee,
    Nor gloom, nor darksome night;
But every soul shines as the sun,
    For God himself gives light.
Thy walls are made of precious stones,
    Thy bulwarks diamond square,
Thy gates are all of orient pearl—
    O God, if I were there!

Right through thy streets with pleasing sound
    The flood of life doth flow,
And on the bank, on either side,
    The trees of life do grow
Those trees each month yield ripened fruit;
    For evermore they spring,
And all the nations of the earth
    To Thee their honors bring.

There the blest souls that hardly 'scaped
    The snares of death and hell,
Triumph in joy eternally,
    Whereof no tongue can tell.

> O mother dear, Jerusalem!
>   When shall I come to thee!
>   When shall my sorrows have an end?
>   Thy joys when shall I see?   F. B. P. 1616.
>
>   (*From " The Sacrifice of Praise." Brick Church
>   Presb. Hymns.*)

No marvel, therefore, that the apostle Paul in view of it exclaimed : " Eye hath not seen, nor ear heard, neither have entered the heart of man, the things which God hath prepared for them that love Him ! " [1]

In the light of these representations, then, may we not ask :—if the Primitive Eden, in all its freshness, and purity, and salubrity, and life-preserving vitality, and beauty, and glory, had been preserved to man, and transmitted to an unfallen posterity through the ages of ages, girded by the expansive belt of the serene Heaven *in* which it floated— we repeat, had all this so been, would it not have been to *you*, reader, a condition of Heavenly Blessedness commensurate with your most enlarged aspirations? Why, even the possession and enjoyment of such a luxurious habitation as abundant wealth can procure in a country villa or a city palace in man's *present state*, could their occupant have an assurance against their loss or decay, and exemption from wearisome toil, carking care, wasting sickness, and the dread of death, may we not doubt whether he would ever desire any other Heaven of happiness?

Indeed, on this subject, we appeal : Is not the above supposition confirmed by the *intensity* of human attachment to

---

[1] 1 Cor. ii. 9.

the things of earth? Whence else, then, the toil, and sweat of brains and of body, and the persevering ardor with which men, year by year, labor to "make haste to get rich?" And, when attained, and in the enjoyment of all that wealth can yield from the abundant store-house of earth's luxuries, how *reluctant* to surrender them up to the relentless hand of death?

And, we once more appeal: Wherefore this predominating propensity in the soul of man? It has its source, we reply, in the very constitution of his complex nature of a physical, as well as an intellectual being. We have only to add, therefore, that the worldling's error and sin consists in this, to wit, a forgetfulness of the *forfeiture*, by a defection from God as his sovereign Head, of his original Eden inheritance, and of his seeking its restoration in an *unlawful* way. He forgets that, by the sin of "the first Adam," he, and in him, his posterity after him, *lost* his primeval lordship in and over the earth, which thenceforward fell into the hands of the satanic usurper of his original rights, leaving him and them powerless, physically, intellectually, and morally, to wrench it from his grasp!

But, praised be God! There is ONE, who is held up to his view, who is declared to be "stronger than the strong man armed," even "THE SECOND MAN, the Lord from Heaven;" who, as the divinely constituted "Heir of all things," steps in between the usurper of His and of man's rights over the earthly "dominion," and who proffers its *restoration* to all who will accept it on His terms—namely, simple faith in Him as the promised seed, Christ, "the Lamb of God," whose atoning blood alone can "take away the sins of the world," and "repentance toward God," accompanied with a holy life.

In man's aspirations to the possession of an "inheritance" adapted to his whole complex nature, physical, intellectual, and moral, therefore, it is only necessary to give a *right direction* to the predominating propensity of which we here speak. In other words, if that propensity be but *sanctified* by the spirit and grace of God, so that, in place of seeking its recovery in and of himself, he looks *by faith* for its accomplishment through the Great Restorer, the Lord Jesus Christ, all will be well. For then, having been " begotten again unto a lively hope by the resurrection of Jesus Christ from the dead," he is made " an *heir* of God and a *joint heir* with Christ," to that "inheritance incorruptible, and undefiled, and that fadeth not away;" or, the LOST PARADISE RESTORED, with infinitely augmented grandeur, and glory, and permanency, and in which, as " the new Heavens and the new earth" which the Lord will " create," there "shall dwell righteousness " eternal.

O PARADISE, O PARADISE.

O Paradise, O Paradise!
Who doth not crave for rest?
Who would not seek that happy land
Where they that loved are blest?
Where royal hearts and true
Stand ever in the light,
All rapture through and through,
In God's most holy sight.

O Paradise, O Paradise !
  The world is growing old ;
Who would not be at rest, and free
  Where love is never cold ?
    Where loyal hearts and true
      Stand ever in the light,
    All rapture through and through,
      In God's most holy sight.

O Paradise, O Paradise !
  'Tis weary waiting here ;
I long to be where Jesus is,
  To feel, to see him near ;
    Where loyal hearts and true
      Stand ever in the light,
    All rapture through and through,
      In God's most holy sight.

O Paradise, O Paradise !
  I want to sin no more—
I want to be as pure on earth
  As on thy spotless shore :
    Where loyal hearts and true'
      Stand ever in the light,
    All rapture through and through,
      In God's most holy sight.

O Paradise, O Paradise !
  I greatly long to see
The special place my dearest Lord
  In love prepares for me ;
    Where loyal hearts and true
      Stand ever in the light,
    All rapture through and through,
      In God's most holy sight.

> Lord Jesu, King of Paradise!
> O keep me in Thy love,
> And guide me to that happy land,
> Of perfect rest above;
> > Where loyal hearts and true
> > Stand ever in the light,
> > All rapture through and through,
> > In God's most holy sight.
>
> *Frederick W. Faber,* 1862. *(From " The Sacrifice of Praise." Brick Ch. Presb. Hymns.)*

In conclusion, then, on this subject, we see the *error* of those who undervalue, despise, and hold in contempt this earth which God has created, and which is destined, according to " His eternal purpose which He purposed in Christ Jesus our Lord" as the God-man, to be the theatre, first, of His *suffering*, and finally of His *glorified* Humanity, to the praise of His infinite attributes, perfections, and works throughout all ages. The poet has truly said—

> "'Tis by comparison an easy task,
> Earth to despise."

But, we submit that we have shown, as a matter of Divine Revelation, that it is inconsistent with man's predestined "Inheritance" on earth in his *resurrected* state, as it is dishonoring God!

SECTION III.

THE SYMPATHETIC RELATIONS EXISTING BETWEEN THE INVISIBLE AND VISIBLE WORLDS.

I. Of the Divine Sympathy between Heaven and Earth.

THE first inspired light reflected on this subject, is the relation of what immediately followed the creation of the earth and the heavens, and of man. We read, that in Eden, " the LORD GOD walked in the garden in the cool of the day," to hold *visible* converse with him whom He had " created in His own image and likeness,"[1] in virtue of His original covenant relation to him.

Of the precise form of this Divine manifestation we know nothing. And, for a little season, it was *interrupted*. Man sinned, and God spurned him from His presence. " O! what a night was that! . . . Not only did God retire, but all Heaven put frowns of anger on. The angels, which had no doubt before been companions of the once happy pair in Paradise, were commissioned with orders and power to *banish* them from Eden. See Heaven and earth separate! See God retire! See Adam and Eve, now fallen, the other path,

——' With wandering steps and slow,
Through Eden take their solitary way.'[2]

Alas! was ever an hour like that? Eden lost! God's favor lost! communication with Heaven closed!"[3]

[1] Gen. i. 26, 27.   [2] Gen. iii. 22, 24.   [3] Harbaugh on Heaven. Page 183.

But, blessed be God! This suspension of the sympathies between Heaven and earth, and God and man, was but for " a little while!" In the promise made to man prior to his expulsion from Eden—"The seed of the woman shall bruise the serpent's head,"—the barrier occasioned by his sin was removed, and the way was opened for a *renewal* of those sympathetic relations which have since existed between the invisible and the visible worlds. We read that, after having expelled man from Eden, JEHOVAH placed that very " cherubim," and that very " sword," the edge of which, turning every way, "*kept the way to* the Tree of Life,"[1] thus adumbrating

---

[1] We read, that, *after* having expelled man from Eden, Jehovah placed at the east that very Cherubim, and that very sword, the edge of which, turning every way, kept the way of (or to) the tree of life. Gen. iv. 24. The whole passage may be analyzed thus:

I. "*And he*" (Jehovah Elohim) "*placed*"—or "*dwelt.*"—(Heb., Ischechinah.). Of the same import with that which speaks of God as having "dwelt" in the burning bush, Exod. iii. 4-6; Deut. xxxii. 16. The proper rendering therefore is, "*dwelt* or *inhabited.*"

II. "*At*" (Heb. from) "*the east*" (Heb., chedem) where the sun is first seen to rise.

III. "*Cherubims.*" The place of habitation of the DEITY; and, as in the Tabernacle and Temple, so at the gate of Paradise.

IV. "*And a flaming sword which turned every way*," or, turning itself (Heb., Emptepechet) every way—i. e., like a rolling flame of fire, it turned itself *within* or *upon* itself.

V. "*To keep the way of* (Heb. or to) *the tree of life.*"

The above may be paraphrased thus: "And the Lord God *dwelt or inhabited*, at or *from* the east, *where the sun is first seen to rise, Cherubims and a flaming sword, the place of habitation for the Deity, which turned every way, like a rolling flame of fire, turning itself within or upon itself*, to keep the way of, or to, the tree of life."

The first clause of the passage Parkhurst reads thus: "And Jehovah Aleim caused to dwell, or placed in a tabernacle at the east of the garden, the Cherubim,"

God's purpose, through the promised seed, Christ, to take the earth and man *back again* into sympathetic covenant relation with Himself !

&c. The word, *Ischechinah*, rendered in the text, " placed," or more significantly, dwelt or inhabited, is that whence we derive the term SCHECHINAH, which is always in Scripture taken for the *Divine " Presence."* The Apostle Paul terms it, "THE GLORY," (Rom. ix. 4.) " So the word," *Ischechinah*, he adds " expresses a Tabernacle, in which the Cherubim and emblematic fire or glory, were placed, *from the fall !*"from which, continues he, " it is certain that the Israelites had a Tabernacle sacred to Jehovah, *long before* that erected by Moses."

The addition *to* the Cherubims of the *flaming sword*, teaches us that as Deity, in the time of Moses and before the erection either of the Tabernacle or Temple, descended and dwelt in the burning bush at Horeb, so in the instance before us. The Divine Presence and Glory curtained beneath the Cherubims appeared at the gate of Paradise, brandishing a flaming sword which turned every way, indicating thereby the *mode* of his personal manifestations in future ages ; intimating thereby the purpose of God to *unite* his ineffable nature with ours in the person of JESUS CHRIST, the *promised seed* of the woman. Hence the following language of the prophet : " *Awake*, O SWORD, *against my* SHEPHERD, *and against* THE MAN that is my FELLOW, saith the Lord of Hosts." Zech. xiii. 7.

The object of these remarks in reference to the above passage, is, to remove from the mind a very common and general error regarding its import ; which is, that " the Cherubims and a flaming sword" are looked upon as emblems of the Almighty's *wrath ;* and messengers of *terror*, sent to execute his *vengeance* upon man, and to *cut off* all further approach *to*, and benefit *from*, " THE TREE OF LIFE." Rather, as is herein shown, they were designed to inculcate the doctrine of *Piacular or Expiatory Sacrifice through the incarnation and sufferings of Christ.* Archdeacon Daubeny on this subject observes—" In conformity with the *mode* of conveying spiritual knowledge through the medium of visible objects, *a certain emblematic representation* under the name of [the SCHECHINAH dwelling beneath the Cherubims] was set up at the east of the Garden of Eden *immediately* after the fall ; for the purpose (as it is recorded) of *keeping or preserving* a way TO the tree of life ; that ' hereby,' as Bishop Horne observes, he might ' be continually *reminded* of the great truths communicated to him, no doubt, from the beginning, viz., that there was *another* and a *better life* than that now led by him in his *terrestrial* temple here below ; and that the *Sabbath* itself was a type of sublimer service and a sweeter rest,' "etc.

No: the earth, while under the curse of sin, though doomed to "bring forth thorns and thistles," and disease, and misery, is not destined to perish for ever! No: Man, under the curse of sin, though doomed to "eat his bread by the sweat of his face till he return to the ground whence he came," is not shut out for ever from all intercourse with his God, nor destined to eternal annihilation! In virtue of the redemptive vicarial sacrifice for sin in the person of the woman's seed, CHRIST JESUS, the interval between "Paradise Lost" and "Paradise Regained," was to be filled up with evidences the most demonstrative, that Man *was not* totally and for ever severed from his God as a thing of naught![1]

The unseen world, so far as we know, is inhabited by three orders of intelligences—Divine, Angelic, and Human. We come now to inquire in what relation *we* stand to each of these, while we are here on earth; and what is the nature of their sympathies with us, and of ours with them. Have we *any communion* with them? And if we have, of what *nature* is it? and in *what way* is it manifested?

Nor let the pious reader be alarmed, as though, in being brought into contact with this subject, he is to be exposed to the horrid and soul-ruining delusion of *modern spiritualism*. He will find instead, that the reflections that are to follow will furnish the *only effectual antidote* to that device of "the spirits of devils, working miracles, which are going forth to deceive them that dwell upon the earth;"[2] and that they cannot fail, if rightly improved, "to bring us consciously near

---

[1] See preceding note, the last two paragraphs.   [2] Rev. xvi. 13, 14.

to the world of spirits," so as " to make us feel that heaven and earth," and God, angels, and men, " are not so coldly related as cold and unreflecting hearts are ready to imagine."[1] Let us then dwell the while on the subject,

I. *Of the Sympathetic Relations which exist between God, the Earth, and Man.*

THE PRESENCE OF GOD WITH MAN.

" O ! wondrous truth to fabling fiction given,
 Of one that *walked on earth*, and fixed His head *in Heaven;*
  Whose stature is eternity,
  His crown the living sky !
 Or rather like a spirit's love,
  Whose form to mortal sense is all invisible ;
 Yet still around doth dwell and move
  Around, yet *how,* we cannot tell."

1. God is present in *Nature's* works. Not in the Pantheistic sense, that Nature is God, but that Nature *reveals* God as present throughout His vast dominions. Thus, " the Heavens declare the glory of God, and the earth showeth forth His handy-work."[2] For, " the invisible things of Him from the creation of the world are clearly seen, being understood by the things that are made, even His eternal power and Godhead."[3] The blazing light of the sun, the silver glimmerings of the moon, and the bright twinkling of the stars, all, all show a *present* God. And so, also, of the

---

1 Harbaugh on Heaven, page 191.
2 Ps. xix. 1. 3 Rom. i. 20.

waving fields of grain, the budding and blooming of the flowers, and the grassy carpet of earth, we may say—

> "These, as they change, ALMIGHTY FATHER, these
> Are but the varied God. The rolling year
> Is full of Thee. Forth in the pleasing spring
> Thy beauty walks, Thy tenderness and love."

And so,

2. God is present in *Providence.* By this we mean, not that providence in the abstract, is God, but that He by His power in providence directs, guides and controls all the affairs of this lower world. In this sense, it is, first, *general.* As His omniscient eye surveys all, so His omnipresence pervades all His works, to uphold, and guide, and control all. He is present in the calm of the evening twilight, in the thunder and the storm. "He is the Governor among the nations." "By Him kings rule and princes decree justice." Hence the exclamation of the Psalmist: "Whither shall I go from Thy Spirit? or whither shall I flee from Thy presence?" He not only fills "the Heaven of heavens," but is present also in the unseen region of "hell," (SHEOL or HADES), while "the remotest parts of the sea" or the midnight "darkness" cannot extend beyond the reach of His hand or the sight of His eye. The same will apply to God's *special* Providence. "Not a sparrow can fall to the ground without His notice," and He "numbereth the very hairs of our head." And, if God cares for sparrows and clothes the fields with lilies, will He not much more care for and clothe us? But, in a more special, exalted, and

sublimely glorious sense, is the most high God present with Man,

3. IN THE PERSON OF THE LORD JESUS CHRIST, and of the HOLY SPIRIT. Yes, the God Triune—Father, Son, and Holy Ghost—as the "Three that bear record in Heaven," each have a sympathy and hold communion with, Man on earth. Else, what is the meaning of these words of the inspired apostle—" Truly *our fellowship* is with the Father?" But the Father has His throne of state in the "highest" or empyreal "Heavens." How then can it be said that we hold communion with Him of whom it is declared that " no man hath seen God at any time ?" The answer is, that while, as the omnipresent infinite Spirit, we can hold no direct communion with Him ; yet, as the manifested God— " GOD IN CHRIST"—every barrier is thrown down, and we are admitted to hold " fellowship with the Father" through our " fellowship with His Son, Jesus Christ." Not that in this divinely appointed and deeply mysterious process, we can separate the operations of the two Divine persons, yet we can distinguish between them, as connected with the great work of our redemption from sin and the curse of God's broken law. Jesus Christ, as MEDIATOR between God and Man,—" God manifest in the flesh"—laid hold upon Heaven with one hand, and upon Man on earth with the other, and thus, " *reconciled* both by His body on the cross." Yes,

HEAVEN AND EARTH RECONCILED.

> —— "The partition wall by Moses built,
> By Christ was levelled, and the Gentile world
> Enter the breach, by their Great Captain led,
> Up to the throne of grace, opening Himself,
> Through his own flesh, A NEW AND LIVING WAY."

Hence, Jesus becomes the *medium* of the restored and perpetuated sympathy between Heaven and earth, God and man. It may be traced in its historic developments to that smile of the Divine complaisance, which fell upon the *accepted* sacrifice of Abel. It was vouchsafed to the antediluvian patriarchs, when "men began to call upon," or rather to be "called by the name of the Lord." Also to Enoch and Noah, who "walked with God." So Abraham in the plains of Mamre, and Lot in Sodom, and Isaac and Jacob and Joseph too, received the assurances of the Divine sympathy, protection, and favor. But especially does this hold true of Jacob, who obtained the most clear and sweetly prophetic pledge of the sympathy ultimately to be established between earth and Heaven, in its higher and more perfect form, when, fleeing from the face of his angered brother Esau towards Paran, while reposing his weary head upon a pillow of stones in the solitary wilderness. There, in his night slumber, " he dreamed, and behold, a ladder set up upon the earth, and the top of it reached to heaven: and behold, *the angels of God ascending and descending upon it.* And behold, THE LORD *stood above it!*" " And Jacob awoke out of his sleep, and he said, *surely the Lord is in this place,* and I knew it not

And he was afraid, and said, How dreadful is this place! This is none other than the house of God, and this is the gate of Heaven!"[1]

In the subsequent history of Abraham's covenant seed down to the Incarnation of the Lord Jesus, we find an *inchoate* verification of the thing thus typically foreshadowed in Jacob's prophetic vision. For example, When the Lord appeared to Moses in Horeb, in the midst of the burning but unconsumed bush; [2] and again in " the pillar of cloud by day and of fire by night," as a guide to the hosts of Israel during their forty years' nomadic wanderings in the wilderness. [3] But more eminently still, when the Divine Presence, in the mysterious form of the SHECHINAH, took up His abode in the Most Holy Place, first, in the tabernacle and afterwards in the temple, curtained beneath the outstretched wings of the cherubims over the mercy-seat, [4] and which is designated by St. Paul, "THE GLORY." [5]

It was reserved, however, for that more perfect display of the Divine sympathy between earth and Heaven, God and Man, which took place in the wondrous scenes which transpired, during the interval from the incarnation at Bethlehem to that on Calvary's Cross. The woman's promised seed, MESSIAH, is born. "The WORD made flesh" is inducted into His public ministry by His baptism. He enters upon His *prophetic* office as the Great Teacher sent from God to the people; performs a series of the most astounding miracles in attestation of the fact of His Messiahship as pointed out by

---

[1] Gen. xxviii. 10-17. [2] Exod. iii. 1-5. [3] Exod. xxxiii. 9-10.
[4] Exod. xxv. 17-20-22. [5] Rom. ix. 4.

the old prophets; and finally being rejected by the Jewish nation, and betrayed by Judas Iscariot, as a priest, He expiates human sin and guilt by His vicarial sacrifice upon the cross—aye, and all this, in proof of the *sympathy* on the part of the Triune Jehovah in behalf of the Earth and of Man! Thus,

> "God, the mighty Maker died,
> For *Man*, the creature's sin."

Yes! "God so loved the world, that He gave His only begotten Son, that whosoever believeth in Him, might not perish, but have everlasting life." [1]

> "O for such love let rocks and hills
> Their lasting silence break;
> And all harmonious human tongues,
> The SAVIOUR's praises speak!"

It remained, however, for the Transfiguration on the Mount,[2] to furnish a still more complete exhibition of this ineffably Divine emotion of sympathy in man's behalf. Here we have, not a type merely, but an *earnest* or *pattern* of that Heavenly Blessedness, when the earth and man shall be fully restored from the effects of the curse, and when once more and for ever, "THE TABERNACLE OF GOD SHALL BE WITH MEN, AND HE WILL DWELL WITH THEM, AND THEY SHALL BE HIS PEOPLE, AND GOD HIMSELF SHALL BE WITH THEM, AND BE THEIR GOD." [3] In the transfiguration, our blessed Lord was manifested in his glorified Humanity as "KING OF KINGS AND

---

[1] John iii. 16.   [2] Matt. xvii. 1-4.   [3] Rev. xxi. 3.

LORD OF LORDS, [1] on such wise that He might be recognized by the Church as the only rightful Sovereign of the Universe. MOSES, raised from the dead, the representative of the *risen dead* in Christ; ELIAS, translated to heaven without seeing death, prefiguring the change and rapture of the *living saints* who remain unto his coming; [2] while PETER, JAMES and JOHN, filled the place in the glorious scene, answerable to those of whom it is said—in reference to "the Holy City, new Jerusalem"—"and *the nations of them that are saved* shall walk in the light of it, and the kings of the earth do bring their glory and honor into it." [3] And, JESUS, as the central object of attraction in the beatific group, the divinely constituted "HEAD OVER ALL THINGS to the glory of God the Father," of "the general assembly of the first-born who are written in Heaven." [4]

But, the true believer has "fellowship with the Father and with His Son Jesus Christ," not only, but also,

4. He enjoys the same "fellowship" or "communion with the HOLY GHOST." [5] As "the Son hath life in Himself," [6] so that "life" is *imparted* to the believer, through the influences of "the Holy Spirit of promise," [7] who enlightens, [8] regenerates, and sanctifies [9] him, and thus brings him into "*fellowship*" with the God Triune. In this manner is formed the "one body," or "the church of the living God," [10] by the one spirit" [11] which influences and quickens all. Hence the *sympathy* between Heaven and earth by and through the office-

---

1 Rev. xix. 16.   2 1 Thess. iv. 14-17.   3 Rev. xxi. 24-26.
4 Eph. i. 22; iv. 15; Col. i. 18.   5 2 Cor. xiii. 14.   6 John v. 26.
7 Eph. i. 13.   8 Ib. verse 13.   9 Titus iii. 5; Rom. xv. 16.
10 Col. i. 18.   11 1 Cor. vi. 17.

work of the Holy Ghost." HE brings all things to our remembrance, whatsoever Jesus has said unto us."[1] "God hath sent forth His spirit into our hearts, whereby we cry, Abba, Father."[2] And so also, "the Spirit beareth witness with our spirits, that we are the children of God ; and if children, then theirs ; heirs of God, and joint-heirs with Christ."[3]

It is, therefore, on these grounds and on such principles, *and on these only*, that Heaven and Earth, God and Man, exchange their sympathies.

We now pass to consider,

II.—*Angelic Sympathies between Heaven and Earth.*

ANGELIC MINISTRATIONS.

"Are they not all ministering spirits, sent forth to minister to them who shall be heirs of salvation?"

> "Millions of angelic beings walk the earth
> *Unseen*, both when we wake, and when we sleep.
> All these with ceaseless praise his works behold,
> Both day and night. How often from the steep
> Of heavenly hill or thicket, have we heard
> Celestial voices to the midnight air,
> Sole, or responsive to each others note,
> Sing their GREAT CREATOR ! Oft in bands,
> While they keep watch, or nightly rounding walk
> With heavenly touch of instrumental sounds,
> In full harmonic numbers joined, their songs
> Divide the night, *and lift our thoughts to Heaven.*

[1] John xiv. 26. [2] Gal iv. 6. [3] Rom. viii. 17.

As we have said, angels are created beings. When they were created, we know not. They are first brought to our notice in connection with the earliest dawn of the Creator's work in the formation of the present heavens and earth out of the chaotic elements of nature, when it is said that "the morning stars sang together, *and all the sons of God* shouted for joy." That they are in their nature, both corporeal and spiritual beings, has been already shown in a previous page. That they are endowed with a *superior order* of intelligence, is evident from the inspired comparison made by the woman of Tekoah, between the wisdom of David and that of an angel: "My lord is wise, according to the wisdom of an angel of God, to know all things that are on the earth."[1] And that they are also endowed with great power, as God's instruments in the execution of His purposes both of mercy and of judgment, is abundantly attested by their agency over and their acts among mortals. The chief dwelling-place of the angelic orders, is around the throne of the Infinite Majesty in the "*highest*" or *empyreal* "Heaven." "In the year that king Uzziah died," the prophet Isaiah in a vision "saw also the LORD, sitting upon a throne, high and lifted up, and His train (angelic) *filled the temple*. Above it stood the seraphims: each one had six wings: with twain they covered their face, and with twain they covered their feet, and with twain they did fly,"[2] etc. Then too, of their number. "The chariots of God are twenty thousand, even thousands of angels."[3] And Jesus, when betrayed into the hands of His murderers, said: "Thinkest thou that I

---

[1] ii. Sam. xiv. 20.   [2] Isa. vi. 1, 2.   [3] Ps. lxviii. 17.

cannot now pray to my Father, and He shall presently give Me more than twelve legions (60,000) of angels?" [1] While St. John says, "and I beheld, and I heard the voice of many angels round about the throne; and the number of them was ten thousand times ten thousand, and thousands of thousands." [2]

Accordingly, dwelling thus in the immediate presence of "the eternal power and Godhead," they are not only in measure acquainted, but they *sympathize* with, all those Divine purposes connected with the great MEDIATORIAL work of the Lord Jesus Christ, in reference to the salvation of lost man. St. Paul tells us that "the angels *desire to look into* these things;" [3] and that, with a view to execute such commands issued from the eternal throne, as are connected with their official work as "ministering spirits, sent forth to minister to them who shall be the *heirs* of salvation." [4]

We have already spoken of the vision of Jacob's ladder. And, what a vision! What a beautiful type of heaven and earth *united!* Now, we have said that it was *prophetic.* That it is so, appears from our blessed Lord's allusion to it in the following prophecy: "Hereafter," says He, "ye shall see Heaven open, and the angels of God ascending and descending upon the Son of man." [5] Here then we are furnished with a golden chain of evidence of that *angelic* sympathy between Heaven and earth, God and man, extending from the time of Jacob, onward to the final triumph of the Great Restorer of all things in Heaven and earth.

[1] Matt. xxvi. 53.   [1] Rev. v. 11.   [3] 1 Peter i. 12.   [4] Heb. i. 14.
[5] Gen. xxviii. John i. 51.

Presuming upon the reader's familiarity with the numerous recorded instances of angelic visitations during the patriarchal and New Testament ages of the church, to save space, we shall omit a particular recapitulation of them. But, from the time of St. John's prophetic visions, all *visible* intercourse between Men on earth and the angelic orders, has been *suspended*. O! "who has not, in those still and thoughtful hours of life which God grants us so graciously, breathed forth" the following—

LAMENT OVER ANGELIC ABSENCE.

"'Why come not spirits from the realms of glory
    To visit th' earth as in the days of old—
The times of ancient writ, and sacred story?
    Is Heaven more distant? or has the earth grown cold?

Oft have I gazed, when sunset clouds, receding,
    Waved like rich banners of a host gone by,
To catch the gleam of some white pinion speeding,
    Along the confines of the glowing sky.

And oft when midnight stars in distant chillness
    Were calmly burning, listened late and long;
But nature's pulse beat on in solemn stillness,
    Bearing *no echo* to the seraph's song.

To Bethlehem's air was their *last anthem* given,
    When other stars before the one grew dim?
Was their *last presence* known in Peter's prison?
    Or where exulting martyrs raised their hymn?

> And are they all within the vail departed?
> There gleams no wing along th' empyrean Heaven:
> And many a tear from human eyes have started,
> Since *angel touch* has to them been given.'"

But, believer, cease thy "lament." True, *visibly*, thou art not permitted to participate in these angelic visitations as did Abraham, and Sarah, and Lot, and Isaac, and Jacob, and Menoah, together with JESUS, and Peter, and Paul, and John. Nevertheless, with the following declarations of Holy Scripture before us, it cannot be said of the *present*, any more than of the preceding dispensations, that the Heaven-bound pilgrim of earth is *cut off* from angelic sympathy. Did David say, "The angel of the Lord *encampeth* round about them that fear Him, and *delivereth* them?"[1] So of the passage already quoted from St. Paul: "Are they not all ministering spirits, sent forth to *minister to them* who shall be the heirs of salvation?"[2] If then, from the greater grossness of our natural vision compared with theirs, we cannot *perceive* their presence, are we hence to infer, that the above inspired apostolic declaration regarding the *sympathy* of angels, is any less true than that of David?

It is clear that, as already intimated, the angelic hosts are God's ministers of state, not only to execute His purposes in the form of judgments, but of mercies also. To argue, therefore, that angelic sympathy towards Man is confined to their visible presence only, would be to *limit* the power of God in the execution of His purposes through them.

---

[1] Ps. xxxiv. 7.   [2] Heb. i. 14.

But, no: if *in Heaven* "there is more" sympathetic "joy among the angels of God over one sinner (on earth) that repenteth, than over ninety and nine just persons that need no repentance,"¹—in which case they are unseen by us—why should it be thought a thing incredible, that the *same* unseen angels should extend their sympathies to the "elect" children of God *upon earth?* As, by their superior intelligence, they are declared to "know all things that are on the earth"—the trials, temptations, sorrows, fears and sufferings, both mental and bodily, of those who are "through much tribulation to enter into the kingdom of God;"² and also the knowledge, power, number, and devices of their great adversary the Devil, together with the malicious machinations against them of "wicked and deceitful men"—so, as their divinely appointed "ministering spirits" on earth, though unseen by them, they still possess the power of an angelic influence—the *sympathy* of an angelic mind brought into contact with the human—in behalf of the Christian warrior in his warfare "against the principalities and powers and spiritual wickedness in high places."

Nor this only. For, acquainted as these angelic beings are with all those *vicissitudes* of life to which God's people are exposed, they are present in the same way to take them by the hand as their guides in seasons of doubt and perplexity; and, thus accompanying them by their *sympathy* during life, in their final exit from this vale of tears—as in the case of the pious Lazarus,—to bear them away as their convoys to "the bosom of Abraham."

1 Luke xv. 7.   2 Acts xiv. 22.

It is reserved, however, for the grand and magnificent scenes of the Great Day of the Lord's coming, to furnish the *crowning evidence* of angelic sympathy between Heaven and earth. " For, then shall appear the sign of the Son of man in heaven : and then shall all the tribes of the earth mourn ; and they shall see the Son of man coming in the clouds of heaven with power and great glory. And He shall *send forth His angels* with a great sound of a trumpet, and they shall gather together His elect from the four winds, from one end of heaven to the other," [1] to enter into the possession of that " INHERITANCE "—" the kingdom prepared for them from before the foundation of the world." [2]

How comforting, therefore, to " the heirs of salvation," such an assurance of the Divine protection in their behalf, through this *sympathetic* ministration of these angelic though invisible agents ! Of the now personally absent Saviour, says St. Peter, " WHOM having *not seen*, ye love ; *in* whom, though now ye see Him not, yet believing, ye rejoice with joy unspeakable and full of glory : *receiving the end* of your faith, even the salvation of your souls." [3] Yea : *faith* lays hold upon Jesus, as our " Great High Priest over the house of God," who in His risen and glorified humanity is now " seated at the right hand of the Majesty in the heavens," there to show His continued sympathy in our behalf as one that is " touched with the feelings of our infirmities," while we are exposed to " the fiery darts " of " the god of this world," the *unseen* " prince of the power of the air," together with

---

[1] Matt. xxiv. 30, 31.   [2] Ib.—xxv. 34.   [3] 1 Pet. i. 8, 9.

all the other combined demoniacal "spirits of wickedness in high places," by "*interceding* for us." Wherefore, then, we ask, should we withhold our faith in the assurance, that the "elect angels," though invisible to us, are also, by *their* sympathy, "about our bed and our path" by night and by day, to "ward off the fiery darts of the wicked one" and "his angels," during our spiritual conflicts on earth? Alas! that our faith in this divinely appointed angelic interposition for our encouragement, support, and comfort, should have been so generally lost to the eye of faith and of trust on the part of the professed "heirs of salvation!"

We have at length reached the last article on this Scripturally revealed though deeply mysterious subject, as follows—

III. *Human Sympathy between the Departed and the Living.*

We introduce the reader to the following beautifully appropriate lines—

HUMAN SYMPATHY PERPETUATED.

"When once we close our eyes in death,
   And flesh and spirit sever:
When earth and father-land and home,
When all their beauty's sunk in gloom-
   Say, shall it be *for ever?*

O! will we (hence) no more review
   Those scenes from which we sever?
Or will our recollection *leap*
O'er *death's dark gulf*, at times to keep
   With (man) acquaintance *ever?*

> In life we love that blessed past,
>   It clings to us as ever :
> The songs of childhood and of home,
> Like music when the minstrel's gone,
>   *Live in our hearts* for ever.
>
> The child's included in the man,
>   And part of him for ever :
> The *past* still in the *future* lives,
> And basis to its being gives,
>   Not it, but *of* it, *ever !* "
>   Anon.

In the second stanzas above, we have taken the liberty to substitute the word (hence), in the place of " in heaven," and also (man), in that of " earth," as in the original. We do this on the ground that the poet, like Dr. Harbaugh and other writers, view the spirits of the departed saints as admitted, " at the instant of death," to a state or condition of *consummated* blessedness in the " highest " or empyreal " heaven where the body of the Saviour now is." Whereas, we claim to have demonstrated, that the place and state of the departed " sleepers in Christ " between death and the resurrection, is an intermediate abode called " Paradise "— " the third Heaven "—" Abraham's bosom," etc., in SHEOL or HADES, where, in a condition of conscious blessedness, they " rest " for " a little season," [1] in *expectation* of their final admittance to that incorruptible inheritance now " reserved IN heaven for them," when body and soul shall be reunited " at the appearing of Jesus Christ." For, until then, as St. Paul declares, the saints departed " shall not be made perfect with-

---

[1] Rev. vi. 9-11.

out us." [1] It is also clear, that, admitting that there *is now*, a sympathetic intercourse between the departed saints and believers on earth ; yet, when ALL the family of the redeemed shall have been admitted to their *final* inheritance in "the world to come," that sympathy which now exists between them, will terminate in the united and eternal companionship of both. This consideration, of itself, is suggestive of the difference in their respective relations now, as contrasted with that of the future. The former is the subject of present remark.

We shall be led to inquire into, I., the *basis* on which this mutual saintly sympathy rests. And II., the *fact* of the existence of this mutual sympathy. Both are included in those comprehensive and universally received words of the Apostle's Creed :—

"I BELIEVE IN THE HOLY CATHOLIC CHURCH, THE COMMUNION OF SAINTS," ETC.

I. The BASIS on which this mutual saintly sympathy rests. Now, if the latter part of the above creed—"The communion of saints" embraces both orders, the *dead* and the *living*, as the source of their mutual sympathy, then there must be *a common principle of union* on which it rests as its basis. But this depends solely upon what constitutes, in a Scriptural sense, "the Holy Catholic Church."

There are some who look upon the church of Christ militant on earth as a mere external organization, or as a congregation of believers united together for purposes

[1] Heb xi. 40.

of convenience. But if, instead, the church is constituted of a real and actual and vital *union* between Christ and true believers, in analogy to that of the fruit-bearing branches of the parabolic vine,[1] or of members to the body,[2] then, and on no other principle, are we furnished with the *true* basis on which rests " the communion of saints " of " the Holy Catholic Church." It is evidently in this sense that St. Paul speaks of the mystical church of Christ as the "Jerusalem, which is above, and which is *the mother of us all*,"[3] whether dead or living. It is incongruous "to speak of children being before their mother, or as constituting her." And so, the apostle in his address to the church at Ephesus, says : " Ye are built upon the foundation of the apostles and prophets, Jesus Christ Himself being the chief corner stone : IN WHOM (i. e., in Christ) all the building," or the church which is His body, " fitly framed together, groweth up into an holy temple in the Lord : in whom ye are also *builded together*, for an habitation of God through the spirit."[4] Again. According to the same apostle, the church is the pillar and ground of the truth."[5] Not, observe, as though the truth is the pillar and ground of the church ; but the church is "its pillar, as it is in and by the church that the truth is sustained, preserved, perpetuated, and unfolded to men for the use of faith and eternal life. Its ground: for it is Christ's mystical body, and He is THE TRUTH ; the church is His presence in the world, through the spirit, in the form of truth and life."

[1] John xv. 1–7.   [2] Rom. xii. 4.   [3] Gal. iv. 26.
[4] Eph. ii. 19–22   [5] i Tim. iii. 15.

Here then we have a *real union* between Christ the Head, and the church which is His body.

CHRIST AND THE SAINTS ONE.

"We are but several parts
  Of the same broken bread ;
One body hath its several limbs,
  But Jesus is the Head."

Ay, He is the head of the living saints, as those branches of the "True Vine," which, "abiding in Him, bring forth much fruit."[1] Nor the less so of those who are departed this life: for, says Jesus, "because *I* live, *ye* shall live also."[2] And thus

"The saints on earth and saints in heaven,
  But one communion make."

Then,

Come, let us join our friends above
  That have obtained the prize ;
And on the eagle wings of love
  To joys celestial rise.

Let all the saints terrestrial sing
  With those to glory gone ;
For all the servants of our King,
  In heaven and earth are one.

One family, who dwell in Him,
  One church above, beneath,
Though now divided by the stream,
  The narrow stream of death.

[1] John xv. 5.   [2] Ib. xiv. 19.

> One army of the living God,
>   To His command we bow;
> Part of His host hath crossed the flood,
>   And part is crossing now.
>
> . . . .
>
> O that we now might grasp our GUIDE,
>   O that the word were given;
> Come, Lord of Hosts, the wave divide,
>   And land us all in haeven.
>
> C. *Wesley*, 1759. (From " *The Sacrifice of Praise.*" *Brick Presb. Church Hymns.*)

This, then, is that basis of "the communion of saints" on earth and in heaven, which forms the channel of their mutual sympathy. It constitutes that *union* of the faithful with Christ and with one another, which takes in the saints of all time, which extends across and beyond the grave, and embraces the whole family of the redeemed "whose names are written in the Lamb's book of life from the foundation of the world."[1] That notable passage of St. Paul, Heb. xii. 22-24, proves the *oneness* of both classes of saints, and the ineffable and undying sympathy which subsists between them:—
"But ye are come unto Mount Zion, and unto the city of the living God, the heavenly Jerusalem, and to an innumerable company of angels, and to the general assembly and church of the first-born which are written in heaven, and to God the judge of all, and the spirits of just men made perfect, and to Jesus the Mediator of the new covenant, and to the blood of sprinkling, which speaketh better things than that of Abel."

[1] Rev. xiii. 8.

Now this passage, in embracing along with the other things enumerated, "the general assembly and church of the first-born," together with "the spirits of just men made perfect," unquestionably embraces that portion of the mystical body of Christ *already departed* this life ; but not to the exclusion of that portion of the same mystical body *still living :* for, addressing himself to the Hebrews of his day, the Apostle says, "YE ARE COME," etc. ; proof decisive, we submit, of that *union* between the classes, which forms the basis of their mutual sympathy as "THE HOLY CATHOLIC CHURCH." And this leads to a consideration,

2. Of the FACT of the sympathy of the departed with the living saints. Take your place in the chamber of the dying saint. Oh, tell me not that one with whom we lived, loved, and struggled in life's conflicts, is, at the instant of his transit, to be shut out from the *human sympathies* of those who are left behind ! Nay, so far from it, that " love which many waters cannot quench, neither the floods drown," looking upon "the dead in Christ" as the only truly living, our language is that applied to David and Jonathan : "lovely and pleasant in their lives, and *in death not divided.*"[1] And so, "our dear sainted friends," torn from us by death, rudely it may be, "are still bound to us by an internal tie. The living consciousness of this fact is not the smallest of those sympathetic influences which, like an irresistible current, are steadily bearing us toward the better land."

[1] 2 Sam. i. 23.

SYMPATHY OF THE DEAD WITH THE LIVING.

> "I feel them with their rustling, sweeping
>   The damp dew gathered on my brow:
> I see them in their lovely vigils keeping
>   Their midnight watch beside me now.
> I know their chainless spirits in their love,
>   *Are gazing on me* from their homes above.'
>
> John L. Chester.

And hence, the sympathy of the *departed* with the living saints. If we believe that

> ———— "The soul, immortal as its sire
> Can never die,"

then it will follow that in the future state, the departed will *retain a recollection* of the present, and of those that they have left behind. "If, at the transit of death, all recollection of the past were blotted out, we would stand on the eternal shore of a new creation, rather than as a being that had a previous life and history, and had just entered upon another state of being." Stilling remarks, that "some dream of an existence that is entirely new, which is better than the present, but upon which his life has *no* influence, and with which it has *no* connection. This whole idea," he adds, "amounts to just the same as an entire *annihilation* at death; for it cannot recollect this life—its fortunes and misfortunes, my wife and children, my friends . . in short, nothing at all." Consequently, "I am no more the same I, no more the same person, but I will be a being *entirely new!* The Lord in mercy preserve me from such a future state! But thanks to his name for ever, the Bible, and the common sense and feeling of men in all ages and in all places, teach directly the contrary."

The rich man in the *Tartarean* abode in HADES, confirms the fact for which we here contend. Abraham calls upon him to "*remember*" that "in this life he had received his good things, and likewise Lazarus evil things." Besides which, as proof positive of his *sympathy* for the living, he remembered his five brethren whom he had left behind, and implored mercy in their behalf." [1] Is it then to be supposed that the departed dead in Christ have *no* remembrance of, and feel *no* sympathy for, those from whom they have been severed by death? The Apostle Paul, Heb. xi. 1, where he alludes to the *spectators* in the Olympic games, over those who strove for the mastery, says: "Wherefore, seeing we also"—i. e., the *living* Hebrew Christians, "are *compassed about* with so great a cloud of witnesses"—meaning the Old Testament saints, all of whom "died in faith," to whom he refers in the preceding chapter—evidently draws an analogy between them and the spectators of said games. The meaning simply is, that this "great cloud" of departed saints, look with intense interest from their abode of "rest," as "*witnesses*" of the hard-fought struggles of the living for an incorruptible crown. More positive evidence than this of the *sympathies* of the departed in behalf of the living saints, cannot be imagined.

And now for the *influence* which this circumstance is

[1] Luke xvi. 28.

calculated to exert over them. The apostle employs it as a *motive* to them, why they should "lay aside every weight, and the sin which doth so easily beset them," that so they might "run with patience the race set before them, looking unto Jesus, the author and finisher of their faith." So also himself, in anticipation of his speedy entrance into that "rest" of which he had spoken to his Thessalonian brethren, (2d Epis. i. 7), and of his final presentation of them as the sheaves of his ministry "in the presence of the Lord Jesus Christ at His coming with exceeding joy," furnishes the evidence that, during that interval of "rest," he would retain the most lively *remembrance* of his ministry among them while on earth, and of his *sympathy* for them and others "to the time of harvest." And finally, those martyr-souls whom St. John "saw under the altar," and whom he "heard cry aloud, saying, How long, O Lord, holy and true, dost Thou not avenge our blood on them that dwell on the earth?" retain the most vivid remembrance of the bloody scenes through which they passed when on earth, and also feel the deepest sympathy in regard to those of their "fellow-servants and brethren who should be killed as they were." [1]

Thus much then of the evidence furnished in Holy Scripture and from the deductions of enlightened reason, of the sympathetic relations which exist between the *invisible* and the *visible* worlds.

In this exhibit of the sympathetic relations existing between the invisible and visible worlds,—whether it relates to

[1] Rev. vi. 11.

the Divine sympathy between Heaven and Earth on the part of the Father, of Christ, or of the Holy Spirit with man ; or between angels and man ; or between the departed and the living—we have *all that Holy Scripture reveals* on this momentous subject. What then, we ask, becomes of the scripture perverted and blasphemous pretences of modern Swedenborgianism and Spiritualism ?

SECTION IV.

Aspirations of the Saints after the Heavenly Blessedness.

"*I am in a strait betwixt two,* HAVING A DESIRE TO DEPART *and be with Christ, which is far better.*"—Philipp. i. 23.

A LONGING FOR HEAVEN.

" Then woke
Stirrings of deep, deep Divinity within,
And, like the flickerings of a smouldering flame
Yearnings of a hereafter. THOU it was,
When the world's din, and passion's voice was still,
Calling the wanderer Home." *Williams.*

" I WOULD NOT LIVE ALWAY."

" I would not live alway, I ask not to stay
Where storm after storm rises dark o'er the way ;
The few lurid mornings that dawn on us here
Are enough for life's woes, full enough for its cheer.

I would not live alway, thus fettered by sin;
Temptation without, and corruption within:
E'en the rapture of pardon is mingled with fears,
And the cup of thanksgiving with penitent tears.

I would not live alway: no—welcome the tomb,
Since JESUS hath lain there, I dread not its gloom;
There, sweet be my 'rest,' till HE bid me arise,
To hail Him in triumph descending the skies.

Who, who would live alway, away from his God,
Away from yon Heaven, that blessed abode,
Where the rivers of pleasure flow o'er the bright plains,
And the noontide of glory eternally reigns?

Where the saints of all ages in harmony meet,
Their Saviour and brethren, transported to greet:
While the anthems of rapture unceasingly roll,
And the smile of the Lord is the feast of the soul?"

Rev. Dr. Muhlenberg, 1823. (From " The Sacrifice of Praise." Brick Pres. Ch. Hymns).

St. Paul said: "I am in a strait betwixt two, having a desire to depart and be with Christ, which is far better." This well agrees with the words of the same apostle—" If in *this life only* we hope in Christ, we are of all men the most miserable."[1] Now, whence these aspirations after the Heavenly Blessedness? Ah, whence indeed, if they spring not up in the soul from an inward consciousness of human sin, and guilt, and wickedness, and the wrecks of all earthly hopes and helps in our present state, on the one hand, and the infinitely pure, and beautiful, and good, now "*reserved*

---

[1] i Cor. xv. 19.

for us" in the blessed "world to come," on the other. Yes, *faith* in God's word produces in the soul those "mournfully pleasant" under tones, characteristic of all those whose "life is hid with Christ in God."[1] Such "declare plainly that they seek a country, that is, an heavenly."[2] The "heart" of such is where his "treasure is."[3] And hence, though oft oppressed with care, and harassed with the wiles and temptations of "the wicked one," and wearied with life's toils and anxieties, and sorrows, and sufferings from "fightings without and fears within," yet his spirit is sustained and cheered by,

THE HOPE OF HEAVEN—

When

"In some lone hour of solemn jubilee,
　The massy gates of Paradise are thrown
　Wide open, and forth come, in fragments wild,
　Sweet echoes of unearthly melodies,
　And odors snatched from beds of amaranth,
　And they that from the crystal river of life
　Spring up on flushed wing, ambrosial gales!
　The favored good man in his lonely walk
　Perceives them, and his silent spirit drinks
　Strange bliss, which he shall recognize in Heaven."
　　　　　　　　　　　　　Coleridge.

And hence, the next theme in course—

[1] Col. iii. 3.　　[2] Heb. xi. 16; xii. 22.　　[3] Matt. vi. 21.

SECTION V.

The Heavenly Blessedness in Anticipation.

"In Hope of eternal life, which God, who cannot lie, promised before the world began."—Titus i. 2.

DEATH—IN VIEW OF HEAVEN.

"A trance of high and solemn bliss,
From purest ether came;
'Mid such an heavenly scene as this,
Death is an empty name." *Wilson.*

The Christian may be said to pass through three stages or conditions of life—the unrenewed, the regenerated, and the glorified states. The second, or regenerated state, partakes of the first and third. A gracious state is not wholly exempt from the remains of that "carnal mind" or "law of the flesh, which warreth against the law of the spirit," and which oftentimes involves the believer "into captivity to the law of sin and death."[1] But, as he "*walks by faith* and not by sight, as seeing Him who is invisible," his language is, "with my mind serve I the law of God, but with my flesh the law of sin."[2] And although, amid the fierceness of the fiery conflict attendant upon this mixed or middle state he oft exclaims—"O wretched man that I am, who shall deliver me from this body of death?" he nevertheless exclaims, "Thanks be unto God who giveth us the victory, through our Lord Jesus Christ." So then, while his life is *retrospec-*

---

[1] See Rom. vii. 23, 24.   [2] See Rom., chap. vii. 25.

tive in regard to sense, it is *prospective* in regard to faith. And, under this last condition, he enjoys a sweet prelibation of the Heavenly Blessedness, which inspires him with a rapturous *anticipation* of his final " abundant entrance into the everlasting kingdom of our Lord and Saviour, Jesus Christ."[1] Yes,

> " Heaven comes down his soul to greet,"

as an " earnest of his inheritance, until the redemption of the purchased possession"[2] is fully conferred upon him. It is the " eternal weight of glory" as revealed *in* him. His faith apprehends it ; while his *hope* lays hold of it ; for it is Christ formed *in* him, the hope of glory."[3] Hence, on the one hand he can say, " blessed be the God and Father of our Lord Jesus Christ, who hath blessed us with all spiritual blessings in heavenly places in Christ ;"[4] on the other, he lives in joyful anticipation of the day, when Jesus " will gather together all things into one IN HIMSELF, both which are in Heaven, and which are on earth ; even in Him."[5] And, while to the carnal Jews such an anticipation is " a stumbling block," and to the philosophysing Greeks " foolishness ;" he can say with the heroic Apostle Paul, when *" ready to be offered up, and the time of his departure was at hand :* I have fought the good fight ; I have finished my course ; I have kept the faith : henceforth, there is laid up for me a crown of righteousness, which the Lord, the righteous judge, shall give me at that day, and not to me only, but unto all

---

[1] ii Pet. i. 11. [2] Eph. i. 14. [3] Gal. iv. 19.
[4] Eph. i. 3. [5] John xi. 52 ; Eph. i. 10.

them that LOVE HIS APPEARING."[1] Nor has "flesh and blood revealed this unto him, but his Father which is Heaven."[2] For, "the secret of the Lord is with them that fear Him, and He will show them His covenant."[3] And thus,

> "The more our spirits are enlarged on earth,
> The deeper draughts can they receive from Heaven."

And so it may be said of them, in view of

HEAVEN ANTICIPATED—

> "The men of grace have found,
> Glory begun below ;
> Celestial fruits on earthly ground,
> From faith and hope may grow.
>
> The hill of Zion yields
> A thousand sacred sweets ;
> Before we reach the Heavenly hills,
> Or walk the golden streets."

Who would not then say—

> Gently, Lord, O gently lead us
> Through this lonely vale of tears ;
> Through the changes *Thou'st* decreed us,
> Till our last great change appears.
>
> When temptation's darts assail us,
> When in devious paths we stray ;
> Let Thy goodness never fail us,
> Lead us in Thy perfect way.

[1] i Tim. iv. 8.   [2] Matt. xvi. 17.   [3] Ps. xxv. 14

In the hour of pain and anguish,
  In the hour when death draws near,
Suffer not our hearts to languish,
  Suffer not our souls to fear.

And, when mortal life is ended,
  Bid us to Thy bosom rest,
Till, by angel-bands attended,
  We awake among the blest.

Thomas Hastings, 1832. (From " *The Sacrifice of Praise.*" Brick Ch. Presb. Hymns.)

SECTION VI.

The Dying Saint at the close of Life.

"O Hades, where is thy victory? O Death, where is thy sting?" (4 Cor. xv. 55.)

THE SAINT'S FINAL EXIT.

" As they draw near to their eternal home,
Leaving the old, both worlds they view."

"The last end
Of the good man is peace. How calm his exit!
Night dews fall not more gently to the ground,
Nor weary worn-out winds expire so soft."

Blair.

What was anticipated of the Heavenly Blessedness by the believer in the preceding section, is *realized* in this, as it regards his release from that " tabernacle," the body, in which he so long " groaned, being burdened "[1] under the cares and

[1] 2 Cor. v. 4.

toils and sufferings of the present life. Having been "troubled," he now enters upon that "rest"[1] in "Paradise" or "the third Heaven," whence he "looks for that blessed hope, the glorious appearing of the great God, even our Saviour Jesus Christ,"[2] to "change his vile body, and fashion it like unto His own glorious body."[3] Like the Psalmist, David, "his flesh rests in hope."[4] Having been "planted in the likeness of Christ's death," he believes that he "shall be also in the likeness of his resurrection."[5] Yea, that he shall be *fully* recompensed "AT the resurrection of Christ."[6] And hence, like the martyr-"souls under the altar," he "rests yet for a little season," until those of his "fellow" Christians who shall "come up out of great tribulation," "shall be fulfilled."[7]

But, let us now go with him to the portal of his abode of "rest," that our spirits may drink in the refulgent and holy light which streams out upon us through the bright vista, as he passes beyond our view in

HEAVEN BEGUN.

"Thus on he moves, to meet his latter end—
Angels around befriending virtue's friend;
Sinks to the grave with unperceived decay,
While resignation gently slopes the way
And, all his prospects brightening to the last,
His Heaven commences ere the world is past."

[1] ii. Thess. i. 7. [2] Titus iii. 13. [3] Philipp. iii. 21.
[4] Ps. xvi. 9. [5] Rom. vi. 5. [6] Luke xiv. 14.
[7] Rev. vi. 9-11.

Ay, you will behold him, in an unearthly rapture, exclaiming—

> "The world recedes, it disappears;
> Heaven opens on mine eyes, mine ears
> With sounds seraphic ring:
> Lend, lend your wings, I mount, I fly;
> O Hades, where is thy victory!
> O Death, where is thy sting!"

While those who still linger behind to await their summons, address to him their

PARTING ADIEU.

"Thou 'rt gone to the grave, but we will not deplore thee;
   Though sorrows and darkness encompass the tomb;
The SAVIOUR has passed through the portals before thee,
   And the lamp of His love is thy guide through the gloom.

Thou art gone to the grave—we no longer behold thee,
   Nor tread the rough path of the world by thy side;
But the wide arms of mercy are spread to enfold thee,
   And *sinners* may hope since the SINLESS has died.

Thou art gone to the grave, and its mansions forsaking,
   Perhaps thy tried spirit in hope lingered long;
But the sunshine of Heaven beamed bright on thy waking,
   And the song that thou heard'st was the seraphim's song.

Thou 'rt gone to the grave, but 'twere wrong to deplore thee,
   When GOD was thy ransom, thy guardian, and guide;
He *gave* thee, and *took* thee, and soon will *restore* thee,
   Where Death has *no* sting, since the SAVIOUR has died."

Anon.

CHAPTER VI.

"Receiving the end of your faith, even the salvation of your souls."

The Saint's Final Admittance to the Heavenly Blessedness.

SECTION I.

HOW THE SAINTS ARE ADMITTED TO THEIR FINAL STATE OF HEAVENLY BLESSEDNESS.

"By the resurrection of Jesus Christ from the dead.

ON CHRIST'S RESURRECTION.

"Sweeter than the notes, when first
   All the stars of morning sang ;
Was that VICTOR song, which burst
   When the sound of triumph rang,
Through the gladdening ranks of light,
As that Sabbath woke from night.

Then the seraph, like a blast,
   Quelled the little vain array,
Shield and sword asunder cast,
   Roll'd the pond'rous stone away—
And the call of Death became,
Birth place of a better name !

Then captivity, which long
　　Chained the soul in gloomy dread,
With the wicked and the strong,
　　Was itself a captive led ;
And the demon powers of harm,
Bent before a VICTOR's arm.

Then were gifts and graces won,
　　For the ransomed slaves of sin ;
With that Sabbath's rising sun,
　　Did a brighter age begin ;
Morning of a reign Divine,
Emmanuel—GOD WITH US—of thine !"

　　　　　　　　　　James Edmonson.

THE resurrection of Jesus Christ from the dead, was a *necessity*. Without it, His perfect obedience to the law, and His atoning sacrifice for sin on the cross, were totally unavailing in securing our pardon and our admittance to the eternal inheritance. Himself had declared, " Marvel not at this : for the hour is coming, in the which all that are in their graves *shall come forth* "—that is, be raised from the dead—" they that have done good, unto the resurrection of life ; and they that have done evil, unto the resurrection of damnation." [1] He had also declared of Himself—" *I* am the resurrection and the life : he that believeth in ME, though he were *dead*, yet shall he *live*, " etc. And, in addition to this, He had predicted concerning Him-

---

[1] John v. 28-29. Comp. Dan. xii. 2.

self—" I will destroy this temple," meaning his body, " and in three days I will *raise* it again." [1] Now then, had not Jesus, who, in such a variety of forms, had taught the *doctrine* of a resurrection, actually risen from the dead on the third day after His crucifixion, what had followed? Why, as St. Paul argues in the xvth of 1st Corinthians : " If the dead rise not"—as the Sadducees against whom he was directing his reasonings allege — " then is not Christ raised : and if Christ be *not* raised, your faith is vain : ye are yet in your sins. Then they also which are fallen asleep in Christ are perished." Nay, more. "If Christ be *not* risen, then is our preaching vain ; yea, and we are found false witnesses against God : because we have testified of God that He raised up Christ : whom He raised not up, IF so be that the dead *rise not*." There is no possibility of evading the deductions drawn from this Pauline logic. It is incontrovertibly clear that, if Christ had not risen, His death had not answered its end. But on the other hand, as the atonement of Christ on the Cross was designedly *vicarious*, it results irresistibly, that His rising again was a token of God's acceptance of it as such, not only, but that it was the *security* and *pledge* of the final and eternal admittance of those who had " fallen asleep in Christ " into their estate of Heavenly Blessedness.

It is not in place here to enter into a detailed proof of the actual resurrection of our Lord. It must suffice to refer to the apostle's averment—" But now *is* Christ risen from the

---

[1] Mark xiv. 58.

dead, and become the first fruits of them that slept." And so, He has redeemed the pledge given, that, by His RESURRECTION on the ever memorable third day, the promised "inheritance of the Saints" is rendered certain. It is secured "by an oath of two-fold immutability, in which it is impossible for God to lie; that they might have strong consolation, who have fled for refuge to lay hold on the hope set before them."[1]

The children of God may therefore sing—

"CHRIST THE LORD IS RISEN AGAIN."

Christ the Lord is risen again,
Christ hath broken every chain;
Hark, angelic voices cry,
Singing evermore on high,
          Hallelujah!

He who bore all pain and loss
Comfortless upon the cross,
Lives in glory now on high,
Pleads for us and hears our cry:
          Hallelujah!

He who slumbered in the grave
Is exalted now to save;
Now through Christendom it rings
That the Lamb is King of Kings:
          Hallelujah!

Now he bids us tell abroad
How the lost may be restored,
How the penitent forgiven,
How we too may enter heaven;
          Hallelujah!

---

[1] Heb. vi. 18.

>   Thou art Pascal Lamb indeed,
>   Christ, Thy ransomed people feed!
>   Take our sins and guilt away,
>   That we all may sing for aye,
>   *Hallelujah!*
>
> *Easter Hymn of the Bohemian Church,* 1531. *Translated by Catherine Winkworth.* (*From " The Sacrifice of Praise." Brick Pres. Ch. Hymns*).

In closing this section, we must invite the reader to accompany us to that spot, where the inspired pensman so graphically describes the sacred scene of

MARY AT THE SEPULCHRE.

> " Love is no more divine,
> Save as it seeks the source whence first it came—
>   Forsakes its mortal shrine,
> And, like the prophet, on a car of flame,
>   Mounts to the holiest! Such, dear saint, was thine,
> When thy expiring Lord endured the cross of shame!
>
>   Thou didst not heed the cry
> Of myriad voices, clamoring fierce for blood!
>   The truest turned to fly,—
> The boldest quailed—but firm the *weaker* stood!
>   Thy heart endured to watch HIS agony,
> Unawed by scoffing priests, and warriors fierce of mood,
>
>   Yes, when his parting groan
> Smote like Death's fearful summons on thine ear,
>   Thou didst not seek alone
> Idly to shed the fond, yet fruitless tear;—
>   By thee, the last sad cares of love were shown—
> Composed the suffering limbs, and spread the decent bier.

The Inheritance Conferred by Christ.

> They laid Him in the tomb
> Thou followedst still—and morning's earliest ray,
>   And midnight's latest gloom,
> Still found thee watching where the SAVIOUR lay;
>   The earth was there thy bed, the cave thy home,
> Till the sealed grave was rent—the stone was rolled away.
>
> THE VICTIM VICTOR ROSE!
> And what, true saint, was then thy meet reward?
>   The eye that watched His woes,
> Was first to hail the rising of the Lord!
>   Oh, when were tears so pure, so blest as those
> Which gushed, when at his feet, she knelt, wept, and adored!"

Yea, verily, "THE LORD IS RISEN INDEED." And, the predestined time is not remote, when He "himself shall descend from Heaven with a shout, with the voice of the archangel, and with the trump of God; AND THE DEAD IN CHRIST SHALL RISE FIRST." [1]

SECTION II.

By whom the Saints will be Finally Admitted to their Estate of Heavenly Blessedness.

"For if we believe that Jesus died and rose again, even so them which sleep in Jesus, will God bring with Him."—(1 Thess. iv. 15).

CHRIST THE SAINTS' HOPE OF HEAVEN.

> "'Prisoner of Hope,'[2] thou art—look up and sing
>   In hope of promised spring.
> As in the pit his father's darling lay,[3]
>   Beneath the desert way,

---

[1] Compare 1 Thess. iv. 16, with Rev. xx. 5.
[2] Zech. ix. 12.   [3] Gen. xxviii. 24.

And knew not how, but knew his God would save
Even from that living grave :—
So, '*buried with our Lord,*' we'll close our eyes,
To the dazzling world, *till angels bid us rise.*"

Keble.

"My faith shall triumph o'er the grave,
And trample on the tombs :
My Jesus, my Redeemer lives,
My God, my Saviour comes ;
Ere long I know he shall appear,
In power and glory great :
And Death, the last of all His foes,
Lie vanquished at His feet.

Then, though the worms my flesh devour,
And make my form their prey ;
I know I shall arise with power,
On the last judgment day :
When God shall stand upon the earth,
Him there mine eyes shall see ;
My flesh shall feel a second birth,
And ever with Him be." *Keble.*

We have, then, the blessed assurance from the risen Christ Himself, in regard to those departed saints who "sleep in Him," that "because He lives, they shall live also."[1] Ay, and that, by no *delegated* power. For, saith He, "I will raise him up at the last day."[2] "For the LORD HIMSELF shall descend from Heaven with a shout, with the voice of the archangel, and with the trump of God : and the dead in Christ *shall rise first.*"[3] Now, wherefore this? It is in

---

[1] John xiv. 19.   [2] John vi. 30.   [3] 1 Thess. iv. 14.

order that, together with those who "are alive and remain unto the coming of the Lord," they may together "be caught up in the clouds to meet the Lord in the air," that they may "ever be with the Lord."[1]

But, as saith St. Paul, "every man in his own order: Christ the first fruits; afterwards, *they that are Christ's.*" Let us now go back to the prophet Malachi, who says: "Then they that feared the Lord, spake often one to another: and the Lord hearkened and heard it; and a book of remembrance was written before Him of them that feared the Lord, and that thought upon His name. *And they shall be mine*, saith the Lord of hosts, *in that day* when I make up my jewels,"[2] etc.

Well: we will suppose that the "DAY" for the gathering in of these "jewels" of the Lord has at length arrived. Ay, Christ's "jewels!" And, how "precious!"[3] St. Paul, speaking of them, says: "Ye are bought with a price."[4] Their value, hence, is to be inferred from the "price" paid for them. This was, "not with silver and gold, . . . but with the PRECIOUS BLOOD OF CHRIST, as of a Lamb without blemish and without spot"—[5]

———"A price, all price beyond."

Reader, can you compute infinity! Then can you, by your arithmetic, measure the "price" paid for the "redemption" of these "jewels" as Christ's "purchased possession,"

---

1 i Thess. iv. 13-17 inclusive.   2 Mal. iii. 16, 17.
3 Ps. xlix. 8; lxxii. 14; cxvi. 15.   4 i Cor. vi. 20; vii. 23.
5 i Pet. i. 19.

for it is written—" GOD purchased" these jewels, " the Church, with His own blood !"[1]

And so we read : "*precious* in the sight of the Lord is the *death* of His saints."[2] It is, therefore, simply monstrous to allege that these "jewels" redeemed at such an infinite " price," will be left for ever corporeally to rot and perish " in the dust of the earth." We have already at some length produced the Scriptural evidence in proof of the *literal* resurrection of the dead at the second coming of Christ. We have now to do with the object or purpose of their resurrection from the dead. This purpose is, to *admit* the saints as the resurrected "jewels" of the Lord—now restored to their entire complex personality by a re-union of soul and body—to the full, perfect, and eternal possession and enjoyment of the HEAVENLY BLESSEDNESS.

Fully to describe this sublimely glorious event, infinitely distances all power of angelic or human thought or utterance. The inspired David, however, furnishes us with some, though feeble glimpses of its grandeur in the xxivth Psalm. This Psalm opens thus :—"The *earth* is the Lord's, and the fulness thereof ; the world, and they that dwell therein." Then he speaks of its *perpetuity :* " He hath founded it upon the seas, and established it upon the floods." He then passes on to describe those who shall *inherit* it. " Who shall ascend into the Hill of the Lord, and who shall stand in His Holy place ? He that hath clean hands and a pure heart : who hath not lifted up his soul to vanity, nor sworn

[1] Act xx. 28.   [2] Ps. cxvi. 15.

deceitfully. He shall receive the blessing of the Lord, and righteousness from the God of his salvation." But, *synchronic* with this, though described in greater detail, is the apocalyptic " NEW HEAVENS AND EARTH," (Rev. xxi.-xxii.), and of its inhabitants, (Rev. xxi. 24-27, and xxii. 14, 15) ; and is identical with St. Peter's " New Heaven and Earth wherein shall dwell righteousness," (2 Pet. iii. 12) : even that "inheritance incorruptible, and undefiled, and that fadeth not away."

Then further. To gather together Christ's "precious jewels" into this state, the Psalmist thus describes the Lord Jesus as the pre-ordained " HEIR OF ALL THINGS," in the act of His triumphant entrance into the possession of His newly recovered Universal Empire. His eye of faith, penetrating through the long vista of the intervening ages onward to the final " restitution of all things," beholds " God and the Lamb," in ineffably mysterious conjunction, taking His seat upon His Imperial throne ; and he exclaims in ecstatic rapture—

> " Lift up your heads, O ye gates ;
> And be ye lift up, ye everlasting doors :
> And the KING OF GLORY shall come in.

Who is the King of Glory ?

> The Lord, Strong and Mighty—
> The Lord, Mighty in battle.
> Lift up your heads, O ye gates :
> Even lift them up, ye everlasting doors ;
> And the KING OF GLORY shall come in.

Who is the King of Glory?

> The Jehovah of Hosts!
> HE IS THE KING OF GLORY!"[1]

But, added to this magnificent enthronement of "God and the Lamb" in the seat of universal empire, is yet another scene. It has to do with the *collective body* of the "precious jewels" of Jesus, as the reward of His sufferings. Here again we turn to the inspired Psalmist. In the xlvth Psalm, having in the most lofty and sublime language depicted the attributes, beauty, grace, majesty, power, and royal habiliments of "the King," David proceeds thus: "King's daughters were among thy honorable women: *upon thy right hand did stand* THE QUEEN *in gold of Ophir*."—(Verse 9).

Now here, a distinction is evidently made between the "King's daughters," and "the Queen"—i. e., a daughter of *pre-eminence* among daughters. Hence it is that the "Queen" is called upon—"Hearken, O daughter, and consider, and incline thine ear; forget also thine own people, and thy father's house." (v. 10). A plain prophetic intimation this, of the call of the Church which was to be "taken out of (or from among) the Gentiles to the praise of Christ's name,"[2] as His redeemed Bride, "THE LAMB'S WIFE."[2] These together constitute that "consecrated host of God's elect" who have obeyed the command, "Come ye out from the world, and be ye separate: touch not, taste not, handle not the unclean thing, and I will receive you, and will be a father unto you, and ye shall be my sons and daughters, saith the

---

[1] Ps. xxiv. 7-10.   [2] Acts xv. 14.   [2] Rev. xxi. 9.

Lord Almighty."[1] Numerically, these, in Scripture, are reputed as "*virgins*,"[2] and, as united into one—"the mystical body of Christ"—are denominated "THE BRIDE." Thus David: "So shall the King greatly desire thy beauty: for He is thy Lord; and worship thou Him." (v. 11). Accordingly, it is said of her, "The King's daughter" (i. e., the King-Father) "is all glorious within: her clothing is of wrought gold." (v. 13). And then it is added, "She shall be brought *unto the King*" (i. e., the King-Father's SON—for which, see the parable of the marriage of the King's Son[3]) "in raiment of needle-work." (v. 1). While, of the other "daughters," it is said, "the virgins her *companions* that follow her, (the Queen) shall be brought unto Thee," (the King). "With gladness and rejoicing shall they be brought: they shall enter the King's palace." (vs. 14, 15).

Keeping in view therefore the above distinction between "the Queen" as the affianced Bride of the "Bridegroom," or the King's Son, and "the virgins her companions," it is of these *latter*, that "one of the elders" in the apocalypse said unto John: "What are these which are arrayed in white robes? and whence came they? And John said unto him, sir, thou knowest. And he said to him, These are they which came out of THE GREAT TRIBULATION, and have washed their robes, and made them white in the blood of the Lamb." In a word, "the BRIDE of the Lamb," being gathered in at the celebration of the nuptials, as described in 1 Thess. iv. 13–17, and Rev. xxi. 2–9, shall be *saved from* "the great tribulation,"

[1] ii Cor. vi. 18. [2] Matt. xxv. i; Rev. xiv. 4. [3] Ps. xlv. 14; Matt. xxii. 2–14.

or that "hour of temptation which," at the close of "the times of the Gentiles," "is to come on all the world, to try them that dwell on the earth."[1] "Only with their eyes shall they behold, and see the reward of the wicked,"[2] while "the virgins her companions" are they who *came up out of* it. Yes. At the crisis of the above ingathering of the elect Bride, being of those who said, "My Lord *delayeth* His coming,"[3] they were left behind, and now are "*saved as by fire*."[4]

But, they shall constitute that number of the redeemed of whom it is said—" And, lo, a great multitude, which no man could number, out of all nations, and kindreds, and people, and tongues, stood before the throne, and before the Lamb, clothed with white robes, and palms in their hands; and cried with a loud voice saying, Salvation to our God which sitteth upon the throne and to the Lamb. And all the angels stood around the throne, and about them the elders and the four living creatures, and fell before the throne on their faces, and worshiped God, saying, Amen : Blessing, and glory, and wisdom, and thanksgiving, and honor, and power, and might, be unto our God for ever and ever."[5]

"Therefore are they before the throne of God, and serve Him day and night in His temple : and He that sitteth upon the throne shall dwell among them ; they shall hunger no more, neither thirst any more ; neither shall the sun light on them, nor any heat. For the Lamb which is in the midst of the throne shall feed them, and shall lead them unto

[1] Rev. iii. 10. [2] Ps. lxli. 8. [3] Matt. xxiv. 48.
[4] Consult i Cor. iii. 12-15. [5] Rev. vii. 9-12

fountains of living waters."[1] "And God shall wipe away all tears from their eyes."[2]

Finally. In the Heavenly Hierarchy, every man is found "*in his own order.*" First. The God-Man Christ Jesus as "the first fruits" of resurrection glory, seated upon the throne of universal empire henceforth in undistinguishable union with the Father—"God and the Lamb."[3] Second. The elect Bride, as "kings and priests unto God and the Lamb," seated with Him "in His throne" as "joint-heirs" in the government of the empire of the redeemed.[4] And third. The saved from "out of the great tribulation" "standing before the throne of God," "bearing palms in their hands," "and serving Him day and night in His temple."[5]

Thus much, then, for the final admittance of the saints into their estate of Heavenly Blessedness, "by the resurrection of Jesus Christ," and for their admission to which, the prayer of the *dying* believer is—

> Thou, whose never failing arm
> Led me all my earthly way,
> Brought me out of every harm
> Safely to my closing day:
> Thou in whom I now believe,
> Jesus, Lord, my soul receive.
>
> From this state of sin and pain,
> From this world of grief and strife,

---

[1] Rev. vii. 15-17.   [2] Ib—xxi. 4.   [3] Rev. vii. 10
[4] Rev. iii. 21; 1, 5, 6; v. 10.   [5] Rev. vii. 9, 15

From this body's mortal chain
  From this weak, imperfect life :
    Thou in whom I now believe,
    Jesus, Lord, my soul receive.

To the mansions of Thy love,
  To the spirits of the just,
To the angel hosts above,
  To Thyself, my only trust :
    Thou in whom I now believe,
    Jesus, Lord, my soul receive.

H. F. Lyte, 1834. (From " *The Sacrifice of Praise*." *Brick Presb. Church Hymns*.)

CHAPTER VII.

"To an inheritance . . ready to be revealed in the last time,

At the appearing of Jesus Christ."

SECTION I.

WHEN WILL THE SAINTS BE ADMITTED TO THEIR ESTATE OF HEAVENLY BLESSEDNESS?

PSALM LXXII.

" Hail to the Lord's ANOINTED!
　Great David's greater Son;
Hail! *in the time appointed,*
　His reign on earth begun!
He comes to break oppression,
　To set the captive free;
To take away transgression,
　And rule in equity.

He comes with succor speedy
　To those who suffer wrong;
To help the poor and needy,
　And bid the weak be strong;
To give them songs for sighing
　Their darkness turn to light,
Whose souls condemned and dying,
　Were precious in His sight.

He shall come down like showers
   Upon the fruitful earth,
And love, joy, hope, like flowers,
   Spring in His path to birth ;
Before Him on the mountains,
   Shall PEACE, the herald, go ;
And righteousness in fountains,
   From hill to valley flow.

Arabia's desert ranger,
   To Him shall bow the knee ;
The Ethiopian stranger,
   His glory come to see :
With offerings of devotion,
   Ships from the isles shall meet,
To pour the wealth of ocean,
   In tribute at His feet.

Kings shall fall down before Him,
   And gold and incense bring ;
All nations shall adore Him,
   His praise all people sing :
For He shall have DOMINION,
   O'er river, sea, and shore ;
Far as the eagle's pinion,
   Or dove's light wing can soar.

O'er every foe victorious,
   He on His throne shall rest ;
From age to age more glorious,
   All-blessing and all-blest :
The tide of time shall never
   His covenant remove ;
His name shall stand for ever ;
   That name to us is—LOVE.   *Montgomery.*

THE preceding section has furnished us with some intimations of *the time*, when the purchased "jewels" of the Redeemer will be admitted to their final "inheritance." Still, there is a need-be for a more specfic statement regarding it.

Now, though it be true that there is *a* gathering together of Christ's saints—those who sleep in Him, and those who are alive and remain unto His coming—that is, "in the last time . . . at His appearing;" yet, that this gathering is but *partial* only; in other words, that it is not THE FINAL ingathering, will appear from the following facts—

1. We have shown that there is a distinction between the physical change to which the globe and its surrounding atmosphere as they now are will be subjected, in adapting them to the Millennial era, and that more complete renovation which awaits them by fire at its close.

2. We have also shown, that the Mediatorial reign of Christ and His risen and raptured saints over the saved nations in the flesh, terminates *at the close* of the Millennial era, when Christ the Son " delivers up the kingdom to God even the Father, that He (God) may be all in all." [1] But

3. Additional evidence of this is derived from the fact, that while, at His ascension, Christ "sat down in His Father's throne;" and also that at His second coming He takes His "seat in His own throne;" [2] we are conducted onward to a third stage, namely, when " cometh the end," that is, of the

---

[1] i Cor. xv. 24-28. [2] Matt. xix. 28; xxv. 31; Luke i. 32; Rev. iii. 21.

Millennial era, when the throne of the universe will be occupied conjointly by GOD AND THE LAMB.

The distinction therefore is this: that while Christ remains seated "in His own throne" during the Millennial age, His mediatorial reign extends over "the twelve tribes of Israel," and the Gentile nations gathered unto them. But the conjoint rule of "God and the Lamb," takes in that "great multitude which no man could number, as gathered out of all nations, and kindreds, and people and tongues," which St. John tells us "stood before the throne *after* the Millennial era had passed away.[1] Hence, the latter can be none other than that FINAL state of Heavenly Blessedness spoken of by our divine Lord when He said: Matt. viii. 11—"And I say unto you, that many shall come from the east and the west, and shall sit down with Abraham and Isaac and Jacob IN THE KINGDOM OF THE HEAVENS," etc.; which condition, it is quite superfluous to add, will not apply to the sealed twelve tribes of Israel, during "the thousand years." For, it is not true of them in regard to that period, that they sat down with Abraham and Isaac and Jacob, together with the twelve apostles. It was of these latter of whom Jesus said—"In the regeneration, when the Son of man shall sit in the throne of His glory, ye shall sit upon twelve thrones, judging the twelve tribes of Israel." The twelve tribes, therefore, during that era, did not rule, but were *subject* to the rule of others—viz., Christ, and His co-reigning saints. But now, that is, *at the* "*end*"[2] of the thousand years, when

---

[1] Rev. vii. 9-17.   [2] i Cor. xv. 24; Rev. xx. 5.

the rectoral rule of the Father, and the mediatorial rule of the Son, are united, and "God and the Lamb" are seated in the same throne; and when God, in the consummated "restitution of all things,"[1] shall have "gathered together *all things in Christ*, both which are in heaven, and which are on earth, even in Him;"[2] THEN, we repeat, in as much as all nations, and kindreds, and people, and tongues are gathered in, the sealed twelve tribes of Israel are joined to them, in constituting that "great multitude which no man could number," in swelling the anthem of praise around the throne of THE UNDIVIDED AND ETERNAL GOD-HEAD through the ages of ages that are to follow.

GLORY TO GOD AND THE LAMB.

"Harp! lift thy voice on high! shout, angels, shout!
And loudest, ye redeemed! GLORY TO GOD
AND TO THE LAMB who bought us with His blood,
From every kindred, nation, people, tongue;
And washed, and sanctified, and saved our souls;
And gave us robes of linen pure, and crowns
Of life, and made us kings and priests to God!
Shout back to ancient time! Sing loud, and wave
Your palms of triumph! Sing, where is thy sting,
O Death! where is thy victory, O HADES!

Thanks be to God, eternal thanks, WHO GAVE
Us VICTORY, THROUGH JESUS CHRIST OUR LORD!
Harp! lift thy voice on high! shout, angels, shout!
And loudest, ye redeemed! Glory to God,
And to the Lamb, all glory and all praise!

---

[1] Acts iii. 21.   [2] Eph. i. 10.

All glory and all praise at morn and even,
That come and go eternally, and find
Us happy still, and Thee for ever blest!
GLORY TO GOD AND TO THE LAMB! AMEN.
FOR EVER AND FOR EVER MORE! AMEN." *Pollok.*

CHAPTER VIII.

"An inheritance, incorruptible."

A GLIMPSE OF THE BEATIFIC VISION:
OR,
The Heavenly Inheritance, in its Relation to the Final Bliss of the Saints.

SECTION I.

THE UNCHANGEABLE NATURE OF THE SAINT'S INHERITANCE, ETC.

I. The incorruptible nature of the Saint's inheritance.

> Jerusalem, the golden:
>   With milk and honey blest;
> Beneath thy contemplation
>   Sink heart and voice opprest.
> I know not, O, I know not,
>   What holy joys are there;
> What radiancy of glory,
>   What bliss beyond compare!
>
> They stand, those halls of Zion,
>   All jubilant with song,
> And bright with many an angel,
>   And all the martyr throng.
> There is the throne of David,
>   And there, from toil released,
> The shout of them that triumph,
>   The song of them that feast.

>   And they who with their LEADER
>   Have conquered in the fight,
>   Forever and forever
>   Are clad in robes of white.
>   O land that seest no sorrow!
>   O state that fear'st no strife!
>   O royal land of flowers!
>   O realm and home of life!
>
>   O sweet and blessed country!
>   The home of God's elect!
>   O sweet and blessed country!
>   That eager hearts expect!
>   JESUS, in mercy bring us
>   To that dear land of rest;
>   Who art, with God the Father,
>   And Spirit, ever blest,
>
>   *Bernard, 1150; translated by I. M. Neale. (From " The Sacrifice of Praise." Brick Presb. Church Hymns.)*

As we have seen, "the Inheritance of the saints" is called a "country," a "kingdom," a "city," etc., all as included in, and hence constituting, that "New Heavens and earth" which, "according to God's promise," He will "create."

Now, its *incorruptibility* or unchangeableness of nature, will consist of the effects produced by its *purification* in passing through the "fire" to which it is "reserved" for the last day. This fiery ordeal will purge from it the dross, and lift from off it the consequences of the curse of sin. Take, for example, one portion of it—St. John's description of the "Holy City, New Jerusalem," which he "saw descending from God out of heaven," bearing the impress of "the glory of God" as its divine Architect and Builder—the twelve foundations of its walls, with their twelve gates garnished with all manner of precious stones; the measurement of the city, which was of pure gold, like unto clear glass; together with its pure river of water of life, clear as crystal, proceeding out of the throne of God and the Lamb; and in the midst of it, and on either side of the river THE TREE OF LIFE, bearing twelve manner of monthly fruits, the leaves of which are for the *healing* of the nations. Constructed of such materials as these, and providing for its blissful inhabitants such perennial, healthful, life-preserving foliage and fruits; banishing from them all tears, all sorrows, all sickness and pain and death; also all night; with the perpetual presence in their midst of "God and the Lamb" as its light: these and the like considerations, we submit, furnish sufficient evidence that the future "Inheritance of the saints" will be, "incorruptible."

But, to particularize, we remark: that the incorruptibility of the Heavenly Inheritance, in its relation to the bliss of the saints—

II. Arises from its *physical* adaptedness to their glorified bodies, and of their glorified bodies to it. This is beautifully expressed in the following lines on

THE IMMUTABILITY OF THE HEAVENLY STATE.

> "There is no death : what seems so is transition ;
>   This life of mortal breath
> Is but a suburb of the life Elysian,
>   Whose portals we call Death." *Longfellow.*

This forms the basis of the relation of the earthly to the heavenly body, when risen and changed. There must be an adaptedness of the one to the other. Take, then, a view,

1. Of the materiality of the risen body. We now speak of the "dissolving" of this present "earthly house of our tabernacle" at death, as raised and changed. The mode of effecting this change is inscrutable to us. As to the question of its possibility, the apostle, for the sake of argument, proposes and answers the question as a matter of *fact*, "How are the dead raised up, and with what body do they come?" To the objector, he says : "Thou fool, that which thou sowest— it may chance of wheat or of some other grain—is not quickened, except it die." And he then argues the possibility, not only, but the certainty of a dead body being raised, from its analogy to the quickening of the dead seed sown. St. Paul's reasoning on this subject has never been confuted.

As to the personal identity of the dead body with the raised body, as drawn from the analogy assumed by the apostle between the dead seed sown and quickened, it is objected, that insect transformation, e. g., that of the butterfly, is against it. But, let us see. On examination, each will be found to pass through the four following stages, thus :—

The Insect. (BUTTERFLY.)		MAN.
1. The Egg.		1. Man, in Embryo.
2. The Larva, or Caterpillar.	Corresponding to	2. " at birth, a crawling worm.
3. The Pupa, or Chrysalis.		3. " at death, his pupa or chrysalis state.
4. The Imago, or perfect state of the butterfly.		4. " at the resurrection, his Imago, or perfect state, when he comes forth clothed with his glorified immortal body.

So that, in view of this subject, well might the Italian poet exclaim—

> " Non v' accorgete voi che noi siam vermi,
>   Nati a forma ! angelica farfalla ?
> " Do you not perceive that we are caterpillars,
>   Born to form the angelic butterfly ?"

And so, the apostle's conclusion, as to the *materiality* and *identity*, both before and after death, of the risen body of the saints. "It is sown in corruption, it is raised in incorruption." Olshausen has said : "As first downward the spirit incarnates itself in the body, so afterwards upward, the body is glorified in the spirit." But a greater than Olshausen has said : "Handle me, and see : for spirit hath not flesh and bones, as ye see me have." And, as is the risen and glorified body of the Lord Jesus, that of the risen saints "shall be fashioned like unto it." And so,

> " Arrayed in glorious grace,
>   Shall these vile bodies shine,
>   And every shape, and every face,
>   Look heavenly and divine."

THE SAINT HAPPY IN DEATH.

" How blest the righteous when he dies !
   When sinks a weary soul to rest,
How mildly beam the closing eyes,
   How gently heaves the expiring breath !

So fades a summer cloud away ;
   So sinks the gale when storms are o'er ;
So gently shuts the eye of day ;
   So dies a wave along the shore.

A holy quiet reigns around,
   A calm which life nor death destroys :
Nothing disturbs that peace profound,
   Which his unfettered soul enjoys.

Farewell, conflicting hopes and fears,
   Where lights and shades alternate dwell ;
How bright the unchanging morn appears !
   Farewell, inconstant world, farewell !

Life's labor done, as sinks the clay,
   Light from its load the spirit flies ;
While heaven and earth combine to say,
   How blest the righteous when he dies !"

Mrs. Barbauld, 1825. (From " The Sacrifice
of Praise." Brick Pres. Ch. Hymns).

We pass to consider,

2. The *spirituality* of the saint's risen body. By this we mean, not that the raised body of the believer is transformed into a purely spiritual entity. This, as we have already shown, cannot be. Like the dead seed sown, it contains the *germ* of an after life, which, when " quickened " by the

resurrecting power of Christ, becomes *spiritualized*, that is to say, it is so highly refined and etherealized, as to invest it with a power of locomotion commensurate with "an eternal round of thought and feeling and action." In all these respects, it will be, not changed into, but made "*equal unto*, the angels." Further than this, we cannot go. In this sense, though "sown a natural body, it is raised a spiritual body." "As is the earthy, such are they also that are earthy. And as is the heavenly, such are they also that are heavenly. And as we have borne the image of the earthy, we shall also bear the image of the heavenly." Yea, "equal unto the angels," in brilliancy and buoyancy, radiant with beauty as the solar light, and free from all sense of weariness, they shall range the universe with them as with a common brotherhood. "They shall mount up with wings as eagles; they shall run and not be weary, they shall walk and not faint."[1]

Again. "The spiritual body is one in which dwells, in a plenary way, the power of the HOLY SPIRIT. And the ancient fathers say of it, that it is a body possessed and actuated by the Holy Spirit, as the natural body is by the animal and vital spirits." Tertullian says, "it is called spiritual as putting on the spirit." "It is spiritual," says Methodius, "as receiving the whole energy and communion of the spirit." And again, "he calls that a spiritual body, which is wholly subject to the spirit." Augustine speaks to the same effect. The Apostle, he says, "Calls that a

[1] Isa. xl. 31.

spiritual body, which is wholly subject to the spirit, and which is free from corruption and death."

The spiritualized body, therefore, like "the kingdom of God," which "is not of this world ($\kappa o\sigma\mu o s$), but from heaven," is "our house which is from heaven." It is not of or by or from man, but of God.

THE SPIRITUALIZED BODY.

> "O glorious hour! O blest abode!
> I shall be near and *like my God!*
> And flesh and sense no more control,
> The sacred pleasures of the soul."

The next subject of remark relates to,

3. The *power* of the risen glorified body. The present body exercises vast power over matter in various ways. It can change its place, mix and mingle it, and by chemical combinations, give to it a different consistency, appearance, and shape; and by uniting, mechanically, one power with another, as in the application of steam, it can produce *motion*, without its immediate co-operation. Yea, by man's power over the *electric fluid*, it can make it subserve its use as THE TONGUE OF THE WORLD, so that, by a *telegraphic* circumvallation of the globe, he can bring the remotest inhabitants of the earth into *hourly* proximity of person and interchange of thought, as around a parlor centre table! In addition to all its subordinate advantages as a medium of ordinary communication, no other human agency under the direction of Providence, has so largely contributed, in these

"last times," to crowd the events of centuries, so to speak, within the narrow limits of months, if not of weeks![1]

And yet man, at least for the most part, may be said to be "compassed about" with so many bodily "infirmities," as to exhale away the most of his life in sighs and groans, in tears and agonies, until he succumbs to the stroke of death, and sinks into the grave, "sown in weakness."

What! never again to be invested with those physical energies for which he was so distinguished in this life? So far from it, they were but the preintimations of a vast augmentation of those same powers, in a risen glorified state; for, the dead in Christ shall be

"*Raised in power.*" Aye, being then for ever freed from all those weaknesses and infirmities which belong to them in the present state, they shall be endowed with an organic power over matter "equal unto the angels."[2] In this life, at least for all purposes of good, while "the spirit is willing, the flesh is weak."[3] But *then*, like the angel Gabriel, who, being sent in answer to the prayer of Daniel, was "caused to fly swiftly;"[4] and like the translated bodies of Enoch, and Elijah, and our blessed Lord, when released from the laws of gravitation, winged their way to the heavens, so with them. The future state of being will be one of pre-eminent *activity*, in which "the redeemed of the Lord" in the glorified immortal body, shall soar as on eagle's pinions among the

---

[1] The world is indebted to our esteemed and highly accomplished fellow-citizen, Professor SAMUEL F. B. MORSE, for the invention and use of the *Telegraph*, which, since the year A.D. 1844, almost begirts the earth both by land and sea.

[2] Luke xx. 36.   [3] Matt. xxvi. 41.   [4] Dan. ix. 21.

"principalities in the heavenly places," to execute without weariness the mandates of their risen Lord.

Again, on this topic, we must subjoin a few remarks on—

4. The *incorruptibility* of the glorified body. This is essential to all the other constituents of this resurrected state. Hence the Apostle: "It is sown in corruption; it is raised in *incorruption*." In this life, in consequence of sin, "corruption" is our common inheritance. Death commences its insidious work with the very first breathings of infancy, and follows us through all the avenues of life. In view of the multitudinous forms of the diseases which prey upon us, it may well be said—

> "'Tis strange that a harp of a thousand strings,
> Should keep in tune so long."

Indeed, their "name is legion." Carking care and anxiety, toil and labor, sickness and sorrow, waste and paralyze the physical energies; while intemperate indulgences in parents often engender hereditary diseases that are transmitted to succeeding generations.

But, in the *resurrected* state, the bodies of the Saints are infinitely removed from all these tendencies to "corruption." The redeemed are blessed with immortal youth, freed from sickness, pain, and toil. They are "raised in incorruption." "Death hath *no more dominion* over them." That "eternal life" of a blessed "immortality which is brought to light by the Gospel," is theirs.

> "No chilling winds nor poisonous breath,
>   Can reach that happy shore;
> Sickness and sorrow, pain and death,
>   Are felt and feared no more."

Finally. The materiality, the spirituality, the power, and the incorruptibility of the risen body of the saints will all be united in the constitution of

5. Its *future "glory."* Ah, yes! The "palace" of humanity in innocence has been sadly marred by sin! Of "the first Adam" we read that, *after* the fall, "he begat a son in his own likeness,"[1] etc: that is, sinful in its nature, and changed in its symmetrical form and beauty compared with its original. "The gold became dim, the most fine gold changed." "*Ichabod*," or "the glory is departed," was stamped upon man's brow. Truly then, as saith the apostle, in its application to the present life, "It is sown in dishonor;" for, "we are conceived in sin," not only, but "we are shapen in iniquity." And so, from the intimate connection of the body with the soul in its fallen state, the virus of sin assimilates that body to its "likeness." But especially does the above declaration of the apostle hold true in its application to the body when laid in the grave—"earth to earth, ashes to ashes, dust to dust." But he adds:—

"*It is raised in glory.*" The word "glory," and its derivative "glorious," convey to the mind the idea of that which is radiant, brilliant, "like the sun in its brightness." We read of the angels who announced to the shepherds the

---

[1] Gen. v. 3.

birth of Christ, that "the *glory* of the Lord shone about them;" and also of the two men (angels) that stood before the women at the sepulchre of Jesus, that they were clad "in *shining* garments."

Now, the apostle, in speaking of the body of the saint that is "sown in dishonor," declares that it shall be "*raised in glory.*" What glory? Not that of the angels. For, Jesus "took not on Him the nature of angels." The nature He assumed was of "the seed of Abraham," whose "children, being partakers of flesh and blood, He also Himself likewise took part of the same." Ay, and that to the end that He as the "stronger than the strong man armed" — by whom the original "palace" of humanity was despoiled of its pristine beauty and glory, might "spoil" him, and again *restore* it to what it was. Hence,

(1.) His work of restoration in its moral aspect, is commenced in man's *regeneration*, when, by the work of the Holy Spirit in the *soul*, he is made a "partaker of the Divine nature," whereby he is made to "bear the image of the heavenly:" that is, Jesus Christ, who is declared to be "the express image" of the infinitely holy God, is stamped upon his renewed soul, when he is said to be "changed from glory to glory, as by the spirit of the Lord." But the saint is also destined to another change, namely,

(2.) That of the *physical* part of his complex nature. On this subject, St. Paul, when discoursing of Christ's second coming, says that its purpose is, that He may "*change* our vile body, and fashion it like unto HIS OWN GLORIOUS BODY."

And St. John says of "the sons of God," that "it doth not yet appear what we shall be; but we know that when He shall appear, we shall be LIKE HIM, for we shall see him as He is."

Now, of our blessed Lord, even in His suffering humanity, it is declared that He was "fairer than the children of men," and "one altogether lovely." Intellectually, morally, and physically, this was true of Him, though "He was despised and rejected" by an unbelieving world, as "one who had neither form nor comeliness." The first Adam in innocence was created as "*the figure* of Him that was to come." But, as he who "buildeth the house hath more honor than the house," so JESUS, "by whom all things were created," as the antitypal "Second Adam, the Lord from heaven"—the manifested shrine of Deity—"the WORD MADE FLESH," even in His *humiliation*, infinitely transcended the original "figure!"

But O! that deeper mystery of the eternal purpose of the incarnate One! It is to restore fallen man, not merely to the "glory" of His suffering, but to that of His resurrected GLORIFIED humanity. Of this, we have an earnest and pattern in Christ's transfiguration on the mount, when, as the true Shechinah, or as the apostle styles it, "*the glory*," "His face did shine as the sun, and His raiment was white as light." To this the revelator John adds: "His head and His hairs were white like wool, as white as snow; and His eyes were as a flame of fire; and His feet like unto fine brass; as if they had been burned in a furnace: and His voice as the voice of many waters."[1]

[1] Rev. i. 14.

And now, to return to the words of the apostle—"shall *change* our vile body;" that is, when it shall be raised from the grave, that it may be "fashioned like unto Christ's own glorious body:" Why, it overpowers all thought and utterance! The day of the Lord's coming only, can reveal it!

THE RISEN GLORIFIED BODY.

"See darkness and doubt are now flying away;
No longer I roam in conjective forlorn:
So breaks on the traveler, faint and estray,
The bright and the balmy effulgence of morn.
See truth, love, and mercy in triumph descending,
And nature all glowing in Eden's first bloom!
On the cold cheek of death smiles and roses are blooing,
And 'GLORY' ETERNAL awakes from the tomb!"

Anon.

Having thus presented a view of the Beatific Vision, or the Heavenly Blessedness, as adapted to the condition of the saints in their risen bodies as materialized, spiritualized, powerful, incorruptible, and glorified: we now proceed to consider in—

CHAPTER IX.

"An inheritance, undefiled."

The Spirituality of the Saints in that State.

' It doth not yet appear what we shall be; but we know, that when He shall **appear**, we shall be like Him, for we shall see Him as He is."—i John iii. 2.

"ARISE AND DEPART: FOR THIS IS NOT YOUR REST."

" It is a weary way! and I am faint:
I pant for purer air, and fresher springs:
O Father, take me Home; there is a taint,
A shadow on earth's present things.
This world is but a wilderness
To me:
There is no rest, my God,
Apart from Thee!'

WE are now to contemplate "the general assembly and church of the first-born," together with " the spirits of just men made perfect," in the aspect—

I. Of the influence which the preceding circumstances have, upon the glorification of the senses, in the saint's estate of Heavenly Blessedness.

By the senses, we mean those faculties in man, which are neither wholly physical nor wholly mental. They "are of a mixed nature, lying between the outer world of matter, and the inner world of spirit." Sensation has to do with the physical, perception with the mental ; and, "through the mental, both meet and exchange their sympathies." Nor can we doubt that these faculties " will continue to hold their place in the glorified body," as in this.

We now observe, that the standard of measurement of these faculties of the risen and glorified saints is the same as that of their bodies. Are their " vile bodies changed and fashioned like unto Christ's glorious body ?" So of their senses. When they " see Jesus as He is, they shall be like unto Him," that is, in regard to all the organs of sense.

1. The EYE. We have evidence, for example, that the eye of our blessed Lord during His humiliation in the flesh, overleaped all barriers arising from distance or the interception of supervening objects, however numerous, so that nothing lay beyond the reach of His all-pervading glance. This is illustrated in the case of Nathanael, who, *before* He had seen Christ, was seen by Him " under the fig-tree," and knew Him as " an Israelite indeed, in whom was no guile ; " which demonstration of the Saviour's *omnipresent visual* power, resulted in Nathanael's believing in Him.[1] And, in His risen and glorified Humanity, He is spoken of as " the Son of God, who hath His eyes like a flame of fire," etc., denoting thereby that they sweep over all worlds, visible and invisible, and all things and beings that are therein.

[1] John i. 45-49.

Now, the eye of man, as the organ of his perceptions, even in the present state, possesses vast power of vision. It has been computed that the nearest of the fixed stars is distant from the eye which sees it 19,200,000,000,000 of miles, and the most remote perhaps twice that distance. And by the aid of the telescope, there are stars so remote from us, that it takes light, which travels 200,000 miles in a single second of time, no less than 4000 years to reach the earth. And yet, the *eye* of man descries, not one star only, but innumerable clusters of these lamps of night which glitter in the firmament of heaven, as they are "taken in at a glance, and pictured upon the retina of the eye, in perfect images, in a space not larger than the diamond that glistens on a lady's finger ring!"

At the same time, man's organ of sight is at present exceedingly limited, obscure and imperfect. God hath purposed that it shall be so. The morning orizon of the pious soul with eye uplifted to the heavens,[1] while it expresses the *desire*, it is prophetic of the certainty of its enlargement and refinement in the *future* life. Even when standing on the "vestibule" of that world of glory to come, as the eye of the dying Stephen "looked up steadfastly into heaven, he saw the glory of God, and Jesus standing in the midst."[2] But, as we "now know only in part, and see through a glass darkly,"[3] of the immensity, extent, and magnificence of the Creator's works; when this "vile body shall be fashioned like unto Christ's glorious body," its visual power "shall be made LIKE UNTO HIS:" not, indeed, as imparting the faculty of

---

[1] Ps. v. 3 ; cxxi. 1.   [2] Acts vii. 55.   [3] i Cor. xiii. 12.

omniscience, but of so intensifying its capacities, that, in their 'celestial pastimes,' as the poet has it, directing each others attention into the boundless distance, where their holy curiosity has descried some objects of new interest, they will address to each other the inquiry which the " elder " put to St. John—" What are these ?"

2. The EAR. Lavater, a German writer, says: "I do not seek to prove it, but I nevertheless say it with the firmest conviction of heart that it is true, that Jesus, our Saviour, the glorified Son of man, does, by the organs of His *hearing* power, at the same time distinctly hear all tones which resound through creation, however infinite in number and confused in the order they may seem to us; so as to hear each one as plainly as if He had only a single one to hear— all songs and adorations of seraphim, and of the inhabitants of all worlds." And so, keeping in view the apostle's statement, that the glorified senses of the redeemed shall be "made like unto His," this "medium of our emotional nature," the *ear*, so entranced even in this state with the power of music; in the world of Heavenly Blessedness shall become one of the chief sources of their eternal joy.

3. The sense of SMELL. The Saviour's *name* is said to be "like ointment poured forth;" and that "the *sacrifices*" of the saints are "a sweet-smelling savor unto Him;" while they are "unto God a sweet-smelling savor of CHRIST." Now, "this sense is active through the organ of odors. . . . . These odorous emissions are of course material, though wonderfully refined; and in the sense of smell there is a meet-

ing of spirit and matter," thus communicating the most delightful sensations to both through the feelings. Who has not experienced this " amid the perfumes of a flower garden, or the many mingling odors of a grove—

> " ' When gentle gales,
> Fanning the odoriferous wings, dispense
> Native perfumes, and whisper whence they stole
> Those balmy spoils,' "

And so, when this sense of the glorified bodies of the saints shall be assimilated to that of Jesus, then "may it be truly said of the church in His presence, 'Much better is the *smell* of Thine ointments than all spices ; and the *perfume* of Thy garments is as the smell of Lebanon.'" [1]

4 and 5. The last two senses, TASTE and TOUCH. These are more immediate in their agencies when brought into contact with spirit and matter, than the sense of smell ; "and yet the contact is scarcely so delicate and refined. *Touch* makes us acquainted with the outward consistency of matter, while *taste* discovers to us more of its inward and hidden chemical qualities."

We now observe, that, as common to the suffering humanity of the Redeemer, we read that He "*touched*" the leprous, the bodies of the sick, the eyes of the blind, the tongues of the dumb, and the bier on which lay the dead. And, on the cross, He "*tasted*" the vinegar mingled with gall that was pressed to His precious lips ! Ah, yes : " He was touched with the feelings of our infirmities." Yea,

[1] Cant. iv. 10.

more. As "the Great High Priest of our profession," now that He is "passed into the Heavens" in His glorified humanity, He carried those sympathetic "feelings" in our behalf with Him. And, when He "returns the second time without sin (or a sin offering) unto salvation," it will be to refine and exalt these, with all the other senses of the glorified bodies of the "just," and which, unitedly, shall be made "like unto" those of "HIS OWN GLORIOUS BODY"—

> "And every passion, every sense,
>   Be heavenly and divine."

> "When God shall stand upon the earth,
>   Him there mine eyes shall see:
> My flesh shall feel a second birth,
>   And ever with Him be.
>
> . . . .
>
> How long, dear Saviour, O how long,
>   Shall this bright hour delay?
> O hasten Thy appearance, Lord,
>   And bring the welcome day."

And so, the weary traveler catches up the prophetic talisman—

> "WATCHMAN, TELL US OF THE NIGHT."
>
> 'Watchman, tell us of the night,
>   What its signs of promise are!
> Traveler, o'er yon mountain's height,
>   See that glory-beaming star!

> Watchman, does its beauteous ray,
>   Aught of joy or hope foretell?
> Traveler, yes; it brings the day,
>   Promised day to Israel.
>
> Watchman, tell us of the night;
>   Higher yet that star ascends!
> Traveler, blessedness and light,
>   Peace and truth its course portends
> Watchman, will its beams alone
>   Gild the spot that gave them birth?
> Traveler, ages are its own;
>   See, it bursts o'er all the earth.
>
> Watchman, tell us of the night,
>   For the morning seems to dawn!
> Traveler, darkness takes its flight,
>   Doubt and terror are withdrawn.
> Watchman, let thy wanderings cease;
>   Hie thee to thy quiet home!
> Traveler, lo! the Prince of Peace,
>   Lo! the Son of God is come!
>
> *Sir John Bowring, Jr.*, 1776. (*From "The Sacrifice of Praise."*
>   *Brick Presb. Church Hymns.*

From this exhibit of the glorification of the senses of the redeemed, we now proceed to consider—

II. The perfection of their MENTAL POWERS in "the world to come."

Saith St. Paul: "We know in part, and we prophecy in part. But when that which is perfect is come, then that which is in part shall be done away. When I was a child, I spake as a child, I understood as a child, I thought as a child: but when I became a man, I put away childish things. For now we see through a glass darkly; but then, face to face: now I know in part; but then shall I know even as also I am known."[1]

Sin has effaced from the soul of man the true knowledge of God. In his *natural* state, man is represented as "having the understanding darkened, being alienated from the life of God through the ignorance that is in them, because of the blindness of their hearts."[2] But, it is the design and work of "the Gospel of the blessed God," to *lift from off the soul* this thick mantle of darkness and its consequent ignorance, by imparting to him "the light of the knowledge of the glory of God, as it shines in the face of Jesus Christ."[3]

Man's utmost attainments in these premises in the present, however, are partial and limited only. He "knows but in part." What is commenced here, is perfected only when he shall "see Jesus face to face, and know even as he is known."

Behold, then, the *source*, the *extent*, the *fulness*, in a word, the *perfection* of this knowledge of the saints in their future glorified state! Its source is from God, through Christ Jesus, who is "the brightness of the Father's glory, and the express image of His person."[4] "Known unto God are all His works, from the beginning of the world."[5] And, "the foundation of God standeth sure, having this seal, the Lord knoweth them that are His."[6] But, when they shall

---

1 i Cor. xiii. 9-13.   2 Eph. iv. 18.   3 ii Cor. iv. 6.
4 Heb. i. 3.   5 Acts xv. 18.   6 ii Tim. ii. 19.

"see Christ as He is," and their mental faculties are brought within the range of influence of His infinite mind, then shall *they* "know even as they are known" to and of God!

Let it not, however, be supposed that the newly-glorified soul is, as by miracle, at once made "perfect" in knowledge on his first admittance to the Heavenly state. True, his mental faculties will have been vastly refined, elevated, expanded. But, as in this life, so then. The acquisition of knowledge by the glorified saints will be *progressive*. This is in accordance with the law both of nature and of grace. The formation of the material earth and heavens was a gradual process. The plan of redemption through Jesus Christ was developed gradually, through successive ages down to the present, and still continues its wondrous unfoldings. When children, we speak, understand, and think as such; and at manhood, having gradually attained towards greater maturity in our knowledge of God and of ourselves, etc., "we put away childish things."

So, in the Heavenly world. The expression regarding "the angels," that they "desire to look into" the stupendous developments of the plan of man's redemption from sin and its curse, indicates a *succession* of mental acts on their part. So with the redeemed. As "the just men made perfect," they cannot take in all the vast, the infinite variety of conceptions in the full brightness and perfection of them, at once. HEAVEN IS A SCHOOL in which they are still pupils. And it is incongruous, and contrary to all analogy, with the developments of the mental faculties in the present life—a circumstance too generally overlooked—to imagine " that all the train of thoughts and ideas, and scenes of joy that shall ever pass through the mind during the long ages of eternity, should be crowded into every single mind the first moment of its entrance into the happy regions." So far from this, " before the eternally advancing spirit, the vast universe of interesting wonders will continue to pass, as a delightful panorama, that shall never for a moment present the same objects to view ; and, in as much as these successive revelations will awaken the adoration and praise of the saints, their songs will never be the same—every one will have a '*new song.*' "

There is, hence, an admirable *adaptation* of this gradual acquisition of knowledge in the heavenly " world to come," to the successive operations of the mental powers. Among " the just men made perfect," there will exist different grades of intellect—a Moses, an Abraham, a David, an Isaiah, a Daniel, a Peter, a Paul, with others, who, either from a want of mental capacity, or from a neglect to improve them to the extent of their ability, have been admitted to the " many mansions in their Father's house" as "babes in knowledge." Now, it is not reasonable to suppose, that these latter will bring into exercise for their improvement the activities of the more highly gifted ; while all, whatever be their mental endowment, will be replenished from the exhaustless treasures of angelic knowledge. Be this, however, as it may. There is nothing surer than that our blessed Saviour continues His PROPHETIC office in the

Heavenly Church; for we read that "the Lamb which is in the midst of the throne *shall feed* them, and shall lead them into fountains of living waters."

It is not therefore to be doubted, that, through these various avenues will be opened up to the redeemed, for their eternal advancement in intellectual culture and the acquisition of knowledge, together with the application of other modes to the same end of which we now know nothing; it will ever hold true of them as of the apostle when he exclaimed—" *O the depth of the riches* both of the knowledge and wisdom of God! How unsearchable are His judgments, and His ways past finding out!"[1]

We will only add, that wherein *we* fail in reaching the illimitable extent, sublimity, and grandeur of this theme—

> "God is His own interpreter,
> And He will make it plain."

There remains in this connection one other article It relates to—

III. The Perfection of the MORAL POWERS of the glorified saints in "the world to come."

"The love of Christ, which passeth knowledge."—(Eph. iii. 19.)

"Lord, Thou knoweth all things: Thou knowest that I love Thee."—John xxi. 15.)

"Thy will be done in earth, as it is done in Heaven."—(Matt. v. 10.)

[1] Rom. xi. 23.

LOVE OF CHRIST, AND LOVE TO CHRIST.

> "O LOVE, DIVINE! how sweet thou art
> When shall I find my willing heart
>   All taken up by THEE?
> I thirst, and faint, and die to prove
> The greatness of redeeming love,
>   *The love of Christ to me.*"

"What are these which are arrayed in white robes? and whence came they? . . . These are they which came out of (the) Great Tribulation, and have washed their robes, and made them white in the blood of the Lamb."—Rev. vii. 13, 14).

Sin hath produced a foul leprosy in the soul of man, so that "the whole head is sick, and the heart faint: from the crown of the head to the sole of the foot, he is naught but wounds, and bruises, and putrifying sores."[1] Nor this only. The will of man which, in an innocent state, acted in harmony with the will of God, is now in rebellion against Him. But, "where sin hath abounded" in despoiling man of his pristine *moral* purity, and in arraying his will in *opposition to* the will of God, "grace has much more abounded" in removing the leprous-spot of sin from the soul, and in subduing the will "to the obedience of Christ."

Still, even in a gracious state, in the present life, the language of the Apostle will apply: "not as though I had

---

[1] Isa. i. 6.

already attained, either were already perfect: but I follow after, if that I may apprehend that for which also I am apprehended in Christ Jesus. Brethren, I count not myself to have apprehended; but this one thing I do: forgetting those things which are behind, and reaching unto those things which are before, I press towards the mark of the prize of my high calling of God in Christ Jesus."[1] The believer's only safety in his warfare with the world, the flesh, and the Devil—those " principalities, and powers, and spiritual wickedness in high places against which he has to wrestle"[2] therefore is, the assurance that he is "*kept by the power of God* through faith unto salvation."[3] On this ground alone he can say, " As for me, I will behold thy face in righteousness: I shall be satisfied, when I awake in thy likeness."[4]

And, this will not, cannot be, until the body and soul are for ever *re-united* in the world of glory. None can find admittance there, save those who constitute that " general assembly and church of the first-born who are written in heaven."[5] As the redeemed GENTILE BRIDE OF THE LAMB, " and the just men made perfect" as her " virgin companions,"[6] who have " come out of (the) great tribulation, and have washed their robes, and made them white in the blood of the Lamb."[7] " For, without are dogs, and sorcerers, and whoremongers, and murderers, and idolators, and whosoever loveth and maketh a lie."[8]

And again. This state of the soul's moral purity will con-

[1] Philipp. iii. 12-14. [2] Eph. vi. 12. [3] 1 Pet. i. 5. [4] Ps. xvii. 15.
[5] Heb. xii. 22-24. [6] Ps. xlv. [7] Rev. vii. 14. [8] Rev. xxii. 15.

sist in "the *glorification* of the will, with all the affections which flow from it;" so that, when "the tabernacle of God shall be with men, and He will dwell with them, and they shall be His people, and God Himself shall be with them and be their God" in that "New Heaven and earth wherein shall dwell righteousness;" then, and not until then, will the "WILL OF GOD BE DONE IN EARTH AS IT IS DONE IN HEAVEN." This is the *completion* of that "consummation of all things which God hath spoken by the mouth of all His holy prophets since the world began." And now, the long "reserved inheritance" of the saints having been conferred upon them, the following lines is expressive of

THEIR FINAL STATE.

"And thou shalt walk in soft, white light,
　　With kings and priests abroad:
And thou shalt summer high in bliss,
　　Upon the hills of God."

CHAPTER X.

"An Inheritance Incorruptible, and Undefiled, and that fadeth not away,

Reserved in heaven for you."

The next topic in course relates to—

SECTION I.

THE SOCIETY OF HEAVEN.

"Ye are come unto Mount Zion, and unto the city of the living God, the Heavenly Jerusalem, and to an innumerable company of Angels, to the General Assembly and Church of the first-born which are written in Heaven, and to God the Judge of all, and to the spirits of just men made perfect, and to Jesus the Mediator of the New Covenant, and to the blood of sprinkling, that speaketh better things than that of Abel."—(Heb. xii. 22-25).

"ONE FOLD UNDER ONE SHEPHERD."

" Fullness of joy IN THEE, my Lord ;
　　Such is the promise of Thy word :
　　　　And fellowship with CHRIST thy Son.
　　O joy, to look that face upon,
　　To hear His voice, and speak my love,
　　Which HE hath won, and will approve.

　　The fellowship of noble men,
　　Refining now, transcendent then,
　　　　In zeal, and power, and purity ;

For this, to all eternity,
When death for life exchanged shall be,
Dear Lord, I'll render thanks to THEE.

Earnest, guileless, and serene,
Of radiant but unworldly mien,
Thoughtful for all, herself forgot,
By such an one have I been taught;
More precious than the ruby even
On earth : *Will she be less in Heaven ?*"

AS already shown, we have seen how, through the medium of that sympathy which, in every age of the Church, there has existed, first, between Heaven and earth ; second, between the Divine and the angelic sympathy towards man ; and third, of its reciprocation between the departed and the living saints—we have seen how it is that the church of the faithful under this dispensation " HAVE COME unto Mount Zion, and unto the City of the living God," etc. It is through " the *grace* of our Lord Jesus Christ" to them, and the "*love* of God" the Father which provided it, and " the *communion* of the Holy Ghost," which applied it, by the exercise of their FAITH in and reliance upon the atoning merits of " the Lamb slain from the foundation of the world." Thus it is that they have a present fellowship with the Father, and with His Son Jesus Christ," " whom, *having not seen*, they love ; in whom, though now they see Him not, yet believing, they rejoice with joy unspeakable and full of glory."

But now, faith is turned into *vision;* hope, into eternal fruition. Yes—

'The battle's fought, the victory's won"—

for it is written: " To him that overcometh will I give of the tree of life," and he " shall not be hurt of the second death ;" but " I will give him to eat of the hidden manna ;" and " I will give him power over the nations ;" and he " shall be clothed in white raiment ;" and " I will make him a pillar in the temple of my God ;" and I will grant him to sit with me in my throne, even as I have overcome, and am sat down with my Father in His throne." And finally, "he that overcometh, SHALL INHERIT ALL THINGS ; and I will be his God, and he shall be my Son."[1]

No : the future predestined "Inheritance of the saints in light," is not an empty, barren, desolate wilderness. "Time does not breathe on its fadeless bloom." The SOCIETY of " the New Heavens and earth wherein shall dwell righteousness" eternal, will consist of countless hosts of the various orders of intelligences, Divine, angelic, and human, " which no man can number."

I. The first in order is, THE GOD TRIUNE—the Father of an infinite Majesty ; His adorable, true, and only Son ; also the Holy Ghost the comforter. God, as the uncreated, infinite, indivisible spirit, " whom no man" as such " hath seen nor can see," having "committed all judgment unto the Son," the last great assize of the resurrected wicked

---

[1] See Rev. chap. ii. and iii.

dead, is now past. And Jesus, having delivered up"—not His Mediatorial office, for He still retains His character as "the Mediator of the new covenant;" together with the continued presentation of "the blood of sprinkling which speaketh better things than that of Abel;" but—the Millennial "Kingdom to the' Father," to the intent that henceforth He "may be all in all," by a conjoint union under the ineffable appellation of "GOD AND THE LAMB." In other words, seated now on the throne of all the restored principalities and powers in the heavenly places, is God the judge of all in *eternal union* with the slain Lamb, and the Mediator of the new covenant, with the blood of sprinkling which speaketh better things than that of Abel, as the perpetually existing monumental evidence of the *source* of salvation to the redeemed, and the *theme* of their ceaseless anthems of praise; while the "ETERNAL SPIRIT,"[1] is present in His "seven-fold" energy,[2] to diffuse His hallowed influences of light and joy and peace and blessedness and glory throughout the vast domains. Then there are,

II. The "*innumerable company of angels.*" As created intelligences, these hold a rank intermediate of God and man. The utmost stretch of our imagination fails us in forming just conceptions of their beauty and glory. No artist's pencil can portray them. Differing in rank, and in the scale and dignity and honor conferred upon them by their Creator, God, they constitute the HIERARCHY of "angels and archangels and all the hosts of Heaven" who surround the throne of "God and the

---

[1] Heb. ix. 14.   [2] See Rev. i. 4; iii. i.; iv. 5; v. 6.

Lamb." When the prophet Daniel gazed upon the splendor of Gabriel's countenance, he could not stand upright, but fell with his face to the ground.[1] Of the angel who descended from heaven to roll away the stone from the mouth of the Redeemer's sepulchre, it is said that "his countenance was like lightning, and his raiment white as snow."[2] The angel who appeared to the Judæan shepherds while watching their flocks by night, proclaiming to them the birth of the new-born Saviour, shone with a resplendance that covered the plains with light.[3] The same beauty of countenance and splendor of form characterize the entire hosts of these first-created angelic "sons of God,"[4] who also "excel in strength, and do the commandments" of "God and the Lamb," "hearkening unto the voice of His word."[5] Then also, possessed of spotless purity of character, with no feeling of envy by the lower toward the higher ranks in the heavenly hierarchy, they are endowed with those social qualities which eminently fit them for companionship with—

III. "*The General Assembly and church of the first born which are written in heaven.*" These are they who constitute what St. Paul styles, "the first-fruits among many brethren,"[6] whom God "did predestinate to be conformed to the image of His Son,"[7] for which they were "taken out of (or from among) the Gentiles to the praise of His name"[8] as "the Bride, the Lamb's wife."[9] Hence "her clothing is of wrought

---

[1] Dan. ix. [2] Matt. xxviii. 3. [3] Luke ii. 8, 9.
[4] Job xxxviii. 7. [5] Ps. ciii. 20. [6] Rom. viii. 29. [7] Ib.
[8] Acts xv. 14. [9] Rev.

gold," in which attire "she is brought unto the King," (Messiah), "in raiment of needle-work."[1] And then there are—

IV. *The spirits of just men made perfect.* Of these St. John tells us, that they "came out of the great tribulation, and have washed their robes, and made them white in the blood of the Lamb." They are composed, consequently, of those "gathered out of all kindreds, and nations, and people, and tongues under the whole heaven," who were among the "left"[2] of the antichristian nations that came against Jerusalem at the time of its last invasion, as described in Zech. xiv. 1, 2, and were therefore "saved, yet so as by fire."[3] And now, as that "great multitude which no man can number, clothed with white robes and palms in their hands,"[4] they form that retinue of "virgins, the companions" of the Bride who "enter into the king's palace.[5]

But, to these we must add yet another, and, in some respects, the most interesting class of the participants of the Heavenly Blessedness, namely:

V. *The Infants in Heaven.* "Three things," says the Rev. Dr. Matthew Henry, "appear to be uninjured by the fall—the song of birds, the beauty of flowers, and the smile of infancy; for it is difficult to conceive how either of them could have been more perfect had man remained holy; as if God would leave us something to remind us of the Paradise we have lost, and to point us to that which we may regain."

[1] Ps. xlv. 14.   [2] Zech. xiv. 16–19.   [3] 1 Cor. iii. 11–15.
[4] Rev. vii. 9, 10, 13, 14.   [5] Ps. xlv. 14, 15.

True, if we except the feebleness of the notes of the warbling minstrelsy of the feathered tribes, the thorns which grow on most flowers, and the fact that since the fall, and as the fruit of it, we are all "conceived in sin and shapen in iniquity." [1] Yes, "by one man's disobedience, many were made sinners." [2] By sin, "the creation is made subject to vanity," so that the whole creation groaneth and travaileth together in pain until now ; " [3] and as to *infants*, lovely as is their smile, yet at birth their very first note is a wail of woe.

Still, "beautiful is an infant, whatever we may picture it to ourselves. Beautiful awake or asleep. Beautiful at play, in the corner of the room, or under the shaded tree before the door. Beautiful as a lamb in the Saviour's arms. Beautiful at the font of baptism. Beautiful beneath the coffin lid ! with its entire face radiant with a smile, which is the imprint of its dying vision !"

Ay, " of its *dying vision !*" For, that smile, however beclouded by the torturing pangs of dissolution, may be viewed as the *seal* of its interest in the ATONING MERITS of Him who, when on earth, received them as the behests of parental affection, took them in His arms, and blessed them and said, " *of such is the kingdom of Heaven*." [4] Yea more. And who on another occasion added in His address to adults —" except ye be converted, and become as little children, ye shall not enter into the kingdom of heaven." [5]

It falls not now within our purpose to discuss the question

[1] Ps. li. 5.   [2] Rom. v. 19.   [3] Ib., viii. 22.
[4] Matt. xix. 13-14.   [5] Matt. xviii. 3.

in detail, whether ALL infants are saved. This we take for granted, and that on the simple ground, that as the soul of an infant is free from the taint of *actual* transgression, it sustains a different relation to the atonement for sin made by Christ, from that of adults. As the participants of original sin, as Irenæus beautifully expresses it, "to infants He (Jesus) became an infant, *sanctifying* infants." That is, in virtue of the merits of Him who "is holy, harmless, undefiled, separate from sinners,"[1] the foul taint of *original* sin in respect of infants is atoned for, and made available to their salvation. In this sense, our blessed Redeemer, "who knew no sin, *was made sin for them*, that they might be made *the righteousness of God in Him*." And so, the spotless righteousness of Jesus, who in His own person "magnified the law and made it honorable," may be said to be "*imputed*" to them; not, indeed, in the same sense as that applicable to adults, to whom "He is the end of the law for righteousness to every one that believeth;" but on the ground that they are included in the covenant promise of redemption from the beginning, that "promise" extending to believing adults, not only, but "to their children."[2] And this "promise" was not only ratified and confirmed by Christ's encircling them in His arms and blessing them, but also by His own declaration that "of such is the kingdom of heaven."

And finally on this subject, in opposition to the unscriptural, the revolting, if not indeed the blasphemous dishonor cast upon the efficacy of the atoning merits of Jesus in behalf of

---

[1] Heb. vii. 26. [2] Acts ii. 39.

such, that "the walls of hell are built with the skulls of infants," it is delightful to turn to the words of the inspired David over the loss of his child: "Can I bring it back again? I shall go to him, but he shall not come to me."[1] The child *as a child* was *saved*. So of the slaughter of the infants by the bloody Herod,[2] which being indiscriminate so far as it relates to the *moral* character of the parents, admits of no exception in respect to them. And so of ALL others.

Does the bereaved parent then exclaim with a sorrowful heart over the absent "little one"—

CASA WADDY?

"The nursery shows thy pictured wall,
Thy bat, thy bow,
Thy cloak and bonnet, club and ball,
But where art thou?
A corner holds thy empty chair,
Thy playthings idly scattered there,
But speak to us of our despair—CASA WADDY!"

Anon.

Peace to thy aching heart, Mother! If thou art a believer in Jesus, thou "needest not mourn as those without hope."[1] From the abode of "Paradise" or "the third heaven" where now "rest" the "little ones" of a bereaved Rachel, "weeping for her children, and refusing to be comforted because they *are not;*" together with that army of the infant martyrs of Bethlehem slain by the bloody mandate of

[1] ii. Sam. xii. 23.   [2] Matt. ii. 16.   [3] i This. iv. 13.

the imperious Herod; the spirit of thy "Casa Waddy" speaks:—"I still live, Mother. True, not as yet enfolded in the arms of Jesus as when on earth in His suffering humanity; that awaits the resurrection of my body which still lies slumbering in 'the dust of the earth,' and its re-union with my now absent spirit, 'at the appearing of Jesus Christ.'"

But, we now contemplate that *re-union* of the body and soul of "Casa Waddy" as consummated,—he having joined the assemblage of

INFANTS IN HEAVEN.

"Infant souls—the sweetest things on earth—
Amid the wonders of the shining thrones,
Yielding their praise in glad but simple tones,
Of tender love beneath the Almighty's wing."

Shall we speak of the *number* of redeemed infants in Heaven? Since all infants who depart this life as such are saved—and we believe they are—then, O! what a countless multitude, what a blessed company, in addition to the others, to magnify the Saviour's triumphs over Sin, Death, and Hades! "According to the computation of Hufeland, one-half of the human race die under ten years of age." Dr. Isaac Watts' says: "the yearly bills of mortality in and near London, show that more than one-third part of the race of man die before the age of two years, and nearly half before five. And let it be remembered, lest it be thought more die there than the usual proportion for want of air and the conveniences of life, that among the savage nations of Asia, Africa, and

America, more of these creatures perish from want of care, or of skill in their diseases, or by the hands of their parents ; so that, take all mankind together, the bills of mortality in London may furnish a pretty just calculation in the matter."

"It has been computed that, at the lowest calculation, there have been one hundred and forty generations who have lived and died since the creation of the world. Counting each generation on an average only one-fifth as many as the present, there would have died in all about 28,000,000,000 ! Truly,

> 'All that tread
> Through the globe, are but an handful of the tribes
> That slumber in its bosom.'

"Considering that *one-half* of the race die in infancy, we have the number of 14,000,000,000 of infants in heaven ! A number which no imagination can grasp. Literally, 'a multitude which no man can number,' for, reckoning at the fastest possible rate that any one could pronounce the numerals in counting, it would take more than 500 years ! To these are added at the rate which infants die from our present population, more than 1,700 every hour, more than 40,000 every day ; about 5,000,000 every year. As on all trees, there are more blossoms in the spring-time than there are ripe fruits in autumn, so there are more infants than adults that drop away from the circles of earthly love. Like those flowers which grow on frail slender vines, bloom but an hour in the morning, and then fold their beauties to the heart from the gaze of earth for ever, so our infants pass quickly and beautifully away—

> 'In the spirit's young bloom,
> Ere earth has profaned what was born for the skies.'

"And—O, transporting thought! THEY ARE ALL IN HEAVEN! Yes, the bereaved parent can truly say of his departed child:—

> 'A lamb, untasked, untried,
> HE fought for thee;
> HE gained the victory,
> And THOU art GLORIFIED!'"

It is a sad reflection, that of the *adult* children of pious parents, not a few, by an abuse of the advantages of early religious culture, "first wander, then despise, and at last perish." And so, "most truly may he repeat, over the newly-made grave of every infant, the touching words of the poet,

ON INFANTILE RESURRECTION.

> 'When the archangel's trump shall blow,
> And souls to bodies join,
> *Millions* shall wish their lives below,
> Had been *as short as thine.*'

"An infant GLORIFIED! The spirit (and body) of an infant made perfect! When we think of our *adult* beloved ones among the saints in light, there mingle with our thoughts of them, even against our own will and wish, some sad memories of their weaknesses and imperfections. We see them not in the future, except through the past. We see them not in Heaven, without some intrusions of earth. But *infants*, so lovely and pleasant in their lives, so untarnished by actual sin, so free from every unpleasant association, they rise before us, in our thoughts of Heaven, the perfection of what was ever here lovely. The beautiful is glorified ! . . . . While, therefore, we may think of the state of patriarchs, prophets, apostles, martyrs, and prominent saints as highest in eminence, we may think of infants as highest in loveliness."

We may, therefore, from this aspect of the subject in hand, without, perhaps, doing injustice to the relative perfection of the more mature "consecrated hosts of God's elect" who are admitted to the Heavenly Blessedness, "suppose that infants enter Heaven with an advantage over adults. Theirs will be a perfection of each 'in his own order'—a perfection not exceeding such peculiarities as enter into personal identity—a perfection, in a word, that admits of degrees." Those, (infants) free from all such peculiarities—they having never been marked with the blemishes of *actual* sin ; and, consequently, approaching nearer to the standard of perfection of the beautiful in holiness : these and the like considerations, we repeat, justify the thought, that as "the smallest planet is nearest the sun, so these stand nearest to God." If the "Bride of the Lamb" as co-heirs with Jesus are admitted to "sit with Him *in His throne*," He nevertheless condescends to "carry the lambs *in His bosom.*" "This thought has been suggested in various ways, and beautifully, for the consolation of those who cherish fondly the memory of

THE EARLY LOST AND SAVED.

'Nearest to God in childhood! It is true,
   For then the heart wears not the deepened stain
That after years bear to it; morn's sweet dew
   Has not yet sought in the blue sky, again
Its first fair home ;—Hope's sunshine is unshaded,
Joy's opening blossoms have not drooped or faded ;
Life's verdant paths have not been sadly trod
By weary feet! *The heart is near to God.*

Yes, *ye are near to God*, ye little ones !
   Nearer than those whose bright eyes have grown dim
With bitter tears—to whose sad heart there comes
   No day unmarked by suffering and sin.
Ye have not found, amid earth's blooming bowers,
Shadows with sunbeams blended, thorns with flowers ;
Ye sport with sinless mirth on the green sod
'Neath the blue sky :—Yes, *ye are near to God !"*

Anon.

And, O, "it is an enrapturing vision that dawns on our faith. See how they rejoice ! Hear how they sing ! Behold how the white-robed infant multitude extend its vast and interminable lines along ' the City of God,' till the last fade from the sight in the dim distant infinitude of bliss : and at the approach of Him who blest all, when He blest those in His arms" when upon earth, "they join the full chorus of the sky :—THE LAMB ! THE LAMB ! WORTHY IS THE LAMB THAT DIED FOR US !"

Finally. These intelligences, then—that is, the God triune, Father, Son, and Holy Ghost, the angelic, and the glorified human in their various "orders," together constitute the society of Heaven—ONE FAMILY—cemented by the most tender, endearing, and enduring union, and assimlated each to the other by that sublimely mysterious process of infinite wisdom and love, the atonement of Jesus upon the Cross! O, love surpassing thought! ONE FAMILY, of which Jesus is the ever-living and glorious Head. Jesus, who "was rich" in the possession and enjoyment of the "glory which He had with the Father before the world was,"[1] having "finished the work which the Father had given Him to do," involving His "becoming poor for our sakes, that we through His poverty might be made rich;" and having "manifested His Father's name to those whom He had given Him out of the world," Himself declares that "He had given that glory to them." Wherefore? The answer is, to the end "that they all may be ONE, even as He and the Father are ONE: He *in* them, and the Father *in* Him: that they all might be made PERFECT IN ONE."[2]

And now, in answer to His prayer:—"Father, I will that they also whom Thou hast given me may be with Me where I am, *that they may behold my glory*, which thou hast given me:—for Thou lovedst Me before the foundation of the world,"[3] this one family of the redeemed, are now *all gathered in* "from the east, and from the west, and from the north, and from the south, to sit down with Abraham, and Isaac, and Jacob, in the kingdom of God"[4] for ever! Nor should we overlook the companionship with this redeemed

[1] John xviii. 5.   [2] John xvii. 4-6, and verses 22-23.
[3] Ib—verse 24.   [4] Matt. viii. 11.

Family, of the "innumerable company" of the hosts of angels and archangels, of cherubim and seraphim, to and with whom they are made "equal," in all the organic, intellectual, and spiritual powers inherent in them.

We close these remarks on the subject of this section, by the following lines :—

LONGING AFTER HEAVEN.

"Ye angels who stand round the throne,
 And view my IMMANUEL's face,
In rapturous songs make Him known ;
 Tune, tune your soft harps to His praise,
HE formed you the spirits you are,
 So happy, so noble, so good ;
While others sunk down in despair,
 Confirmed by His power, ye stood.

Ye saints that stand *nearer* than they,
 And cast your bright crowns at His feet ;
His grace and His glory display,
 And all His rich mercy repeat :
HE snatched you from hell and the grave,
 HE ransomed from death and despair ;
For *you* He was mighty to save,
 Almighty to bring you safe there.

O, when will the period appear,
 When I shall unite in your song?
I'm weary of lingering here,
 And I to my Saviour belong.
I'm fettered and chained up to clay ;
 I struggle and pant to be free ;
I long to be soaring away,
 My God and my Saviour to see.

I want to put on your attire,
    Washed white in the blood of the Lamb;
I want to be one of your choir,
    And tune my sweet harp to His name:
I want, O I want to be there,
    Where sorrow and sin bid adieu;
Your joy and your friendship to share,
    To wonder and worship with you."

SECTION II.

The Worship, Employments, and enjoyments of the Society of Heaven.

"All dominions shall serve and obey Him." (Dan. vii. 27.)

"And there shall be no more curse: but the throne of God and the Lamb shall be in it: AND HIS SERVANTS SHALL SERVE HIM." (Rev. xxii. 3.)

"Therefore they are before the throne of God, AND SERVE HIM DAY AND NIGHT in His temple: and He that sitteth on the throne shall dwell among them." (Rev. vii. 15.)

"And I heard as it were the voice of a great multitude, and as the voice of many waters, and as the voice of mighty thunderings, saying—ALLELUIA, for the Lord God omnipotent reigneth." (Rev. xix. 6.)

WE HAVE NO HOME BUT HEAVEN.
(Heb. xi. 16.)

"We have no home but Heaven; a pilgrim's garb we wear;
Our path is marked by dangers, and strewed with many a care;
Surrounded with temptation, by varied ills oppress'd,
Each day's experience warns us, that this is not our rest.

We have no home but Heaven; then wherefore seek one here?
Why murmur at privation, or grieve when trouble's near?
It is but for a season, that we as strangers roam,
And strangers must not look for the comforts of a home.

We have no home but Heaven ; we want no home beside !
Our God, our Friend and Father, our footsteps thither guide ;
Unfolds to us its glory, prepares us for its joy,
Its pure and perfect friendship, its angel-like employ.

We have a home in Heaven ; how cheering to the thought !
How bright the expectation which God himself has taught !
With eager hearts we hasten the promised bliss to share ;
In earnest through redeeming love to find an entrance there."

From " Hymns for the Church on Earth."

Surely, "the testimony of Jesus is the spirit of prophecy." [1] Daniel, of the Old Testament, and St. John of the New, join in setting forth the triumphs of "the Man Christ Jesus over His and the church's enemies, and of her enjoyments and employments, when, "in" and "before the throne of God and the Lamb," they shall "serve Him in His temple, to go out no more for ever." And, as the Lord Jesus is now seated on the throne with God, "the brightness of His Father's glory and the express image of His person," as one still "touched with the feelings of our infirmities," He the kinsman, the elder-brother of "the family of the first-born," Himself the reflection of the image of the ineffable God-head. Nor is He there as one placed at an infinite remove from the feelings and sympathies that pervade the bosoms of the redeemed family of Heaven : but is, on the contrary, mingling with them in the utmost condescension of fraternal holy familiarity. Then too, the Holy Spirit, the illuminator, regenerator, and sanctifier of the faithful, "is the fire from off heaven's high and holy altar, which glows so

[1] Rev. xix. 10.

intensely and so unquenchably in the bosom of every child of God, descending in living currents upon all the inhabitants of the world of glory, enabling them, with the full and ever-gushing aspirations of gladdened hearts, to pour forth, to the Father, Son, and Holy Ghost, their anthems of adoration and praise."

We cannot, therefore, be amazed that men should at times be moved to know somewhat of the *employments* and *enjoyments* of the saints, in their estate of Heavenly Blessedness. Nor is such a desire—call it curiosity, if you please—unlawful, if restrained within reverential limits. We should not forget, however, that "eye hath not seen, nor ear heard, neither hath it entered the heart of man, the things which God hath prepared for them that love him." [1] "Secret things belong unto the Lord our God." It is only "the things that are *revealed*, that belong to us and our children." [2]

Within these limits, then, to him who has been for years hungering and thirsting and panting for *holiness*, "as the hart panteth after the water-brook," [3] the assurance that he is about to attain to a complete and full realization of Him who has inspired and who alone can slake this thirst, is a momentous assurance. To him who has long, patiently, and thoroughly studied the works of God; to him who has emulated angelic eagerness in looking into the wonders of redemption; to him who has to the utmost endeavored to develop the beauty of holiness in the redeemed; to him who has sounded the depths of all terrestrial provisions for the

---

[1] 1 Cor. ii. 9.   [2] Deut. xxix. 29.   [3] Ps. xlii. 1.

cravings of an immortal soul, and found that it is neither in persons nor things to fill the void, it is an assurance full of hope. In him who loves the Lord Jesus Christ with a love that many waters cannot quench nor floods drown, with a love that enlists all his energies and drinks up his very being, the promise of dwelling in ' His presence, where there is fullness of joy, and at His right hand, where there are pleasures for ever more,' and of worthily serving Him, will have power to kindle every sensibility, and to portray a heaven equal to the highest aspirations of the loftiest imagination."

We will only add, that as the *employments* of the saints in glory are the sources whence flow his *enjoyments*, in treating of this subject, we shall use them as inseparable. The following lines will be found to beautifully illustrate this combination :—

THE FLOCK OF CHRIST.

" Thou SHEPHERD OF ISRAEL, Divine,
   The joy and desire of my heart ;
For closer communion I pine,
   I long to reside where THOU art :
The pasture I languish to find,
   Where all who their Shepherd obey
Are fed, on Thy bosom reclined,
   And screened from the heat of the day.

Ah, show me that happiest place,
   The place of Thy people's abode,
Where saints in an ecstacy gaze,
   And joy in the presence of God.

> Thy love for a sinner declare,
>   Thy passion and death on the tree;
> My spirit to Calvary bear,
>   To suffer and triumph with Thee.
>
> 'Tis there with the lambs of Thy flock,
>   *There only I covet to rest;*
> To lie at the foot of the ROCK,
>   Or rise to be hid in Thy breast.
> 'Tis there I would always abide,
>   And never a moment depart,
> Concealed in the cleft of Thy side,
>   Eternally held IN THY HEART."
>
> Charles Wesley.

To proceed. We observe that, strictly speaking, it may be a matter of indifference as to what will be the *precise* occupations of the saints in "the world to come," since they all derive their interest and impart their pleasure from the relations which they sustain to that end. To a Christian, whether in the present or the future state, GOD IS THAT END; and the Christian's employments and enjoyments are interesting to him, in proportion to their discoverable relations to God's pleasure therein. And, it being a matter of consciousness that, as already shown, they are in complete union with "the God Triune," it will be found that the all-comprehending characteristics of the occupations of the redeemed and their enjoyments thence arising, will consist,

I. Of *acts of pure benevolence.* These will be exhibited in the life, and regulated by the precepts and example of the

Lord Jesus Christ. When upon earth in his suffering humanity, we read that our blessed Lord "went about doing good," and as the great "Teacher sent from God," instructing the people. And although, in Heaven, we behold Jesus in His glorified humanity, yet, "the *principles* embodied in His life and in His teachings, are, in their nature, eternal and unchangeable."

"JESUS CHRIST, THE SAME YESTERDAY, TO-DAY, AND FOR EVER."
(Heb. xiii. 8.)

"There's nought on earth to rest on,
  All things are changing here,
The smiles of joy we gaze on,
  The friends we count most dear.
One friend alone is changeless,
  The One too oft forgot,
Whose love has stood for ages,
  JESUS, who changeth not.

The sweetest flower of summer
  That sheds its fragrance round,
Ere evening comes oft withers,
  And lies upon the ground.
The dark and dreary desert,
  Has only one green spot ;
'Tis found in living pastures,
  With CHRIST who changeth not.

Clouds soon o'ercast our sunshine,
  So beautiful, so bright !
And while we still admire it,
  It darkens into night.

One sky alone is cloudless,
   There darkness enters not,
'Tis found alone with JESUS,
   And JESUS changeth not.

E'en friendship's smile avails not,
   To cheer us here below,
For smiles are oft deceitful,
   They quickly ebb and flow.
One smile alone can gladden,
   Whate'er the pilgrim's lot,
It is the smile of JESUS,
   For JESUS changeth not.

And thus our bark moves onward,
   O'er life's tempestuous sea,
While Death's unsparing finger,
   Is stamped on all we see.
But *faith* has found a refuge,
   Where *hope* deceiveth not,
Our life is hid with JESUS,
   In HIM who changeth not.

There's naught on earth to rest on,
   All things are changing here,
The smiles of joy we gaze on,
   The friends we count most dear.
One Friend in Heaven is changeless,
   The One too oft forgot,
Whose love has stood for ages,
   JESUS, WHO CHANGETH NOT."

F. *Whitfield.*

And, as we are assured that in Heaven we "shall be changed and fashioned like unto" our divine Lord in soul and in body, these eternal and unchangeable principles will constitute THE LAW of action of the redeemed for ever. But chiefly,

II. The saints in "glory everlasting" will be occupied in rendering *ceaseless praises* to the TRIUNE JEHOVAH—Father, Son, and Holy Ghost. These will be found recited by St. John in the Apocalypse, in the form of a series of divine songs or anthems, ascribed to all the various acts of "the God Triune," as connected with the stupendous works of Creation, and Providence, and Grace, which have been appropriately paraphrased thus:

ANTHEM I

(Rev. xv. 3, 4.)

A Sabbath Hymn of Triumph, declaring that God only is Holy, and ought alone to be worshiped.

" *Sing unto the Lord,* for He hath done marvellous things;
  Ascribe ye greatness unto our God.
The Lord JEHOVAH is our strength and our song,
  He also is become our salvation:
A God of truth, and without iniquity,
  Just and right is He:
  His Name only is excellent,
And His praise above heaven and earth.
Glorious in Holiness, fearful in Praises, doing wonders!
All nations whom Thou hast made, shall come and worship
  before Thee:
And shall glorify Thy name.

The Lord hath made known His salvation,
His righteousness hath He openly showed in the sight of
the people.

ANTHEM II.

(Rev. iv. 2.)

An Anthem, celebrating the Glory of God as the Creator.

"Give Glory to God in the highest,
And praise Him in the firmament of His power;
Praise Him for His mighty acts,
Praise Him for His excellent greatness:
The Lord hath made the Heavens,
And laid the foundations of the earth.
All things were created by Him and for Him,
And by Him all things consist:
Glory and worship are before Him,
Praise and honor are in His sanctuary."

ANTHEM III.

(Rev. vii. 10, 12, 13.)

A Song of the Redeemed, celebrating the Glory of God as the Redeemer.

"And they sung a new song, saying:
Thou art worthy to take the Book,[1]
And to open the seals thereof;
For Thou hast loved us and given Thyself for us,
An offering and a sacrifice to God for a sweet-smelling savor,

---

[1] The Book of the Prophet Daniel. See chap. xii. 9.

> Thou hast redeemed us to God by Thy blood,
> And hast taken us out of every nation,
> To be a people for Thy name;—
> And to purify to Thyself
> A peculiar people, a chosen generation, a royal priesthood;
> And that the kingdom and dominion,
> And the greatness of the kingdom under the whole heaven,
> Shall be given to the saints of the Most High,
> Whose kingdom is an everlasting kingdom,
> And all dominions shall serve and obey Him."

To this the semi-chorus cry with a loud voice, (v. 12,, saying—

> "All power, and riches, and Wisdom, and strength,
> And honor, and glory, and blessing,
> Be unto THE LAMB OF GOD,
> Who taketh away the sin of the world."

Then comes in the full chorus, (v. 13), of universal adoration—

> "The blessing, and the honor,
> The glory, and the power everlasting,
> Be unto HIM that sitteth upon the throne,
> And unto the LAMB for ever."

ANTHEM IV.

(Rev. vii. 10–12.)

A Song of the Redeemed, ascribing Salvation unto God, and unto the Lamb.

> "Thou hast saved us now, O Lord, and we will praise Thee:
> Thou hast heard us, and become our salvation.

> Salvation belongeth unto the Lord;
> To the Lord only, and to His anointed.
> He was brought as a LAMB to the slaughter;
> He humbled Himself, and became obedient unto death:
> Wherefore, God hath highly exalted Him,
> He hath crowned Him with glory and honor."

To this is added the Angelic Chorus or Doxology, (v. 12).

> "The blessing, the glory, the wisdom,
> The thanksgiving, the power,
> The honor, the might,
> Be ascribed unto our God for ever and ever. Amen."

ANTHEM V.

(Rev. xi. 17.)

A Song of the Redeemed, celebrating the Glory of God, in the establishment of His Kingdom.

> "Blessed be the Lord God,
>   Who only doeth wondrous things;
> And blessed be His glorious Name for ever!
> Let the whole earth be filled with His glory!
>   For the Kingdom is the Lord's.
> He is the Governor among the nations;
> The heathen raged, the Kingdoms were moved,
>   He uttered His voice, the earth melted."

ANTHEM VI.

(Rev. xii. 10-12.)

A Song of Triumph.

" Now have we seen Thy salvation, O Lord !
Thy Kingdom is come, and Thy power,
And the authority of Thine Anointed.
The evil one is banished low,
Who spake evil of the saints before God.
But they have overcome the wicked one ;
For they believed in JESUS, the Son of God :
They confessed Him with their mouth,
That God had raised Him from the dead.
They loved not their lives ; they resisted unto blood.
Praise ye the Lord in the Heavens,
Praise Him in the heights :
Praise Him, all His angels,
Praise Him, all His hosts."

ANTHEM VII.

(Rev. xix. verses 1, 2, and 3.)

The Last Grand Chorus of the Heavenly Hosts.

" Hallelujah ! in the Lord is salvation :
To His Name be the praise.
To the Lord our God be the Honor,
And the Glory, and the Power ;
For just and true are His judgments ;—
For He hath judged the great Harlot,
Which destroyed all the earth
With the wine of her fornication.

> He hath revenged the blood of His servants,
>   Which was found in Her ;
> He hath recompensed Her according to her works.
>   And again they said—HALLELUJAH !"

SECTION III.

Various Orders and Degrees of Blessedness, in the Society of Heaven.

" There is one glory of the sun, and another glory of the moon, and another glory of the stars ; for one star *differeth* from another star in glory. So also is the *resurrection* of (or from among) the dead " (ones). (1 Cor. xv. 41, 42).

" A certain Nobleman went into a far country to receive a kingdom, and to return. And he called his ten servants, and delivered unto them ten pounds, and said unto them, OCCUPY, TILL I COME. And it came to pass, that when he was returned, having *received* his kingdom, that he commanded these servants to be brought unto him, to whom he had given the money, that he might know how much every man had gained by trading.

" Then came the first, saying, lord, thy pound hath gained *ten pounds*. And he said unto him, Well done, thou good servant, because thou hast been faithful in a very little, have thou authority over TEN CITIES. And the second came, saying, lord, thy pound hath gained *five pounds*. And he said likewise unto him, Be thou also over FIVE CITIES. And another came, saying, lord, behold, here is thy pound, which I have kept laid up in a napkin. . . And he said unto them which stood by, *Take from him* the pound, and give it unto him that hath ten pounds.
For, those mine enemies, which would not that I should reign over them, bring hither, and *slay before me*." (Luke xix. 11–27.)

DIFFERENT ORDERS AND DEGREES IN HEAVEN.

> " If loftier post superior state declare ;
>   More virtuous acts if ampler meeds requite ;
>   If brightest crowns on noblest prowess light,
>   And well-sown fields a fuller harvest bear ;

> If thrones, dominions, princedoms, powers, that are,
>   Which God's inferior hosts excel in might ;
>   If day's bright orb outshine the lamps of night,
>   And Hesper's radiance the remotest star :
>   Then shall the younger brethren of the sky,
>   If right I scan the record of their fate,
>   *In varied ranks of social harmony*
>   God's Mount encircle. Glorious is the state
>   Ev'n of the lowest there : but seats more nigh
>   The sovereign throne His greater servants wait."
>
> Bishop Mant.

The subject of this section is not a vain and profitless inquiry. It will be found, if we mistake not, that there are *various orders and degrees* among the redeemed—A HEAVENLY HIERARCHY—corresponding to the diversities of apostles, prophets or teachers, evangels, pastors, helps, governments,[1] and the like, which have obtained in the progressive stages of the church on earth. Indeed, the things of the earthly, are but the faint copies of the Heavenly. Hence it is, that "the irrepressible energies of a soul animated with the hopes of an endless life beyond death, instinctively sends it voice of ardent inquiry through the darkness which hangs over the tomb," in order "to know what it can of the things to come."

If what we have said of the resurrected state of the saints be true, then it follows that the future life is but a *continuation* of the present. This forms the basis of the Scriptural doctrine of FUTURE RETRIBUTION. It has been justly said, that "when the soul leaves the body, it will retain the

---

[1] i Cor. xii. 28 ; Ep. iv. 11.

consciousness of whatever passed within it while here upon earth. It carries along with it into the future world, the ideas, the knowledge, the habits, which it possessed here. And so it takes also *good* and *evil* from this life into the next, as its own property, and there receives the fruit of it"—as illustrated in the case of the rich man and Lazarus—when re-united in body and soul *at* the resurrection.

It hence follows, that the glorified saints will occupy a *higher* or a *lower* grade of official dignity and honor, and a higher or a lower stage of happiness, according as he attained in this life a more exalted or limited degree of excellence. While one will be invested "with authority over ten cities," another will be limited to " five cities," with corresponding diversities of honor and dignity, in analogy to the varying "glory of the stars" of heaven.

Nor does this view militate against the idea of the *full measure* of the blessedness enjoyed by each. "When it rains, more drops fall upon the wide-spread oak than in the cup of the violets, and yet both are watered ; so, when glory streams from all the heavens upon the spirits of the saints, those of widest capacity will receive most, while all will be fully blest and fully satisfied. Or, to use an illustration of the old divines, vessels of different sizes *may all be full*, and yet some contain much more than others."

Nor is it to be inferred, that the circumstance of these diversities of orders, rank, condition, etc., will awaken feelings of *jealousy* among the redeemed. It will be with them as the Rev. Richard Baxter said of the two angels, that "if one was sent down from heaven to govern an empire, and another to sweep a street in it, they would not wish to exchange occupations."

It is almost superfluous to remark, that the Scriptures plainly teach that there are diversities of *punishment* in the place of final torments. The Saviour himself declared that it "should be *more tolerable* for Sodom and Gomorrha in the day of judgment, than for those cities in which His mighty works were done." [1] And so, "a *sorer* punishment" awaits those "who have trodden under foot the Son of God, and counted the blood of the covenant wherewith he was sanctified an unholy thing, and hath done despite to the spirit of His grace," than those who, "at the mouth of two or three witnesses, died without mercy under Moses's law." [2] For, "unto whomsoever *much* is given, of him shall *much* be required." [3]

The same equitable principle has its analogy in *the degrees of blessedness* in "the world" of glory "to come." The ways of God "are equal." [4] If the very wicked are punished more, "receiving the greater damnation," [5] then the very good must be rewarded more. Like the stars, some mild, like the eyes of love, some bright as glory, some burning in light as if to consume themselves in their own blazing brightness—so it is declared of those that be wise, that they "shall shine as the brightness of the firmament, and they that turn many to righteousness, as the stars for ever and ever." [6]

---

[1] Matt. x. 15. [2] Heb. x. 29. [3] Luke xii. 48.
[4] Heb. ii. 5. [5] Ezek. xviii. 25-29. [6] Dan. xii. 3.

The Apostle Paul, in speaking of "that day which shall try every man's work of what sort it is," says: that then "every man's work shall be made manifest," and that every man shall receive his own reward, *according to* his own labor."[1] Now, it would be incongruous, in the light of this principle, to suppose that those who, in that day, having built upon the true "foundation," which is Christ, "wood, hay, and stubble," in a way of false doctrine and practise, though at the last "saved, yet so as by fire," and thus enters Heaven with a great loss, just as one who escapes out of a burning house: that such an one, we repeat, should be admitted to and enjoy the *same degree* of blessedness with an Abel, an Enoch, a Noah, an Elijah, together with Abraham, Isaac, Jacob, Joseph, David, the prophets and apostles—James, Peter, Paul, and John, and the unnumbered army of worthies enumerated in the xith of Hebrews, who, having "through faith subdued kingdoms, wrought righteousness, obtained the promises, stopped the mouths of lions, quenched the violence of fire, escaped the edge of the sword, out of weakness were made strong, waxed valiant in fight, and put to flight the armies of the aliens;" with "others who had trial of cruel mockings and scourgings, yea, more, of bonds and imprisonments; who were stoned, were sawn asunder, and tempted, and slain with the sword; wandering about in sheepskins and goatskins in mountains and dens and caves of the earth, being destitute, afflicted, tormented, and of whom the world was not worthy:" it would be in the

[1] i Cor. iii. 12-14.

highest sense incongruous, if all these eminent saints and suffering martyrs, and all those who have since their time suffered "much tribulation"[1] for Christ's sake, should be placed in the same ranks with the others.

Nor are the Scriptures wanting in *direct proofs* in these premises. Take for example, in the first place, the following passages : "Whosoever shall break one of the least of these commandments, and shall teach men so, shall be called the *least* in the kingdom of Heaven ; but whosoever shall do and teach them, shall be called *great* in the kingdom of Heaven."[2] Again. "He that receiveth a prophet in the name of a prophet, shall receive a prophet's reward ; and he that receiveth a righteous man in the name of a righteous man, shall receive a righteous man's reward."[3] Our blessed Lord, further, in speaking of John the Baptist as equal to any that were "born of woman," says : "Notwithstanding, he that is *least* in the kingdom of Heaven, is *greater* than he."[4] And finally, in referring to the scene which is laid immediately at the time of His return from Heaven, to reward His servants, He says : "In as much as ye have done it unto one of the least of these my brethren, ye have done it unto me."[5]

Now, surely, in these and similar passages, the use of the terms "least" and "greatest," taken in connection with the final rewards of the saints in their glorified state—for they all refer to that state—must be understood to indicate *different degrees* of honor and glory and blessedness as then conferred upon and enjoyed by them. And this is in exact accordance

---

[1] Acts xiv. 22.   [2] Matt. v. 19.   [3] Ib.—x. 41.   [4] Ib.—xi. 41.
[5] Matt. xxv. 40.

with that principle of eternal rectitude, which has characterized all God's dealings with the saints in this life. And, that it will be so in the life to come, is clear from that declaration of our Lord : " For the Son of man shall come in the glory of His Father and with His angels ; and then shall He reward every man *according to his works.*"[1]

But, this will appear further from the fact, that God, with *emphasis*, calls Himself " the God of Abraham, and Isaac, and Jacob." He also conferred distinguished honors and favors upon such of the old patriarchs as Enoch, and Noah, and Moses, and Elijah, and David, with others ; which may be viewed as prophetic assurances, that the eminence which distinguished saints enjoyed in a state of grace, will be enjoyed by them in a state of glory. Yes, "they that sow in tears shall reap in joy. He that goeth forth and weepeth, bearing precious seed, shall doubtless return again, bringing his sheaves with him."[2] Precious promise ! Of every self-denying, cross-bearing, and suffering laborer in the vineyard of the Lord it may in truth be said, " God is not unrighteous, to forget your work and labor of love."[3] With the apostle, each one, in the retrospect of his having " turned many to righteousness," whether through the pulpit or the press, or by any other instrumentality, can say : " For what is our hope, or joy, or crown of rejoicing ? are not even ye *in the presence of our Lord Jesus Christ at His coming?* For *ye* are our glory and joy."[4]

[1] Matt. xvi. 27 ; see also Rom. ii. 6; i Cor. iii. 8-16; Rev. ii. 23 ; xx. 12.
[2] Ps. cxxvi.   [3] Heb. vi. 10.   [4] i Thess. ii. 19, 20.

What is decisive, however, on this subject, is the following: When Peter, in contrast with the conduct of the covetous rich young ruler, who refused to comply with the command of Christ to sell all that he had and give to the poor, and to follow him, reminded his divine Master that he and his brethren had left all to follow Him, and asked: "What shall we have therefore? Jesus said unto him, "Verily I say unto you, that ye who have followed me in the regeneration, when the Son of man shall sit upon the throne of His glory, *ye shall sit upon twelve thrones, judging the twelve tribes of Israel.*"[1] Dr. SCOTT on this passage says—" Our Lord assured the Apostles, that they who had followed Him in the regeneration, should be advanced and honored at length in a peculiar manner. They will be His ASSESSORS in judgment; the world and the church will be judged according to their doctrine; and they will be distinguished in an especial manner from their brethren in Christ." And Dr. MATTHEW HENRY on this passage says: "There are higher degrees of glory for those who have done and suffered most." We ask, therefore, Will not St. Paul, who was counted worthy to *do* and to *suffer* so much for Christ and the salvation of men, be happier, *and be raised* to a *higher* post of dignity and honor than the thief upon the cross, who aside from his repentance and acceptance of Christ's mercy, had not perhaps one good deed to follow him? "Not, indeed, that these labors and sufferings *merit* any reward, but that they are the *measure* of it" by and through the sovereign grace of God.

[1] Matt. xix. 27, 28; Luke xxii. 28, 31.

Finally. For the crowning evidence of the great truth herein maintained, let us repair to the mount of TRANSFIGURATION, for a type and earnest of, the divers honors and degrees of blessedness and glory of the redeemed in "the world to come." There, JESUS appeared, transfigured into His glorified humanity, as the KING or SOVEREIGN of universal empire Moses, as the representative of the *raised dead* in Christ ; Elias, as that of the *living translated* saints. While in the persons of Peter, James, and John, we have the representatives of those over whom the raised and raptured saints as *assessors* with Christ shall for ever reign.

Enough ! Think, O my soul, of that "New Heaven and earth wherein shall dwell righteousness" eternal, as THE FINAL ABODE of the redeemed !" There is the star of Bethlehem, like a sun of righteousness blazing in mid heaven, upon the crowned head of our adorable Jesus, shedding its imperial glory over all the heavenly places ! There are the patriarchs, and prophets, and apostles, and martyrs, and saints of every class and capacity, shining as stars differing in magnitude and brilliancy, with imperishable lustre and glory. There are some humble saints, *unknown* on earth, but *known* in Heaven. They had but "two mites" on earth as their "living," but they gave it all to Christ.[1] They were "faithful over a *few* things, but are now set over *many* things."[2] By exhibiting the beauty of holiness in a holy, though humble life, they wooed "many to righteousness." And see !

---

[1] Mark xii. 42.   [2] Matt. xxv. 21.

they are shining with a bright though even beam, "like stars in the firmament for ever and ever!"

THE FUTURE PEACE AND GLORY OF THE CHURCH.—Isa. lx. 15-20.

"Hear what God the Lord hath spoken,
  O my people, faint and few,
Comfortless, afflicted, broken,
  Fair abodes I build for you;
Thorns of heartfelt tribulation
  Shall no more perplex your ways;
You shall name your walls salvation,
  And your gates shall all be praise.

There, like streams that feed the garden,
  Pleasures without end shall flow;
For the Lord your faith rewarding,
  All His bounty shall bestow.
Still in undisturbed possession,
  Peace and righteousness shall reign;
Never shall you feel oppression,
  Hear the voice of war again.

Ye no more your suns descending,
  Waning moons no more shall see;
But, your griefs for ever ending,
  Find eternal noon in ME,
God shall rise, and shining o'er you,
  Change to-day the gloom of night;
He, the LORD shall be your glory,
  GOD, your everlasting light.   *Cowper.*

———

As a suitable appendage to the preceding sections on the state of the redeemed, in connection with the employments and enjoyments of the Heavenly blessedness, we now add, in further illustration of it, that of—

SECTION IV.

The Scriptural Doctrine of the Saints Mutual Recognition in Heaven.

" For now we see through a glass darkly ; *but then, face to face* : now we know in part, *but then shall we know even as we are known.*"—1 Cor. xiii. 12.

HEAVENLY RECOGNITION.

" Some tell us all earthly love must *die*,
   Nor enter the heavenly land ;
That friendship is *lost* in the blissful sky,
   'Midst the happy and joyous band.
And can it be so ? On that blissful shore,
Shall we meet with the lov'd, we have lost, no more ?

They tell us that those unseen on earth
   Shall be dear as an only child ;
And the Mother belov'd who gave us birth,
   Shall be met as a savage wild !
And can it be so ? In that land of love,
Are there no joys of re-union above ?

They tell us the Pastor, who taught us the way
   To the blessed abode of the just ;
Shall know us no more in eternity's day,
   Though the body's redeemed from the dust.
And can it be so ? in that world of bliss ?
Shall we love less there than we do in this ?

They tell us the martyr, who fell on the shore,
　'Mid the war-cry and horror untold,
Shall meet his lov'd flock with joy no more
　Than the merchant who traffics for gold.
And will it be so? in that golden street
Where Williams, and all he held dear shall meet?

Is ignorance found in the spirit home?
　Is memory left in the dust?
Then shall we not feel that we stand alone,
　As strangers among the just?
And can it be so? in that city of light,
Where love is unfolding, and joy ever bright.

Is darkness found in that cloudless sky,
　Veiling the life just past?
Forgotten the friends who saw us die,
　All faithful and true to the last?
And can it be so? shall we meet no more
When this feverish dream of life is o'er?

Then where is the Pastor's crown of joy?
　And where the reward of the saints' employ?
And why do we cherish this restless love,
　If all will be lost or forgotten above?
Oh! *can it be true*—in that blissful place,
Where we see the redeemed ones "*face to face?*"

This beautiful effusion of the poet is argumentative. While some *doubt*, it supposes that others *deny*, the doctrine of the saints' recognition in the better land, and then suggests the striking and forcible arguments in its defence.

We view the question :—Will the saints who have once been associated in this life,

RECOGNIZE EACH OTHER IN THEIR RESURRECTED AND GLORIFIED STATE IN THE LIFE TO COME ?

as one which claims special attention at our hand. It is one in which all classes—parents, children, brothers and sisters, pastors and their people, masters, servants, neighbors, rulers and the ruled—feel an equal interest. Indeed, the emotions of each of these, as they stand weeping over the death-bed of their departed loved ones, is happily expressed in the following stanzas :—

A MOTHER'S LAMENT.

"I loved thee, daughter of my heart ;
  My child, I loved thee dearly ;
And though we only met to part—
  How sweetly ! how severely !
Nor life, nor death can sever
My soul from thee for ever.

Thy days, my little one, were few ;
  An angel's morning visit,
That came and vanished with the dew,
  'Twas here—'tis gone—*Where is it ?*
Yet did'st thou leave behind thee
A *clue* of love to find thee ?

SARAH ! my last, my youngest love,
  The crown of every other !
Though thou art born in Heaven above,
  I am *thine only Mother !*
Nor will affection let me
Believe thou wilt forget me.

> Then, thou in Heaven, and I on earth—
> May this one hope delight us,
> That thou will hail my second birth,
> When death shall *re-unite* us,
> Where worlds no more can sever
> Parent and child for ever."
>
> *Montgomery.*

On the other hand, the *animus* of the objection to this doctrine, is significantly expressed in the following lines :—

THE SCEPTIC'S SORROW.

> I have heard you say,
> That we shall see and know our friends in Heaven.
> *If that be true,* I shall see my boy again !
> For since the birth of Cain, the first male child,
> To him that did but yesterday suspire,
> There was not such a gracious creature born.
> But now, will *canker sorrow* eat my bud,
> And chase the native beauty from my cheek,
> And he will look as hollow as a ghost ;
> As dim and meagre as an ague fit ;
> And so he'll die : and rising so again,
> When I shall meet him in the Court of Heaven,
> *I shall not know him :* therefore, never, never,
> Must I behold my pretty ARTHUR more !"
>
> *Shakspeare.*

I. First, then. We shall consider the *objections* alleged against the doctrine of the recognition of saints in Heaven. It is urged,

1. That if it were true, *the Scriptures would have more clearly revealed it.* The truth however is, that the very obscurity which apparently overshadows this doctrine in

Holy Scripture, furnishes the strongest proof of it. Grant that there are but a few incidental allusions to it, instead of plain, positive, and explicit declarations regarding it. It were as consistent to deny the doctrine of the soul's immortality, of the Divine Trinity, of the Sabbath, of the right of females to communion in the church, etc., etc., neither of which are explicitly set forth in Scripture, as to deny the doctrine in question. The fact is, that the *incidental* allusions to it, rest upon the ground that it was universally believed in the church at the time when it was thus alluded to. It is hence to be received by us as in the case of the other truths spoken of—*faith in* it as the way to a *knowledge of* it.

2. It is urged, that the condition of the glorified in Heaven, will so far transcend that on earth, as to *supercede* all pre-existing earthly relations. How is it, then, that the *prior* relations of man to man in his unrenewed state in this life, are not superceded by his relations to them in the higher regenerated and sanctified state? which no one will pretend. And, surely, the transfer of the saint from the present to the future life, does not destroy his *personality;* and though that transfer raises him to an infinitely more exalted state of being, we can see no just reason why it should sever him forever from those relations which he held to his fellow saints when on earth. Again.

3. It is urged, that saintly recognition in Heaven, and the intercourse thence arising, *would interfere with our supreme love to Christ*, and that therefore it cannot be true. Now, this is hypothecated of the theory, that Heaven is not a

place, but a *state* only. Hence, such are wont to speak of the "pure spirituality" of that State, " affirming, that where Christ is, there is Heaven, even if it were on earth or in Hell;" and that the saints "shall do nothing there but stand like statues and gaze at Him." But, as the error of such superficial and extravagantly affected zeal of love to Christ, is evident from its tendency to overthrow the principle enjoined by our blessed Lord upon His saints on earth—" *Thou shalt love* THE LORD THY GOD *with* ALL *thy heart, and soul, and mind, and strength, and thy neighbor as thyself;*"[1] so it denies the *perpetuity* of that love or " charity" which the inspired Apostle Paul declares "never faileth," as the basis of the eternal exercise of it by the saints in Heaven. We ask here: is the love of the saints to and for each other on earth, any disparagement towards " Him who, having not seen, we *love*, and who, though *now* we see Him not, yet believing, we rejoice with joy unspeakable and full of glory?" It is then, we are compelled to say, little less than a hallucination of the mind, to imagine that *supreme* love to Christ in Heaven, will form any the least barrier to the exercise of love by the saints towards each other. Further.

4. It is urged: That the recognition of saints in Heaven, *would interfere with their social relations, by producing partiality among them.* There is an apparent plausibility in this objection. But it supposes the existence among the saints in glory of *a spirit of jealousy*, which cannot be. A late writer has well said: " Particular individual attachments are

[1] Matt. v. 43.

not uncongenial in a perfect state of society. On the contrary, it is one of the most prominent and delightful features of grace in this life, that it begets and increases general love to all, and particular love to some." And he asks: "Will glory divide what grace has united?" Nay, verily. For, "as the moon, in moving round the earth, does not the less move, with all the other planets, round the sun; so the saints in Heaven, who cluster, by sweet silent attraction, round the objects of their peculiar attachments, will not thereby fail to move on, with all saints"—and that, without any emotions of jealousy—"round the Saviour, as the sun of righteousness, in the general harmony of Heaven." Once more.

5. It is urged: That *second marriages* militate against this doctrine. This objection supposes, that a first wife, to meet and recognize the second in Heaven, would scarcely be able to look with complaisancy and composure upon her successor in the connubial relation. And hence, to avoid this, to them, disagreeable meeting and recognition, such writers take shelter in an entire disbelief of the doctrine. It rests for its foundation, however, upon those low and gross conceptions of the bonds of saintly unions in Heaven, upon which the Sadducees relied, to disprove the doctrine of a *literal resurrection*, in the case of the woman who had been the wife of seven husbands. They demanded of our Lord—" whose wife shall she be of the *seven?* for they all had her." To this Jesus replied: "Ye do err, not knowing the scriptures, nor the power of God: for *in the resurrection,* they

neither marry nor are given in marriage ; for they are equal unto the angels."[1] Now, in this reply, Christ does not say that the saints *shall not know* each other, but only that "they shal not marry nor be given in marriage ;" and that, for the simple reason, that "they are" equal unto the angels, "between whom, there are no marriage relationships. All the saints, like them, will be merged into *one common union and fellowship*, in virtue of their union to Christ," IN whom, "there is neither *male* nor *female*."[2] Not the least intimation is given, "that the affections begotten and friendships formed" by the marriage relations in this life, "shall be renewed and continued in the Heavenly society. Hence, those emotions that are erroneously supposed to exist between a *first* and *second* wife in Heaven, can no more find a lodgment in the hearts' affections of the saints, than in the bosoms of 'angels' to whom they are 'equal.'"

6. It is urged : That *the change in the resurrection bodies of the saints will be so great*, as to render mutual recognition impossible. This objection, at the first view, is a strong one. But a little consideration will show its utter fallacy. We ask then : great as was the change that took place in the resurrection body of our blessed Lord, was He not recognized as the same person who had been crucified three days before, by Mary Magdalene and the other woman ? And did not Jesus, in proof of the reality of His resurrection say to His doubting disciples, "handle me and see : for spirit hath not flesh and bones as ye see Me have ?" And did He not

[1] Matt. xxii. 30. [2] Gal. iii. 28.

eat in their presence "a piece of broiled fish and a little honey-comb?" Yea, though "the fashion of His countenance was altered, and His raiment was white and glistening, and His face did shine as the sun," yet Peter, James, and John, on the mount of Transfiguration knew Him, and readily distinguished Him from Moses and Elias, for they beheld His "excellent glory, and were eye-witnesses to His Majesty." But we are assured, that the Lord Jesus, in His risen and glorified humanity, is the PATTERN, in all things, of His saints. For, "He shall change our vile body, and fashion it *like unto* His own glorious body. If then, HE was recognized as above in that body, on what principle can it be denied that the saints in resurrection glory shall not be able each to recognize the other?

We would only add in conclusion on this subject, that "as in life a person is changed from a sinner to a saint, while he still retains, to a great extent, the *same* external features; so, the elements of power, glory, and immortality may be unfolded to us, in our glorification, without producing any more change in the appearance on the side of our being with which we were wont to converse with our friends, than the positive condition of electricity does upon that which it fills with its mysterious fluid."

> "Gently—so have good men taught—
> Gently, and without grief, *the old shall glide
> Into the new.*

"Thus, the change which awaits us, so far from *hindering* us in recognizing our friends in Heaven, will be the means of facilitating it." When we shall "see Jesus as He is," and be made "like unto Him," all the organic senses, together with the moral faculties, being intensified to the highest possible attainments of the resurrected state, no interval of separation, no transformation of the persons of the redeemed, will avail, on the grounds of the above objection, to estrange them each from the other.

PERSONAL IDENTITY IN HEAVEN.

"And shall I e'er again thy features trace,
  Beloved friend ; thy lineaments review ?
  Yes : though the sunken eyes, the livid hue
And lips comprest, have quenched each lively grace,
Death's triumph ; still I *recognize the face*
  Which thine for many a year affection knew :
  And what forbids, that, clothed with life anew,
It still on memory's tablet holds a place ?—
Tho' then thy cheek with deathless bloom be sheen,
  And rays of splendor wreath thy sunlike brow,
That change I deem shall sever not between
  Thee and thy former self ; nor disallow
That love's tried eyes *discern* thee through the screen
  Of glory then, as of corruption now."
Bishop Mant.

7. We add : It is urged—that if this doctrine of Heavenly recognition be admitted, the blessedness of the saints in glory will be greatly marred, *by missing some of the loved ones* whom we knew on earth, and especially that it will be accompanied with the reflection that they are *lost*. This objection presents a difficulty of no small magnitude, and one which is by no means diminished when we consider that it

finds a place in every bosom. But, when traced to its source, we shall see that it is founded upon a misapprehension of the difference between *mere natural* affection towards kindred and friends, and the higher affections of the *spiritual* life. This distinction is clearly brought to view in the following passage: "as is the *earthy*, such are they also that are earthy; and as is the *heavenly*, such are they also that are heavenly." And again. "As we have *borne* the image of the earthy, we shall also *bear* the image of the heavenly." And again. "Now this I say, brethren, that flesh and blood,"—that is, in its earthly or unrenewed state —"cannot inherit the kingdom of God."[1]

To this we add in the next place, that between the "earthly" or sensual affections, and the spiritual or religious, there is *no* union, communion, or sympathy. For, "what fellowship hath righteousness with unrighteousness? and what communion hath light with darkness? and what concord hath Christ with Belial? and what part hath he that believeth with an infidel?"[2] The reason of this is, that in the case of mere natural affection, it is a matter of *feeling* only. "All religious or moral motives to love are suspended, by the strong flow of instinct or nature" which is common alike to the heathen, and to that affection which is peculiar to the marriage relation of persons in an unrenewed state. While, on the other hand, that Pauline injunction, "Be ye not unequally yoked together with unbelievers," implies, not only, but is predicated of, that *change* which is effected by the

---

[1] i. Cor. xv. 50. [2] ii Cor. vi. 15.

grace of God, in *lifting man above* the merely natural or
"earthly" affections, into the higher regions of the "heavenly,"
to the end that a *spiritual concord* may subsist, in cementing
that holy relationship. Not that this change from the
earthly to the heavenly *destroys* the flow of the natural affections, but only that they become absorbed or included in
grace. Ay, and so absorbed and included by grace *in this
life*, that the natural or "earthly" affections become *subordi-
nated* to, the divine or "spiritual;" so that supreme love to
God, and acquiescence to His will in all things, form the
ruling motive in all our actions.

Now, of these, take the first—*supreme love* to God. It is
illustrated in those strong and emphatic words of our blessed
Lord : "If any man come to me, and *hate not* his father and
mother, and wife, and children, and brothers, and sisters, yea,
and his own life also, he cannot be my disciple."[1] The
meaning here is, not that we should "hate" our kindred in
the absolute sense, but that we should love them with a less
intensity of affection than that which we exercise towards
God. "Son," says he, "give ME thine heart." Yes, God
will have the heart, the whole heart, and nothing but the
heart, or we can have *no* saving interest in His salvation!
Is this, then, the feeling of him who would sit in Heaven and
weep for God's enemies, or grieve at the exercise of His justice, even if those enemies are our nearest kindred according
to the flesh?

Take the other—*acquiescence to God's will in all things.*

[1] Matt. x. 37.

This involves the idea of separation between the "earthly" or unrenewed state, and those of the "heavenly," who are in a state of grace. It is beautifully illustrated by the following words of our Lord: "While he yet talked with the people, behold, His mother and His brethren stood without, desiring to speak with Him. Then one said unto Him, Behold thy mother and thy brethren stand without, desiring to speak with thee. But He answered and said unto them, Who is my Mother? and who are my brethren? And He stretched forth His hand toward His disciples, and said, Behold my Mother and my brethren! For whosoever shall *do the will* of my Father which is in heaven, the *same* is my brother, and sister, and Mother."[1] Now, some have been wont to censure these words of our Lord as cold, or as wanting in natural affection toward His kindred. But so far from this, they were intended merely to intimate that there are ties *higher* than kindred; and that, while these affections still live with Him, they lived in a higher sphere than mere instinctive nature; in a sphere of *grace*, in which He had stronger affinities of love toward all that did God's will.

We find a striking and appropriate illustration of this, in the command of Moses to Aaron and his two sons, Eleazar and Ithamar, on the occasion of the destruction of Nadab and Abihu, his other two sons, by fire from heaven, for their having "sinned in offering strange fire before the Lord, which He commanded them not :—*uncover not your heads, neither rend your garments, lest ye die, and lest wrath come upon all*

[1] Matt. xii. 46-50.

this people!" "No: not a tear for the enemies of the Lord, when He judgeth them, even though they be your children and brethren! lest ye show that your mind is not with God's mind, *your* will is not as God's will. '*And they did according to the words of Moses.*'"[1] But, the Christian's prayer is, that God's "will may be done *in Heaven*, as it is done on earth;"[2] which could not be, if the disposition to acquiesce in God's will on earth is not *transplanted*, "with them, to that Heavenly soil. Besides, this is in exact harmony with the disposition of the glorified 'elect angels,' who, though they once loved those of their number who kept not their first estate, but left their own habitation,"[3] experience *no* interruption of their joys, now that they know them to be confined to their Tartarean abodes of darkness, "*reserved* for chains unto the day of judgment and perdition of ungodly men,"[4] for whom there awaits a similar doom.

And, finally. It is so with our adorable Saviour, who, although when upon earth He "wept" over the Holy City,[5] and "endured the contradiction of sinners against Himself,"[6] yet experiences *no* diminution of His ecstatic blessedness, now that they are shut up in the blackness of despair for ever. "May not WE expect a similar change in our feelings?" or, will any one say that Christ's love for the lost, "was not as strong as ours can possibly be for any of our friends?" Surely then, nothing will hinder us from falling in fully with *all* His ways; we shall approve, not only what we now see

[1] Lev. x. 1-8. [2] Matt. vi. 10. [3] Jude, verse 6. [4] 2 Pet. iii. 7.
[5] Luke xix. 41. [6] Heb. xii. 3.

to be right, and what we now feel able to approve ; forgetting all creatures, and filled with the one idea of God, as great, and wise, and good, we shall be able to join heartily in the exclamation :—" Great and marvellous are thy works, Lord God Almighty : *just and true* are all Thy ways, THOU KING OF SAINTS." [1]

THE WILL OF THE SAINTS IN HEAVEN, IN ACCORD WITH THE WILL OF GOD.

" Fear not the prospect of the realms of woe
   Shall mar thy bliss, or thence sad thoughts arise
   To blunt thy sense of Heavenly ecstacies.
There, if thy heart with warm devotion glow
   Meet for thy place, 't will solace thee to know
   No friend of thine, 'mid those keen agonies,
   In that dark prison-house of torment lies :
For none is there, but is of GOD the foe,
   An alien thus from thee. The ties of blood,
   And earth's most sacred bonds, are but a twine
Of gossamer, compared with what is owed
   To Him, THE LORD OF ALL ! On Him recline :
He shall thy heart from every care unload,
   He bids thy day with cloudless lustre shine."

Bishop Mant.

There yet remains another, and the final objection in this category, which merits animadversion :

8. It is urged : That *nothing would be gained* by the recognition of our friends in Heaven. The reply to this is, that it would be immeasurably more difficult to tell what we gain,

[1] Rev. xv. 1.

than what we would lose by it. "We would *lose* the delight of meeting, in circumstances of peculiar gladness, those dearly beloved ones from whom we were parted in our chamber of bereavement and sorrow; and we would be deprived of the joy of dwelling with those, through eternity, in a home which is a high realization of the last and dearest hope of dying humanity. Nay, there is something dreary and desolating and blighting to the warm, longing, social emotions of the heart, in the very supposition, that we *may not*, in a future state, recognize those we loved upon earth: and if the hope is to bear *no* fruit, then, in that case, we do well to bid them farewell at death; for, if there be not the recognition of friends in Heaven, I am never to meet them again so as to *know* them; or in other words, we are parted with them for ever! They *may* exist: but they are *lost* to us—absolutely, eternally lost!" But no, a thousand times, No! For, "we need not sorrow, even as others which have no hope," [1] as by faith we look forward to a—

REUNION OF SAINTS IN HEAVEN.

"If death my friend and me divide,
  Thou dost not, LORD, my sorrow chide,
    Nor frown my tears to see;
  Restrained from passionate excess,
  Thou bidst me mourn in calm distress,
    For them that rest in THEE.

I feel a strong immortal "hope,"
  Which bears my mournful spirits up,
    Beneath its mountain load;

[1] i Thess. iv. 13.

> Redeemed from death, and grief, and pain,
> I soon shall find my friend again,
>   Within the arms of God.
>
> Pass the few fleeting moments more,
> And Christ the blessing shall restore
>   Which death hath snatched away:
> For me thou wilt the summons send,
> And give me back my parted friend,
>   In that eternal day!
>
> *Charles Wesley.*

The preceding replies to the objections urged against the doctrine of the recognition of saints in Heaven, may by some be deemed a sufficiently satisfactory proof of it. They are designed, however, simply as *inductive* evidence of its truth. The importance of the subject will justify us in proceeding,

II. To produce the *direct arguments* on which the doctrine rests. As preliminary to what is to follow, it may be well in passing, to advert—

1. To the *Traditionary legends of the Pagans* regarding it. We have already treated of their ideas respecting Heaven, as derived traditionally from the Sacred Records. The same ideas hold true of their belief in the *mutual recognition* of each other in a future state, and the renewal and perpetuation of their earthly friendships and affections. We find it in the writings of the ancient Greek poetry of Homer—

> "The blind old man of Scio's rocky isle."

Also of Socrates, and of the Roman orator, Cicero, and of

Virgil, "the plaintive bard of Mantua," extending from the nine hundredth to the fiftieth year before Christ. "In his Æneid, Virgil makes frequent allusion to the state of the dead. In the VIth Book, he represents the *Sibyl* as conducting Æneas through the SHADES below; where, as he passes along among them—

> 'He saw his friends, who, whelm'd beneath the waves,
>   Their funeral honors claimed, and ask their quiet graves.
>   The lost Leneaspis *in the crowd he knew*,
>   Whom, on the Tyrrhene seas, the tempest met,
>   The sailor's mastered, and the ship o'erset.
>   Amid the spirits Palinurus pressed,
>   Yet fresh from life, a new admitted guest,
>   Who, while he, steering, saw the stars, and bore
>   His course from Afric to the Latian shore,
>   Fell headlong down. The Trojan fixed his view,
>   And scarcely through the gloom, the sullen shadows knew.'"

"Virgil, passing along through the lower and more sombre Hades, the regions of those who are only partially blest, they enter at length the 'verdant fields' of the higher and happier regions. Here too, he *recognizes* those whom he knew upon earth :—

> 'Here found he Teucer's old heroic race,
>   Born better times, and happier years of grace.
>   Assaracus and Ilus here enjoy
>   Perpetual fame, with him who founded Troy.'

Still, he is not satisfied. . . He longs especially to see his father Anchises! He is at last found in a flowery vale, viewing, with a kind of holy pride, his race of illustrious descendants, as they pass in review before him. The scene is tender and moving. The sire sees Æneas coming, and

> 'Meets him with open arms and falling tears.
> 'Welcome,' he said, 'the god's untroubled race!
> O long-expected to my dear embrace!'

This rapture of meeting is warmly and affectionately reciprocated by the son. Is it not exactly what we feel to be natural, when, after a long separation, we meet our friends in the realms of bliss? Æneas exclaims with holy joy—

> 'Reach forth your hand, oh parent shade! nor shun
> The dear embraces of your darling son!
> He said: And falling tears their face bedew:
> Then thrice around his neck his arms he threw.'"

Now what, we ask, are these "Pagan Ideas," but "voices in the wilderness, like that of John the Baptist, which do not contradict the teachings of Him who is to come," but which, as the "deep, earnest voices and whispers of the human heart, are always prophetic" of the future? Then,

WEEP NOT FOR THE DEAD.

> 'Oh, weep not for the dead!
> Rather, oh! rather give the tear
> To those that darkly linger here,
>   When all besides are fled.
> Weep for the spirit withering
> In its cold cheerless sorrowing;
> Weep for the young and lovely one
> That ruin darkly revels on;
>   But never be a tear-drop shed
>   For *them*, the pure enfranchised dead."

2. We have already intimated, that the sublime doctrine of the mutual recognition of saints in Heaven, is one which characterizes the belief, hope, and desire of all classes—the high and the low, the rich and the poor, the bond and the free, whether Jew, Pagan, Mohammedan or Christian—ay, and that to the intent that when all things shall be subdued to the authority of the Triune Jehovah, the ONE FAMILY of the redeemed may unite with one mind and will and act in prostrating themselves at the feet of their common Saviour,

"And crown Him LORD OF ALL."

"For this purpose, God breaks our hearts into tenderness and tears, by a common sorrow, that our affections may—

"Like kindred drops, be mingled into *one*."

And thus it is that we can realize the soul-inspiring truth of

OUR ONENESS IN CHRIST.

" The saints on earth, and all the dead,
But one communion make ;
All join in CHRIST, their living Head,
And of His life partake.

With such society as this,
My weary soul would rest ;
The man that dwells where JESUS is,
Must be forever blest."

3. We now add a few remarks on the aspect in which this subject may be viewed in the light of Reason, or *Natural Religion*. In this view, we must respectfully demur to the

reasoning of that class of writers, who argue the doctrine in hand from this stand-point.

Apart from Revelation, men have in all ages believed in the existence of the soul, after death. Man's *immortality* is a doctrine of Natural Religion. Not so, however, of the *resurrection* of the body. This is purely a matter "brought to light *by the Gospel*,"[1] even that "Gospel which was preached unto Abraham."[2] And we have demonstrated, we submit, the reservation of "the inheritance of the saints in light" in its fulness, until the souls of the departed in their intermediate abode "under the altar"—or which is the same thing, in "Paradise," "the third heaven," or "Abraham's bosom"—shall be *re-united* to their bodies when raised by the power of God "AT the appearing of Jesus Christ." That generally trust-worthy writer, Dr. Harbaugh, in his work on "the Heavenly Recognition"—and from which we have quoted with approbation in several places—when treating of this subject in the light of reason, refers us to "the Heidelberg Catechism"—"the Shorter Catechism"—"the Westminster Confession," etc., in proof that the souls of believers are, at death, immediately "received into the highest Heavens;" and adds, that, "instead of this consoling doctrine, the existence of a 'middle place' is imagined, where the spirits are detained until they receive their bodies. Hence, he continues, it has been thought necessary, in proper respect to this imagination, to inquire whether recognition will take place among disembodied spirits in this 'middle state' *before* the resurrection," etc.

[1] ii Tim. i. 10.   [2] Gal. iii. 8.

To this we deferentially submit, however, that, so far as the question of the resurrection of the body is concerned, reason alone can cast *no* light whatever on the subject. As to the statement of this learned writer, that "the existence of any such a 'middle place' having no foundation either in reason, Scripture, or the teaching of the church, except where these have been made to speak under the influence of pagan philosophy," is a mere begging of the question. We have shown that in connection with what "*reason*" has discovered in regard to the immortality of the soul, the pagans also believed in an intermediate place and state of the departed, both good and bad.

Hence also their ideas as it respects the mutual recognition of the souls of the departed. But when we come to treat of the resurrection of the body, if we except the belief of it by the ancient Persians—who filched it from the writings of the prophet Daniel—the pagan world had *no* knowledge of it. Indeed, this writer himself concedes—"even if the spirits of the saints at death, being then made perfect in holiness, are received into the highest Heavens"—but which we have shown cannot be—"still, being disembodied, there may seem to be difficulties in the way which will not exist *after* the resurrection," etc. We affirm that there *are* such "difficulties;" Ay, and difficulties which, on the hypothesis of a *denial* of an intermediate place and state of the departed between death and the resurrection, are, in our judgment, absolutely insuperable.

Let it then be admitted, that the spirits of the departed

while separated from the body can and do recognize each other; yet, what we affirm is, that this recognition does not and cannot transpire in its consummated form until *after* the re-union of body and soul AT the resurrection. And *this* heavenly recognition, we repeat, is not the discovery of "the Light of Reason," and that for the reason, that the *resurrection* of the body, as a revealed cardinal truth, lay infinitely beyond its province. The basis of the spiritual recognition of saints, is founded on the principle of that ineffable union which subsists between the Lord Jesus Christ as "the True Vine," and His mystical body, the church, as "fruit-bearing branches," the which, abiding in Him,[1] whether dead or living, hold "*fellowship* with the Father and the Son," and with one another. And so, united by this bond of heavenly recognition, the apostle's benediction will apply to both estates:—"The *love* of God, and the *grace* of our Lord Jesus Christ, and the *communion* of the Holy Ghost, be with you all. Amen."[2]

Finally, we pass—

4. To a consideration of the *positive teachings of* HOLY SCRIPTURE, in reference to this subject of Heavenly Recognition. And,

First. Of the *Old Testament*. We now speak of "Christ and the church which is His body," as a whole. As we have said, there is a sense in which the church militant "have come unto mount Zion, and to the heavenly Jerusalem," etc. Hence the "fellowship" and "communion" which, through the med-

---

[1] John xv. 1–7. [2] ii Cor. xiii. 14.

ium of that sympathy of the Divine with the human, which subsists between Christ and the members of that "body" of which He is "the Head." And here, surely, there is a *recognition* of saint by saint on earth, and of Christ by all through faith.

But we are now treating specially of that *future* state of the saints, when "that which is in part, shall be done away :" when faith is turned into sight, and hope into fruition.

And here, it is refreshing, to turn from the dim, confused, and obscure traditionary legends of the pagan world, to the clearer sun-light of the inspired pages, as our future guide. We begin with,

I. The doctrine of Heavenly Recognition, as taught by God's covenant people, THE JEWS, concerning the—

JEWISH HOPE OF HEAVENLY RECOGNITION.

"Oh, wondrous times! those palmy days of old—
When God with prophets spake, and angels walked
With men—when Heaven, with mild and radiant eye,
Through dreams, and types, and shadowy visions looked,
And smiled on all who sought a better life.
Though darkly hung the mystic vail that hid
The better world ; yet, through it, *faith* beheld,
On the celestial side, the lovely forms
Of sainted friends in blessed pastimes move.
They mourned, *but still in hope,* for those beyond ;
And smiling through their tears, in meekness said,
They cannot come to us, *but we shall go*
To them."

Admitting that, to the ancient Hebrews or Jews, the doctrine of immortality was but obscurely revealed compared with after times—that they

> "Through dreams, and types, and shadowy visions looked,"

as the source of their knowledge of another life; yet, the translations of "Enoch the seventh from Adam," and of Elijah, of the preaching of Noah, and of the fact as stated by St. Paul, that the pious patriarchs, antediluvian and postdiluvian, "all died in faith," which is "the substance of things hoped for and the evidence of things not seen;" is proof decisive, that so far from being ignorant of, "they desired a better country, that is, an heavenly," though they "beheld it afar of."[1]

We now observe, that the deeply seated affection of the pious patriarchs towards their deceased; the contiguity of their places of sepulture, and their mode of speaking of their departed friends; all go to prove a belief in their final union and recognition in that "better country." Take the following in illustration. We read that "Abraham died, and was gathered unto his people."[2] "Jacob yielded up the ghost, and was gathered unto his people."[3] God said to Moses, "Get thee up and die in the mount whither thou goest, and be gathered unto thy people: as Aaron thy brother died in mount Hor, and was gathered unto his people."[4] Now the expression, "gathered unto thy people," as already explained, refers not to the entombed bodies of the patriarchs, to the

---

[1] Heb. xi. The reader will also do well to turn to the following passages in this connection:—ii Kings ii. 1-8; Job xix. 25-28; Ps. xvi. 10; xvii. 15; xlix. 15; lxxiii. 24-26; Eccles. xii. 7-14; Isa. xxvi. 19; Ezek. xxxvii. 1-10; Dan. xii. 1-3.

[2] Gen. xxv. 8.   [3] Ib—xlix. 33.   [4] Deut. xxxii. 50.

exclusion of their souls: the grave or sepulchre being the receptacle of dead bodies *generally*, whether Jew or Gentile, good or bad. Not so with the departed *spirits* of the just. These, to use Jewish phraseology, "rest from their labors" "in Abraham's bosom," or which is the same thing, "under the altar," *until* the time come that their bodies are raised from the dead among whom they have been mingled, and re-united to their souls. And so, their having "all died in faith" of that " better country, even an heavenly," which they " beheld afar off, involves their *belief in the doctrine of mutual recognition* in the future state—that Abraham shall know Isaac, Jacob, etc. In this faith, "Joseph buried his father Jacob in Canaan, in the cave of the field of Machpelah, which Abraham bought with the field for a possession of a burying place, of Ephron the Hittite, before Mamre." [1] And in this faith, "Joseph took an oath of the children of Israel, saying, God will surely visit you, and ye shall carry up my bones from hence." [2] This was accomplished 430 years after, at the time of the exode of the Israelites from Egypt under Moses. [3] There is, therefore, a hallowed solemnity, a solace, a sweetness about the phrase, "gathered to thy people," or "to thy fathers.",

> "How blest the righteous when he dies!
> When sinks a weary soul to rest;
> How mildly beams the closing eyes,
> How gently heaves the expiring breast!"

Of *spirit* recognition in the HADES of the departed, we

[1] Gen. l. 13.   [2] Gen. l. 25.   [3] Exod. xiii. 19; xii. 40, 41; Gal. iii. 17.

have a most graphic illustration, in Isaiah's prophecy of the final exultation of Israel over their mystical oppressor, the LAST ANTICHRIST—"Lucifer, son of the morning, who said in his heart, I will ascend into heaven, I will exalt my throne above the stars of God . . . I will be like the Most High,"¹ etc. The prophet says: "The whole earth is at rest, and is quiet; they break forth into singing. Yea, the fir-trees rejoice at thee, and the cedars of Lebanon, saying, Since *thou* art laid down, no feller is come up against us."² And then he adds: "SHEOL (Hell) from beneath is moved at thee, even all the chief ones of the earth, *to meet thee at thy coming*: it hath raised up from their thrones all the kings of the earth. All they shall speak, and say unto thee, Art *thou* become as weak as *we?* art *thou* become like unto *us?*"³

And so, David says of his dead child: "*I shall go to him, but he shall not return unto me.*"⁴ This expression surprised the servants of the king. It has its explanation, not in David's being laid beside his child in the grave, free from trouble; but in his being re-united to and recognizing it in the world of glory.

From these last two references, we learn, *first*, that as the scene of the prophet Isaiah is laid among the *lost*, the general features of human life among the wicked, "are carried over the grave, and are represented as existing under the same general type. . . . Hence in the shades, or in the mysterious world of the departed, this passage discovers the *continuation*

---

1 Isa. xiv. 9, 12. Compare ii Thess. 8-10.   2 ii Sam. xii. 23.
3 Isa. xiv. 12, 13, 14. Compare ii Thess. ii. 1-4.   4 Isa. xiv. 7, 8.

of the social life of earth in its general features. Kings are still known and recognized as kings, great ones as great ones, friends as friends." And so, *second*. The same great truth stands out in equally bold relief, in respect to the long line of patriarchs and prophets and other of God's dear people of the pious Jews. "Precious in the sight of the Lord, is the death of His saints." [1] We now pass to,

Second. The *New Testament*. Here, first in order, it will be our business to inquire—

2. What Christ taught on this subject. We open with the following

POETIC CHALLENGE.

"Is friendship then unfit for Heaven! would love—
That holy impulse which in Jesus dwelt, and streamed
From Him into the souls of those who touched
His loving heart—would it pollute the place?
If that which buds in grace, is not to bloom
In bliss, and thou canst prove it—say on!"

We have already intimated, that "when a doctrine is assumed as the basis of any reasoning, or appears to be casually wrought into the texture of an illustration, it is evidently supposed to be true: nay, such a use of the doctrine amounts to a positive affirmation of it, since it originates in a belief that it is too obvious, or too generally received, to require that it should be made the subject of explicit statement or formal discussion."

Now, precisely of this character are the teachings of our blessed Lord, on the subject in hand. He alludes to it and

---

[1] Ps. cxi. 15.

speaks of it, as a generally received and acknowledged truth. He constituted the church of the present dispensation on the basis of *unity, fellowship,* and *communion* of the members with "the Head, which is CHRIST."[1] "There is *one* Lord, *one* faith, *one* baptism, *one* God and Father of all, who is above all, and through all, *and in you all.*"[2] And hence His declaration to His disciples: "I call you not servants; for a servant knoweth not what His Lord doeth: but I have called you friends; for all things that I have heard of my Father, I have *made known* unto you."[3] Here, then, we have a beautiful illustration of the Divine sympathy with the human, demonstrative of the union, fellowship, and communion of the church "with the Father and the Son" *on earth.* Ay, and this too, sealed by the immutable assurance, "Lo, I am with you *alway,* even unto the end of the ($αἰωνως,$) world,"[4] age or dispensation. An assurance that, as one another, "like stars in the gloom of this life, daily grow fewer," they "shall fade away into the morning light of—

A BRIGHTER HEAVEN.

' Thus star by star declines,
   Till all are passed away,
As morning high and higher shines,
   To pure and perfect day;
Nor sink their stars in empty night,
But hide themselves in Heaven's pure light.'"

Accordingly, in our Saviour's allusions to the "Better Land," the now reserved inheritance of the saints, He said to

---

[1] Ps. cxxxiii. 1.   Eph. iv. 3, 13.   Acts ii. 42.   i John i. 3.   ii Cor. xiii. 14.
[2] Eph. iv. 5, 6.   [3] John xv. 15.   [4] Matt. xxviii. 20.

His desponding disciples: "Let not your hearts be troubled. . . . . In my Father's house are many mansions; if it were not so, I would have told you. I go to prepare a place for you. And if I go and prepare a place for you, I will come again and receive you unto Myself; *that where I am, there ye may be also.*"[1] A declaration this without meaning, if they are not to *know* one another!

Then further. In harmony with this representation, Jesus proceeds to direct our eye of faith to the *social intercourse* founded upon the mutual recognition of the redeemed in the world of glory, under the aspect of a *feast*. "I say unto you, that many shall come from the east and west, *and shall sit down with* Abraham, and Isaac, and Jacob, in the kingdom of Heaven."[2] St. Luke adds, "And all the prophets."[3] And again. "Verily I say unto you, that ye which have followed Me in the regeneration, when the Son of man shall sit in the throne of His glory, *ye also shall sit upon twelve thrones,* judging the twelve tribes of Israel."[4] St. Luke adds, in the parallel passage—"That ye may *eat and drink with Me at My table* in the kingdom of God."[5] So also, when, having "received His kingdom, He returns from a far country, to reckon with His servants."[6] To those who had ministered meat to the hungry, drink to the thirsty, and shelter to the stranger, which He represents as having been done unto Himself; He gives to them the welcome: "Come, ye blessed of My Father, *inherit* the kingdom prepared for you, from the foundation of the world."[7]

---

[1] John xiv. 1–3. [2] Matt. viii. 11. [3] Luke xiii. 28. [4] Matt. xix. 28.
[5] Luke xxii. 30. [6] Luke xix. 12. [7] Matt. xxv. 31-40.

Yes: Heaven is a *social* place. But it could not be such, separately from and independently of a *mutual recognition* of the ingathered multitude of patriarchs, prophets, apostles, and martyrs, and saints of every age and country," whose names are written in Heaven. Ay, and we must add, that "those *angels* who, in the palmy patriarchal times, stood in the shade of a tree at the door of Abraham's tent—whose "feet he washed"—who ate of his "morsel of bread," of his "cakes on the hearth," of "butter and milk," and "calf tender and young" . . . will feel at home sitting down with Abraham and Isaac and Jacob, with all the prophets and apostles and us, at those holy festivities in the spacious "many mansions" of our "Father's house." But there are other allusions in our blessed Lord's teachings in this connection, of which, take the following: The transfiguration on the Mount, Moses and Elias, who appeared in that enrapturing scene, "*spake* of the Lord's decease which He should accomplish at Jerusalem;" while Peter, James, and John exclaimed, "It is good for us to be here,"[1] etc. But we must proceed to notice,

3. What the *Apostles* teach of the recognition of saints in Heaven, concerning—

GENERAL HEAVENLY RECOGNITION.

"Prophets, priests,
Apostles, great reformers, all that served
Messiah faithfully, like stars appear
Of fairest beam: round them gather, clad

[1] Matt. xvii. 4; Mark ix. 5; Luke ix. 33.

> In white, the vouchers of their ministry—
> The flock their care had nourished,
> Fed and saved."
>
> *Pollok.*

One grand feature in the teachings of the Apostles was, that they preached "*Jesus and the resurrection.*"[1] Hence the frequency with which they point the eye of faith of the believer to a "looking for that blessed hope, the glorious appearing of the Great God and (or even) our Saviour, Jesus Christ,"[2] believing, that when He comes, He will "change our vile body, and fashion it like unto His own glorious body;"[3] and that to the end, that they might "*present every man perfect* in Christ Jesus."[4]

And so, in accordance with this teaching, St. Paul, in writing to the Church of Corinth, says: "We are your rejoicing, even as ye are ours *in the day* of the Lord Jesus."[5] And again. "Knowing that He which raised up the Lord Jesus, shall raise up us also by Jesus, and shall *present us* with *you*."[6] So also in his epistle to the Thessalonian saints: "For what is our hope, or joy, or crown of rejoicing? Are not even ye *in the presence* of our Lord Jesus Christ AT HIS COMING? for *ye* are our glory and joy."[7] He also presents this great truth as a motive to faithfulness, in his letter to the saints at Philippi: "That I may rejoice *in the day* of Christ, that I have not run in vain, neither labored in vain."[8] And he again associates himself with these converts in the following passage: "And to *you* who

---

[1] Acts iv. 2, 33.   [2] Titus ii. 13.
[3] Philipp. iii. 21.   [4] Col. i. 28.   [5] ii Cor. i. 14.
[6] ii Cor. iv. 14.   [7] i Thess. ii. 19, 20.   [8] Philipp. ii. 16.

are trouble drest with *us*, when the Lord Jesus shall be revealed from Heaven with His mighty angels in flaming fire," etc., for then, " to them which trouble you, God will give as a recompense, tribulation ;" while " He shall come to be glorified in His saints, and to be admired in all them that believe . . . in that day."[1] And finally, he sums up all, in that remarkable passage, penned for the comfort of his Thessalonian brethren in the midst of their bereavements by martyrdom at the hands of their pagan persecutors : " I would not have you ignorant, brethren, concerning them which are asleep, that ye sorrow not, even as others which have no hope. For if we believe that Jesus died and rose again, even so them *which sleep in Jesus*, will God bring with Him. For this we say unto you by the word of the Lord, that we which are *alive and remain* unto the coming of the Lord, shall not prevent (or go before) them which are asleep. For the Lord Himself shall descend from heaven with a shout, with the voice of the archangel, and with the trump of God : and the dead in Christ shall rise first : then we which are alive and remain, shall be *caught up together* with them in the clouds, to meet the Lord in the air : and so shall we *ever be with* the Lord. Wherefore comfort one another with these words."[2]

These various statements, therefore, are without meaning, on any other construction than that of a final union of pastor and people, and of their *mutual recognition* in that state of

[1] ii Thess. i. 6-10.   [2] i Thess. iv. 13-18.

Heavenly Blessedness where "the wicked cease from troubling, and the weary are at rest"[1]

CONSUMMATION OF THE PASTOR'S HOPE.

"Such, Christian Pastor, is thy heart's delight,
　To serve thy God, and see thy people share
　His service, led by thee : with them how bright
　The joy to come, let holy Paul declare ;
A joy, a glory, and a crown of light,
Which kings might envy, and exult to wear !"

At the opening of the fifth apocalyptic "Seal," the Apostle John "saw under the altar the *souls* of them that were slain for the word of God and for the testimony which they held." And he heard them "cry with a loud cry, saying, How long, O Lord, holy and true, dost Thou not judge and avenge our blood on them that dwell on the earth? And white robes were given unto every one of them ; and it was said unto them that they should rest yet for a little season, *until* their fellow-servants and brethren, that should be killed as they were, should be fulfilled."[2] On this passage we observe, first, that these were the martyr-souls of the patriarchs, prophets, apostles, and other saints, who had not counted their lives dear unto themselves,[3] from the time of the righteous Abel, to the penning of the vision by the Apostle in the isle of Patmos in A.D. 96, "that they might

---

[1] Job iii. 17.　　　[2] Rev. vi. 9-11.
[3] See Heb. xi.

obtain a better resurrection."[1] Second. The happy condition of these martyr-souls "under the altar," is indicated by the term "rest," and by their being clothed "in white robes," significant of "the righteousness of the saints." Third. The expression, that they should rest yet for a little season, until their fellow-servants and brethren who should be killed as they were should be fulfilled, and their loud cry for vengeance upon their enemies, etc., show 1st, their *recognition* of one another in that state. 2nd, their *knowledge* of men on earth. 3rd, their *continued interest* in behalf of their still suffering brethren here below. And, though last not least, 4th, that they had not yet attained to that state of consummated blessedness yet in "reserve" for them at "the resurrection of the just."[2]

But we now remark, that in another vision—that of Rev. xx. 4, 5, the Apostle sees these *same* martyr-souls with others, not "under the altar," but "*seated upon thrones of judgment*," and of whom it is declared, that "they lived and reigned with Christ a thousand years." And, of these reigning "souls" St. John says: "THIS IS THE FIRST RESURRECTION." That is, they are the same with those of whom St. Paul speaks, 1st Thess. iv. 13-17, viz., "the dead in Christ," or those who "sleep in Jesus" whom he declares "shall rise first," and of whom St. John says, Rev. xx. 6, 'Blessed and holy is he who shall have a part in the first resurrection; for over them the second death shall have no power," but they shall be priests of God and of Christ, and shall reign with Him a thousand years."

[1] Heb. xi. 35. [2] Luke xiv. 14.

This leads to another remark, regarding the *different stages* in the state or condition of the resurrected and the translated living saints. Now, true, when first "caught up to meet the Lord in the air," those whom "God brings with Him," "shall ever be with the Lord." But, as we have seen, the Millennial reign of Christ and His saints over the saved nations in the flesh, is limited to "a thousand years." This state of the redeemed in glory, therefore, is depicted in Rev. xi., where "the temple was opened in Heaven," and St. John heard "the seventh angel sound; and there were great voices in Heaven, saying, "The kingdoms of this world are become the kingdoms of our Lord and of His Christ," etc.

That this, however, is not the *eternal* state of the redeemed, is evident from the fact that the above vision carries us onward to the close of the Millennial era, called by St. Paul "the end," i. e., of time. For, the four-and-twenty elders which sat before God on their seats, fell upon their faces and worshiped God, saying, "We give Thee thanks, O Lord God Almighty, because Thou hast taken to Thee Thy great power and *hast* reigned." Yes, "the end," that is, of the Millennial era, is now fully come. In other words, *time now ends*, and the eternal state of the glorified begins. It is that stupendous season of the closing up of "God's great mystery," when "the nations are angry;" that is, those nations which constitute the last or *post*-millennial Apostate Magogean army, described in Rev. xx. 8, 9, "and God's wrath is come, and the time of the dead," (that is, the rest of the [wicked] dead who lived not again until the thousand years were *finished*," verse 5), "that they should be judged, and that Thou shouldst give reward unto Thy servants the prophets, and to the saints, and to them that fear Thy name, small and great; and shouldst destroy them that destroy the earth."[1] For *at this time*, Jesus will have delivered up the Millennial kingdom to God, even the Fathers, that He may be all in all."[2] Hence it is *after* the sealing of the 144,000 of the twelve tribes of Israel,[3] that St. John "beheld, and lo, a great multitude which no man could number, of all kindreds, and nations, and tongues, and people, stand before the throne, and before the Lamb, clothed in white robes, and palms in their hands, and who cry with a loud voice, saying, "Salvation to our God which sitteth upon the throne, and to the Lamb." Yea, these are they of whom "one of the elders asked of John, What are these which are arrayed in white robes? and whence came they?" And upon his answering, "Sir, thou knowest," said: "These are they which have come up out of the great tribulation, and have washed their robes, and made them white in the blood of the Lamb."[4]

Having thus, therefore, finally reached the ETERNAL STATE of the Heavenly Blessedness, what, we ask, is *the bond of union* which cements and actuates this social society of the redeemed each to the other, and all to the now eternally conjoined "God and the Lamb," seated upon the throne of "the principalities and powers"—including that of the restored

[1] Rev. xi. 18.   [2] i Cor. xv. 24-28.
[3] Rev. vii. 1-8.   [4] Ib.— verses 13-14.

"new heavens and earth," with "the Holy City, new Jerusalem"—"in the heavenly places?" St. Paul answers in the following words: It is "CHARITY THAT NEVER FAILETH." Yes, when faith and hope are turned into vision and fruition, then "charity" still "*abideth*." It is eternal as GOD, who is the fountain of love, whence it takes its source, is eternal!

LOVE, THE LAW OF HEAVEN.

" The Law of Heaven is Love : and though its name
   Has been usurped by passion, and profaned
   To its unholy uses through all time,
   Still the eternal principle is pure."

Southey also lends his poetic genius in the following contribution on "the eternal nature of love." Most strongly does he reprove those who deny its continuance after death. We quote it the more gladly because of the touching manner in which he makes it bear on the *Heavenly recognition* of saints.

LOVE ETERNAL.

" They sin, who tell us love can die ;
  With life all other passions fly,
    All others are but vanity.
  In Heaven ambition cannot dwell ;
  Nor avarice in the vaults of hell ;
  Earthly these passions of the earth,
  They perish where they have their birth ;
    But *love is indestructible*—
  Its holy flame for ever burneth,
  From Heaven it came, to Heaven returneth :

> Too oft on earth a troubled guest,
> At times denied, at times opprest,
>   It there is tried and purified,
> Then hath in Heaven its perfect rest.
> It soweth here in toil and care,
> But the harvest time of love is there.
> Oh! when a Mother meets on high
> The babe she lost in infancy,
> Hath not she then for pains and fears—
>   The day of wo, the watchful night—
> For all her sorrows, all her tears,
>   An overpayment of delight?"   *Robert Southey.*

Ay :—

> " Bright in that happy land
>   Beams every eye ;
> Kept by a Father's hand,
>   *Love cannot die.*"

Finally, on this subject. The fact that the rich man in Hell (Hades) had a perfectly distinct and minute knowledge as well of Lazarus as of himself, together with Abraham, and they also of him, is proof demonstrative of the doctrine herein maintained in reference to the *personal recognition* by each other, both of the saved and the lost, in "the world to come." But it is of the ONE FAMILY, as redeemed by the precious blood of "the Lamb slain from before the foundation of the world" out of "all kindreds, and nations, and people, and tongues," that we would sing of

THE ETERNAL REUNION IN THE BETTER LAND.

" If yon bright stars which gem the night,
    Be each a blissful dwelling sphere,
Where kindred spirits *reunite*,
    Whom death hath torn asunder here,
How sweet it were at once to die,
    To leave this blighted orb afar ;
Mixt soul to soul to cleave the sky
    And soar away from star to star.

But oh ! how dark, and drear, and lone,
    Would seem the brightest world of bliss,
If, wandering through each radiant one,
    We fail to find the loved of this !
If there no more the ties shall twine
    Which death's cold hand alone could sever,
Ah, those tears in mockery shine,
    More hateful as they shine for ever !

It cannot be—each hope, each fear,
    That lights the eye or clouds the brow,
Proclaims there is a happier sphere,
    Than this cold world that holds us now.
There is a voice which sorrow hears,
    When heaviest weighs life's galling chain,
'Tis Heaven that whispers—dry your tears,
    The pure in heart shall meet again."

Leggett.

St. Paul's triumphant declaration, at the close of his self-sacrificing apostolic career, will form an appropriate close to the subject of this section :—" For I am now ready to be offered, and the time of my departure is at hand. I have fought the good fight, I have finished my course, I have kept the faith : henceforth there is laid up for me a crown of righteousness, which the Lord the righteous judge shall give me at that day ; and not unto me only, but unto all them that love His appearing." [1]

Now, this inimitably sublime passage, we submit, is decisive against the theory of those who allege that, immediately at death, the soul of the departed saint is admitted to the full and consummated state of Heavenly Blessedness. It is clear from the above language of the apostle, that he did not expect the conferment upon himself or others of the " crown of righteousness," *until* " at the day" of Christ's " appearing," when " He shall Himself descend from heaven with a shout, with the voice of the archangel, and with the trump of God," to " raise first those who sleep in Him." Until *then*, their " vile bodies" could not be " changed, and fashioned like unto Christ's glorious body." Until *then*, there could be no reunion of soul and body, without which restored complex personality in its completeness, they could not be put in a capacity for the enjoyment of a state of consummated blessedness in Heaven. And, that this view is sustained throughout the entire body of the New Testament Scriptures, will appear from the following :—

1. " *Charity*," as we have seen, is represented by St. Paul as the most pre-eminent of the Christian graces, and therefore that which will obtain the highest recompense. Accordingly, the motive by which our blessed Lord would excite us to the

[1] 2 Tim. iv. 6–8.

cultivation and exercise of it runs thus :—"Thou shalt be recompensed AT the resurrection of the just." [1]

2. Those who *suffer persecution and martyrdom* for the sake of Christ and the salvation of men, are promised a great reward in "the world to come :" but this reward the apostle Peter declares, will not be conferred upon them until "the trial of their faith shall be found unto praise and honor and glory AT the appearing of Jesus Christ." [2] Onward to that event, the "souls of them that were slain for the Word of God and the testimony which they held," are represented as remaining "under the altar." [3] So also,

3. To those who "*feed the flock*" *of Christ*, a glorious recompense is promised, even "a crown of glory, which fadeth not away :" [4] but it is conferred then only, "*when* the Chief Shepherd shall appear." A reward is to be bestowed upon the servants of God, "the saints and prophets ;" but it is conferred only "*when* the time comes that the dead in Christ shall be raised and judged." [5] The apostles and faithful are to have their "many mansions" with Christ ; but it is not until He "comes again" from heaven : for then, saith He, "I will receive you unto Myself, that where I am, there ye may be also." [6]

4. The *retribution* to every man according to his works, is also to be made : for, "the Son of Man will come in His own glory, and with the glory of the Father, and with the glory of the holy angels ;" [7] and *then* "He will reward every man

---

[1] Luke xiv. 14.   [2] 1 Pet. i. 7.   [3] Rev. vi. 9.   [4] 1 Pet. v. 4.
[5] Rev. xi. 18.   [6] John xiv. 1–3.   [7] Matt. xvi. 27.

according to his works: to them who by patient continuance in well doing seek for glory and honor and immortality, eternal life . . . to every man that worketh good ; to the Jew first, and also to the Gentile : but unto them that are contentious, and do not obey the truth, but obey unrighteousness, indignation and wrath, tribulation and anguish, upon every soul that doeth evil ; to the Jew first, and also to the Gentile." [1] And this act of retribution takes place, observe, at " the end of the world"—not, mark, κοσμος, the globe or earth, but αιωνως, age or dispensation—in " the morning" of which, as " the day of the Lord" or " day of judgment," " the upright" [2] shall be judged ; while the " many" of their enemies who shall then be " slain" of the Lord, [3] being numbered among " the rest of the (wicked) dead," shall " not live again," i. e., be raised and judged, until the thousand years are finished," [4] or the evening of that day. Finally,

5. We hence find in Scripture, that *the time* of recompense and the time of judgment run parallel with that " day of the Lord" which is reckoned by Him " as a thousand years." [5] It will be the time of glory and of the apparition of our Lord, as in the words, " When Christ who is our life shall appear, *then* shall ye also appear with Him in glory." [6] The time of Christ's appearance and our salvation : For, " He shall appear *the second time* without sin unto salvation." [7] The time of His appearing and of our beatific vision : For,

---

[1] Rom. ii. 7-10.   [2] Ps. xlix. 14.   [3] Isa. lxvi. 15, 16.
[4] Rev. xx. 5, and verses 7-15.   [5] ii Pet. iii. 8, 10.   [6] Col. iii. 4.
[7] Heb. ix. 28.

"*when* He shall appear, we shall be like Him, for we shall see Him as He is." [1] And finally, the time also, "*when* them which sleep in Jesus, will God bring with Him;" and "when we which are alive and remain unto the coming of the Lord," together with "the dead in Christ who shall rise first," "shall be caught up with them in the clouds to meet the Lord in the air, and so shall be ever with the Lord." [2]

Nor this only. For, there is *the judgment upon the wicked*, called "the day of judgment," "the great day of His wrath," etc. This *opens* with the pouring out of the vials of the Divine indignation upon the living antichristian nations of earth in "the morning" of that day. For, "the Lord Jesus shall be revealed from heaven in flaming fire with His mighty angels, to take vengeance on them that know not God, and that obey not the gospel of our Lord Jesus Christ" —that is, the idolatrous heathen and the impenitent of the gentile nations of Christendom—"who shall be punished with everlasting destruction from the presence of the Lord, and from the glory of His power." [3] For that judgment-day will commence by "the Lord's pleading with all flesh with fire and with the sword," as stated above, "and the slain of the Lord shall be many;" and, being consigned to their Tartarean abode in Hades, shall be "reserved for chains under darkness against the day (that is, the final act) of judgment and perdition of ungodly men" [4] at the *close* of "the thousand years." [5]

We close with the following appropriate lines on the—

[1] John iii. 2.   [2] 1 Thess. iv. 13-17.
[3] 2 Thess. i. 7-9.   [4] ii Pet. ii. 4.   [5] Rev. xx. 5, and verses 7-15.

LAST JUDGMENT.

"Day of judgment, day of wonders!
   Hark! the trumpet's awful sound;
Louder than a thousand thunders,
   Shakes the vast creation round!
     How the summons
Will the sinner's heart confound!

See the JUDGE, our nature wearing,
   Clothed in majesty Divine;
You who long for His appearing,
   Then shall say, 'This God is mine!'
     Gracious Saviour,
Own me in that day for THINE!

At His call the dead awaken,
   Rise to life from earth and sea;
All the powers of nature shaken,
   By His looks prepare to flee;
     Careless sinner,
What will then become of thee?

Horrors past imagination,
   Will surprise your troubled heart;
When you hear your condemnation,
   Hence, accursed wretch, 'Depart!'
     Thou with Satan
And his angels have thy part.

But to those who have confessed,
   Loved and served the Lord below;
He will say, 'Come near, ye blessed,
   See the Kingdom I bestow:
     You for ever
Shall My love and glory know.'"

CHAPTER XI.

Preparation for the Heavenly Blessedness.

SECTION I.

The Scriptural Motives to Faith, Repentance, and a Holy Life.

"Believe in the Lord Jesus Christ, and thou shalt be saved."
"And they went out and preached every where, that men should repent."
"Follow peace with all men, and holiness, without which no man can see the Lord."

THE question before us—and it is a momentous one—is, what are the *true Scriptural motives* to faith, repentance, and a holy life, as preparatory to a state of future Heavenly Blessedness?

This is a purely practical subject. It forms a necessary, as it will prove an acceptable appendage to the preceding discussions.

We observe, then, that it is conceded by all evangelical Christians, that faith and repentance are indispensable to our justification before God through the atoning merits of Christ, while the genuineness of both these graces are manifested in our progressive sanctification or holiness of heart and of life, in rendering us mete for "the inheritance of the saints in light."

But, in effecting a moral change in man from a natural to a gracious state, the Gospel addresses itself to man's understanding, by a presentation of suitable motives to that end. In no other way can it commend itself to his acceptance, or subdue his natural rebellion of will to the obedience of Christ, or turn the current of his affections from unholy to holy objects, desires, and pursuits.

In *what*, then, do these motives consist? If we rely upon the current theology of the day, the motives to faith, repentance, and holiness, are alleged to be drawn from the necessity of our preparation for death; while meditations on the glories of heaven and the pains of hell, are a secondary class of motives for preserving the mind and heart in a proper state for the future Heavenly Blessedness. Any other motive besides these, is denounced as of a purely theoretical character, and that it tends only to fanaticism and delusion. But let us see—

I. The alleged *preparation for death* as the primary motive to an exercise of faith, repentance, etc. This motive of preparation for death, it is affirmed, is predicated of the alleged *identity* of that event with the second coming of Christ. On this point, we respectfully demur, on the ground that, however appropriate and effective a presentation of the brevity and uncertainty of the tenure of human life as a motive to the exercise of the above named graces, yet that it is *in no way* identical with Christ's coming to them at death. Let us put this to the test, in its application,

1. As a motive to the exercise of *faith* in Christ, in regard to the *unregenerate*. Here we find the grand and leading motive is, *not* Christ's coming to the sinner at death, but, "*believe* in the Lord Jesus Christ, and thou shalt be saved." This was urged by Paul and Silas upon the "Jailor."[1] It pointed him to the necessity of an exercise of *faith* in and reliance upon the atoning merits of Christ as "the Lamb of God who taketh away the sins of the world."[2] This formed the basis and burden of apostolic preaching, the theme of which had been furnished by Christ Himself, in the declaration, "He that *believeth* in Me, hath everlasting life."[3] And again. "I am the resurrection and the life: Whosoever *believeth* in Me, though he were dead, yet shall he live,"[4] etc. And so, instead of death being held up as a motive to an exercise of faith in Christ, we are pointed to His *resurrection from* the dead, and of our resurrection in, by, and through Him, as the guarantee of our eternal life. Accordingly, St. Peter declares that the apostles were ordained to be "the *witnesses* of His resurrection,"[5] in virtue of which, St. Paul affirms "how that God had opened the door of faith to the Gentiles."[6] Nor this only. This last named apostle places faith in the preaching of "the resurrection of the dead and of eternal judgment," as among the fundamental "principles of the doctrine of Christ."[7] No, we repeat: it was not preparation for death, as a motive to faith in Christ, but the "preaching through Jesus of the resurrection from the dead !" It

---

[1] Acts xvi. 51.   [2] John i. 29.   [3] Ib—iii. 36, vi. 47, v. 24.
[4] John xi. 25–26.   [5] Acts i. 22. ii. 32.   [6] Ib—xiv. 27.
[7] Heb. vi. 1–2.

was this preaching that so grieved the people, the priests, and the captain of the temple, and the Sadducees, as to lead to the imprisonment of Peter and John." [1] So also the persecution of Paul by "the high priest Ananias, with a certain orator named Tertullus," who denounced him as "a pestilent fellow, and a mover of sedition among the people," etc., because he "cried, standing among them, touching the resurrection of the dead." [2]

Still it is urged, do we not read, "*Be ye also ready*, for in such an hour as ye think not, the Son of man cometh?" And does not this mean *His coming to us at death?* We reply: So far from it, we have in this passage the declared unexpected return, *personally*, of the Son of man from heaven, and not His coming to us at death, as a motive of preparation to meet, not "the king of terrors," [3] but, "THE SON OF GOD." And not, further, to meet the Son of God as though HE came to us at death: which would be to transform Him into "the king of terrors," that is, "the Devil, who has the power of death," and whose work it is—under the permissive providence of God—to inflict upon us the *penalty* of death due to our sins. From such a revolting transformation as this of "the Son of man" to serve a popular theory, the enlightened mind shrinks with instinctive horror! Again then we say, No: the purpose for which the dear "Son of God" came into the world was, "to *destroy* the works of the devil, and to *deliver* them who, *through fear of death*, were all their life-time subject to bondage," [4] by enabling them through

---

[1] Acts iv. 1-2.   [2] Ib. xxiv.   [3] Job xviii. 14.   [4] Heb. ii. 15.

faith in the atoning merits of Christ as the ground of their pardon and salvation, to exclaim—O ᾅδης, (Hades, not grave) where is thy victory! O death, where is thy sting!"[1]

FAITH IN CHRIST.

"Not all the blood of beasts
   On Jewish altars slain,
Could give the guilty conscience peace,
   Or wash away the stain.

But CHRIST the heavenly Lamb,
   Takes all our sins away;
A sacrifice of nobler name,
   And richer blood than they.

My *faith* would lay her hand
   On that dear head of THINE;
While like a penitent I stand,
   And there confess my sin.

My soul looks back to see
   The burdens THOU didst bear;
While hanging on the cursed tree,
   And hopes her guilt was there.

Believing, we rejoice,
   To see the curse remove;
We bless the LAMB with cheerful voice,
   And sing His bleeding love."

Watts.

[1] i. Cor. xv. 55.

But in the next place—

Let us consider the motive to an exercise of faith, as it respects the *regenerate*. Now, so far from Christ's coming to the saints at death, their souls, disenthralled from their earthly "tabernacle,"[1] *go to Him*. Hence like Paul, their "desire to depart, that they may be with Christ," [2] "whom," as St. Peter has it, "having not seen, ye love; in whom, though now ye see Him not, yet *believing*, ye rejoice with joy unspeakable and full of glory, receiving the *end* of your faith, even the salvation of your souls, AT HIS APPEARING." [3]

Besides: death, in any view we may take of it, is *unnatural* to us. God at the first did not make man to die, but to live. Hence the placing of "*the tree of life*" in the centre of Eden. Death is the legitimate offspring of sin. "By *sin* came *death*." And so, death having robbed us of our pristine state, is become our greatest enemy. For this reason it is that we dread death. Accordingly, "the glorious Gospel of God," which "brings life and immortality to light through the Gospel," instead of preaching *death* to us as a motive to faith, etc., points our eye of faith to HIM who, at His first appearing in the flesh, came to *disarm* death of its terrors by His triumphant resurrection from the dead; and who, when He shall "appear the second time," comes as "the Judge of the quick (or living) and the dead;" seated on His "white horse" and wearing "His many crowns" as He whose "name is Faithful and True," to receive His ransomed ones to Himself forever.

[1] ii Cor. v. 1.   [2] Philipp. i. 23.   [3] i Pet. i. 7–9.

FAITH'S TRIUMPH OVER DEATH.

"Come, thou long-expected JESUS,
   Born to set thy people free ;
From our fears and sins release us,
   Let us find our rest in THEE.

Israel's strength and consolation,
   Hope of all the earth Thou art ;
Dear desire of every nation,
   Joy of every longing heart!

Born thy people to deliver,
   Born a child, and yet a king ;
Born to reign in us forever,
   Now Thy glorious kingdom bring.

By thine own eternal Spirit,
   Rule in all our hearts alone ,
By Thine all-sufficient merit,
   Raise us to Thy glorious throne !"

We now pass to an application of this alleged motive to the next text, namely—

2. The exercise of the grace of *repentance towards God.* "And they," that is, the apostles, "went out and preached every where, that men should *repent.*"

Now, as it is the province of faith to apprehend Jesus Christ in His mediatorial work, in reconciling us to God by His sin-atoning sacrifice upon the cross ; so it is "*repentance towards God*" that secures our pardon and "justification from all things from which we could not be justified by the deeds of the law." This faith in and reliance upon the merits of Christ to "save us from our sins," produces in us that "godly sorrow for sin, which worketh *repentance* towards God that needeth not to be repented of."[1] Therefore it is that "Him hath God highly exalted, to *give repentance* unto Israel"—and to the Gentiles as well—"and remission of sins."[2]

Do you then ask: What is the Scriptural *motive* to repentance? The answer is, that it is derived, not from the presentation of *death* to our view, but that which is infinitely paramount to it, viz, the SECOND PERSONAL COMING OF CHRIST. Thus the apostle Peter, in his address to the crucifiers of our Lord: "*Repent* ye, therefore, and be converted, that your sins may be blotted out, when the times of refreshing"—not death—"shall come from the presence of the Lord; and He *shall send* Jesus Christ, which before was preached unto you:" that is, when you repented and were converted—"whom the heavens must receive, *until* the times of restitution of all things which God hath spoken by the mouth of all His holy prophets since the world began."[3] Obviously here, the motive to repentance presented by the apostle to his unconverted auditors is drawn, not from any contingency of mortal existence, however impressive in itself, but from that incomparably transcendant and glorious event into which all others converge—"the restitution of all things" by the *revelation* of the Lord Jesus from "the heavens." While at the same time, the "blotting out of sins" and their "conversion" to God, was made to hinge, so to speak, upon

---

[1] ii Cor. vii. 10.   [2] Acts v. 31.   [3] Acts iii. 19–21.

their "repentance" at the foot of the cross. This grace is forcibly expressed in the following lines—

REPENTANCE AT THE CROSS.

The voice of the *Beloved* sounds
Over the hills and rising grounds,
   Unweary in His cry :
Ho, ye guilty, starving poor,
Who dwell in sin at hell's dark door,
   Turn, turn, or thou shalt die.

Why do ye spend your strength for naught,
And money, that which can't be bought—
   Food for your starving soul?
While I have wine and milk to give,
That without price you may receive ;
   Eat, and you shall be whole.

LORD, help my poor heart to believe,
Thy heavenly gift I will receive,
   The gift of offered grace ,
Repentant at Thy feet I fall,
And on Thy name sincerely call,
   For pardon and for peace.

Peter Naylor, 1870.

Finally. The last test of this motive is that which relates to—

3. *Personal holiness* of heart and of life, as a preparation for the Heavenly Blessedness. The requisition here is— " Follow peace with all men, and holiness, without which no man can see the Lord." God is a God of peace and holiness,

and Heaven is the abode of peace and holiness. It is "the peace-makers and the pure in heart" alone, that shall "see God." Do you here again ask: What are the *motives* for the cultivation of these divine graces, in order to our preparation for heaven? The answer is, that they are derived, not from depicting to the imagination the solemnities of death, but those which are derived from FAITH IN THE SECOND PERSONAL COMING OF CHRIST. Indeed, it will be found that this class of motives, as predicated of the above named event, will apply to the whole range of *practical* godliness.

(1.) Is it, to *love* Christ? "If any man *love not* the Lord Jesus Christ, let him be anathema, maranatha:" and the motive to this love is, "*the Lord is at hand.*"[1]

(2.) Is it, to the *mortification* of sinful lusts? The motive is, "When Christ who is our life *shall appear*, then shall ye also appear with Him in glory. Mortify *therefore* your members which are upon the earth," etc.[2]

(3.) Is it, to *spirituality of mind?* The motive is, "For our conversation ($πολίτευμα$, or citizenship) is in heaven, whence we *look for the Saviour*,"[3] etc.

(4.) Is it, *to love one another?* "And the Lord make you to increase and abound in love one toward another, and toward all men, even as we do toward you:" and the motive is, "to the end that He may stablish your hearts unblameable in holiness before God, *at the coming* of our Lord Jesus Christ with all His saints."[4]

---

[1] 1 Cor. xvi. 22.
[2] Colos. iii. 4, 5. Titus ii. 11–13.
[3] Philipp. iii. 20, 21.
[4] 1 Thess. iii. 13.

5. Is it, to *works of mercy?* The motive is, "When the Son of man *shall come in His glory,* . . . THEN shall He say to them on His right hand, Come, ye blessed of my Father, inherit the kingdom," etc.; for, I was an hungered and ye gave me meat; I was thirsty and ye gave me drink," etc.: for as much as ye have done it unto one of these little ones, ye have done it unto Me." [1]

6. Is it, to *watchfulness* against temptation? etc. The motive is, "Let your loins be girded about, and your lamps burning"—for, "blessed are those servants whom the Lord, *when He cometh,* shall find so doing."[2]

7. Is it, to *moderation and sobriety?* "Let your moderation be known unto all men:" And the motive is, "*The Lord is at hand.*" [3]

8. Is it, to *ministerial fidelity and diligence?* "For what is our hope, or joy, or crown of rejoicing?" The motive is, "are not even ye in the presence of our Lord Jesus Christ at His coming?" [4]

9. Is it, to *patience and long suffering?* "Be ye also patient: stablish your hearts:" and the motive is, "For *the coming of the Lord draweth nigh.*" [5] Finally,

10. Is it, to *general obedience and holiness* of heart and of life? The motive is, "We know that, *when He shall appear,* we shall be like Him, for we shall see Him as He is. And

---

[1] Matt. xxv. 31-36. [2] Luke xii. 35-37. i Thess. iv. 5. Rev. xvi. 15.
[3] Philipp. iv. 5. i Pet. i. 13.
[4] i Thess. ii. 19. Matt. xxiv. 46. i Tim. vi. 13. ii Tim. iv. 1, 2. i Pet. v. 1-4.
[5] James v. 7, 8. ii Thess. i. 4-7. Heb. x. 36, 37. i Pet. i. 6, 7.

every man that hath this hope in him, purifieth himself even as He is pure." [1]

HOLINESS OF HEAVEN.

"Nor eye hath seen, nor ear hath heard,
    Nor sense nor reason known,
What joys the Father has prepared,
    For those who love His son.

But the good Spirit of the Lord
    Reveals a Heaven to come;
The beams of glory in His word,
    Allure and guide us home.

Pure are the joys above the sky,
    And all the region peace;
No wanton lip nor envious eye,
    Can see or taste the bliss.

Those holy gates for ever bar
    Pollution, sin, and shame;
None shall obtain admittance there
    But followers of the LAMB.

He keeps the Father's book of life—
    There all their names are found;
The hypocrite in vain shall strive
    To tread the Heavenly ground."   *Watts.*

In the light of these Scriptural statements, therefore, we submit, is furnished the most positive evidence, that the *primary* motive to the exercise of faith, repentance, and a holy life is derived, not from a presentation of Christ's com-

---

[1] i John iii. 2, 3.   Ib. ii. 28.   Matt. xvi. 27.   Rev. xxii. 12.

ing to us *at death*, but, of "our gathering together unto Him"[1] AT HIS SECOND APPEARING to "judge the quick (or living) and the dead"[2] at the last day."[3]

Let us now proceed to consider the next article—

II. *Meditations on the glories of heaven and the pains of hell*, as a second class of motives to prepare and preserve the mind in a proper state for Heaven. Now, doubtless, such meditations are highly beneficial for the purpose here alleged. But, if we overlook the fact of the peculiar state or condition of the departed soul *during its separation* from the body at the instant of death, the motives inspired by such meditations, being founded upon a *false* basis, cannot but fail to prove operative in securing the benefits alleged. Being of a nature kindred to the other, which affirms that Christ *comes to us* at death, it supposes that the believer, immediately at the moment of the soul's departure from the body, is admitted to a state of consummated blessedness in the "highest" or empyreal Heaven.

Now, that the souls of the pious departed do, immediately at death, enjoy a state of blessedness which "passeth understanding," and that they do visibly behold the Lord Jesus seated upon His Mediatorial throne at "the right hand of the Majesty in the heavens," we fully believe. But both these classes of motives alike overlook the fact, that Christ is still exercising His priestly office as our "INTERCESSOR," and that as such, He is "received into the Heavens," only "until the times of restitution of all things," when God will *again*

---

[1] ii Thess. ii. 1.   [2] ii Thess. ii. 1.   [3] Acts x. 42.

"send Jesus Christ" from heaven "with a shout, with the voice of the archangel and with the trump of God," to *raise the dead* who sleep in Him, *re-unite* their risen bodies to their previously separated souls, and change and translate the living saints who remain unto His coming; and that, this accomplished, He is thenceforth to "REIGN" OVER THE SAVED NATIONS IN THE FLESH during "a thousand years," or "until He has made all His enemies His footstool." Then, that is, at "*the end*" of this period, having "delivered up" the Millennial "kingdom to God, even the Father, that He may be all in all," the one united family of the redeemed will enter upon the employments and enjoyments of their consummated state of Heavenly Blessedness.

It follows, that all motives that are derived from a meditation of the glories of Heaven, etc., which *fall short* of this, must be founded in fundamental error. Instead, the Scriptures teach throughout, that the only proper motives to that end, are drawn from the *faith* and *hope* of the church, Patriarchal, Jewish, and Christian, as pointing to and centered in, Christ Jesus the Lord, as THE COMING ONE to restore all things, when,

————— "in pomp and majesty ineffable."

He will "appear the second time without sin unto salvation," to *complete* in "eternal glory," what He purchased for the redeemed out of all nations and kindreds and tongues and people by His vacarious sacrifice on the cross. As we read of the Old Testament saints, that they "*all died in faith*" of those "better promises which they beheld afar off;"[1] so of those of the New Testament, we read, that they "looked for,"[2] and "loved the appearing," and "hastened unto the coming and kingdom of God,"[3] "eternal and in the heavens."[4]

THE SAINT'S PERPETUAL THEME.

"Tell me the subject of their lays—
And whence their loud, exalted praise?
Jesus, the Saviour, is their theme,
They sing the wonders of His name."

Ay, and so, the believer shall be

"FOREVER WITH THE LORD."

"Forever with the Lord!"
 Amen : so let it be ;
Life from the dead is in that word ;
 'Tis Immortality.

Here in the body pent,
 Absent from Him I roam :
Yet nightly pitch my moving tent
 A day's march nearer home.

My Father's house on high,
 Home of my soul! how near,
At times, to faith's foreseeing eye,
 Thy golden gates appear !

"Forever with the Lord!"
 Father, if 'tis Thy will,
The promise of that faithful word,
 E'en here to me fulfill.

---

[1] Heb. viii. 6.   [2] Ib. xi. 13.   [3] ii Tim. iv. 8; ii Pet. iii. 12.   [4] ii Cor. v. 1.

> So, when my latest breath
>   Shall rend the vail in twain,
> By death I shall escape from death,
>   And life eternal gain.
>
> Knowing as I am known,
>   How shall I love that word,
> And oft repeat before the throne,
>   " FOREVER with the Lord !"
>
> <div align="right"><i>James Montgomery</i>, 1825. (From " The Sacrifice of Praise." Brick Pres. Ch. Hymns).</div>

"Time gone, the righteous saved, the wicked damned,
  And God's ETERNAL GOVERNMENT approved." *Pollok.*

SECTION II.

" The Conclusion of the whole matter." [1]

We ask, then, in conclusion: What think you, reader, of that "Inheritance which is incorruptible, and undefiled, and that fadeth not away, reserved in Heaven" for all those who are "begotten again unto a lively hope by the resurrection of Jesus Christ from the dead?" We have shown you in Part I. of the treatise, *Where* that Heaven is, "IN" which will be found that "eternal inheritance" of the redeemed, as it will be when *restored* by the power of "the second Man, the Lord from heaven." We have also shown in Part II, IN WHAT the inheritance "in the heavenly places" will consist —even that "New Heaven and New Earth wherein shall

---

[1] Eccles. xii. 13.

dwell righteousness" eternal, together with the "Holy City, New Jerusalem, which cometh down from God out of heaven" as the *capital* of universal empire. And we have also furnished you with a glimpse, however limited and imperfect, into the BEATIFIC VISION of that Heavenly Blessedness "where the wicked cease from troubling, and the weary are at rest."

While, therefore, at first view, the momentous truths enunciated in these pages may not all meet with your unhesitating concurrence—for doubtless, placed in contrast with the current theology of the day in these premises, they may be thought to wear the aspect of novelty—yet, taking it for granted that you believe that there *is* a Heaven of Blessedness "reserved" for the faithful in Christ Jesus; and a Gehenna of future misery for the finally impenitent; we repeat, in conclusion—

What is *your* present character, condition, hopes, and prospects, as to your admission "into the everlasting Kingdom of our Lord and Saviour Jesus Christ?" Are *you* "looking for that blessed hope, the glorious appearing of the Great God, and (or even) our Saviour Jesus Christ?" Is *your* "lamp trimmed and burning?" Are *you* "like unto those who are making ready to go forth to meet the BRIDEGROOM AT HIS COMING?" "As the hart panteth after the cooling water-brook," is *your* "soul panting" for an abode in that blessed "world" or habitable earth "to come" of which St. Paul speaks?

Consider, reader: "What a pure world for the pure! What forms of holy beauty bloom in sight beneath the upper skies! How different from this sin-soiled earth! 'There, no idol temples pollute groves and mountain-tops. There, no spirit of horror broods over ancient (or modern) battle-fields, and spots where dark deeds were done. There, no frightful Golgothas, or places of skulls, waken up remembrances and associations of guilt and death. There, no dark spirits rule in the air, or dwell among desolations and tombs. There, is no ground which once drank the blood of Martyrs, or of God's own Son. There, no serpents hiss under the tree of life, or bruize the heads of those white-robed ones that stray by the fountains of living waters. There, no foul worms creep forth from the heart of ripening fruit, and no poisonous, softly stealing death revels on the cheek of beauty. Bright, pure, and blessed world! Life without death. Beauty without blemish. Bloom without decay.'"

THE BETTER WORLD.

"There is a better world, they say,—
  O, so bright! O, so bright!
Where sin and want are done away,—
  O, so bright! O, so bright!
Music fills the heavenly air,
And angels with bright wings are there!
With harps of gold in mansions fair—
  O, so bright! O, so bright!

No clouds there pass along the sky,
  Happy land! Happy land!
No tear-drop glistens in the eye,—
  Happy land! Happy land!

They drink the gushing streams of grace,
And gaze upon the Saviour's face,
Whose glory fills that holy place,—
   Happy land! Happy land!

And wicked things, and beasts of prey,
   Come not there! Come not there!
And ruthless death, and fierce decay,
   Come not there! Come not there!
There all are holy, all are good,
And hearts unwashed in Jesus' blood,
And guilty sinners unrenewed,
   Come not there! Come not there!

And though we're sinners every one,
   Jesus died! Jesus died!
And though our crown of peace is gone,
   Jesus died! Jesus died!
We may be cleansed from every stain,
We may be crowned with bliss again,
And in that land of pleasure reign,—
   Jesus died! Jesus died!

Then, parents, brothers, sisters, come:
   Come away! Come away!
We long to reach our Father's home,
   Come away! Come away!
O come; the time is slipping past,
And men and things are fleeting fast,
The Judge will surely come at last,—
   Come away! Come away!

This world is—O, so dark and drear,
   Take us there! Take us there!
We never can be happy here,
   Take us there! Take us there!

> O listen to that music sweet,
> It comes so rich from yonder seat,
> Where all the good in glory meet,—
> Take us there! Take us there!
>
> *(An English Author—Anonymous.)*

Reader, again we ask: Are *you* prepared for it? Then, oh! then, though still "wrestling against principalities and powers and spiritual wickedness in high places," for your encouragement in the mighty conflict, turn your eye for the moment to the death-bed scenes of the Lord's faithful ones—

> "One gentle sigh their fetters break,
> We scarce can say, 'they're gone!'
> Before their willing spirits take
> Their mansion near the throne."

And so the weary, way-worn traveler to the "Better Land" may sing—

> "Lo, He comes, with clouds descending,
> Once for favored sinners slain:
> Thousand, thousand saints attending
> Swell the triumph of His train:
> Hallelujah!
> God appears on earth to reign!
>
> Every eye shall now behold Him,
> Robed in dreadful majesty;
> Those who set at naught and sold Him
> Pierced, and nailed Him to the tree,
> Deeply wailing,
> Shall the true Messiah see.

Every island, sea, and mountain,
  Heaven and earth shall flee away;
All who hate Him must, confounded,
  Hear the trump proclaim the day:
    Come to judgment!
  Come to judgment, come away!

Now Redemption, long expected,
  See in solemn pomp appear!
All His saints, by man rejected,
  Now shall meet Him in the air:
    Hallelujah!
  See the day of God appear!

Answer Thine own Bride and Spirit;
  Hasten, Lord, the general doom;
The new Heaven and earth to inherit,
  Take Thy pining exiles home:
    All Creation
  Travails, groans, and bids Thee come!

Yea, Amen! let all adore Thee,
  High on Thy eternal throne:
Saviour, take the power and glory,
  Claim the Kingdom for Thine own:
    O come quickly,
  Everlasting God, come down!

Variation by Martin Madan, 1760.
From Charles Wesley and John Cennick.
(*From* " *The Sacrifice of Praise,*" Brick Presb.
Ch. Hymn 589.)

Finally, of the ingathering upon "Mount Zion, the heavenly Jerusalem," of "the innumerable company of angels, and the general assembly and Church of the first-born which are written in Heaven, and the spirits of just men made perfect, and God the judge of all, and Jesus the mediator of the new covenant, and the blood of sprinkling which speaketh better things than that of Abel," to which by faith *" we are even now come,"* we may sing—

> " Egypt, and Tyre, and Greek and Jew,
> Shall there begin their lives anew;
> Angels and men shall join and sing
> The Hill where living waters spring.
>
> When God makes up His last account
> Of nations in His Holy Mount,
> 'Twill be an honor to appear
> As one new-born and nourished there!"

We add: that the *alternate emotions* of hope and fear, and of joy and sorrow which ofttimes agitate the mind and heart of the believer at the near prospect of death, are beautifully pictured forth in the following

MOTHER'S LAMENT OVER HER DYING BOY.

Boy.

" My Mother, my Mother, O let me depart,
Your tears and your pleadings are swords to my heart;
I hear gentle voices that chide my delay;
I see lovely visions, that woo me away.
My prison is broken, my trials are o'er!
O Mother, my Mother, detain me no more!

Mother.

And will you then leave us, my brightest, my best?
And will you run nestling no more to my breast?

The Summer is coming to sky and to bower ;
The tree that you planted will soon be in flower ;
You loved the soft season of song and of bloom ;
O, shall it return, and find you in the tomb?

Boy.

Yes, Mother, I loved in the sunshine to play,
And talk with the birds and blossoms all day ;
But sweeter the songs of the spirits on high,
And brighter the glory round God in the sky :
I see them, I hear them, they pull at my heart,
My Mother, my Mother, O let me depart !

Mother.

O, do not desert us ! Our hearts will be drear,
Our home will be lonely, when you are not here ;
Your brother will sigh 'mid his playthings, and say
I wonder dear William so long can delay :
That foot like the wild wind, that glance like a star—
O, what will this world be, when they are afar?

Boy.

This world, dearest Mother—O, live not for this ;
No, press on with me to the fulness of bliss !
And trust me, whatever bright fields I may roam,
My heart will not wander from you and your home.
Believe me still near you on pinions of love ;
Expect me to hail you, when soaring above.

Mother.

Well, go, my beloved ! the conflict is o'er ;
My pleas are all selfish, I urge them no more ;

Why chain your bright spirit down here to the clod,
So thirsting for freedom, so ripe for its God?
Farewell, then, farewell, till we meet at the throne,
Where love fears no parting, and tears are unknown.

Boy.

O Glory! O Glory! What music! What light!
What wonders break in on my heart, on my sight!
I come! blessed spirits! I hear you from high;
O frail, faithless nature, can this be to die!
So near! what, so near to my SAVIOUR and KING,
O, help me, ye angels, HIS GLORY TO SING!

In conclusion, permit the writer to advert once again to the solemn and momentous fact of the Coming of the Bridegroom as *imminent*, and of the consequent importance of an earnest and vigilant preparedness to meet HIM.

" Rejoice, rejoice, believing,
 And let your lights appear;
The evening is advancing,
 And darker night is near:
The BRIDEGROOM is arising,
 And soon He will draw nigh:
Up! pray, and watch, and wrestle
 At midnight comes the cry.

See that your lamps are burning,
 Replenish them with oil;
Look now for your salvation,
 The end of sin and toil;

> The watchers on the mountain
>   Proclaim the Bridegroom near;
> Go meet Him as He cometh,
>   With hallelujahs clear.
>
> O wise and holy Virgins,
>   Now raise your voices higher,
> Till, in your jubilation,
>   Ye meet the angel-choir.
> The MARRIAGE-FEAST is waiting,
>   The gates wide open stand;
> Up, up, ye heirs of glory!
>   The Bridegroom is at hand!
>
> Our hope and expectation,
>   O JESUS, now appear;
> Arise, Thou SUN so longed for,
>   O'er this benighted sphere!
> With heart and hands uplifted,
>   We plead, O Lord, to see
> The day of Earth's Redemption,
>   And ever be with Thee!"
>
> *Laurenti, 1690. Translated by Jane Borthwick. (From "The Sacrifice of Praise," Brick Pres. Ch. Hymns.)*

The following appropriate lines, from the pen of Mrs. L. H. Sigourney, are added in closing, as presenting an epitome, so to speak, of the leading truths brought to view in this treatise, as connected with the separation of the body and soul at death, and their re-union in a state of immortal Heavenly Blessedness:—

FAREWELL OF THE SOUL TO THE BODY.

" Companion dear ! the hour draws nigh,
  The sentence speeds—to die, to die ;
  So long in mystic union held,
  So close with strong embrace compell'd,
  How can'st thou bear the dread decree,
  That strikes thy clasping nerves from me?
  To Him who on this mortal shore,
  The same encircling vestment wore,
  To Him I look, to Him I bend,
  To Him thy shuddering frame commend.

  If I have ever caused thee pain,
  The throbbing breast, the burning brain,
  With cares and vigils turn'd thee pale,
  And scorn'd thee when thy strength did fail—
  Forgive ! Forgive ! thy task doth cease,
  Friend ! Lover ! let us part in peace.

  That thou didst sometimes check my force,
  Or trifling stay mine upward course,
  Or lure from Heaven my wavering trust,
  Or bow my drooping wing to dust,—
  I blame thee not ; the strife is done,
  I knew thou wert the weaker one,
  The vase of earth, the trembling clod,
  Constrain'd to hold the breath of God.
  Well hast thou in my service wrought,
  Thy brow hath mirror'd forth my thought ;
  To wear my smile thy lip hath glow'd,
  Thy tear to speak my sorrows flow'd ;
  Thine ear hath borne me rich supplies
  Of sweetly varied melodies ;

Thy hands my prompted deeds have done,
Thy feet upon my errands run ;—
Yes, thou hast mark'd my bidding well,
Faithful and true ! farewell, farewell !

Go to thy rest.   A quiet bed
Meek mother Earth with flowers shall spread,
Where I no more thy sleep can break
With fever'd dream, nor rudely wake
Thy wearied eye.
                    Oh ! quit thy hold,
For thou art faint, and chill, and cold,
And long thy grasp and groan of pain
Have bound me pitying in thy chain,
Though angels urge me hence to soar,
Where I shall share thine ills no more.

Yet we shall meet.   To soothe thy pain,
Remember, we shall meet again ;
Quell with this hope the victor's sting,
And keep it as a signet-ring.
When the dire worm shall pierce thy breast,
And naught but ashes mark thy rest,
When stars shall fall, and skies grow dark,
And proud suns quench their glow-worm spark,
Keep thou that hope, to light thy gloom,
Till the last trumpet rends the tomb.
Then shalt thou glorious rise, and fair,
Nor spot, nor stain, nor wrinkle bear,—
And I with hovering wing elate,
The bursting of thy bonds shall wait,
And breathe the welcome of the sky—
' No more to part, no more to die,
Co-heir of Immortality.' "

www.ingramcontent.com/pod-product-compliance
Lightning Source LLC
Chambersburg PA
CBHW022108300426
44117CB00007B/633